Computer Architectures for Spatially Distributed Data

NATO ASI Series

Advanced Science Institutes Series

A series presenting the results of activities sponsored by the NATO Science Committee, which aims at the dissemination of advanced scientific and technological knowledge, with a view to strengthening links between scientific communities.

The Series is published by an international board of publishers in conjunction with the NATO Scientific Affairs Division

A Life Sciences **B Physics**	Plenum Publishing Corporation London and New York
C Mathematical and Physical Sciences	D. Reidel Publishing Company Dordrecht, Boston and Lancaster
D Behavioural and Social Sciences **E Applied Sciences**	Martinus Nijhoff Publishers Boston, The Hague, Dordrecht and Lancaster
F Computer and Systems Sciences **G Ecological Sciences**	Springer-Verlag Berlin Heidelberg New York Tokyo

Series F: Computer and Systems Sciences Vol. 18

Computer Architectures for Spatially Distributed Data

Edited by

Herbert Freeman

Professor of Computer Engineering, Rutgers University
New Brunswick, NJ 08903, USA

Goffredo G. Pieroni

Professor of Computer Science, University of Houston
Houston, TX 77004, USA

Springer-Verlag Berlin Heidelberg New York Tokyo
Published in cooperation with NATO Scientific Affairs Division

Proceedings of the NATO Advanced Study Institute on Computer Architectures for Spatially Distributed Data held in Cetraro (Cosenza), Italy, 6–17 June 1983

ISBN-13:978-3-642-82152-3 e-ISBN-13:978-3-642-82150-9
DOI: 10.1007/978-3-642-82150-9

Library of Congress Cataloging in Publication Data. NATO Advanced Study Institute on Computer Architectures for Spatially Distributed Data (1983 : Cetraro, Italy) Computer architectures for spatially distributed data. (NATO ASI series. Series F, Computer and systems sciences ; vol. 18) "Proceedings of the NATO Advanced Study Institute on Computer Architectures for Spatially Distributed Data held at Cetraro, Cosenza, Italy, 6–17 June 1983"—Verso t.p. "Published in cooperation with NATO Scientific Affairs Division." 1. Computer architecture—Congresses. 2. Data structures (Computer science)—Congresses. I. Freeman, Herbert. II. Pieroni, Goffredo G. III. Title. IV. Series: NATO ASI series. Series F, Computer and systems sciences ; no. 18. QA76.9.A73N36 1983 004.2'2 85-27643
ISBN-13:978-3-642-82152-3

Softcover reprint of the hardcover 1st edititon 1985

2145/3140-543210

PREFACE

These are the proceedings of a NATO Advanced Study Institute (ASI) held in Cetraro, Italy during 6-17 June 1983. The title of the ASI was *Computer Architectures for Spatially Distributed Data*, and it brought together some 60 participants from Europe and America. Presented here are 21 of the lectures that were delivered. The articles cover a wide spectrum of topics related to computer architectures specially oriented toward the fast processing of spatial data, and represent an excellent review of the state-of-the-art of this topic.

For more than 20 years now researchers in pattern recognition, image processing, meteorology, remote sensing, and computer engineering have been looking toward new forms of computer architectures to speed the processing of data from two- and three-dimensional processes. The work can be said to have commenced with the landmark article by Steve Unger in 1958, and it received a strong forward push with the development of the ILIAC III and IV computers at the University of Illinois during the 1960's. One clear obstacle faced by the computer designers in those days was the limitation of the state-of-the-art of hardware, when the only switching devices available to them were discrete transistors. As a result parallel processing was generally considered to be impractical, and relatively little progress was made.

It was not until well into the 1970's, as large-scale integrated circuits (LSI) and then very-large-scale integrated circuits (VLSI) became a reality, that the prospect of building true spatial-data computers appeared to be both practically and economically feasible. This has led to a vast increase in research activity in recent years. Attention is being devoted not only to the design of the architectures themselves, but also to suitable data structures for spatial data, to appropriate fast spatial-data algorithms, and to new programming systems for parallel processing.

By 1980, a number of large spatial-data computers were in various stages of design or construction around the world. Though, many unanswered questions remained as to preferred design philosophies, data structures, and programming methods. It was with this in mind that the editors decided it to be an opportune time to organize a NATO ASI devoted to this topic. The ASI would have the dual purpose of bringing together the leading researchers in the field for a two-week program of intensive interaction as well as serving to disseminate information about the current issues facing the field.

The lectures presented here are concerned primarily with different architectures for the parallel processing of spatial data and with novel data structures for facilitating such processing. Discussions of applications lean generally to those in image processing, pattern recognition, solid modeling, and computer cartography. This simply reflects the dominant interests of the lecturers. There is no intent to imply that these are the only important application areas for spatial-data computers.

The presentations are diverse, and some of the approaches described may seem to be in conflict with each other. This is only natural for a proceedings of this type. Rather than cause the reader any concern, it should evoke in him an appreciation for the youth and vigor of this developing field and a recognition that much work still lies ahead.

The Editors

TABLE OF CONTENTS

ALGORITHM-DRIVEN ARCHITECTURE FOR PARALLEL IMAGE PROCESSING

Per-Erik Danielsson
Department of Electrical Engineering
Linkoping University
S-581 83 Linkoping
SWEDEN

Abstract

Arrays with a large number of bit-serial processors have long been suggested for high speed image processing. The set of necessary algorithms and operations seem to require a number of new features in the architecture. Of special importance are the so-called distributed processor topology for fast neighborhood access, and index arithmetic for table-look up. From a hard-ware point of view, however, the added complexity of the processors is also a threat to the bit-serial approach.

1. Introduction

With its large operands (the images) and the seemingly uniform way to handle them, image processing is a natural target for parallel computer architecture. Although special-purpose image processors use to be pipe-lined to obtain necessary speed and simplicity, for the general-purpose case, a processor array with a large number of very simple bit-serial processors has had several advocates in the past. However, it seems that systems of this type have had a very limited success. The reason may be that they have not taken into account all the operations and algorithms necessary for a complete image processor. Ideally, such a design must be efficient for

- Input/Output of images
- Neighborhood operations (parallel)
- Propagation (recursive neighborhood operations)
- Feature extraction (counts, event coordinates)
- Table look-up
- FFT-type operations
- Geometry corrections
- Data-dependent traversal (e.g. border tracing)
- Data-dependent neighborhood operations

The two last operations are almost excluded by definition for a parallel processor array in SIMD-mode. The remaining ones can be implemented but require several changes with respect to existing designs of type CLIP IV and MPP [4], [6]. Some of these changes will be demonstrated in the following sections.

2. Image-to-array mapping for neighborhood operations

In all realistic cases the size m x m of the array is much smaller than the size n x n of the image we want to process. Thus, we have to adopt a mapping rule between image and array or, equivalently, decide which pixels of the image should be stored in the top left-most memory module. There are two basic methods for this mapping [1].

The most common one is to store every m:th pixel (in both coordinates) of the image in the same memory module. This is the method used in CLIP IV and MPP. It is illustrated by Figure 1 for a 4 x 4 array and we see that the principle is to distribute the image over the Processing Elements (PE's). Each memory module holds n/m pixels of the image found on intervals of m pixel units in both coordinates. It

NATO ASI Series, Vol. F18
Computer Architectures for Spatially Distributed Data
Edited by H. Freeman and G. G. Pieroni

leads to a "densly packed" activity situation where all processors are simultanously processing neighboring pixels of an m x m window.

If we assume 8-connected PE:s, 3 x 3 neighborhoods work fairly well. Access of a larger neighborhhod requires either connections over longer distances (which is probably unrealistic) or shifting of data. The last method will increase the number of cycles by at least with a factor of 2 compared to immediate access. Also, it does not allow efficient access to a more scattered or irregular neighborhood.

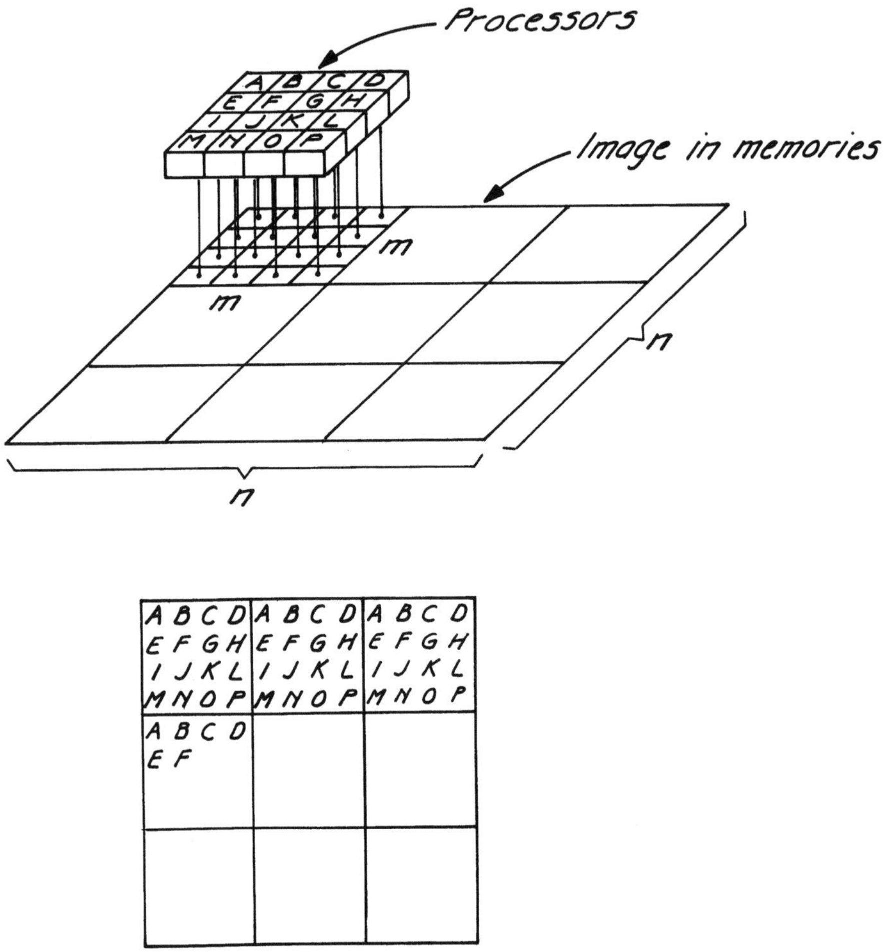

Figure 1 Image distributed over the PE:s

The most difficult problem to overcome, however, is the special edge conditions. By necessity, the single global address is correct and sufficient only as long as all processors want data from the same m x m window. However, for the border PE:s their respective neighborhoods extend over to other subimages the pixels of which are found on other memory addresses. Consequently, individual address modifiers have to be introduced (+1, -1, +m, -m etc). Alternatively, these border pixels have to be brought into play with separate and selective access cycles. In either case complex and time-consuming overhead develops.

For the MPP a circumvention of this problem has been suggested [7]. The full image is stored outside the array and only one window of 128 x 128 is brought in at time. For a 3 x 3 operation 126 x 126 valid results can be produced, which means that subsequent windows have to be overlapping.

The problem of the "densely packed" array of Figure 1 can be summarized by the fact that the processors almost stand on each other's toes when it comes to neighborhood access. The alternative is to distribute the processors over the image and this case is illustrated by Figure 2. Each processor roams over its own subimage of size n/m x n/m under control of the same global address pointer. Neighborhoods (even large ones) that overlap the adjacent subimage are reached by nearest neighbor connection.

The steering of data from neighboring memory modules to the processors is easily controlled by the same central mechanism that delivers global addresses. Note that when one processor "reaches" out for a bit, say, to the east and grabs something

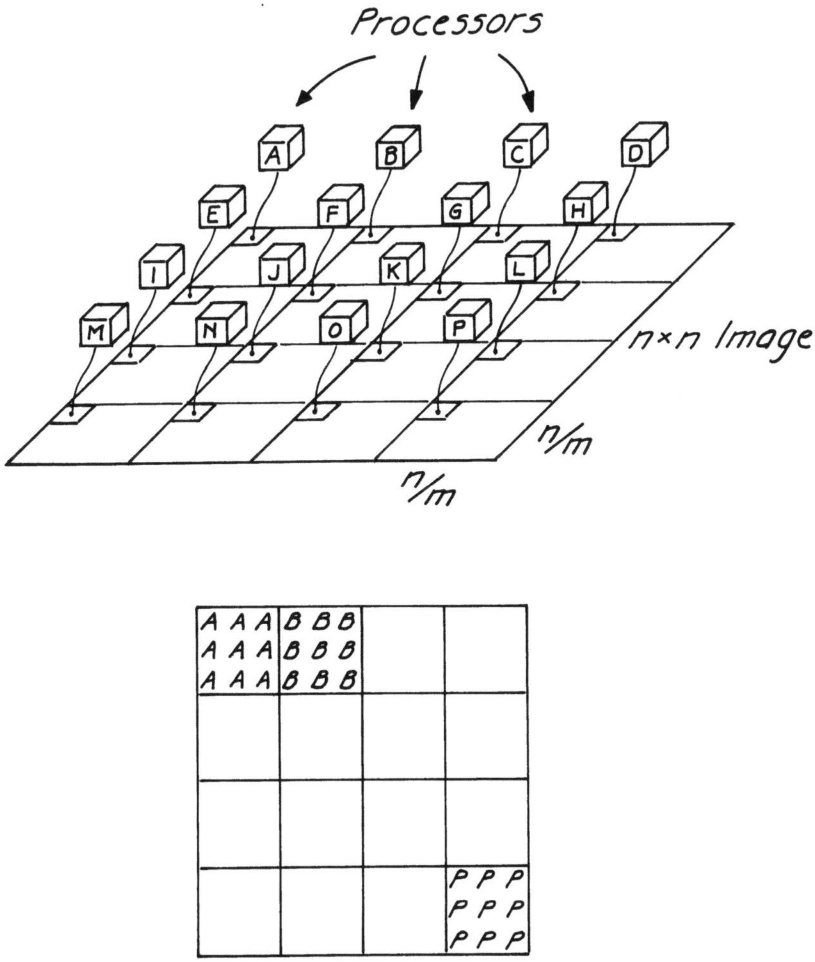

Figure 2 Distributed processor topology

from this memory module, the neighboring processor to the west is doing the same using the memory of the first one. For all realistic cases, huge neighborhoods become accessible. For instance, a 512 x 512 image on a 16 x 16 array results in 32 x 32 subimages and max neighborhoods of 65 x 65.

One of several interconnecting schemes is shown by Figure 3. Note that we emphasize the memory to processor interconnection rather than the processor to processor interconnection.

In Figure 3a) the processors are on top of the memory modules of their own. A case where each processor reads information from its north-west neighbor memory is illustrated by the dashed data paths. Only four double directed lines are necessary.

It seems that distributed processor topology is drastically enchancing the potential of image parallelism. It was first suggested for DAP [5] although the efficient neighborhood access and control seems to be lacking in this machine as is evident from [8]. Recent examples of processor arrays of this type are LIPP [2] and GRID [12], [13].

It should be noted that so called pyramid or cone processing [9] is easily accommodated for in the topology of Figure 2. Demagnifying the n x n image in steps of 2 can go on inside the array storing the new subimages at new memory positions. However, the top of the pyramid above the m x m level has to be handled outside

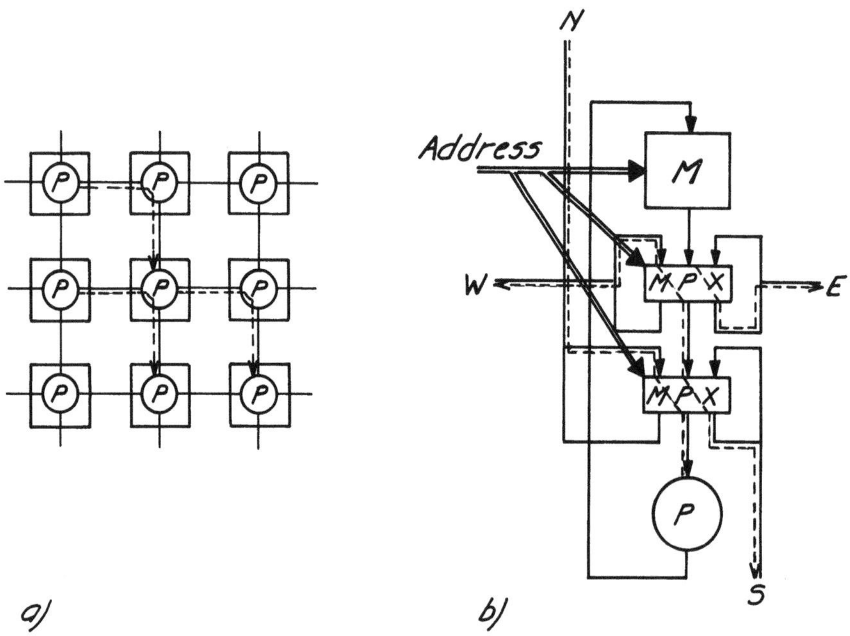

Figure 3 Only four interconnecting lines are necessary for memory to processor interconnection

the array. Since the amount of data is very small in these top levels this is readily done without time penalty.

The virtue of distributed processor topology might be disturbed by input problems. The normal raster scan serial format outside the array does not immediately lend itself to be stored in the format of Figure 2. Similar problems arise also in Figure 1 for that matter which is one good reason for the so called staging memories of MPP. We will return to the I/O-problem in section 5 below.

3. Convolution

As an example of the virtues of free random addressing in a large neighborhood and the benefits of bit-serial processing we will now analyze the performance of the common convolution operation. The performance is measured in terms of speed, or, to be component independent, in the number of cycles to produce one output pixel per processor.

The convolution should produce for each output pixel a sum of products due to the formula

$$A_1 \cdot X_1 + A_2 \cdot X_2 + \dots + A_L \cdot X_L$$

where $A_1, A_2, \dots, A_L$ are constant filter coefficients and $X_1, X_2, \dots, X_L$ are the pixels in a neighborhood of the input image. The sum of products can be pictorially described by the total accumulation scheme of Figure 4a) where each horizontal block is one data word (of 4 bits only in our simple case). Now, a certain bit, e.g. a_{12}, being 0 means simply that nothing but 0 will be accumulated in this row, while $a_{11} = 1$ means that incrementing or not is determined by the data bits. Also, the order of the different accumulations are insignificant. Therefore, we can a priori cancel the blanks of Figure 4a) and reorder the nonblank bit contributions to the shape of Figure 4b).

These remaining accumulations can now be picked up in order top-down, right-left and accumulated in a down-shifting up-down counter as in Figure 5. After each vertical "scan" in Figure 4b), one output bit is ready to be shifted out and stored. Note that the constants $A_1, A_2, \dots, A_L$ are compiled into the microcode in the form of a proper addressing sequence together with the control signals for the counter.

By just assuming random distribution (50%) of 1's and 0's in the bits of the constants the number of cycles will be

$$L \cdot N \cdot K/2 + N + K + {}^2\log L$$

where

N = number of bits in a data word X
K = number of bits in a constant A
L = number of points in the convolution kernel

The last three terms correspond to the maximum number of significant bits in the output.

Now, as have been shown in [10] by representing the coefficients in Canonical Signed Digit Code (CSD-code) the average number of 0-digits can be raised from 50% to approx 65%. On top of this we know that many filter coefficients have low magnitude which further increases the number of 0-digits in CSD-code to about 75%.

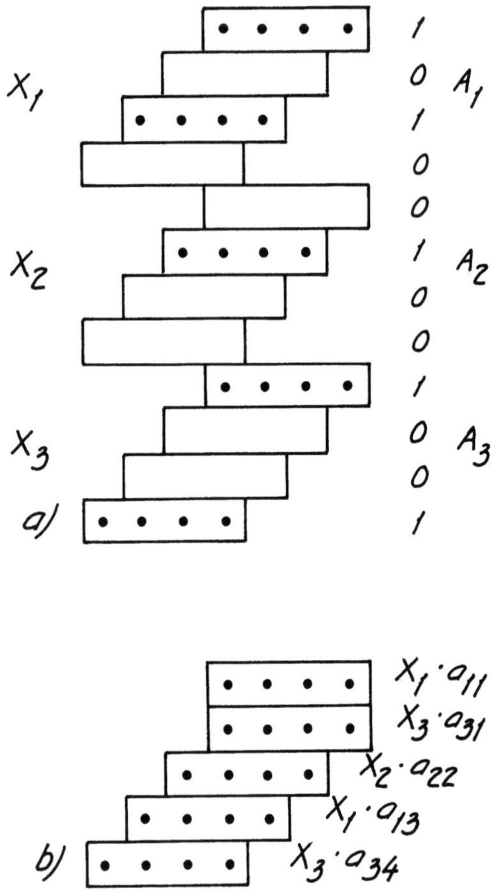

Figure 4 The accumulation process in the convolution operation

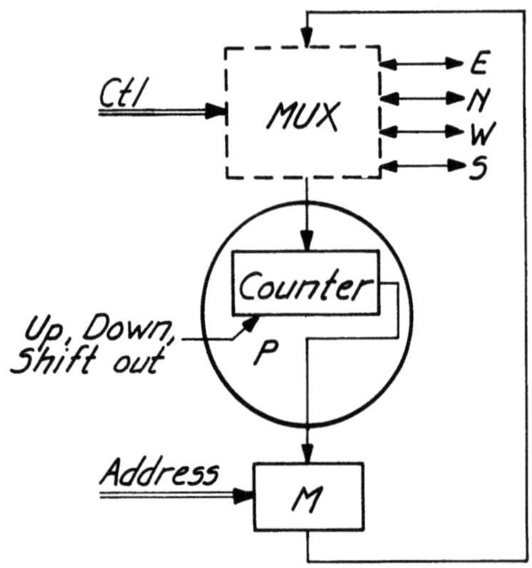

Figure 5 Bit-serial convolution with a down-shifting up/down counter

Hereby, the number of cycles is reduced to

$$L \cdot N \cdot K/4 + N + K + {}^{2}\log L$$

The mixing of incrementing and decrementing events is of no consequence since we already assumed an up/down counter in Figure 5.

A typical case, for which the MPP performance has been estimated is a 3 x 3 convolution on 8-bit data and with 8-bit coefficients. For Figure 5, the formula above gives us

$$9 \cdot 8 \cdot 2 + 21 = 163 \text{ cycles}$$

The corresponding number for MPP is 2110 cycles (deduced from [7]) which is inferior by a factor of about 13.

A pleasant feature of the above bit-serial method is that simple filters (few-point kernels, low-precision coefficients) are executed very fast. Execution time follows complexity.

4. Table look-up

Just as in any other kinds of data processing, table look-up has become extremely common in image processing as a result of the ever decreasing cost of memory. Examples of table look-up that are hard to abstain from are the following.

- Arbitrary grayscale mapping.
- Boolean function on a 3 x 3 binary neighborhood.
- Histogram functions.
- Multiply with a constant.

However, a large variety of other image processing algorithms can also make good use of table look-up as shown in [2].

The implementation requires an index register in each PE. The global address is a pointer to the beginning of the table and the individual offset values in the index registers are added to the global address. This operation may seem to require a major extension of the PE-hardware.

However, if index arithmetic will be used for table look-up only, we can spare the adder completely. See Figure 6.

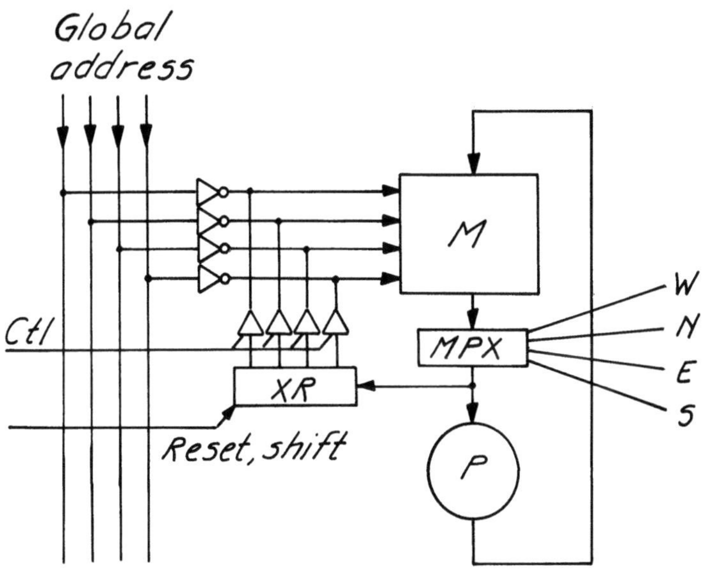

Figure 6 Simplified index arithmetic

For simplicity assume a 16 bit memory. Let all tables occupy 2, 4, 8 or 16 bits and let a 2-bit table start at XXX0, a 4-bit table start at XX00 etc. Then, we can shift in the offset, MSB first, in XR and reach the table entry by simple concatenation implemented as wired-OR.

Table look-up was one feature of ILLIAC IV. Quite probably it is a necessary ingredient in any competitive image parallel architecture.

Any Boolean function (= logic operation) on a 3 x 3-neighborhood can be implemented by a 512 x 1 bit entry look-up-table. The number of cycles per output pixel is easily deduced from Figure 7.

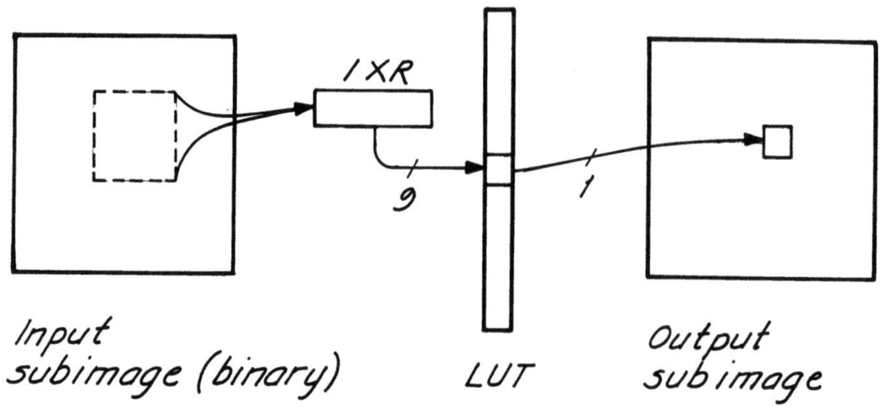

Figure 7 Look-up table for Boolean neighborhood operation

First the nine bits are brought to the index register which takes nine cycles. Next, the global address points at the look-up table and with the index offset the output bit is fetched. Finally this bit is stored in the output image. In total this requires 11 cycles and for a 32 x 32 subimage (512 x 512 image, 16 x 16 PE array) this amounts to 11264 cycles or 1.1264 ms assuming a cycle time of 100 ns.

Let us also estimate the time required for collecting the histogram of a 512 x 512 x 8 bit image on a 16 x 16 array. The operation takes place in three steps. See Figure 8.

i) Local histogram collect. Each subimage is 32 x 32. Thus each bin (table entry) has to be 11 bits. To read out a pixel value to XR takes 8 cycles and to update the entry value and store it back takes 22 cycles. In total 1024 (8 + 22) = 33972. Figure 8a).

ii) Merging of four neighboring 256-tables. Every second PE in each row is given an XR-value of 128. Half of the tables are then moved in their lower part, half in their upper part to their neighbor. Figure 8b). (Assume a torus connected array). All tables now contain pairs of entries that can be merged, i.e. added. Figure 8c). The procedure is repeated columnwise. Figure 8d,e). The total number of cycles becomes 128 x 22 + 128 x 34 + 64 · 24 + 64 · 37 = = 12072.

iii) Each PE now holds a table of 64 entries of 13 bits. These are shifted out over the edge and merged into one table in 16 x 64 x 13 = 13312 cycles. Figure 8f). This requires hardware of type All 1's Count logic and shifting accumulators outside the array.

The total number of cycles becomes 59356.

Assuming a 100 ns cycle like in the MPP we arrive at a histogram collect time of 5.94 ms equivalent to approx 43 Mpixels/sec.

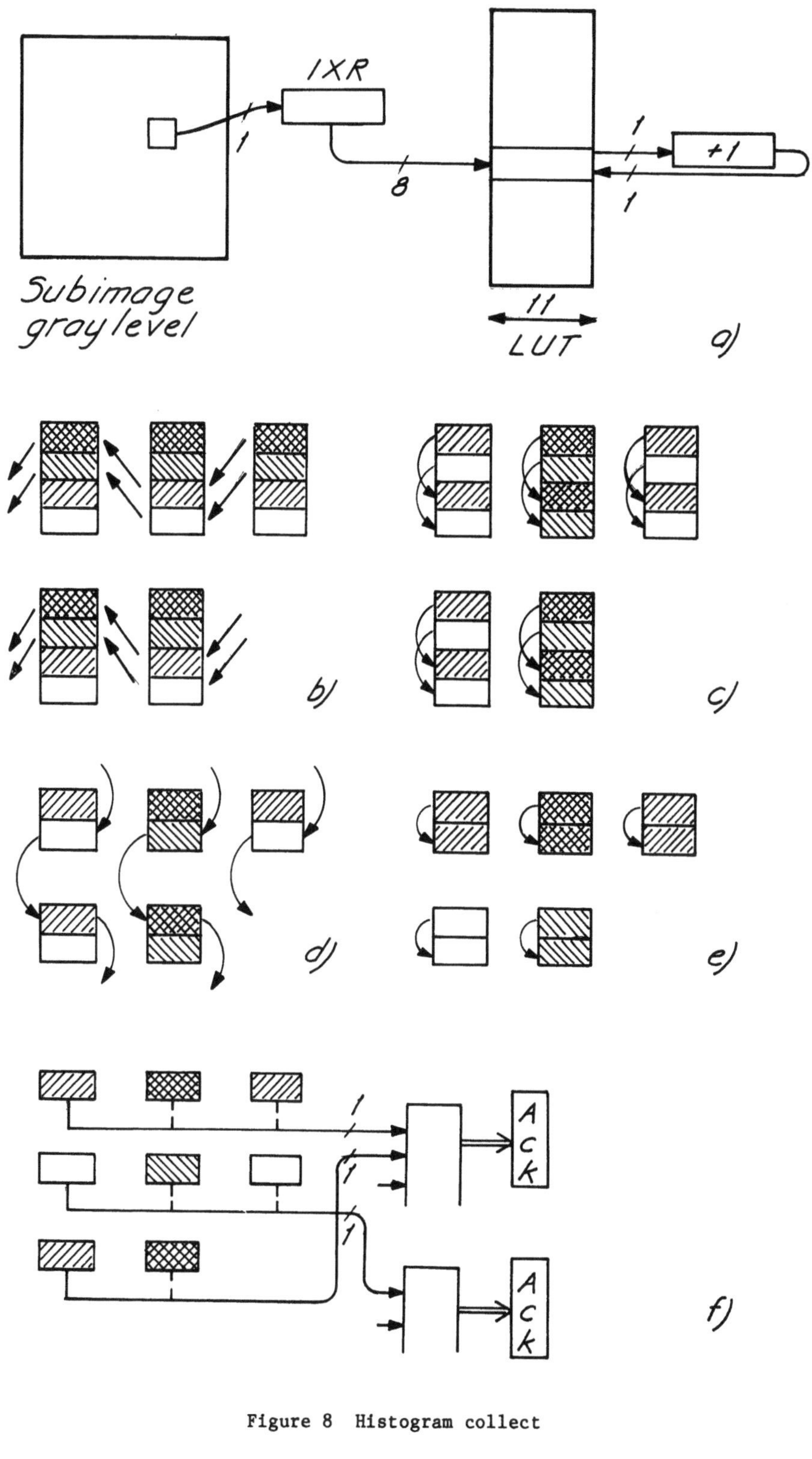

Figure 8 Histogram collect

5. Input/output

An input/output problem arises since we have to face the fact that images outside the array exist in raster scanned format. Without further precautions the input data rate would be limited by the bandwidth of one single memory module. Since the bandwidth while processing is m x m higher (the array size being m x m) this bottleneck has to be removed.

A natural way is to enter a set of m bits at a time over one of the edges of the array which would increase the I/O-bandwidth with a factor of m. However, if the first rasterscanned m bits are shifted in over the horizontal (or vertical) edge of the array, followed by the next m bits, then the pixels will be stored as in Figure 9 that shows a simple case of a binary 16 x 16 image stored in a 4 x 4 array. Note that we assume that the RAM modules of the array are connected to the edge over a bus system. Hereby, we can steer each set of 4 bits to the correct vertical position although horizontally the pixels will not be in the right place. The correct allocation is shown by Figure 10. The process of transforming the data to this desired format will be referred to as orthogonalization.

We will now show an orthogonalization method where the basic steps are executed with full m x m-parallelism. The time consumption should be small compared to the primary I/O-operation which employs m-parallelism only.

We presume that each PE has an address modifier where the common global address can be adjusted modulo m according to the content of an index register. Thus, for the present purpose our needs are slightly different from the look-up table case above. Also, we presume nearest neighbor connections that enable the processors to fetch data from the memory modules of their own and their neighbors as well as to shift data between themselves. These hardware features are shown in Figure 13 below. For brevity reasons we are only showing the neighbor connections in the horizontal direction.

The first step is to move data, m x m bit at a time from the subimage areas depicted in Figure 9 to the small m-bit buffer areas depicted in Figure 11. Thus, this is something that takes place within each MPE and proceeds in m cycles, each cycle moving m x m bits. Storing in the buffer areas takes place with modified addressing so that one set of m bits from Figure 9 appears as a skewed line of bits in Figure 11.

The second step is to read out data from the buffer areas without address modifications, m x m bits at a time and shift them until they arrive at the positions of Figure 12. To go from the state of Figure 11 to the state of Figure 12 we need 0, 1, 2, ... or m/2 steps depending on the positions. For instance, the bits 0, 5, 10, 15, 64, 69, ... require no shifts while 1, 6, 11, 12, 65, 70, ... require one left shift. Note that we assume wrap-around connections between the vertical edges of the array. With two shift directions and m being an even number the average number of shifts is m/4 for each bit-plane of m x m bits.

The third step is to move the content of the buffer areas back to the original subimage area. Again, this takes place within each MPE. Reading from the buffer areas is done with address modification as indicated in the bottom of Figure 12. It is readily seen that we now arrive with data in the desired positions of Figure 10.

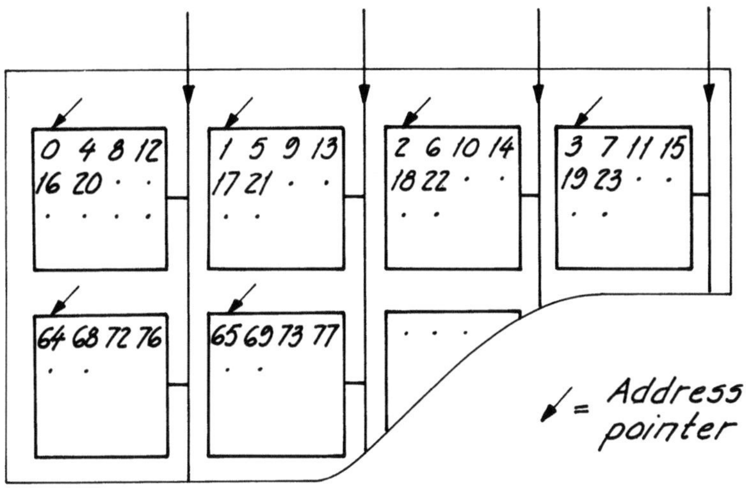

Figure 9

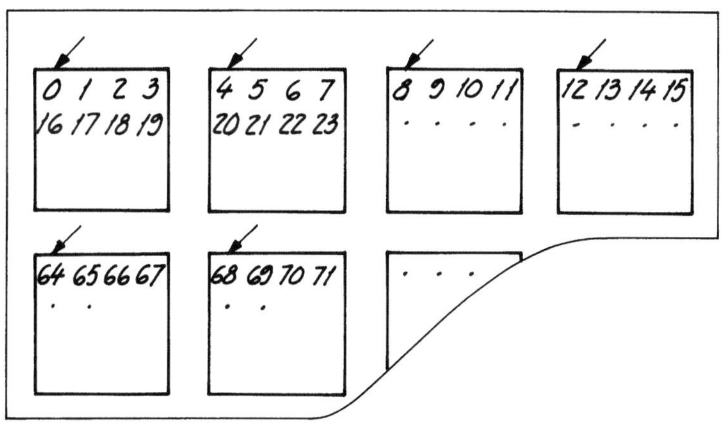

Figure 10

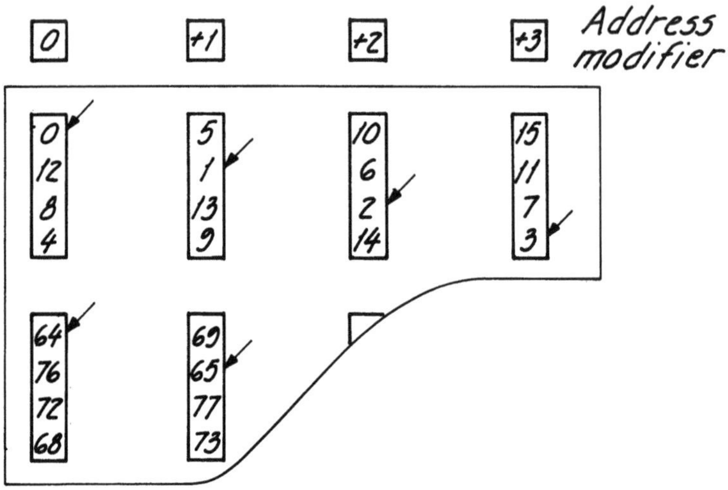

Figure 11

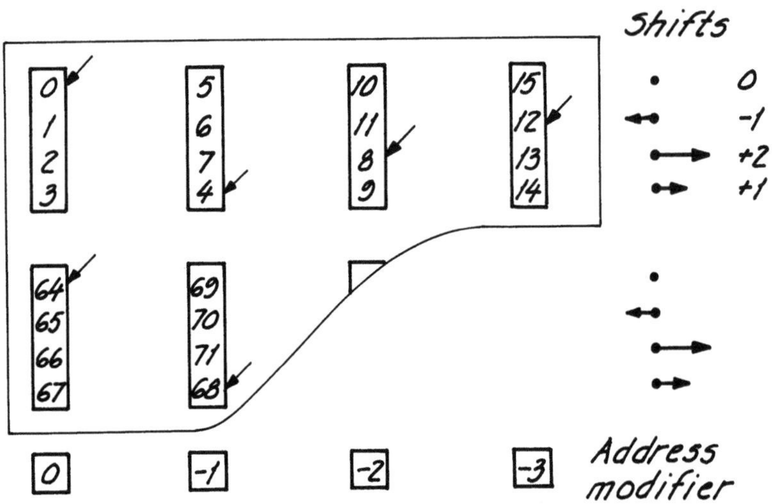

Figure 12

As a summary we can list the total I/O-sequence as follows. The number of cycles holds for one bitplane of m x m bits.

	# cycles
- Primary move over the array edge to subimage area in each memory module	m
- Load from subimage area (Figure 9)	1
- Store in buffer area with data skewing (Figure 11)	1
- Shift buffer area content to new positions (Figure 12) in average	m/4
- Load from buffer area with deskewing	1
- Store in subimage area (Figure 10)	1
Total	4 + 5m/4

Thus, the effective I/O-bandwidth equals $m^2/(4 + 5m/4)$

which for m = 16 gives us a bandwidth gain of 2 m/3 times over the single memory module. This factor approaches 4 m/5 for large m.

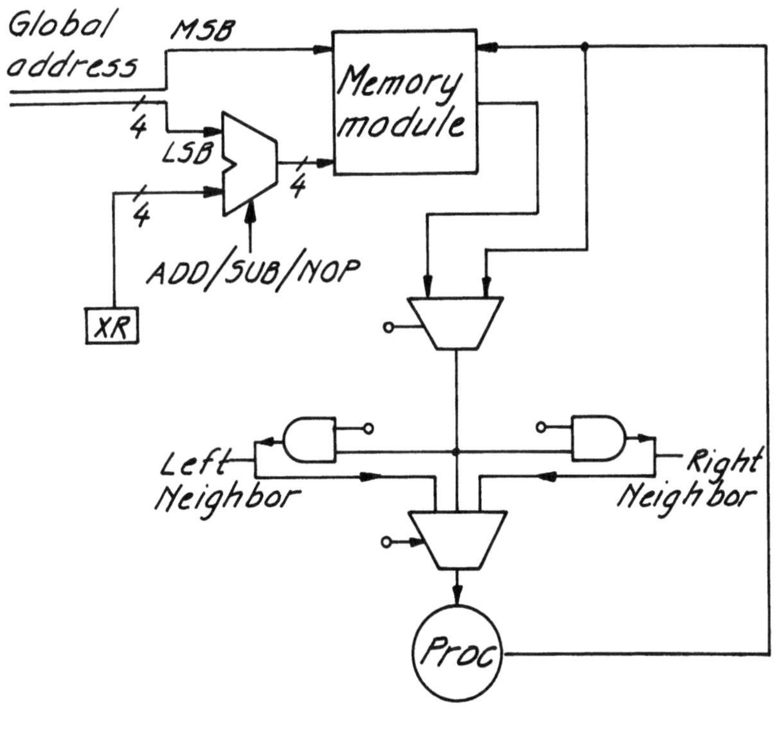

Figure 13

6. Recursive operations. Propagation

Contradictory to common belief, propagation-type operations like shrinking, thinning, labelling etc cannot be performed by image parallel machines with full efficiency. This is best understood if we consider two extreme cases dealing with an n x n image, namely the uni-processor versus the n x n processor system.

The uniprocessor may traverse the image top-down with double-directed line scans followed by a second bottom-top scan. See Figure 14. This is 2 n^2 operation steps but since the neighborhood is halved it is equivalent in complexity to n^2 normal (parallel non-recursive) operations. The effect is propagations along straight lines over the entire image, i.e. over n pixel distances.

Now consider the n x n processor array. In one time step a propagation wave moves only one pixel distance in spite of the fact that n^2 operations are performed. The efficacy is only 1/n and the speed-up factor relative to the uniprocessor system is n rather than n^2.

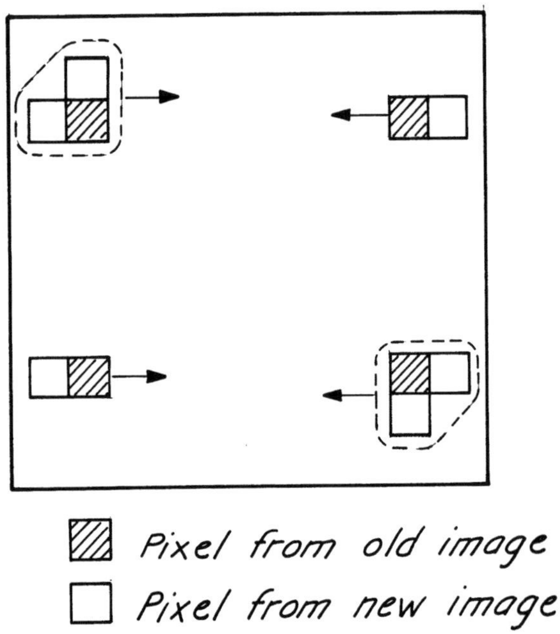

Figure 14 Recursive, propagating operation with a simple neighborhood operator

ILLIAC III [3] and CLIP IV [4] have implemented combinatorial "flash-through" which brings down the cycle time considerably for propagation type operations. However, only the simplest logic operations can be set up in this manner.

Now consider image parallel machines with distributed processor topology (Figure 2) having an m x m array operating on an n x n image. The processors can work with full recursive efficacy inside the n/m subimages. However, at the subimage borders the behaviour is more like a parallel system. Clearly, to propagate across a subimage we need (n/m x n/m) operations and a propagation wave that should traverse the whole image requires

$$m(n/m \times n/m) = n^2/m \text{ time steps}$$

Thus, the speed-up factor is m rather than m^2 which means that the efficacy is 1/m as could be expected. It is inversely proportional to the number of processors.

The given numbers may be overly pessimistic. Propagation over the entire image may be an exceptional case. For reasonably large values of n/m it seems likely that the objects are of the same size as a subimage, i.e. overlapping two subimages. In such a case the image parallel machine works close to full efficacy.

7. Conclusions

It has been shown that SIMD architecture for image processing is a viable concept. However, the architecture should be algorithm-driven. Algorithms and the fundamental operations have to be verified in terms of performance. Such verification loops may indicate that the design has bottlenecks and pitfalls. The most severe pitfall of all seems to be to lump the processors together which restricts their access capability and imposes exemptions from true SIMD-mode for neighborhood operations. In contrast, an even distribution of the processing power over the image results in smooth and uniform processing without overhead.

One may then ask if the road is now paved for the success of bit-serial image processing architectures with a large number or processors. The answer may very well be <u>no</u> for a reason that is not coming from above (algorithm-driven) but from below (hardware-driven). Consider the following.

Image processing systems of the future have to be equipped with huge RAM:s (64 Mbytes or more) to cope with the ever increasing appetite for large images (satellite imagery, radiology, newspaper editing etc). Therefore these systems cannot utilise fast and expensive memory components but relatively slow and cheap ones with cycle times on the order of 400 ns.

Processors can easily run at a clock rate of 10 MHz today (probably 20 MHz in the future). In 100 ns a processor can even perform 16-bit arithmetic. Thus it will seem that there is something like a 64-fold missmatch in speed when a bit-serial processor is performing only <u>one</u> bit operation for each memory cycle. See Figure 15.

Assume that the two systems in Figure 15 both have the same simple task of doing one ADD and one STORE on 64 16-bit words. Evidently this can be done in 32 memory cycles in the bit-serial system of Figure 15a). In Figure 15b) it takes 128 operations for the 16-bit ALU but thanks to its 4-fold speed it can match the memory bandwidth and also do the task in 32 memory cycles.

Since the time complexity is the same let us now discuss the processor complexity. In Figure 15b) it seems reasonable to equip the processor part with say 8 or 16 fast registers. Since there are four channels to the memory this corresponds to 2 or 4 registers per channel. The same outfit in Figure 15a) becomes very costly. In the first place, we need at least one 16-bit shift register per processor so that we don't have to use three memory accesses for a simple accumulate. Then, if we want to be as "advanced" as in Figure 15b) everything else also has to come in multiples of 64. It seems that the set of processors in 15a) will be at least 16 times as complex as the single processor of Figure 15b).

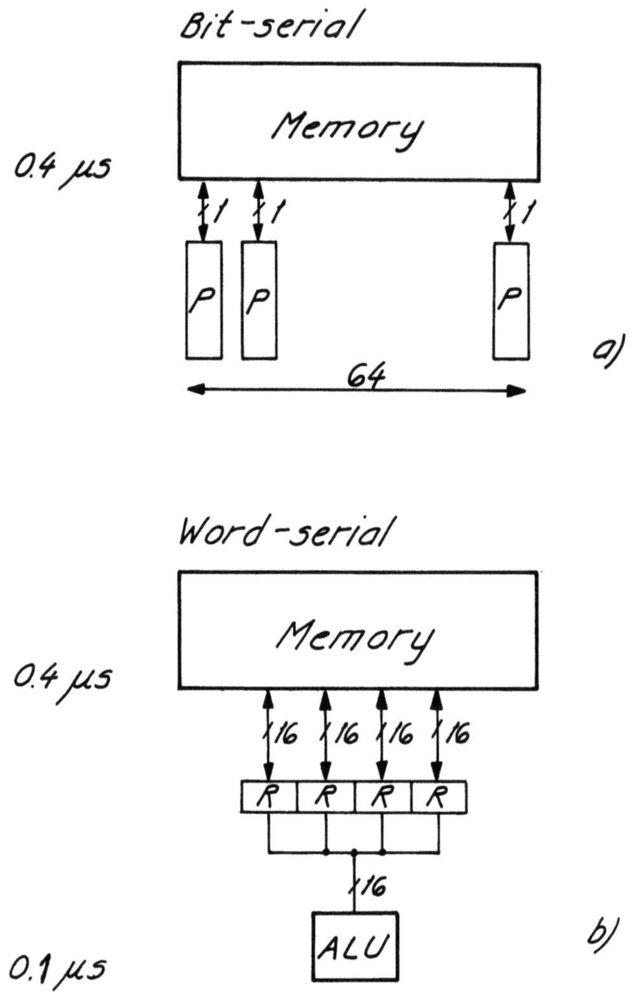

Figure 15 Comparison between bit-serial and word-serial processing

This discussion speaks against bit-serial processing and it is interesting to comment on the arguments for bit-serial processing brought forward in [11], pp. 147-152. Here the operands are brought directly from memory to the logic and back without any help of registers in the memory. Therefore, everything is memory bounded. No time-sharing of the resources by several data streams are forseen as in Figure 15b). Also, since registers are non-existent the 16-fold complexity of Figure 15a) does not show up in [11]. It then follows as a consequence that bit-serial word-parallel and bit-parallel word-serial systems are equivalent in speed. However, the history of computers shows that a majority of operations and algorithms benefit greatly from registers and extra datapaths inside the processor. This is the Achilles' heal of the bit-serial approach.

In summary, the bit-serial architecture with distributed processor topology seems able to exploit many elegant algorithms and take advantage of the short and varying word-lengths in image processing. It is not obvious however, that this can outweigh the high costs for necessary enhancements of processor capabilities like more ALU-functions, index registers, counters and the like.

8. References

[1] P.E. Danielsson, S. Levialdi, "Computer Architecture for Pictorial Information Systems", Computer, Vol 14, pp 53-67, November 1981.

[2] P.E. Danielsson, T. Ericsson, "LIPP - proposals for the design of an image processor array", in "Computing Structures for Image Processing", M.J.B. Duff (ed.), Associated Press, 1983.

[3] B.H. Mc Cormick, "The Illinois Pattern Recognition Computer - ILLIAC III", IEEE Trans. Computers, Vol EC-12, pp 791-813, December 1963.

[4] M.J.B. Duff, "Parallel Processors for Digital Image Processing", in "Advances in Digital Image Processing", P. Stücki (ed.), Plenum Press, New York, pp 265-276, 1979.

[5] S.F. Reddaway, "The DAP approach", in "Infotech State-of-the-Art Report on Supercomputers", Vol 2, pp 309-329, 1979.

[6] K.E. Batcher, "Design of a Massively Parallel Processor", IEEE Trans. Computers, Vol C-29, pp 836-840, September 1980.

[7] J.L. Potter, "Continous Image Processing on the MPP", IEEE Computer Society Workshop on Computer Architecture for Pattern Analysis and Image Database Management, pp 51-56, 1981.

[8] P. Marks, "Low-level Vision Using an Array Processor", Computer Graphics and Image Processing, Vol 14, pp 281-292, 1980.

[9] S.L. Tanimoto, T. Pavlidis, "Hierarchical Data Structure for Picture Processing", Computer Graphics and Image Processing, Vol 14, pp 104-119, 1975.

[10] A. Peled, "On the hardware Implementation of Digital Signal Processors", IEEE Trans. Vol ASSP-24, pp 76-86, 1976.

[11] R.W. Hockney and C.R. Jesshope, "Parallel Computers", Adam Hilger Ltd, Bristol, 1981.

[12] D.K. Arvind, I.N. Robinson and I.N. Parker, "A VLSI Cellular Array Processor", Proceedings of 1983 International Symposium on VLSI Technology, Systems & Applications, Taipei, Taiwan, March 1983.

[13] D.K. Arvind, I.N. Robinson and I.N. Parker, "A VLSI Chip for Real-Time Image Processing", Proceedings of 1983 IEEE Symposium on Circuits & Systems, Newport Beach, CA, May 1983.

ARCHITECTURES OF SIMD CELLULAR LOGIC IMAGE PROCESSING ARRAYS

M. J. B. Duff
Image Processing Group
University College London
London, England

1. INTRODUCTION

The use of parallelism in the design of computer architectures specialised for image processing is now recognised as a necessity, especially as interest grows in the potential applications of real-time image analysis. A conventional (von Neumann) serial processor is clearly unable to achieve processing rates which would keep up with the data flow from standard television image sequences. Suppose that it is required to perform a simple, 3 x 3 local neighbourhood operation on a new 512 x 512 pixel image every one twenty-fifty of a second. This operation would involve, at every pixel, fetching nine pixel values and performing at least eight additions (although there would most likely be multiplications involved as well), concluding with a store operation. Over and above this activity in the arithmetic logic unit, input and output operations would also be required. Thus in one second, the minimum number of processor operations would be 25 x 512 x 512 x (8 additions + 9 memory accesses), i.e. more than 100 million operations each second. Improvements in semiconductor technology can be expected to go some of the way towards enhancing computer performance towards rates in this region, but the bulk of the gain must still be found elsewhere and, specifically, in improved architectures.

Fortunately, image data are organised in a very structured manner with the structure pointing the way to the design of efficient processor assemblies. A typical image operation is one in which the value of every pixel in the processed image is found by calculating a simple linear or non-linear function of the values of a set of pixels in the neighbourhood of each corresponding pixel in the original image. In many cases, the neighbourhood will be the 3 x 3 group surrounding and containing each pixel. Performed sequentially, this image operation would involve scanning through each image, repeating the same sequence of operations N^2 times in each N x N pixel image. Clearly, there is no reason, other than the cost of the hardware, why separate processors should not be assigned to each pixel location, the processors all performing identical sequences of operations on their own local subset of

NATO ASI Series, Vol. F18
Computer Architectures for Spatially Distributed Data
Edited by H. Freeman and G. G. Pieroni

of the image data. Programming such an array of N x N processors need not be any more difficult than programming a single processor since each processor is to perform the same set of instructions.

In conventional computer systems, much time can be lost in address computation, both in 'scanning' through the pixels as each is re-evaluated, and in fetching pixel values from local neighbourhoods. Some minicomputer based image processors have been upgraded by incorporating address computation hardware, but their performance is usually still quite inadequate for real-time applications. For an array of processors, however, the possibility exists of assigning a small amount of 'local' memory to each processor, so that a fetch operation would involve the same address at all points in the array, the address being relative to the position of the processor itself, in the same array. Processor arrays of this type have been classified by Flynn (1) as Single Instruction stream, Multiple Data stream (SIMD), using a simple classification scheme which has been widely accepted even though it does seem not to describe some of the newer architectures particularly accurately or completely.

2. COMPONENTS OF AN SIMD ARRAY

Although there have now been many proposals for SIMD array designs, few have actually reached the point of construction. It is also remarkable that those that have been constructed, or are in the process of being constructed, are all very similar in their essential details. The main features can be summarised as follows:

a) Processor design

The 'heart' of each processor is a single-bit arithmetic and/or logic unit capable of performing a full-add or Boolean functions on two binary input variables (together with a 'carry' bit input where appropriate). Options include duplicating the processor to allow the generation of a second function for transmission to neighbouring processors, shift registers to facilitate compound arithmetic such as multiplication or division, and an 'activity bit' used to render selected processors inoperative for certain parts of a program.

b) Array design

All processors are driven by the same set of control lines and therefore simultaneously execute the same program instructions. Communication between processors is usually limited to immediate neighbours in the array, the options being four, eight or six neighbours (the latter being found in hexagonal arrays). Selected subsets of interconnections are determined by the program so that in a particular instruction, say, only connections to the processor immediately to the North may be enabled at every processor.

c) Storage

Data is stored in memory associated with each processor, the association typically being physical as well as logical. Thus a particular address broadcast to the array will locate single bits of data in each processor's memory, the whole forming a single bit-plane in an image.

d) Input/Output

In most cases, it will be required to input and output single bit-planes, the operation being repeated six times for a 64 grey-levels image. A convenient method for this is to link single-bit registers in each row of processors so as to form N shift-registers in an N x N array. The bit-plane can then be shifted across the array, column by column, in N cycles, after which it can be transferred into local memory in a single parallel operation.

e) Instruction Store and Controller

These are usually separate units and not part of the array as such, although in at least one SIMD machine, I C L's DAP (2), the designer has chosen to use the local memory to store instructions as well as image data.

Some of the above features are illustrated in the small section of an 8-connected array shown in Fig. 1.

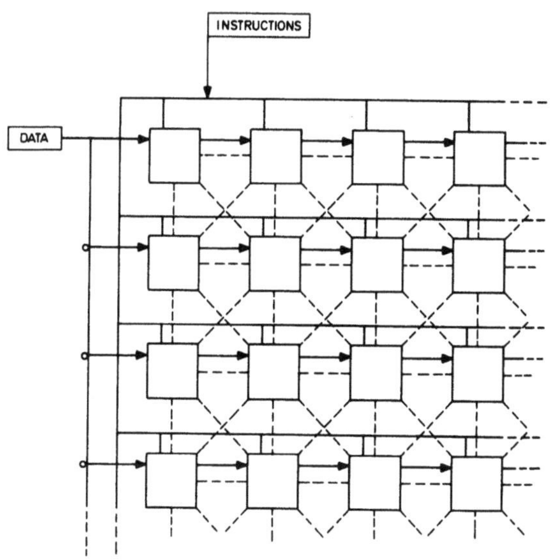

Fig. 1 Principal connections in an 8-connected SIMD array

The dotted lines represent the bidirectional processor interconnection paths. The square boxes represent both processors and memory as combined units.

Nothing has yet been said about the number of processors to be included in an array. Ideally, for the processing of an N x N image, there would be N x N processors, but this would imply that an array of over one quarter of a million processors would be needed to process a 512 x 512 image. At current prices, even the simplest processors, packed eight to an integrated circuit, might be expected to cost about 50 pence each, implying a total processor cost of the order £130,000, not including printed circuit boards, etc. More realistically, arrays ranging from 32 x 32 to 128 x 128 in size have been constructed, larger images being dealt with by scanning the processing array through blocks of image data, each block matching the processor array dimensions. Edge conditions call for special treatment and each system offers its own solution to this problem. In essence, it is necessary to provide additional storage both to present appropriate neighbourhoods to all active processors and also to preserve signals propagated out of the array block, for subsequent injection into neighbouring blocks. Obviously, scanned arrays are bound to be of considerably lower performance than complete arrays, but economics may compel their use.

3. CURRENT ARRAY DESIGNS

At the time of writing, only three SIMD image processing arrays are believed to be constructed and in operation : CLIP4, DAP and MPP. Fountain (3) has reviewed and compared these and other recent proposals in his survey of bit-serial array processor circuits, and includes a discussion of five other systems : CLIP5 (4), the NTT array processor (5), GRID (6), PCLIP (7) and LIPP (8). This survey and the original reports should be consulted for detailed information on specific systems. The similarities between such processor designs can easily be seen from Fig. 2 which shows the logic structures of CLIP4, DAP and MPP, the diagrams being reproduced from Fountain's survey paper. Further minor variations appear in the designs not illustrated here, LIPP being more different than most. Full particulars of CLIP4 (9), DAP (2) and MPP (10) can also be found in the literature. One of these (CLIP4) will now be described in more detail in order to show how a typical processor design evolves from the basic requirements imposed by the data and by the algorithms used to process the data.

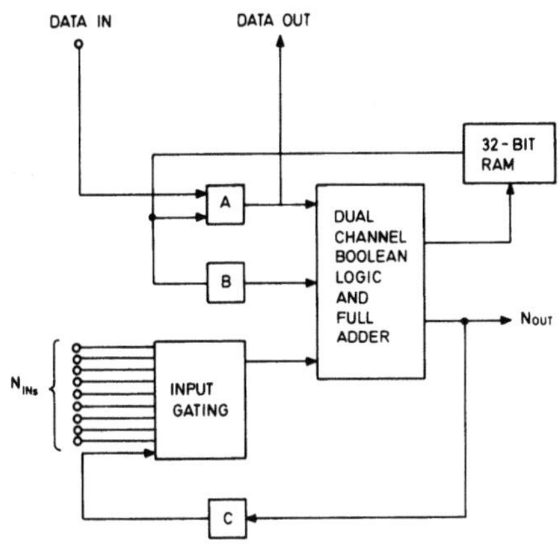

Fig. 2(a) The CLIP4 processor

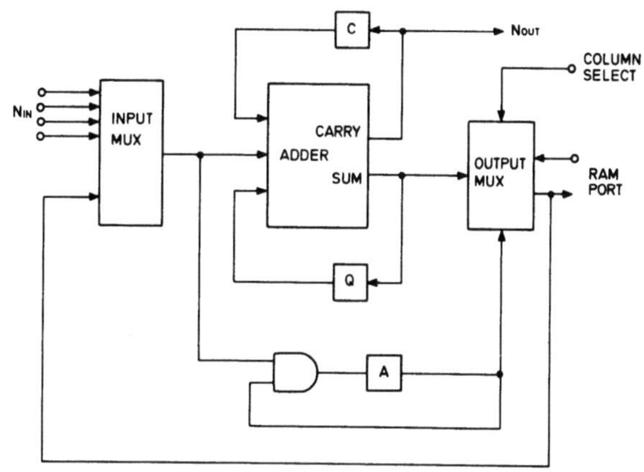

Fig. 2(b) The DAP processor

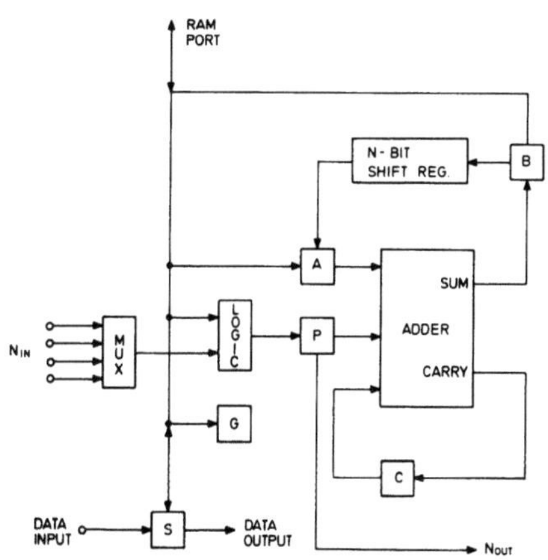

Fig. 2(c) The MPP processor

4. THE CLIP4 PROCESSOR

It is convenient to consider the operation of the CLIP4 processor in four stages, looking only at the active parts of the processor corresponding to each stage. The four stages are: (a) pointwise Boolean operations, (b) local neighbourhood Boolean operations, (c) labelled propagation operations, and (d) arithmetic operations.

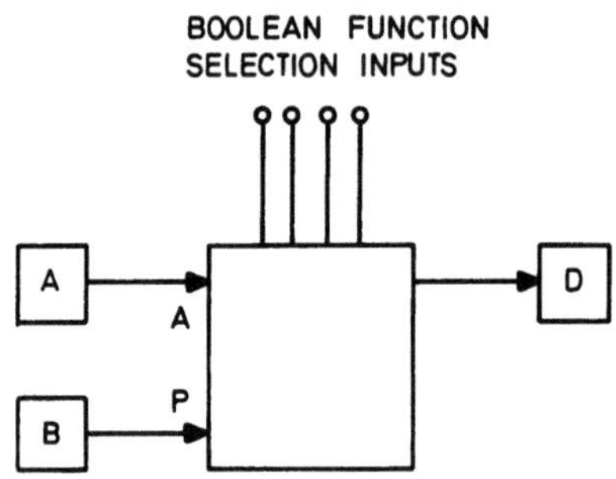

Fig. 3 Pointwise Boolean operations

(a) Pointwise Boolean operations

Each processor is provided with two single-bit buffers, labelled A and B in the diagram. Thus the arrays of these buffers can be loaded with binary images, or bit-planes. Image data are stored in memory with addresses DO to D31, one bit at each address residing with its corresponding processor. The four control lines to the processor select one of the sixteen possible Boolean functions of A and B, the result appearing at D for reloading into the desired D address. The short program sequence following takes binary images stored in D3 and D5, ORs them together and returns the result to D7, the last instruction signifying 'Process and Store':

```
LDA 3
LDB 5
SET A + B
PST 7
```

The read operations are non-destructive.

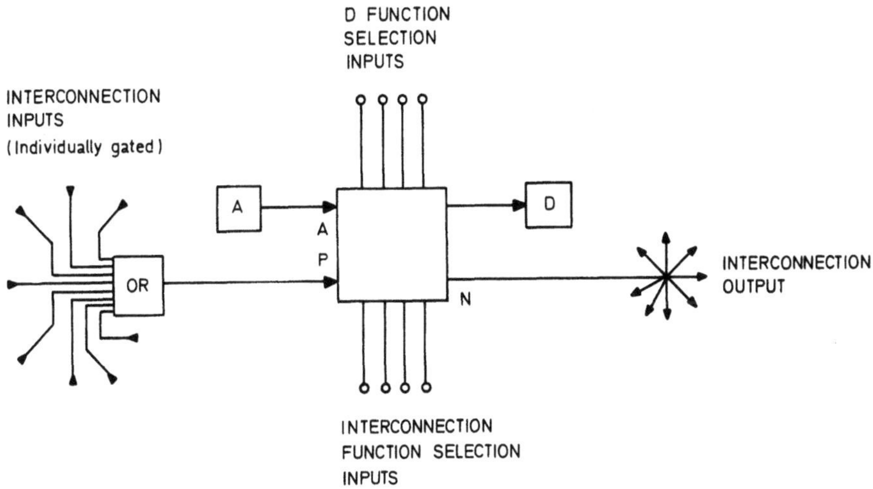

Fig. 4 Local neighbourhood Boolean operations

b) Local neighbourhood Boolean operations

The second input B is now replaced by another binary input, P. Two independent Boolean functions are formed from the two inputs A and P. These are D, as before, and N, and the second output N is immediately sent to all eight neighbouring processors. On arrival at the neighbours, the function N is summed into an OR-gate along with the N outputs from the other seven neighbours. Each direction is individually enabled so that any selected subset of the neighbour outputs can be combined in the OR-gate. The SIMD operation requires that the same subset is involved in every processor. Thus the function P is the OR of a set of N outputs from selected neighbours. A 'chicken and egg' situation is prevented by holding all the P inputs to zero at the start of each process and by disallowing Boolean functions which would, by inverting P into the output N, give rise to oscillatory conditions (assuming there could be a return path to the processor, through the array neighbours).

An example of a local neighbourhood Boolean operation is the removal of isolated 1-elements from a binary image. Suppose the image is in D1 and the 'noise-cleaned' image is to be written back into the same address. The required code would be:

```
LDA  1
SET  P.A, (1-8)A
PST  1
```

The format of the SET instruction here requires some explanation. If B_n and B_d are the Boolean functions of P and A for N and D respectively and L is a list of interconnection directions to be enabled, then the instruction is of the form:

$$\text{SET} \quad B_d, \quad (L) \quad B_n$$

the directions being labelled 1 to 8 for propagation directions proceeding in the sequence SE, S, SW, W, etc. directed towards each processor. In the example given, therefore:

$$N = A$$
$$D = P.A$$

This implies that, since all 1-elements produce an output at N which enters all neighbouring processors, the D output will only be 1 where the element itself is 1 and at least one neighbour is also 1, i.e. isolated 1-elements will not produce a 1 output and will be eliminated.

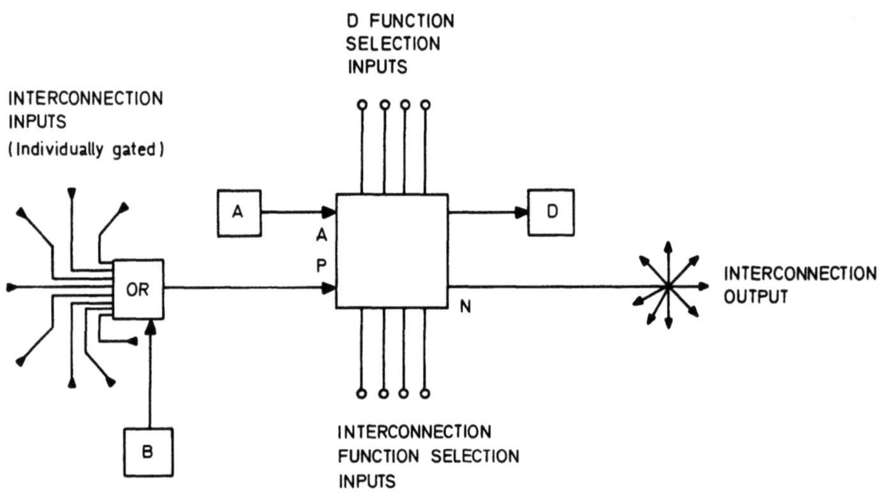

Fig. 5 Labelled propagation operations

c) Labelled propagation operations

As will be seen from the illustration, the only difference here is that the B register, containing a second binary image, is output into the interconnection signal OR-gate. To understand this configuration, consider the two functions:

$$N = P.A$$
$$D = P.A.$$

Since P will be everywhere zero at the start, then so will N. The output image D will therefore also be zero everywhere. If, however, B has the value 1 in any part of the array where A is also 1, then propagation will be initiated in that processor and parts of the input image may appear as 1-elements in the output. As an example, assume that A is loaded with an image containing several isolated objects, each being a connected group of 1-elements. Background elements are 0-elements. Assume also that the image in B is one or more 1-elements out of just one of the objects in A. If the two images are in D1 and D2 and the result image is to be returned to D3, the following short sequence would produce an image containing only the one 'labelled' object D1 of which a few elements were known and in D2:

```
LDA  1
LDB  2
SET  P.A, (1-8B) P.A.
PST  3
```

(The B in the brackets with the direction list enables the connection between the B register and the OR-gate).

Another way in which propagation can be initiated is provided by a bus running around the four array edges. All interconnection inputs from missing neighbours are taken from this bus. If E is placed at the end of a SET instruction, the bus will be set equal to 1; otherwise it is at zero. An example of the use of this bus would be:

```
LDA  1
SET  P̄.A, (1-8) P.A, E
PST  3
```

This sequence would eliminate objects touching an array edge, by passing a propagation signal through such objects and then outputting 1 only where there are 1-elements that had not received a propagation signal. Note the bar over the P in the B_n function, implying inversion.

d) Arithmetic operation (Fig. 6)

A grey-tone image consists of a stack of bit-planes, so that a 6-bit image might be stored in the array in locations D0 to D5, the least significant bits of the binary representations of the grey-levels of each pixel being in D0, and the most significant in D5. Let this image be I1 and let there be another 6-bit image I2 in D6 to D11, with its least significant bits in D6. Averaging the intensities of these two images would involve averaging corresponding pairs of pixels by summing them and dividing by 2, so that the new image I3 is given by a pointwise (pixelwise) computation of $I3=\frac{1}{2}(I1 + I2)$.

To perform a binary addition, the least significant bit-planes are loaded into A and B respectively and a bit-plane produced at D which contains the least significant bits of every summed pixel. The N output is a plane of carry bits, each either 0 or 1.

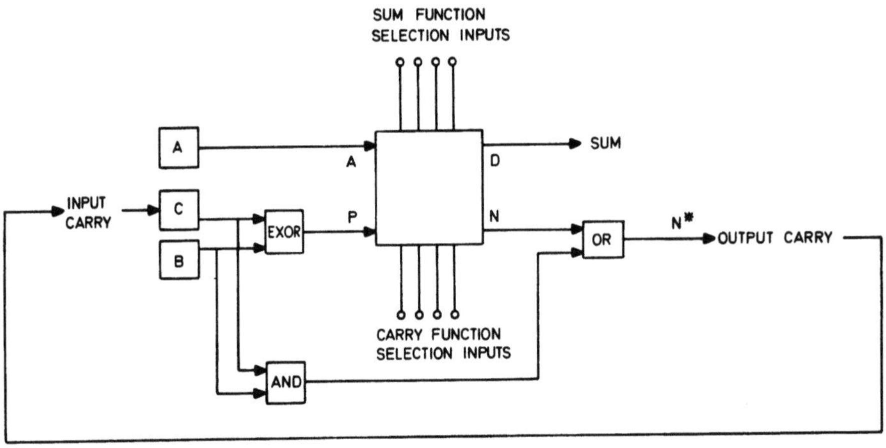

Fig. 6 Arithmetic operations

The program is:

```
LDA  0
LDB  6
SET  P @ A, (BC) P.A
PST  12
```

(The C within the brackets loads the carry plane into the C register and the symbol @ implies 'exclusive OR').

In the next stage, A and B are loaded with the next planes in each stack and a full addition carried out by enabling the extra gates shown in the figure. This is effected by including R in the SET instruction. The next program segment is:

```
LDA  1
LDB  7
SET  P @ A, (BCR) P.A
PST  13
```

and subsequent bit-planes are similarly treated. It can be deduced that the expressions for the sum and carry are those required for full addition:

SUM = C @ B @ A

NEW CARRY = (B @ C).A + B.C

A small variation in the sequence results in subtraction. Division by 2 merely involves addressing the summed image as though the most significant plane is an additional empty plane, <u>i.e.</u> by ignoring the least significant plane. Thus the 6-bit averaged image I3 will have its least and most significant bit-planes in D12 and D17 respectively.

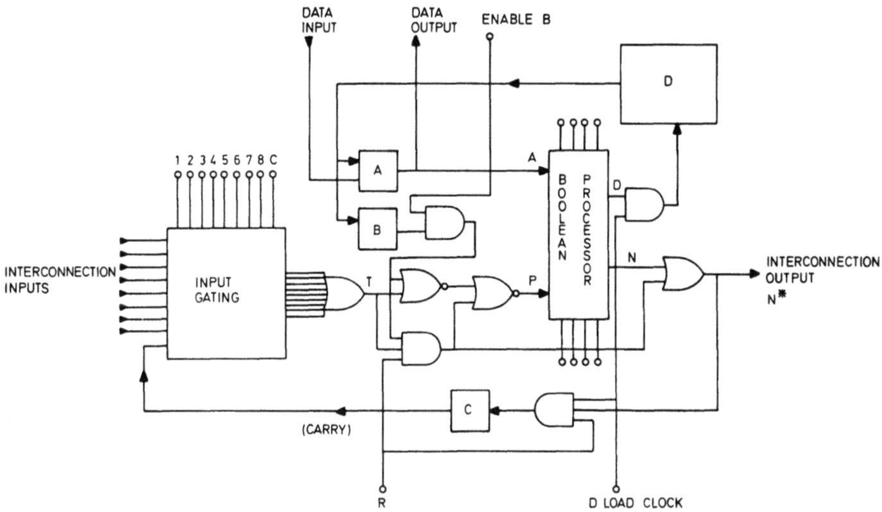

Fig. 7 The complete CLIP4 processor logic

The four stages outlined above each involve different parts of the full processor structure. The complete structure is shown in Fig. 7, the only additional parts being enable lines for the various modes of operation.

5. THE COMPLETE IMAGE PROCESSOR

In the previous section, the operation of a single processing element (usually abbreviated in the literature to 'PE') was described in some detail. Nevertheless, many important aspects of the complete system were ignored. For example, in order to input an image into the array, it may be necessary to have available a television camera, an analogue to digital converter, an image store, and an image reformatter. This latter item takes each bit-plane of the stored image and restructures it as a set of N single bit pixel strings, each N pixels long (as required by the shift-registers for inputting the image). The outputting of images, single bit-planes at a time into an image store, is effected in a manner similar to inputting, and is followed by digital to analogue conversion for display purposes. Alternatively, images can be passed to and from disk and tape files.

The CLIP4 system is able to stand alone but is, in fact, hosted by a DEC PDP 11/34 running under the UNIX operating system. This permits easy communication with the array and multiple use of editing facilities, for example.

Finally, any worthwhile image processing system will be expected to support at least one high-level language. CLIP4 is predominantly programmed in IPC which is an image processing variant of C, developed at University College London by Reynolds and Otto (11).

The detailed description given above refers specifically to CLIP4 but illustrates the principles involved in most SIMD image processor designs, the differences being mainly in emphasis rather than principle. Some of the problems involved in designing efficient algorithms for such systems are discussed in the next section.

6. PARALLEL ALGORITHMS

Cellular logic arrays for image processing have been discussed in detail in the earlier sections of this paper. In the following sections the ways in which such arrays can be used to process images will be reviewed, giving particular attention to the problem of designing algorithms which are efficient when implemented on SIMD machines.

Novel architectures have a bad reputation in that it is generally assumed that they must of necessity be difficult to program. It is certainly true that any new computer, especially when developed non-commercially in a research laboratory, is unlikely to offer the software support which has come to be expected of the more widely available marketed machines. Equally, the absence of user-experience will imply that not all the 'bugs' will be out of the system. But the prejudice runs deeper than this; it is thought that there must be inherent difficulties in programming which are rooted in the architecture itself, not in the early state of development of the software facilities.

Some systems have exactly this disadvantage. MIMD machines, comprising assemblies of autonomous processors, each of which can be running different program segments, present enormous difficulties which tend to make the process of efficient compiler writing close to impossible. A consequence of this is that a compromise may have to be struck between ease of use on the one hand and maximum utilisation of processors on the other. However, it is not the purpose of this paper to discuss these and other more complex systems, but rather to study the much more manageable task of programming SIMD arrays. First, it is well to consider the motivation for programmers faced with this exercise, and to point out certain causes for misunderstanding.

7. CHOOSING AN ALGORITHM

Before discussing how algorithms are designed, the reasons for selecting a particular algorithm should be carefully examined. In many cases, the programmer has an image processing task to perform but, rather than starting with the task specification, the starting point becomes an algorithm which was originally written for a very different type of computer architecture. This algorithm may have tacitly assumed constraints which are actually not present in the SIMD structure and, equally, may ignore constraints which are present. In a properly devised system, all programs should be executable, but the time penalties for failing to appreciate the constraints might be, and usually are, severe.

As an example, consider the problem of finding all the edge elements in a binary image comprising several black objects (some with holes) on a white background. Various ingenious border-following algorithms have been proposed for serial computation and these could be implemented on an SIMD array. In practice, this is never done since it is only necessary to give each processor an instruction sequence which says: output a black element if the input element is black and there is at least one neighbouring white element. This obviously short instruction sequence takes full advantage of the array architecture and is therefore optimally efficient. It would probably not be so efficient on a conventional serial machine since much time would be wasted exploring all black or all white regions of the image. In fact, many of the array's processors are similarly fruitlessly occupied but, since they cannot, under an SIMD regime, be freed to do anything else, no usable processing power is wasted.

SIMD architectures have been criticised for exactly this point, that although all the processors are busy most of the time, much of their business is dissipated in parts of the image which are not required to be processed. Proponents of these architectures point to a similar 'misuse' of memory in serial machines, and also complain that serial computation is inherently more wasteful than parallel computation, in that a substantial part of the workload derives from the need to calculate addresses in the image data - an activity largely unnecessary in SIMD machines. Furthermore, it could reasonably be argued that although it may be academically challenging to produce systems and algorithms which give 100% utilisation of the available resources, in practical terms this may be a fruitless exercise. What is actually required is a system which can be manufactured (and sold) cheaply, programmed simply, which does not take up too much space or use excessive amounts of power, and which performs image processing tasks rapidly. There is no reason to believe that 100% resource utilization will necessarily result in the achievement of these aims.

Whatever the computer architecture in use, it is self-evident, but not always readily appreciated, that certain algorithms will be unsuitable for implementation in a line-by-line translation. The important step which must be taken is to go back to the task specification. Even this may not be far enough back. For example, the optical inspection techniques which are in current use are almost all intended for human vision. The human visual system is immensely powerful for pattern recognition, for discrimination between slightly differing grey-tones, and for detection of low light levels. It is extremely poor for counting and for measurement of lengths and areas. Classification of biological cells, or the detection of disease in cells and tissues, might therefore be expected to be performed best in completely different ways by Man and Machine, since machine-based vision has an almost complementary set of strong points to offer. The difficulty for the image processing expert is to convince potential users of his system to abandon their well-tried and provenly successful techniques for faster but relatively unassessed automatic methods.

8. THE STRENGTHS AND WEAKNESSES OF SIMD

Just as it should not be surprising that the mammalian retina has peak spectral sensitivity near the peak of the Sun's emission, so it should not be unexpected that SIMD architecture can be easily programmed to provide efficient image processing. These architectures were proposed and originally developed with image analysis as an objective. Algorithms suitable for SIMD arrays were suggested long before the arrays themselves could sensibly be constructed (12-15), so that machine designers already had guidance as to what might be required of them.

Looking at current SIMD systems, proposed or in operation, certain common features emerge:

a) Strengths

Most SIMD arrays are particularly good at handling binary images, mainly because of their bit-serial structure. Point Boolean operations between pairs of binary images, and single array position shifts of binary images, are the fundamental, lowest complexity operations which can be performed. It can easily be shown that all conceivable image functions can be built up from finite sequences of these two types of fundamental operations.

Simple arithmetic functions of one or more images can be calculated in order (B) time, where B is the number of bits/pixel in the result image. Multiplication and division are based on address shifting and additions and will require order (B^2) time, except in more advanced systems, such as CLIP7, which will make use of multi-bit processors (16).

The implementation of local (immediate) neighbour operations involves the shifting of data from each of the neighbours to the central processor of each neighbourhood. Some array structures simplify the process for binary images by permitting simultaneous interconnections into some form of arithmetic or logical gate. An early array, CLIP3, provided both options (17) by incorporating a summing and thresholding unit in each processor. More typically, a neighbourhood operation on B-bit images with a neighbourhood with L elements, will require B.L shifts, L B-bit multiplications and L additions in which the largest will involve B+logL bits. Although this is non-trivial, it should be remembered that the complete sequence need only be performed once for the entire image (assuming a full coverage array of processors).

Propagation in arrays can lead to extremely efficient algorithms. In a propagating operation, a binary signal is passed from processor to processor conditionally upon the state of the image at each processor. Referring to the CLIP4 code used earlier in this paper, if B_N contains the variable P (or $\bar{P}$), propagation may take place. Propagation, often referred to as 'global propagation' in this context, has many useful and sometimes surprising applications. Consider, for example, the generation of so-called 'ramps'. If an array is filled with 1s and loaded into the A buffer of CLIP4, propagation can be caused to take place by specifying the SET instruction: SET P @ A, (8) P @ A (where @ implies exclusive OR as before). This causes the propagation signal to alternate between 1 and 0 at consecutive elements in each row of the array. The same values are then stored and reloaded into A. The next SET instruction is: SET $P.\bar{A}$, (8) A, and this has the effect of generating and storing a 1 after each 1-0 transition along the rows of data in A. These pairs of instructions are then applied consecutively and repeatedly until an empty array is formed, the data arrays generated after the odd number operations (i.e. the SET instructions involving exclusive ORs) being treated as the planes of a bit stack. Although not intuitively obvious, it can be shown that the numbers stored in the bit stacks at each array element are equal to the x coordinates of each element. The y coordinates can be formed by an equivalent process with direction 6 substituting for direction 8 in the SET instructions.

Propagation takes place without memory references and is therefore very fast (typically 10 times faster than other operations). It thus provides a means of transporting data rapidly across the array. A detailed discussion of propagation is given in (18).

Object counting can be achieved by sequences of array operations, but these tend to be not particularly efficient. A much faster method is used in CLIP4 which takes advantage of the parallel input-output lines (one in each row) of the array. Single bit-planes are clocked out of the array, column by column, into a 'tree' of adding units, so that the sum is obtained in the highest node of the tree a few clock cycles after the bit-plane is out of the array. In an N x N array, the time taken for summation is thus order (N).

Many useful image operations are based on the various processes described above. Convolution merely involves image shifting and simple arithmetic; it is consequently not often necessary to move into the Fourier domain, particularly as much information about spatial frequences can be found by employing sequences of shrink and expand functions. A fuller account of these and other local neighbourhood operations is given in (19).

b) Weaknesses

As may be deduced from the description of SIMD arrays as 'parallel processors', any process which is inherently serial in its nature, particularly 'pixel-serial', will not be efficiently performed in an SIMD system. The situation can be aggravated by lack of memory assigned to the individual processors. For example, replacing grey-levels by table look-up is a trivial operation if there is room to store the table in each pixel's memory, otherwise the operation must involve a large, serial component. In general, remapping either in intensity or position, is not efficiently performed by SIMD arrays.

A second weakness concerns shifting data across the array by preselected amounts. Unless propagation can be used (and this will not normally be possible except for binary images), the process will involve shifting each bit plane by series of unit steps. An attempt to eliminate this weakness has been made by designing pyramid structures, giving order (logN) steps for any shift by N positions. This property has been discussed by several authors; see for example Uhr in (20).

Finally, the long, involved conditional programs concerned with structural form in scenes and images are not easily or even sensibly handled by arrays and more usually are implemented in the serial machine hosting the array.

The SIMD array does not provide answers to all image processing problems. Nevertheless, its performance on many of them has ensured its place in image laboratories for many years to come.

9. REFERENCES

1. Flynn, M J, Some computer organizations and their effectiveness; IEEE Trans. Comput., C-21, pp. 948-960, 1972.

2. Reddaway, S F, DAP - a distributed processor array; First Annual Symposium on Computer Architecture, Florida, pp. 61-65, 1973.

3. Fountain, T J, A Survey of bit-serial array processor circuits; In Computer Structure for Image Processing (ed. M J B Duff), Academic Press, pp. 1-14, 1983.

4. Fountain, T J, Towards CLIP6 - an extra dimension; IEEE Computer Society Workshop on Computer Architecture for Pattern Analysis and Image Database Management, Hot Springs, Va., pp. 25-30, 1981.

5. Sudo, T and Nakashima, T, An LSI adaptive array processor; IEEE International Solid-State Circuits Conference, pp.122-123 & 307, 1982.

6. Robinson, I N and Moore, W R, A parallel processor array architecture and its implementation in silicon; Proceedings of IEEE Custom Integrated Circuits Conference, Rochester, N.Y., pp. 41-45, 1982.

7. Tanimoto, S L and Pfieffer, J J, Jr., An image processor based on an array of pipelines; IEEE Computer Society Workshop on Computer Architecture for Pattern Analysis and Image Database Management, Hot Springs, Va., pp. 201-208, 1981.

8. Danielsson, P-E and Ericsson, T, Suggestions for an image processor array; Internal Report LITH-ISY-I-0507, Linköping University, Sweden, 1982.

9. Duff, M J B, Review of the CLIP image processing system; Proceedings of the National Computer Conference, pp. 1055-1060, 1978.

10. Batcher, K E, Design of a Massively Parallel Processor; IEEE Trans. on Comp., C-29, pp. 836-840, 1980.

11. Reynolds, D E and Otto, G P, Software tools for CLIP4; Image Processing Group Report 82/1, University College London, 1982.

12. Unger, S H, A computer orientated toward spatial problems; Proc. IRE, 46, pp. 1744-1750, 1958.

13. Slotnick, D L, Borck, W C and McReynolds, R C, The SOLOMON Computer; Proc. Western Joint Comp. Conf., pp. 87-107, 1962.

14. McCormick, B H, The Illinois pattern recognition computer ILLIAC III; IEEE Trans. Electron. Commun., EC-12, pp. 791-813, 1963.

15. Levialdi, S, "CLOPAN": a closedness pattern analyzer; Proc. IEE, 115n, no.6, pp. 879-880, 1968.

16. Fountain, T J, CLIP7 - The development of a multi-valued array processor, Internal Report 82/7, Image Processing Group, University College London, 1982.

17. Duff, M J B, Watson, D M, Fountain, T J, and Shaw, G K, A cellular logic array for image processing; Pattern Recognition, 5, pp. 229-247, 1973.

18. Duff, M J B, Propagation in Cellular Logic Arrays; Proc., IEEE Workshop on Picture Data Description and Management, Pacific Grove, Ca., pp. 259-262, 1980.

19. Duff, M J B, Neighbourhood operators; in Physical and Biological Processing of Images (eds. O J Braddick and A C Sleigh), Springer-Verlag, pp. 53-72, 1983.

20. Uhr, L, Schmitt, L and Hanrahan, P, Cone/pyramid perception programs for arrays and networks; in Multicomputers and Image Processing (eds. K Preston, Jr., and L Uhr) Academic Press, pp. 179-191, 1982.

CLASSIFICATION SCHEMES FOR IMAGE PROCESSING ARCHITECTURES

V. Cantoni

Dipartimento di Informatica e Sistemistica
Università di Pavia
Strada Nuova 106/c
27100 Pavia (Italy)

ABSTRACT

Over the last years a number of classification schemes for image processing architectures have been presented, five of them are discussed here with the purpose of pointing out the design principles of the existing systems. These five schemes focus the attention on different structural characteristics: matching to data or computation structures; interprocessor communication modes; levels of parallelism; subarrays composition; image memory storage and management. The main features of machines belonging to each class of the five taxonomies are pointed aut and a few examples of each class are chosen.

1. INTRODUCTION

During the 1960s and 1970s a wide variety of different computer architectures for image processing have been designed for research purposes. In the late 1970s and early 1980s the first commercial systems appeared. Coupled with the evolution of these machines is the increase in the number of types. Over the last years several attempts of classification of these architectures have been made, in order to observe commonalities, trends and consequences of various design decisions.
The classification scheme of organisms which best reflects the totality of similarities and differences is called taxonomy, because, in accordance with the biological theory of evolution, all species are descended from single species characterized by different "taxa". A taxonomy of image processing architectures is more difficult because

NATO ASI Series, Vol. F18
Computer Architectures for Spatially Distributed Data
Edited by H. Freeman and G. G. Pieroni

it is necessary to identify the "taxon" referring other than to the existing examples, also to the future advances that modern technologies will provide.
In what follows, the "taxa" of five classification schemes described in literature will be highlighted and a few examples of each class are chosen.

2. GENERAL PURPOSE COMPUTER CLASSIFICATION SCHEMES

Many attempts have been made to overcome the bottleneck of the Von Neumann traditional computer architecture (1) since the 1960s. Several different parallel machines have been suggested and built. In 1972 a first attempt to classify the wide variety of machines in discussion has been made by Flynn (2). The taxonomy of Flynn is based on how to overcome the Von Neumann bottleneck. In fact, the processor-memory channel of the sequential machine is used in one-word-at-a-time style for both the instruction and the data streams. Separating the data stream from the instruction stream, four classes of architectures can be defined according to whether the instruction or the data streams are single or multiple.
The taxonomy of Flynn is briefly presented here because it has been widely discussed and applied in the image processing area, and the associated terminology has become part of the language of computer science.
- SISD (Fig. 1.a) - Single instruction stream / Single Data stream. This is the uniprocessor system class in which there is one stream of instructions and a single stream of the related arguments and results. The DEC PDP 11 computers is an example of this kind of machine.
- MISD (Fig. 1.b) - Multiple Instruction stream / Single Data stream. This is the class of particular data-flow architectures using just one linear data stream. Each processor executes a predefined instruction stream. Common I/O image devices working in raster scan format are suitable for this architecture: as raw data streams in, processed data streams out. The IBM 360/91 and the Cytocomputer are two examples of this kind of machines.
- SIMD (Fig. 1.c) - Single Instruction stream / Multiple Data stream. This is the case of a single global control which drives several processing units. The common instruction stream is fed by

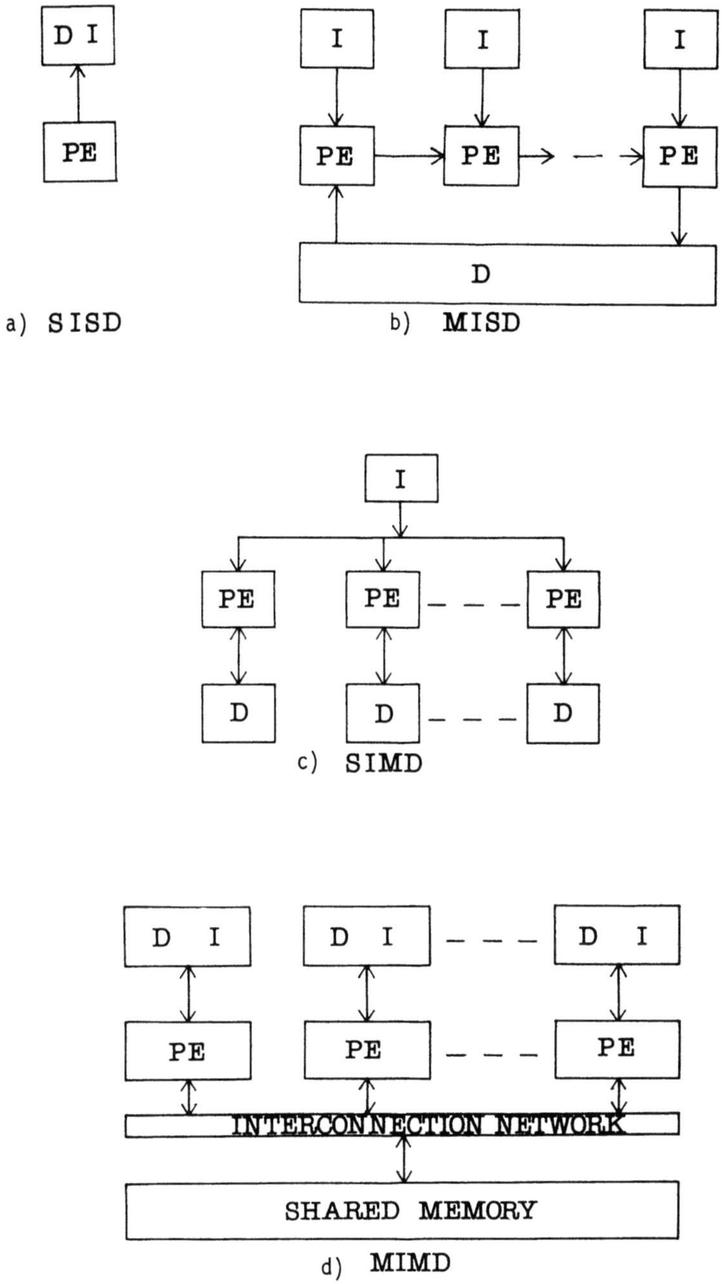

Fig. 1. The four classes of the Flynn's taxonomy.

the control unit to the processor units that operate indentically on separated data streams. In image processing the principle described here, is to distribute the image over the processing units (3,4), often the alternative solution, to distribute the processor units over the image is used; this second case can be included in this class though it is doubtful whether this is appropriate. The ILLIAC IV, CLIP 4, MMP are examples of this kind of machine.

- MIMD (Fig. 1.d) - Multiple Instruction stream / Multiple Data stream. This is the class of multiple processor systems in which the processors execute different instruction streams on different data streams. In this case different tasks are executed by each processor in parallel, with moderate communication between processors because of the difficulties of synchronization. The UNIVAC 1108 and ZMOB computers are examples of this kind of machine. A subclass is the Multi-SIMD, in which the system can be structured as two, or more, independent SIMD machines. The PASM computer is and example of this architecture.

Nevertheless, several well known architectures cannot be fitted clearly into this classification and others may be equally fitted in different classes. Many other classification schemes have been proposed, a second one will be introduced here because of the importance of the information on which it is based: the levels of parallelism. Four levels of possible parallelisms to improve the computer's effectiveness have been recognized (5): complete jobs level, tasks within a job, basic operations within a task (instruction level), sub-operations (arithmetic or bit level).

Without taking care of the connection between processors and memory, the Erlangen (6) classification is based on the following three consequent processing levels:

- PCU - Program Control Unit for the exploitation of the first two types of parallelism

- ALU - Arithmetic Logical unit for the basic operations within a task

- ELC - Elementary Logic Unit for the sub-operations execution

A machine architecture can include several PCU's. Each PCU can control several ALU's, each one executing the same operations. Each

ALU can contain several ELC's each one dedicated to one bit position. The one introduced here corresponds to an "horizontal" replication of PCU, ALU, ELC a "vertical" replication by pipelining is possible at all the levels described (6), obtaining respectively: macro-pipelining, instruction pipelining (or "instruction look-ahead"), arithmetical pipeline.
Using the Erlangen classification scheme a computer class is evaluated by six independent measures of parallelism, as summarized in the following equation:

$$t = (k \times k', d \times d', w \times w')$$

number of:

PCU's in parallel	(multi-processor)
PCU's in pipelining	(macro-pipelining)
ALU's in parallel	(array computer)
ALU's in pipelining	(instruction pipelining)
ELC in parallel	(wordlength)
ELC in pipelining	(arithmetic pipelining)

This classification form the basis of a taxonomy that is easy to apply to varied computer architectures, from the simple scalar microprocessor, through the multi-unit pipeline vector computer, to the highly replicated processor array.

3. IMAGE PROCESSING ARCHITECTURES: CLASSIFICATION APPROACHES

A number of classification schemes for image processing architectures have been presented, five of them are discussed here with the purpose of clarifying the design principles of these systems. These five schemes focus the attention on different structural characteristics: matching to data or computation structures; interprocessor communication modes; levels of parallelism; subarrays composition; image memory storage and management.

Task matching approach

Image processing is often characterized by the repetition of the same computation on a well defined regular data structure: the array of image points. In order to speed-up the execution of programs, the Von Neumann architecture has been modified so as to match the data structure and the algorithm structure. From this standpoint machines may be classified in terms of how much this matching has been achieved (7).

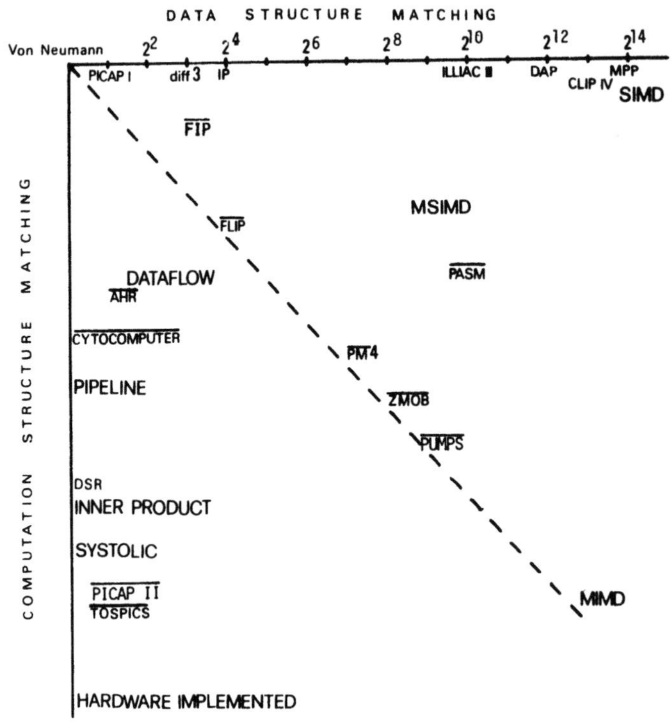

Fig.2. Matching representation for different architectures of image processing systems. Machines having a black line on the top of their name are byte oriented machines, the remaining one are bit oriented. Classes of machines are indicated using larger characters.

In fig. 2, a "matching plane" representation has been introduced where the X-axis give the data structure matching index and the Y-axis the computational structure matching index, so allowing us to plot, as points, the different machines suggested and constructed for fast, convenient image processing. On the origin, the one word-at-a-time (either data or instruction access) processing mode is represented by the Von Neumann computer, whilst moving away from this point we may plot more powerful and better matched architectures to fulfill image tasks.

Along the data structure axis a number of machines which fall into the SIMD class and contain array organizations of processors are placed, in increasing number of processing elements, up the maximum value of 128x128 belonging to the MPP. The geometrical structure of these machines includes: hexagonal plane tessellation which produces 6 (diff3) and 4/8 (all the other) neighbors for each pixel; different local storage values (the maximum amount is 1Kbit for the MPP). The higher the number of processing elements in the array, the higher the amount of memory per processor must be to handle typical operations (such as histogramming, computation of region properties, etc).

The MIMD class of machines is represented along the line at 45 degrees. These machines have the possibility of executing simultaneously a different instruction on each processor, but this feature creates difficulties when designing their operating system since the concurrency of execution by means of the resources present in the machine creates both synchronization and data transmission problems. These machines are mainly based on a channel (bus) communication system between processors (for instance the conveyor belt in ZMOB) which allows a fast, flexible connection, in byte parallel mode so ensuring efficient computation on a dynamically configurable system. Each unit may process data both from its own local memory (of the order of several thousands of bytes) or from other memories including those of the other processors.

The octant defined between the SIMD and MIMD representation lines identifies the Multi-SIMD class of Machines. This architecture may be seen as containing different SIMD machines each executing its own program, sharing resources like memory and communication bus. Furthermore a processor in the system may perform as a controller or even dynamically reconfigure the system alterating the SIMD partition size as a function of the problem requirement. The configuration manager has available the low-level information from the single SIMD groups enabling the system to perform higher level tasks. For these reasons MSIMD and MIMD machines appear more suitable for pattern recognition and artificial intelligence applications than SIMD

machines which are particularly tailored for image processing.
The other octant (comprised between the MIMD representation line and the computation structure matching index axis) generally identifies architectures which more direclty implement the algorithm structure either by hardware oriented construction or by an open end cascaded set of programmable units.
The first set of machines includes systems which contain special function units that perform typical image processing algorithms or sets of related functions by hardware. The inner product computer and the systolic chip are two families of very fast devices that outperform by one order of magnitude the equivalent programmed versions of the same machines. One application of the first family is in computerized tomography and specifically in the reconstruction of 3-D human organs from a given set of their projections (see DSR of Mayo Clinic project). The second family includes pipeline and data flow machines where the computation is decomposed a-priori in elementary subtasks, performed respectively in a sequential mode by a linear chain of processors (each one having its own program), or in a data selected more mode where the subtask (template) is triggered by the data for every requested instance.

Interprocessor communication

Advances in VLSI technology provided both hardware oriented implementations (architectures belonging to the area away from the origin, nearby the Y-axis, in Fig.2) and powerful general purpose architectures. The X-axis of Fig.2 shows SIMD machines in increasing numbers of processors; the set of machines in the first part was fabricated ten years ago, new machines such as CLIP 4 and MPP are characterized by 9216 and 16384 processing elements respectively. The higher the number of processors and memory units, the greater the role in system design of communications among processors, and among processors and local/global memories. In this connection a taxonomy has been presented (8) (Fig.3) based on combining two classification criteria: the former referring to flexibility, between homogeneous or general purpose programmable architectures and heterogeneous or functionally dedicated architectures; the latter, instead referring to the interconnection structure of the system. With regard to the second criteria, three major classes of physical communication systems are used: fixed interconnection structures, bus interconnection structures and reconfigurable interconnection structure. The main classes of the taxonomy are briefly discussed here concerning the latter criteria. General considerations about the flexibility characteristic have been discussed in the previous chapter: in fact, the octant of Fig.2 compressed between the data structure axis and the MIMD representation line, broadly corresponds to the homogeneous general purpose architecture, and the other octant represents the heterogeneous functionally dedicated systems.

- Homogeneous programmable/fixed interconnected structures. In these architectures each processing element is connected to n neighbors ($1 \angle n \leq$ number of processors). Cellular arrays based on regular meshes, or hexagonal or eight connected square plane tessellations belong to this group. The efficiency of this machine is drastically decreased when communication between processors cannot be realized in a "tightly orchestrated way". In (9) it has been shown that in several practical cases the SIMD structure has a communication time higher than its computation time. Methods for efficient propagation across cellular array have been developed and one of most interesting is that of using a "pyramid" structure, with each plane of processors half the size of the preceding layer. Each processor is connected to a cell of the "father" plane and to four cells of the "son" plane. In this case the speed of communication is increased at the expense of an increment of connection complexity and a higher number of processors (33% more than in the array structure). However a higher computational speed can be obtained, due to the pyramid structure, in several practical applications. Another family of machines belonging to this class utilizes for interprocessor communication a ring shift register (n=2); ZMOB is an example. Tasks well suited for the execution of these machines are those in which control and communication are a negligible fraction of the computational depth of the algorithm.

- Homogeneous programmable/bus oriented structures. A common solution for data transfer in a distribuited processors' system is provided by the bus structure. On the bus a logical link creates a communication path between processors. Buses represent shared resources and in tasks with frequent data transfer contention may arise (obviously communication proceeds one at a time). Referring to the previous classes of SIMD architectures, in this case the degree of concurrency in communication is lower, but higher speed buses with larger bandwidth are possible, so that the global computation times are often comparable. FLIP is an example of these machines.

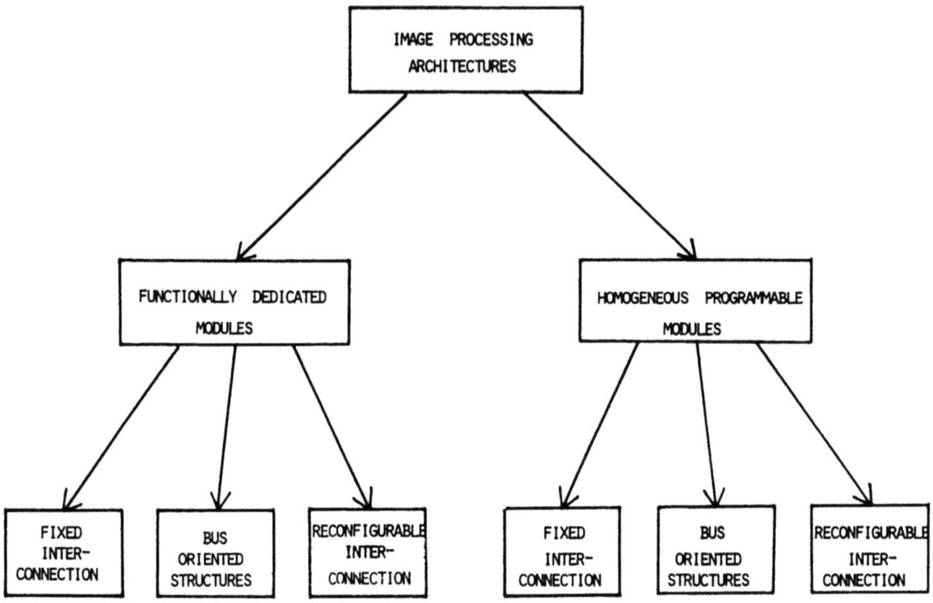

Fig. 3. Classification scheme based on flexibility and communication structure.

- Homogeneous programmable/reconfigurable interconnection structures. A number of reconfigurable interconnection structures have been proposed: such as the crossbar network (N^2 switching element with a delay equal to one level of switching), the Banyan,the Omega and the Delta networks (0.5 $N\lg_2 N$ switching elements with a delay equal to $\lg_2 N$ levels of switching), etc. Systems of this class can be reconfigured into different forms of SIMD, MSIMD or MIMD machines. Obviously, the possibility of different modes of operation enables the system to "match" computing or data flow structures. Nevertheless, these architectures are not very efficiently organized for low level image processing, since much hardware is devoted to asynchronous data communication between units, and the common neighborhood access requested for every pixel in this kind of problem can become a real bottleneck. Examples of this class are PASM, PUMPS, PM4.

- Heterogeneous functionally dedicated/fixed interconnection structures. Advances in VLSI provided the possibility of developing these architectures. Two approaches have been followed: to map algorithms directly onto silicon using a single chip for each functional primitive; to use few different types of cells interconnected in a regular pattern. Particularly suitable for this implementation are low level algorithms, where the sequence of operations independent of the data has to be executed for every pixel. In such cases communication is performed by dedicated link, and control is mainly concerned with the flow of the data between modules. Examples of these systems are the Cytocomputer and the systolic arrays.

- Heterogeneous functionally dedicated/bus oriented structures. These machines consist of an host system and a set of special processing function units. A special function processing unit is a special purpose hardware for implementing a single function or a set of related functions. In these machines communication is mainly concerned to the transfer of data to and from the units, and synchronization is necessary only for initiating and terminating functions. TOSPICS and PICAP II are two examples of this class of architectures.

Levels of parallelism

This classification has been presented by Danielsson-Levialdi (10), and corresponds for image processing machines to the Erlangen classification previously described. In this case four dimensions of parallelism may be introduced:

- the seguence operations	(operator parallelism = pipelining)
- the image coordinates	(image palallelism)
- the neighborhood points	(neighborhood parallelism)
- the pixel bits	(word conventional parallelism)

To some extent these dimensions correspond to the classes of parallelism discussed in paraghraph 2. The operator parallelism corresponds to "task within a job", the image and neighborhood parallelisms corresponds to the level of "basic operations within a task", and lastly the pixel bits dimension corresponds to the "sub-operations" level. The total parallelism of a given architecture can be then measured by four indices Ko, Ki, Kn, Kp. Explicit examples of the four levels are shown in Fig. 4. The product of the four parameters gives information about the potential speed of a given architecture. The actual system capacity, obviously, is at last determined also by the internal processor design and the technologies used. As an example of this taxonomy the amounts of parallelism of the well known Cytocomputer and MPP machines are given respectively by the following quaterns:

N. stages word size

$$K_{Cytocomputer} = 88 \times 1 \times 9 \times 8 = 6336$$

$$K_{MPP} = 1 \times 16384 \times 5 \times 1 = 81920$$

N. PE's N. neighbors

Subarrays composition

The image size can vary widely, there are applications such as robotics, in which a resolution of 64x64 pixels is usually sufficient, and other applications such as the case of satellite imagery, in which the size can be 2500x3000 (Landsat), up to the GOES weather satellite having 15000x15000 pixels per image. Systems containing enough elements to match the maximum practical size are very unlikely. Therefore, the image often has to be distributed over the processors using windowing. In the case of local operations, the solution of the window border problem is requested and in some cases, as in iterative operations, the difficulties grow. A large portion of low level image processing is of the local operations type and "the neighborhood access problem is the Von Neumann bottleneck of image processing" (3).
In this connection the existing architectures can be grouped (Preston (11)) in four major architectural types: the single subarray sequential processor, the multiple subarray processor, the full array

processor and the pipeline processor.

- Single element subarray machines. By means of suitable shift-register as data streams in, a subarray of the immediate neighbors (four or eight for the cartesian tessellation and six for the hexagonal one) scan the image and provides the processing element with immediate access in a window centered in each pixel, so synchronously processed pixel streams out. Such machines are practical only for particular tasks because the time response can be effective only for a small number of operations per pixel and small image size (on-line processing obviously limits burdensomely the number of operations per pixel). The Cellscan and GLOPR are two example of this kind of machine.
- Multiple element subarray machines. This class of machine has a number of processing elements, each one having a parallel neighborhood logic that provides access to the bits of its neighbors. Due to the moderate number of processors, a suitable approach is that of distributing the processors throughout the image, so that each one has a portion of the image. In this manner the computation rate can rise by a factor equal to the number of processors. Obviously an overhead due to the border problem and to the coordination of the processing units must be taken into account. During the 80's the complete experimentation and consolidation of ultra high speed technologies, such as the subnanosecond gallium arsenide, will possibly provide for this class of machine (11) an operation time of less than 100 picosecond per pixel using a single circuit board. The diff3 and PHP II are two examples of this kind of architecture.
- Full array processor. This class corresponds to that of the SIMD machines in the Flynn's taxonomy. The approach is to set up systems using the largest number of processors (compatible with economical and technological reasons) operating in parallel, by simplifying the single processing unit (usually in these cases the arithmetic is bit-serial). Up to now the maximum array built is the MPP (Goodyear Aerospace for NASA) that contains 128x128 processing units. Also in this case, often, only a small portion of the image can be processed simultaneously, so the approach is to distribute the image to the processors one block at a time. Performing local operations, difficulties arise in the border processors, and in the case of iterative local operations, the useful part of the array propagates inward at every operation. In the future, VLSI technology will permit larger arrays, but it is highly unlikely that systems with full image will

be built in the next decade (11). The impact of VLSI technology on these machines is limited by the fact that the number of processing elements integrated on one chip has a bond with the number of pins required for the connection to all neighbors. The MPP and CLIP IV are two examples of this class of architecture.

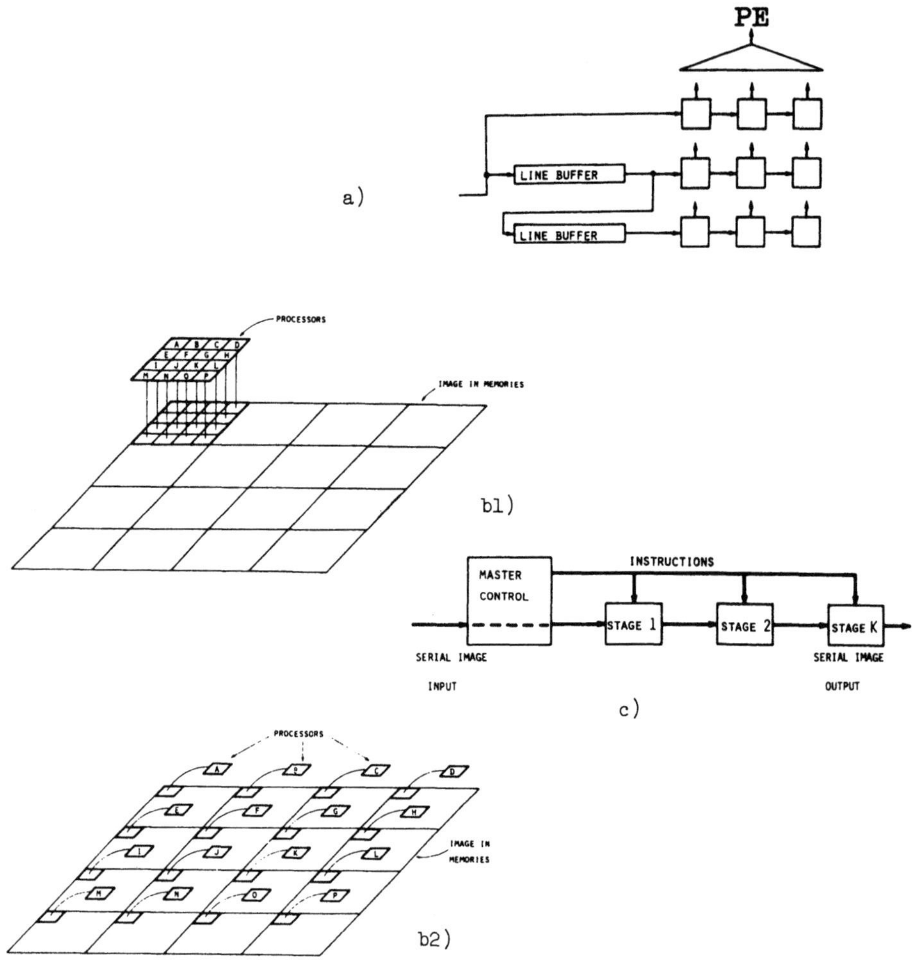

Fig. 4. Examples of the three higher levels of parallelism: a) operator parallelism; b) image parallelism (b1: image distributed over PE's; b2: PE's distributed over image); c) neighborhood parallelism.

- Pipeline architecture. This class of architecture is in a way complementary to the previous one, and resembles the MISD class of Flynn's taxonomy. The subarray units are linked together in a linear unilateral structure, and the computation is decomposed a priori in elementary subtasks, performed respectively in a sequential mode as the data flows downstream. Common I/O devices can easily interface these machines. If there are fewer program steps than processors, a number of "idle" elements pass the data they receive to the output and the machine is not fully utilized. On the contrary, if there are not enough units available, data has to be recycled with remaining steps loaded. In any case, for dedicated image processing systems where the processing is well defined and understood, this architecture offer the greatest economy and speed. An example of this class is the Cytocomputer.

Image memory storage

As we have previously pointed out, one image can require large amounts of data storage that often exceed the capacity of standard general purpose computers based on the stored program theory. Image processing systems built around these computers have an overhead time for transferring image data between core memory and mass memory that is, in some tasks, higher than the computation time. Image processing machines should have either a memory large enough to contain the image data, or high speed data transfer mechanisms. Existing commercial systems for Image Processing have been (Kidode (12)) grouped according to the solutions found for this problem. Seven classes can be defined, four explicitly oriented to image processing tasks and three that can be efficiently employed in this field, even if they were built for other purposes. In the first set there are:

- Computer with embedded image memory. In these machines the core memory works as image memory for I/O image operations with standard equipment such as TV cameras or monitors. Preprocessing and standard operations such as histogramming, convolution etc., can often be exploited by special hardware.
- Display oriented image memory. These systems are usually composed by standard host mini or microcomputers, and an interactive image processing part composed by a display oriented image memory. Special

features of these systems, usually provided are zoom, pan, roam capabilities, look-up tables for gray scale and color or pseudocolor modification; high performance systems can also include real time video processing modules such as pipeline arithmetic processor for simple low level image processing.

- Image memory with local parallel processor. This class of architecture covers both the single and multiple subarray machines of the previous taxonomy. Using line-buffer, local parallel processing and sequential scanning control can be matched to the I/O devices and memory. Several machines have been built using different sizes, different local windows, different number of local processing modules programmable or hardware implemented.
- Image-parallel processor. This is a class of machine widely quoted and discussed previously, that corresponds to the SIMD class of Flynn's taxonomy. Each processor operates on the data in its own dedicated memory. Some difficulties arise in the I/O of images; particular components have been developed to reformat data in order to use the parallel array efficiently.

In the second set of the Kidode classification scheme, which is less interesting for the purposes of this paper, there are:

- Computer with array processor or special attached processor. In these cases we have a sequential general purpose architecture which, in order to obtain high level computation performance, contains some hardware for vector and array calculations such as internal product, transformation, matching and correlation.
- Multiprocessor system. Multiprocessors or multicomputers have been designed for artificial intelligent, scientific matrix computation, associative processing purpose. High level vision processing is well suited to these machines.
- Special purpose devices with image processing capability. Several special purpose implementation of image analysis functions have been realized in a wide range of applications, such as automatic inspection, robotic vision, remote sensing, etc.

In (12) a number of machines are described for each one of the classes of this taxonomy.

4. CONCLUSION

Different attempts to group image processing architectures have been reviewed. Each one is characterized by a particular selection logic that points out some design details. In describing these taxonomies, characteristic features of the classes have been emphasized, and some prototypes have been quoted. Despite the usefulness of understanding computers according to the architectural composition it is essential to remember other fundamental properties that characterize it such as cost (13), ease of use (13), and performance evaluation (5).

REFERENCES

1. J. Backus: "Can programming be liberated from the Von Neumann style, a functional style and its algebra of programs". Comm. of ACM, vol.21, No 8, 1978, p.613-41.

2. M.J. Flynn: "Some computer organizations and their effectiveness", IEEE Trans. on Computer, C-21, 1972, p.948-60.

3. P.E. Danielsson: "Vices and virtues of image parallel machines", Proc. Conf. on Image Analysis and Processing, Selva di Fasano, 1982.

4. A. Rosenfeld:"Parallel image processing using cellular arrays", Computer, vol.16, No 1, 1983, p.14-20.

5. R.W. Hockney, C.R. Jesshope: "Parallel computers", Adam Hilger publ., Bristol, 1981.

6. W.Handler: "The impact of classification schemes on computer architecture", Proc. IEEE Int. conf. on Parallel Processing, 1977, p.7-33.

7. V. Cantoni, S. Levialdi: "Matching the task to an image processing architecture", Computer Vision Graphics and Image processing, vol. 22, N. 2, 1983, p. 301-309.

8. K. Palem, S. Yalamanchili, L.S. Davis, J.K.Aggarwal, A.J. Welch: "Image processing architectures: a taxonomy and survey" University of Texas and Austin, TR-82-6.

9. V. Cantoni, S. Levialdi, C. Guerra: "Towards an evaluation of an image processing system", Computational Structures for IP, (M.J.B. Duff Ed. Academic Press), 1983, p.43-56.

10. P.E. Danielsson, S. Levialdi: "Computer architectures for pictorial information system", Computer, vol.14, No 11, 1981, p.53-67.

11. K. Preston, Jr:"Cellular logic computer for pattern recognition", Computer, vol.16, No 1, 1983, p.36-47.

12. M. Kidode: "Image processing machines in Japan", Computer, vol. 16, No 1, 1983, p.68-80.

13. M.J.B. Duff: "Special Hardware for pattern processing", Proc. 6th Int. Conf. on Pattern Recognition, Munich, 1982, p.368-379.

References on IP Computers

14. AHR: A Guzman: "A parallel heterarchical machine for high level language processing", in Languages and Architectures for IP (M.J. Duff and S.Levialdi, Eds.), Academic Press, New York, 1981, p. 229-224.

15. CELLSCAN GLOPR: K.Preston, Jr.: "Application of Cellular Automata to Biomedical Image Processing", Computer Techinques in Biomedicine and Medicine, Auerbach Publishers, Philadelphia, 1973.

16. CLIP IV: T.J. Fountain: "Clip IV: A progress report", in languages and Architectures for IP (M.J. Duff and S. Levialdi, Eds.), Academic Press, New York, 1981, p. 283-293.

17. CYTOCOMPUTER: R.M. Lougheed, D.L. Mc Cubbrey, and S. R. Sternberg: "Cytocomputers: Architectures for parallel image processing", Proceedings of the Workshop on Picture Data Description and Management, Pacific Grove, California, 1980, p. 281-286.

18. DAP: P.M. Flanders, D.J. Hunt, S.F. Reddaway and D. Parkinson: "Efficient high speed computing with the distributed array processor", in High Speed Computing and Algorithm organization (D.J. Kuck, D.H. Lawrie, and A.H. Sameh, Eds.), Academic Press, New York, 1977, p. 113-127.

19. diff3: M.Ingram, P.E. Norgen, and K.Preston: "Automatic differentiation of white blood cells", in Image Processing in Biological Science (D. M.Ramsey, Ed.), Univ. of California Press, Berkeley, Calif., 1968, p. 97.

20. DSR: B.K. Gilbert, R.A. Robb, and L.M. Krueger: "Ultra high speed recontruction processors for X-ray computed tomography of the heart and circulation", Real-time Medical Image Processing, p. 23-40.

21. FLIP: K. Luetjen, P. Gemmar, and H. Ischen: "FLIP: A flexible multiprocessor system for image processing", Proceedings of the 5th International conference on Pattern Recognition, 1980, Miami, p. 326-328.

22. ILLIAC III: B. H. Mc Cormick: "The Illinois pattern recognition computer - ILLIAC III", IEEE Tranc Comput. EC-12, 1963, p. 791-813.

23. IP: H. Matsushima, T. Uno, and M. Ejiri: "An array processor for image processing" in Real time/Parallel Computing (M. Onoe, K.Preston, adn A. Rosenfeld, Eds.), Plenum Press, New York, 1981, p. 325-338.

24. MPP: L. W. Fung: "A massively parallel processing computer", in High Speed Computer and Algorithm Organization (D.J. Kuck et al., Eds.), Academic Press, new York, 1977, p. 203-204.

25. PASM: H. J. Siegel: "PASM: A reconfigurable multi-microcomputer system for image processing", in Languages and Architectures

for IP (M.J. Duff, and S. Levialdi, Eds.), Academic Press, New York, 1981, p. 257-266.

26. PHP: J.M. Herron et al.: "A General-Purpose High-Speed Logical Transform Processor", IEEE Trans. Computers, Vol. C-31, No. 8 Aug. 1982, p.795-800.

27. PICAP II: B.Kruse, B. Gudmundoss, and D.Antonsson: "FIP: The PICAP II filter processor", Proceedings of the 5th International Conference on pattern Recognition (1980), Miami, p. 484-488.

28. PM4: F. Briggs, K. S. Fu, K. Huang, and J. Patel: PM4: A reconfigurable multiprocessor system for pattern recognition and image processing", AFIPS Conference Proceeding (1979), Vol. 48, p. 127-137.

29. PUMPS: F.A. Briggs, K. Hwang, K.S.Fu, M. Dubois: "PUMPS architecture for pattern analysis and detabase management", Proc. pattern Recognition an Image Processing Conf., Dallas, (1981), p. 178-187.

30. PCLIP: J. Tanimoto: "Towards a hierarchical cellular logic: design consideration for pyramid anachines", TR-81-02-01 University of Washington, Seattle, (1981).

31. TOSPICS: K. I. Mori, M. Kidode, H. Shinoda, and H. Asada: "Design of local parallel pattern processor for IP", AFIPS Conference Proceedings (1978), Vol. 47, p. 1025-1032.

32. ZMOB: C. Rieger, ZMOB: "Doing it in parallel!" Univ. of Maryland, TR-1099, 1981.

REPRESENTATIONS OF SPATIALLY PARALLEL ARCHITECTURES

David H. Schaefer
George Mason University
Fairfax, Virginia 22030 U.S.A.

INTRODUCTION

Spatially parallel architectures utilize both logical and geometric concepts. In the usual representation of spatially parallel structures, only the logical components are formalized. In exactly the same sense that there are logical components, there are also components of a strictly geometric nature. In the construction of hardware, these geometric components are lost, becoming a "part of the wiring." This paper looks at spatially parallel structures as being collections of two-dimensional logic and geometric components. The geometric components perform such tasks as providing communication paths between elements of an array of a given dimension, and providing selection or replication functions that allow data to pass from an array of one dimension to an array of a greater or lesser dimension. Logical components perform operations on arrays of identical dimensions.

Spatially parallel architecture is computer architecture in which a large number (usually many thousands) of computations are performed simultaneously, and which has in its organization the concept of an X, Y matrix. The maximum number of simultaneous computations for existing computers (1983) is 16,384. The basic computational entity of a spatially parallel computer is a binary image or array as opposed to a binary bit that is the basic computational entity of conventional computers. Examples of computers with spatially parallel architectures are the CLIP (Duff, 1978) the MPP (Batcher, 1980; Schaefer et al., 1982), and the DAP (Reddaway, 1979).

In this paper (1) a set of two-dimensional components will be defined; (2) historical and present SIMD machines will be described in terms of these components; and (3) the representation of pyramid structures will be examined.

BUSES

In a spatially parallel structure a collection of wires is the transmission path for arrays of binary information. Figure 1 shows

NATO ASI Series, Vol. F18
Computer Architectures for Spatially Distributed Data
Edited by H. Freeman and G. G. Pieroni

pictorially a data bus containing nine wires in a 3 X 3 element array and its schematic representation, the "3 X 3" notation indicating the number of wires and their arrangements. This symbolism will be used for any bus of dimension m x n. The CLIP IV for example, will be described in terms of a 96 X 96 element bus, and the Massively Parallel Processor in terms of a 128 X 128 element bus.

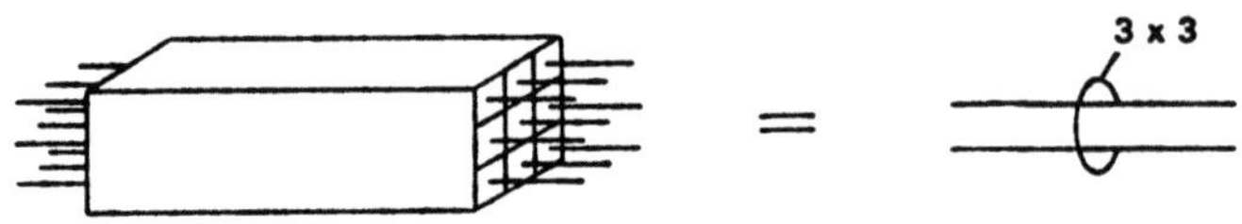

Figure 1 - Bus Containing 9 Wires

These buses can be branched as shown in Figure 2(a), each branch being of the same dimension as the input bus. Output from each limb of the branch will be identical to the input. Buses can also be combined as shown in Figure 2(b). It is assumed that only one branch (for any element) has a signal. The other branch must be an open circuit.

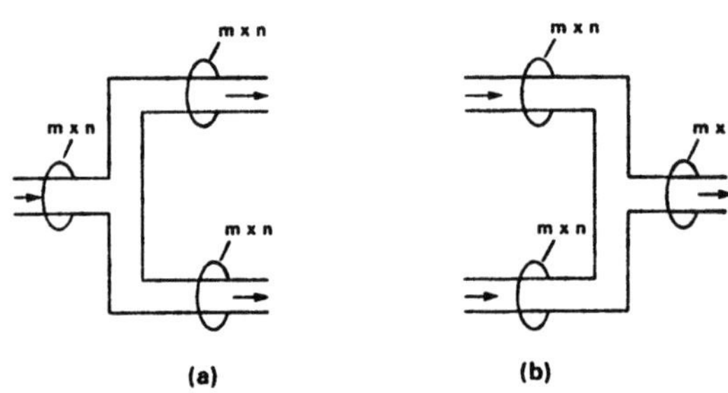

Figure 2 - Branching & Combining of Buses

<u>LOGIC COMPONENTS</u>

Two-dimensional logic components perform logic on binary arrays of data input. In the two-dimensional negation device represented in Figure 3 any element in the output array of this component has the value of the complement of its corresponding input element. Figure 3 shows both a pictorial representation of the negation component, and its schematic representation.

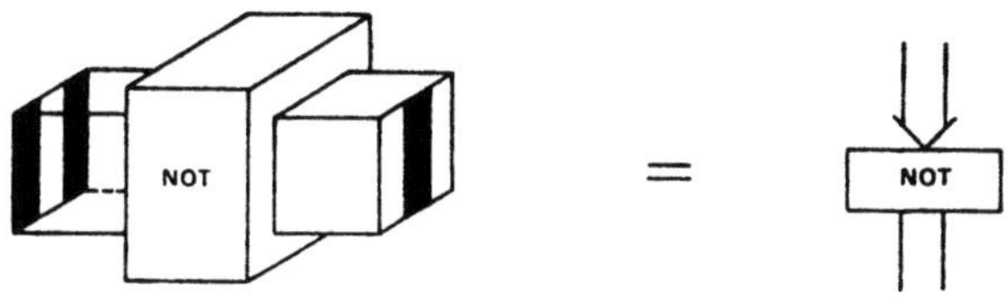

Figure 3 - Negation Component

The basic two-dimensional components that perform logic operations on two array inputs are AND and OR components (Figure 4). The full adder component (Figure 5) produces at its left output an array consisting of sum bits formed by the addition of the three input arrays, and at its right output the array of carry bits.

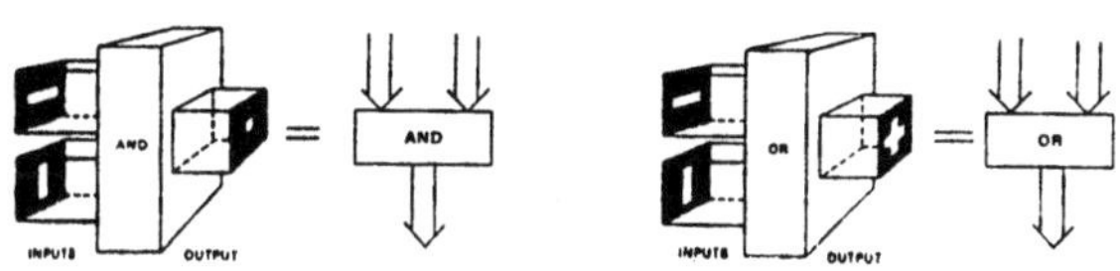

Figure 4 - AND and OR Components

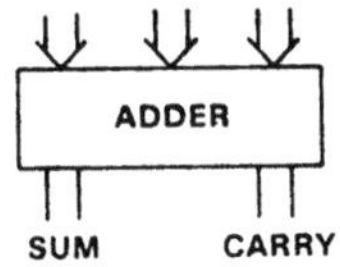

Figure 5 - Full Adder Component

A generalized logic component that can produce all sixteen boolean functions of two array inputs is shown in Figure 6. The instruction to this generalized logic specifies which of the sixteen functions will be performed. The fish-like symbol indicates that one instruction is replicated many times, once for each element of the component, as is the case for SIMD machines. The generalized logic component can, of course, be even further generalized to accept any number of array inputs.

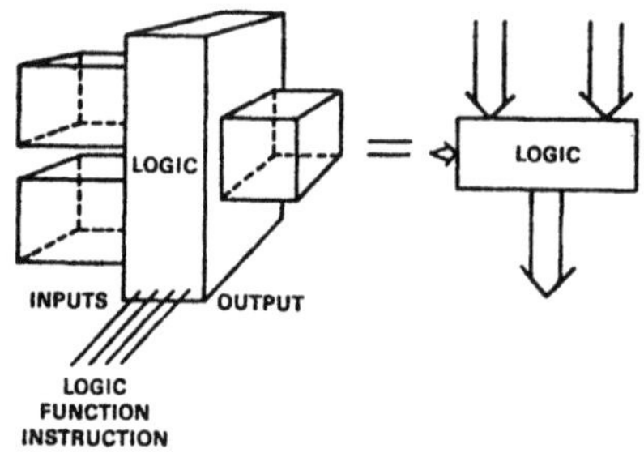

Figure 6 - Generalized Logic Component

Arrays of tristate switches provide the needed open circuit function to control the flow of data into bus junctions such as shown in Figure 2(b). Figure 7 shows schematically such an array of switches in a data bus. Each switch (one for every element in the bus) provides either a conducting or non-conducting link. Figure 7 represents the case in SIMD computers where all switches respond to a single "open" or "close" instruction.

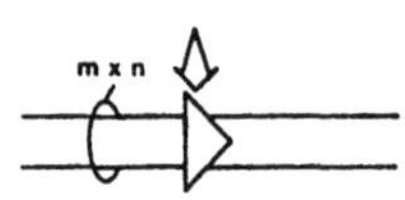

Figure 7 - Array of Switches

Figure 8(a) is the schematic representation of a device called the "zero selector" which can be instructed to either transmit data undisturbed, or present a field of "0's" at its output. Figure 8(b), a "one or zero selector" contains the added capability to present a field of "1's" at its output.

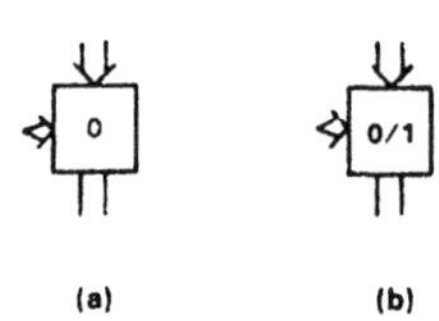

Figure 8 - Components that Generate Fields of all-1's and all-0's

MEMORY COMPONENTS

A "single plane memory", the basic two-dimensional memory component, is an array of flip-flops or one bit registers. Figure 9 is an example of a single plane memory containing nine flip-flops.

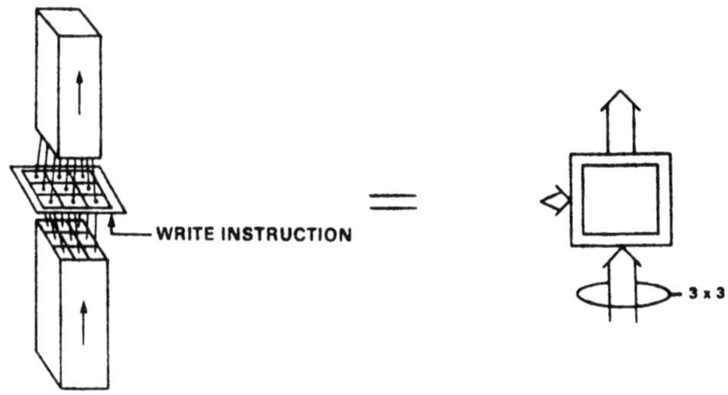

Figure 9 - Single Plane Memory

A two plane memory (Figure 10(a)) consists of two single plane memories. A multi-plane memory containing 1024 planes, each plane consisting of 16,384 flip-flops arranged as a 128 X 128 array, is represented in Figure 10(b). In alternate terms, Figure 10(b) is a 128 X 128 array of 1024 bit random access memories.

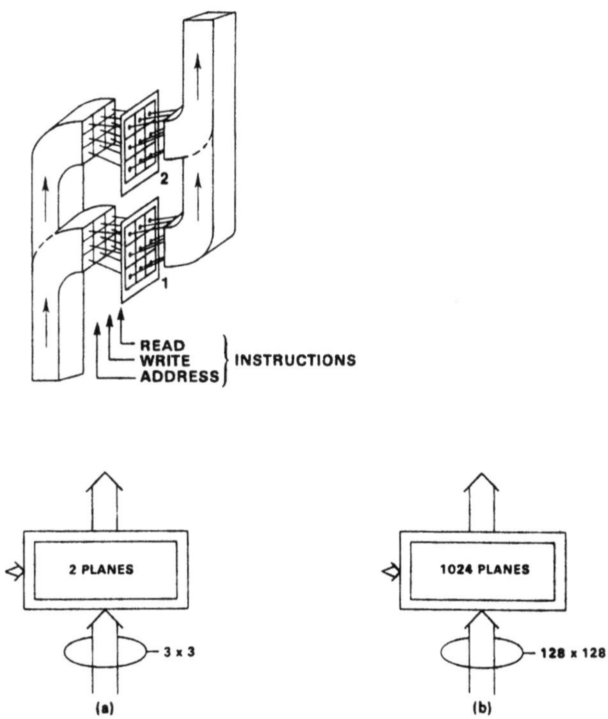

Figure 10 - Multi-plane Memory

A unique type of two-dimensional memory is an array of shift registers (Figure 11). Such a device consists of memory planes similar to those shown in Figure 10, but with the limitation that each plane can only receive input from the plane immediately below.

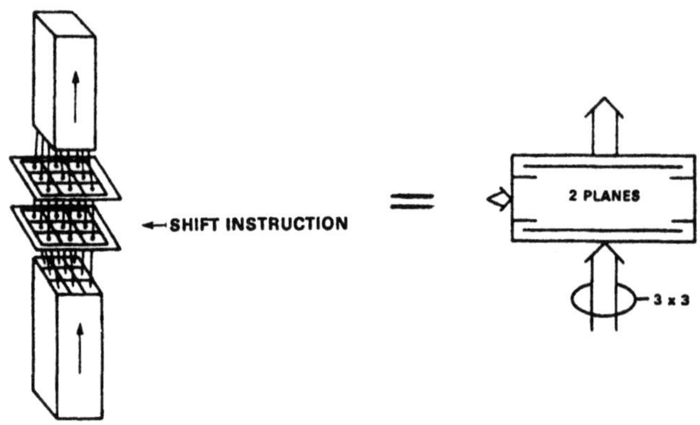

Figure 11 - Array of Shift Registers

COMMUNICATION COMPONENTS

Communication components transform an input array into a different output array (of the same dimension) by changing the coordinates of the input elements. A communication component consists exclusively of wires. No logic of any sort is performed in these devices. They provide a means for transfering information from one element of an array to another element. The simplest such device is the sliding component (Figure 12) where output is a geometrically translated version of the input array. A slider can be visualized as two permanently attached data buses, one offset from the other.

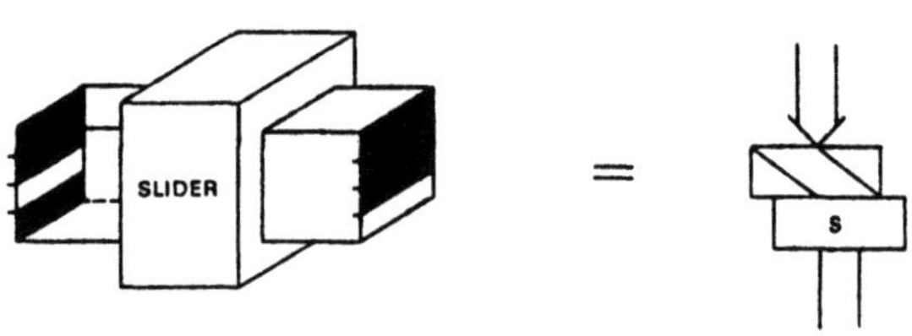

Figure 12 - Slider Component

Figure 13 presents this concept pictorially and indicates the schematic representation of sliding components that translate an image one element to the north, south, east and west. There are also components (not shown) that translate an image diagonally (i.e. a translation to the northwest or southeast) by one element.

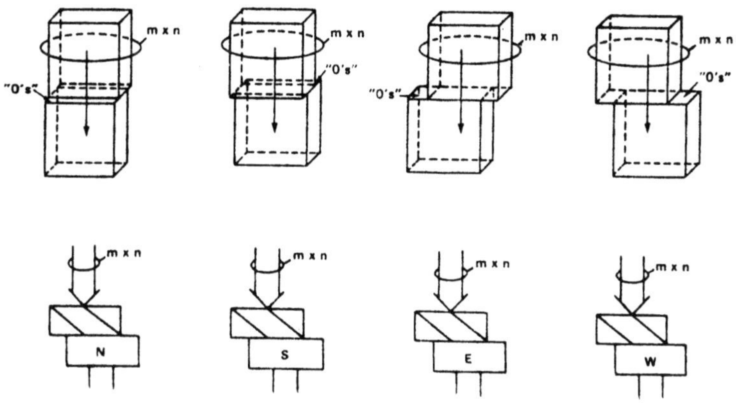

Figure 13 - Slider Representation

In the "basic" slider just described, one row or column at the edge of the input array is lost and the output array receives, at the opposite edge, a row or column of 0's. In contrast to this, a "loop slider" does not lose information. Instead, the row or column that would be lost in a basic slider moves to the opposite edge of the output array. Figure 14 shows this concept.

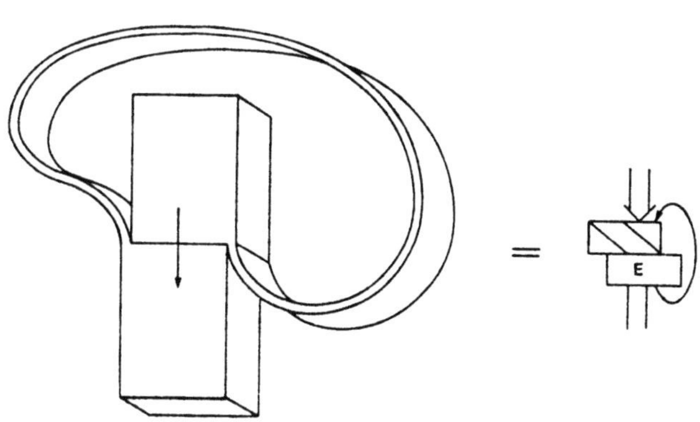

Figure 14 - Loop-Slider

The "leftover wires" of a slider can be used for input and output of single rows or columns of data. Figure 15 shows such an "input-output" sliding component.

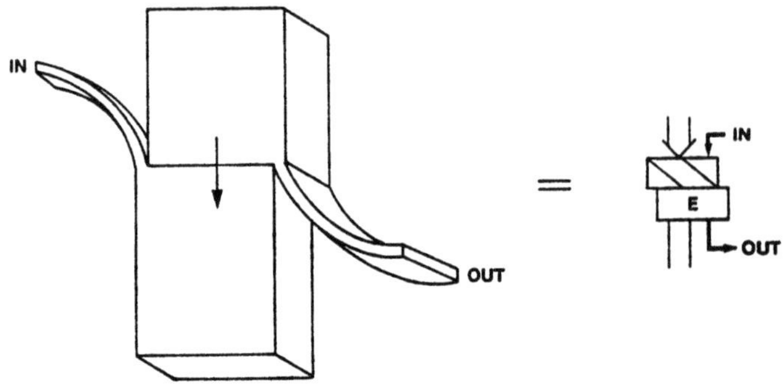

Figure 15 - Input-Output Slider

Sliders in existing machines translate an image only one element in a given direction. Conceptually, however, there can be sliders that translate an image any number of elements. These sliders can be visualized in a manner identical to that of the single element slider, but with the output bus being offset from the input bus by more than one element. In Schaefer and Strong (1977), a generalized arithmetic unit was presented that assumed a collection of sliders capable of sliding an image 2^n elements in any direction.

There are a large number of intercommunication schemes for spatially parallel structures in addition to sliders, such as the perfect shuffle (Stone, 1971). These communication components can be visualized as a "weave" of wires that produce the desired output. They can be represented in a manner similar to the representation of the sliding components.

COMPONENTS THAT MODIFY THE DIMENSION OF ARRAYS

In order to build advanced architectures (such as pyramids), it is necessary to change the spatial dimensions of arrays of data. When moving from an array of small dimensions to one of greater dimensions, a replication of wires (or signals) must take place. When moving from an array of large dimension to one of lesser dimensions, a selection process of some sort must take place.

Replication components increase the size of an array. An example of such a component is the "one to four" replication component shown in

Figure 16. In the pictorial representation a 2X2 array is transformed into a 4X4 array. The transformation shown is conceptually accomplished by simply "unbraiding" the input wires so that each input signal arrives at the output on four separate wires in a square neighborhood.

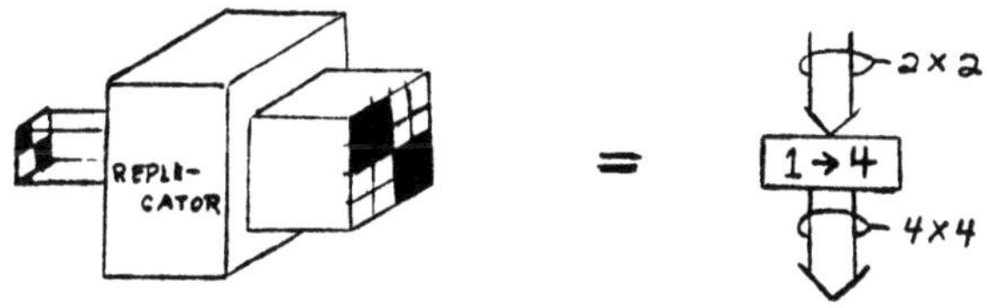

Figure 16 - "One-to-four" Replication Component

Selection components decrease the size of an array. A wide range of selection functions are possible. For instance, one could reduce the dimensions of an array by simply choosing quadrants of the large array as input to a smaller one that is one quarter the size. Another selection function (which we will utilize later) is to divide the large array into a set of two by two squares, and provide as output four smaller arrays, each from elements in a given location of each of the two by two squares. This is illustrated in Figure 17. The effect of this "sorter" selector is to put neighbors in the large array into separate smaller arrays.

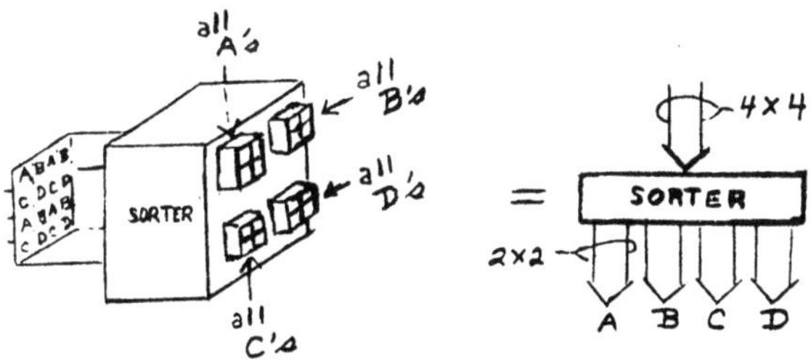

Figure 17 - Sorter Selector

ELEMENTARY CONFIGURATIONS USING TWO-DIMENSIONAL COMPONENTS

A circuit consisting of a single plane memory and an input-output slider (Figure 15) is shown in Figure 18. Upon application of a "write" instruction to the flip-flop array, each flip flop assumes the data value of its western neighbor. This is simply a shift register that shifts data from west to east. This sliding circuit should not be confused with the shift register memory component of Figure 11, which is a storage device located at single elements in the array.

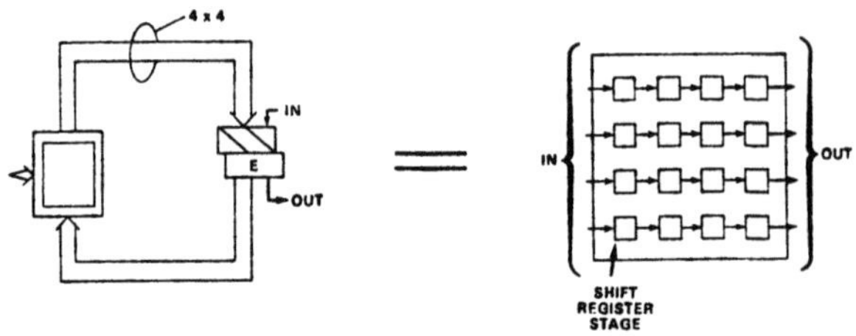

Figure 18 - Translation Register

A "four way programmable slider" capable of sliding north, south, east or west (the direction selected by command) can be constructed from arrays of switches and elementary sliding components as shown in Figure 19. The nomenclature of this figure will be utilized later.

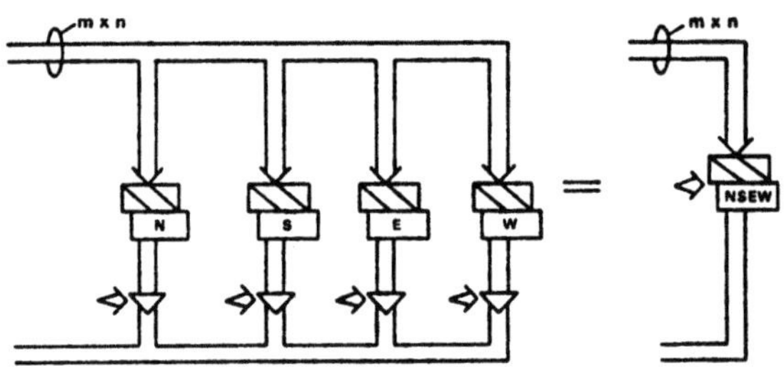

Figure 19 - Four-Way Slider

If feedback is applied to a sliding element as shown in Fig. 20, then information is slid and ORed in an unclocked, asynchronous manner.

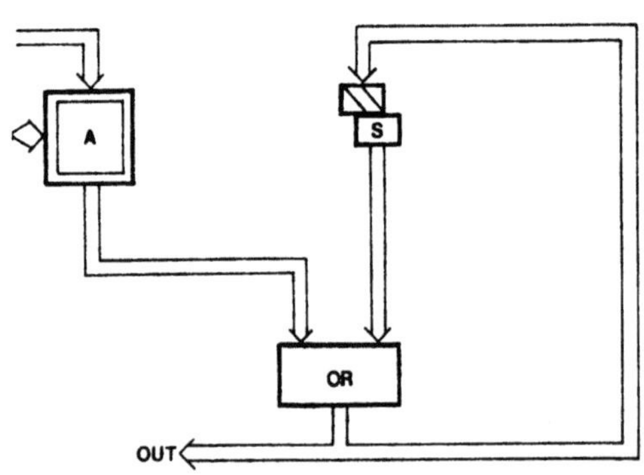

Figure 20 - Asychronous Slide Circuit

The action of the repeated sliding and ORing propagates information from one element to its neighbor. Thus, if register component A of Fig. 3 contains the image P (Figure 21(a)), then the image presented at the terminal marked "out" is image R (Figure 21(b)). This image is a "dripping paint" version of image P, in which every white (one) element has been propagated to the south. Asynchronous sliding is utilized in the CLIP and Unger computers.

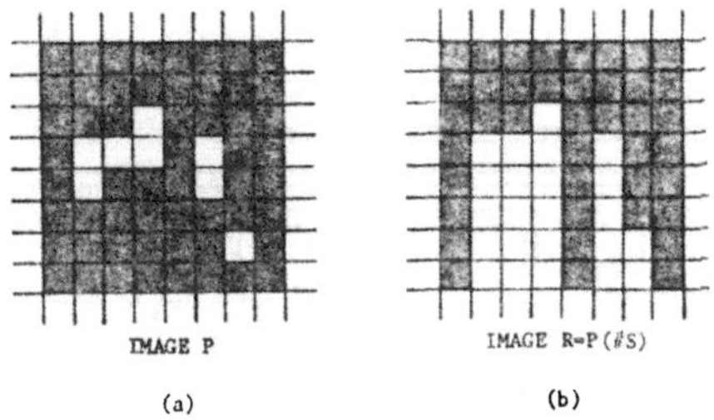

Figure 21 - Result of Asynchronous Sliding Operation

The final configuration we consider is the "Sum-OR" component. This component "OR's" together all elements of the input array to produce a single binary element as output. If any element of the input is a "one", the output of the Sum-OR component will be a "one". Only an all zero array as input will produce a "zero" output. The Sum-OR component has reduced the dimension of a large array down to dimension of 1 X 1. To accomplish this, there must be a series of selection and logic operations. Figure 22 shows how this is accomplished using sorters and OR components.

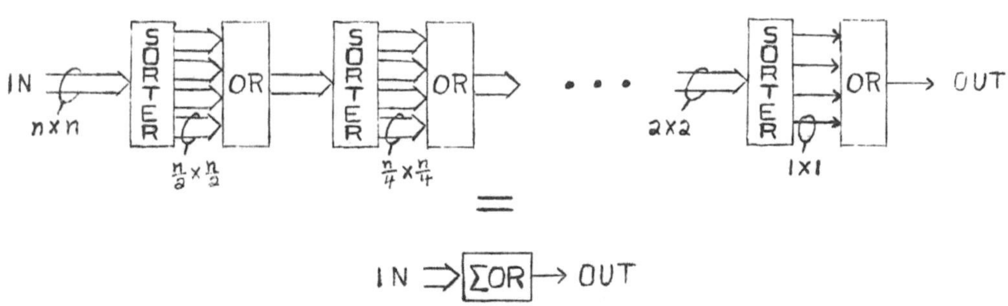

Figure 22 - Sum-OR Circuit

COMPUTER DESCRIPTIONS

A spatially parallel computer was described by S.H. Unger twenty-five years ago (Unger, 1958). He noted that "pattern recognition is an area in which present day machines cannot match the performance of their designers." To meet this need he designed his "Spatial Computer" shown in the two-dimensional representation in Figure 23.

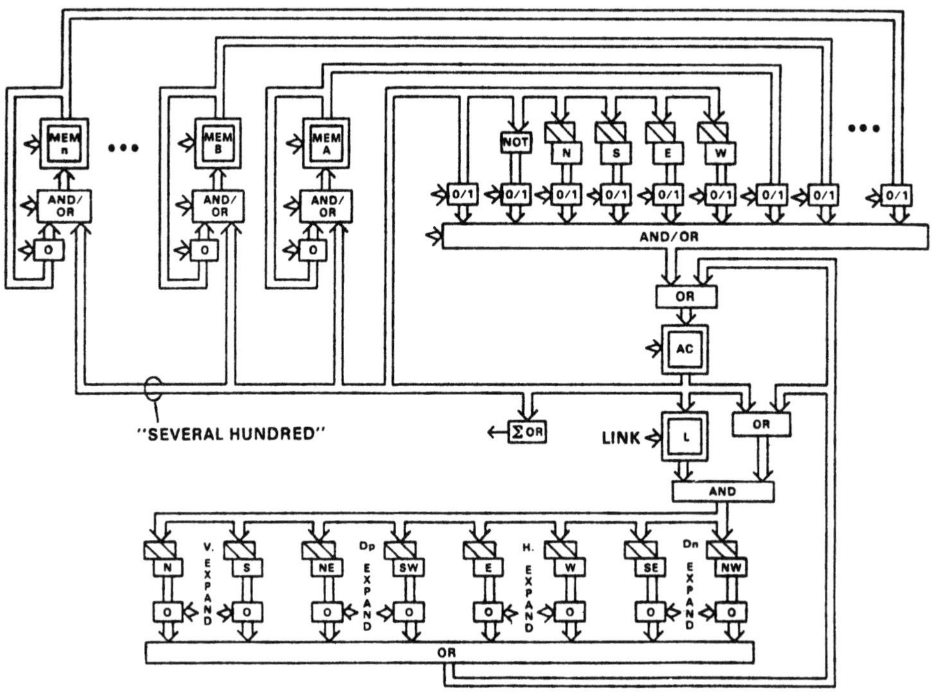

Figure 23 - Unger Spatial Computer

Input was assumed to come from an array of photodiodes directly into AC, his "accumulator" array. The machine is unique in that all memory planes can have logic performed upon their contents simultaneously by ORing or ANDing with the contents of AC. By the same token, AC can be logically combined with any or all of the memory planes and with slide versions of itself all in one machine cycle.

The lower portion of Figure 23 contains circuitry to perform Unger's LINK and EXPAND operations. The LINK command stores the contents of AC in array L. At some later time an EXPAND command will allow data in AC to "expand" along existing (horizontal, vertical, positive diagonal or negative diagonal) paths or "chains" of adja-

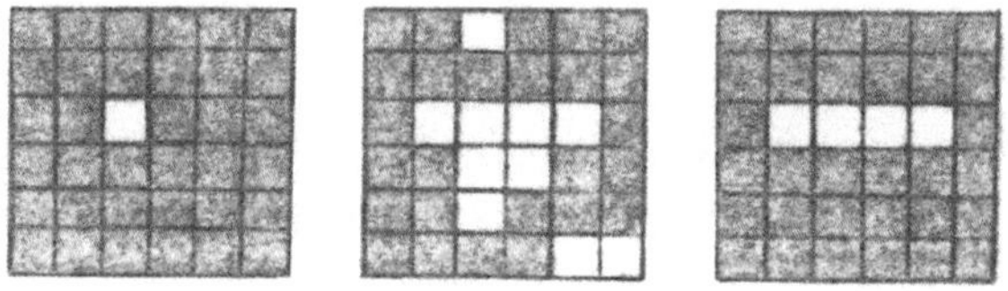

(a) (b) (c)

Figure 24 - Illustration of EXPAND Function

cent 1's stored in L. Figure 24 presents an example of a horizontal expansion. Figure 24(a) shows data in AC, Figure 24(b) the data in L, and Figure 24(c) the output of the bottom OR component of Figure 23. The expansion grows from the 1 in AC that coincides with a 1 in L. Growth along a chain of 1's in L then takes place by asynchronous propagation of data through the sliders in the lower portion of Figure 23 (in this example, the east and west sliders). This growth is constrained at each end by the action of the lower AND gate. The asynchronous propagation attribute of the link circuit manifests itself by the presence of a loop containing sliding components and no memory planes.

The Cellular Logic Image Processor (CLIP IV) is shown in Figure 25. An example of its logical capabilities is its ability to perform

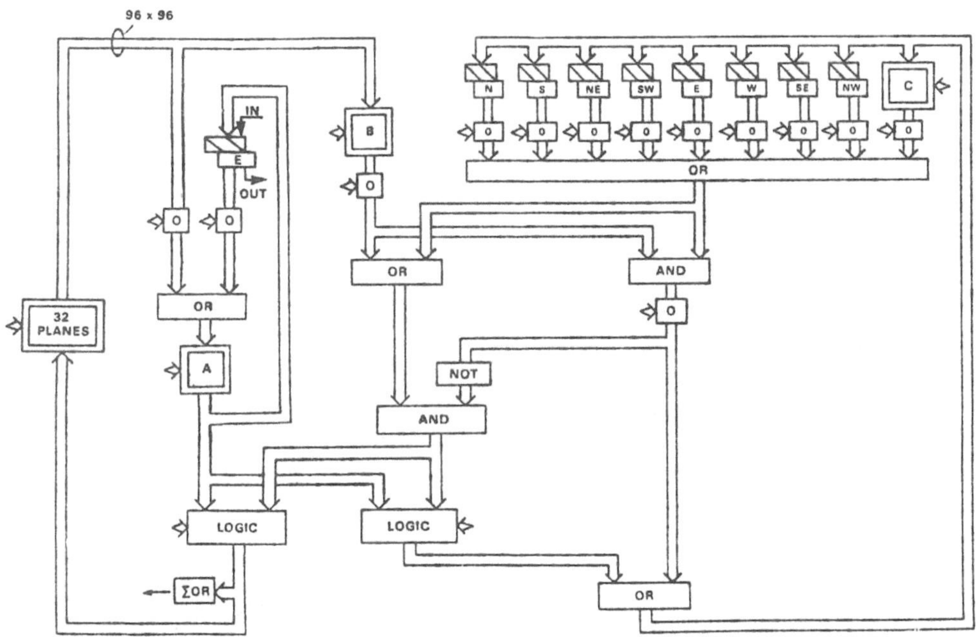

Figure 25 - CLIP IV Computer

the Unger EXPAND operations. For these operations memory plane B assumes the role of Unger's L plane, and A substitutes for AC. Propagation takes place through the right hand logic component programmed as an OR. When CLIP IV adds grey level images, the left-hand logic component assumes the Exclusive OR function, while the right hand logic device is programmed to AND. Arrays of carry bits are fed to the C memory plane to be used in the succeeding cycles of the bit serial addition.

The Massively Parallel Processor (MPP) (Figure 26) has been fabricated for NASA by the Goodyear Aerospace Corporation and is presently in operation at the Goddard Space Flight Center. The MPP contains distinct areas for arithmetic operations, logical operations, and input-output operations allowing these three types of operations to be performed simultaneously. The primary use of the shift register memories are for multiplication and floating point addition. The length of shift register paths can be any one of 2,6, 10,14,18,22,26 or 30 stages depending upon which components are bypassed. The input-output circuitry is on the right hand side of the figure.

The primary communication element of the MPP is the four-way slider in parallel with the logic component. This slider can be programmed to be either a standard or a loop slider. The "corner

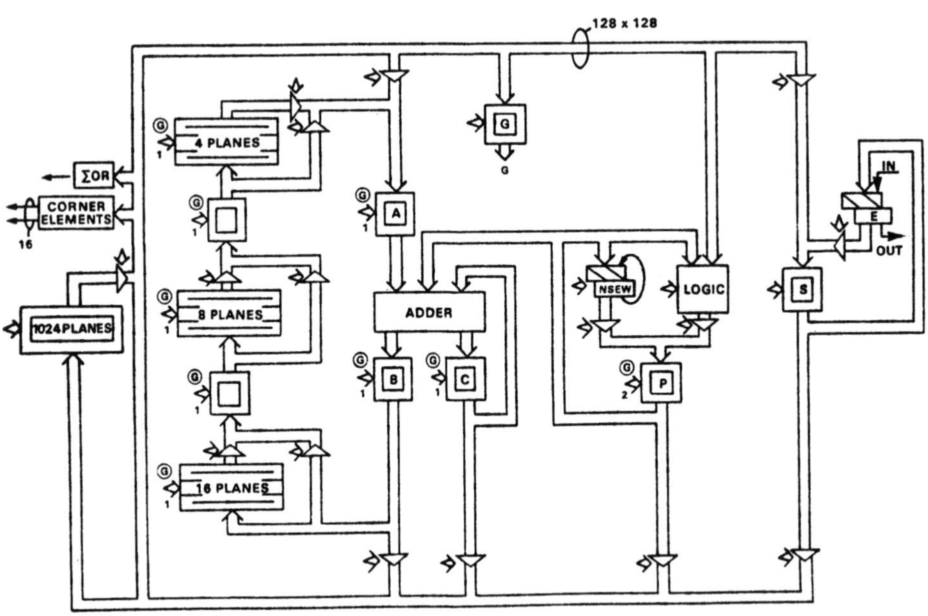

Figure 26 - The Massively Parallel Processor

element" component selects sixteen elements from the corners of 32 X 32 subarrays of the 128 X 128 data bus for use by the control unit.

The encircled "G" that appears above certain instruction symbols indicates that the instruction is "maskable." In the MPP a masked instruction is executed by elements where the G register is a "one." A "no-op" occurs at elements where G equals zero. The MPP control unit issues both masked and "unconditional" instructions.

Pyramid Structures

Pyramid computer structures provide interesting examples of the use of the two dimensional representation of circuits. These pyramid structures are characterized by having several layers of arrays, the upper arrays being of a smaller dimension than those below. An example of a very simple pyramid architecture has already been presented in the description of the Sum OR component (Figure 22). In the Sum-OR structure, information flows only upward (from arrays of large dimensions to those of a smaller dimension) and only one type of operation is performed on outputs of the SORTER, that being the OR operation.

Tanimoto (1982) has described a nonoverlapped pyramid machine called the "PCLIP". Any array of processing elements has four times as many elements as the array immediately above. Each processing element in the machine has connections to its eight neighbors on the plane, to four children below and to one parent above. Therefore each element has connections to 13 other elements. The interconnection of PCLIP's "propagation registers" on three adjacent levels is shown in Figure 27. The 13 connections to each element of the registers can be seen. Information flows from the base up the pyramid through the sorters. Information flows down from the top of the pyramid through the "one to four" replication components. In this system all movement of data is clocked into the arrays of flip-flops. There can be no asynchronous propagation of data between layers of the structure.

Various pyramid computer designs are possible. At George Mason University consideration is being given to building a pyramid computer that utilizes custom chips developed for the Massively Parallel Processor. One possible design is shown in Figure 28. Here data paths between layers of the pyramid are connected directly to the data buses of each level. This allows asynchronous propagation from layer to layer. For instance, data at the top of the pyramid can be broadcast to all processing elements of the pyramid with only the propaga-

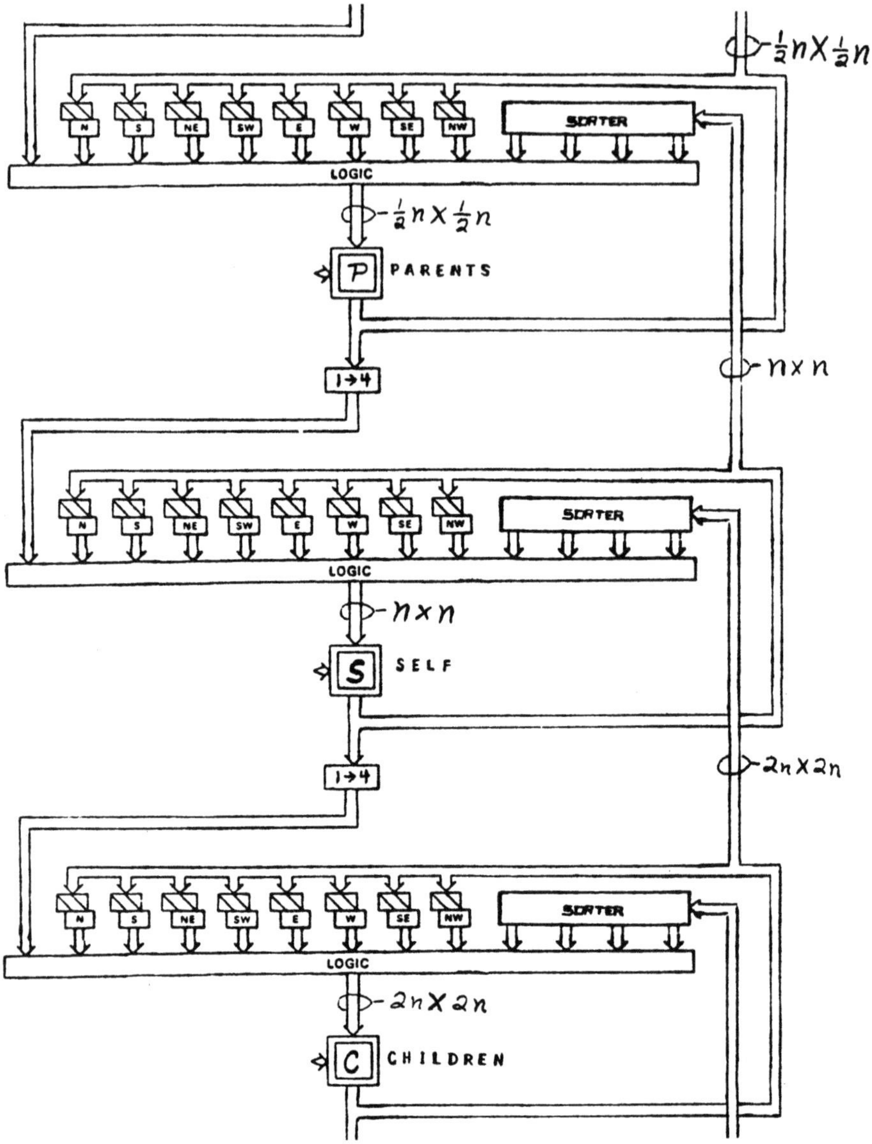

Figure 27 - Pyramid Structure

tion delays of the tristate switches slowing this broadcast. In a similar manner the value of any given element in the base can be sent directly to the top of the pyramid. The penalty of communication from bus to bus rather than from register to register is that n cycles are required to transfer unique information from all levels to all higher (or lower) levels in an n stage structure. In Figure 27 such unique level to level transfers can take place simultaneously.

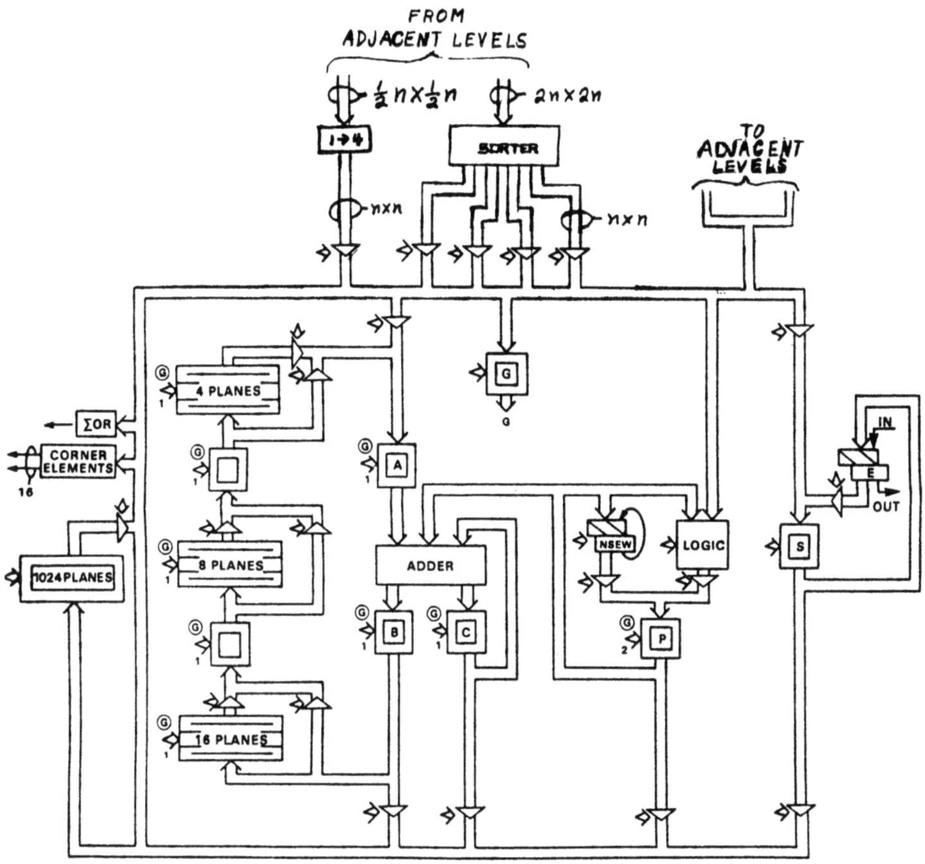

Figure 28 - Pyramid of MPP Processing Elements

CONCLUDING REMARKS

The method presented here of representing spatially parallel structures explicitly shows both the logical and geometrical properties of these machines, provides a unified method of characterizing these structures, and allows for a graphic visualization of their operation. The use of this representation has been demonstrated for both single level architecture and for computers that have a hierarchy of processing arrays.

ACKNOWLEDGMENTS

The descriptions of single level structures in this paper are from a 1981 unpublished report entitled "Spatially Parallel Computers - Ensembles of Two-Dimensional Components" prepared by the author and James R. Fischer of the Goddard Space Flight Center. Dr. James Strong of Goddard shared in the origination of the concepts presented here (Schaefer and Strong, 1977). The impetus to address multi-level structures came from discussions at Cetraro with Dr. C.K. Chow of IBM, Dr. S. Goldwasser of the University of Pennsylvania, and Dr. S. Tanimoto of the University of Washington. Preparation of this paper would have been impossible without the help of my wife, Maxine Schaefer.

REFERENCES

Batcher, K.E. (1980), "Design of a massively parallel processor," IEEE Trans. Comput., Vol 28, pp. 836-840.

Duff, M.J.B. (1978), "Review of the CLIP image processing system," Proc. National Computer Conference, pp. 1055-1060.

Reddaway, S.F. (1979), "The DAP approach," Infotech State of the Art Report on Supercomputers, vol. 2, 1979, pp. 309-329.

Schaefer, D.H. and Strong, J.P. (1977), "Tse Computers," Proc. IEEE, Vol 65, No. 1, pp. 129-138.

Schaefer, D.H., Fischer, J.R. and Wallgren, K.R. (1982), "The massively parallel processor, Journal of Guidance and Control, May/June, pp. 187-190.

Stone, H.S. (1971), "Parallel processing with the perfect shuffle," IEEE Trans. Comput. vol C-20, pp. 153-161.

Tanimoto, S.L. (1982), "Programming Techniques for Hierarchical Parallel Image Processors." In Multicomputers and Image Processing, Preston and Uhr (Eds.), Academic Press, New York, pp. 421-428.

Unger, S.H. (1958), "A computer oriented toward spatial problems," Proc. IRE, Vol. 46, pp. 1744-1750.

COMPUTER ARCHITECTURE FOR INTERACTIVE DISPLAY OF SEGMENTED IMAGERY

S.M. Goldwasser

Department of Computer and Information Science
The Moore School of Electrical Engineering
University of Pennsylvania, Philadelphia, PA 19104

Abstract

This work addresses aspects of several topics related to the general problems of hardware architecture for high performance interactive display systems for computer processed imagery. The general characteristics important for such systems are outlined with emphasis on multiple format object oriented structures. A special purpose multiprocessor architecture is then described which facilitates the real-time display and interactive manipulation of shaded three dimensional objects or object surfaces on a conventional raster scan CRT. Finally, a summary of some possible alternative technologies for system implementation is presented including a concept proposal for a true three dimensional display system based on hybrid techniques. General comments follow encouraging the active investigation and development of emerging non-traditional technologies for use in architectures for spatially distributed data.

Introduction

Future directions in man-machine interaction will be heavily influenced by the development of improved display systems for the presentation of computer processed information. Such information includes continuously changing images, photographs, graphics, and text, in 2 and 3 dimensions - as well as non-visual information. For the purposes of this paper, the term 'display' refers to the entire processing chain from the image or object database through to the actual output device. This includes mechanisms for accessing and manipulating the graphical database, for processing and reconstructing the spatial information, and for presenting the resulting visual output in a dynamic, esthetically pleasing format. The physical world is not, however, inherently based on scanned techniques nor is it a Flatland.

The three parts of this paper address related aspects of this problem. Part I briefly summarizes some of the requirements which we believe are important for current and future interactive display systems and which are essential in achieving the objectives of an effective display presentation. Part II describes a particular architecture which represents one approach which is being investigated in achieving these goals for display and manipulation of three dimensional objects with hidden surface removal on a conventional raster scan CRT. The emphasis is on objects derived or reconstructed from real world data, in particular, medical imagery. Part III gives some examples of possible non-traditional technologies for application to special purpose computer architectures. A conceptual proposal for a true three dimensional display system is outlined which, while theoretically possible, would need substantial engineering advancement to be achieved in practice and to be cost effective. Finally, the potential importance of new emerging hybrid technologies is discussed with emphasis on application to the processing and display of spatially distributed data.

NATO ASI Series, Vol. F18
Computer Architectures for Spatially Distributed Data
Edited by H. Freeman and G. G. Pieroni

Part I - General Requirements for Interactive Display

Graphical interaction with computation systems has evolved continuously with the development of improved technology in both the hardware and software areas. Early machines were fitted with cathode ray tube (CRT) point plotting displays which were essentially oscilloscopes driven by D/A interfaces hooked to CPU internal registers. As computer technology evolved, these systems became increasingly more sophisticated offloading much of the processing burden from the main CPU to peripheral display processors capable of complex high speed generation of wireframe images including the capability for interactive geometric transformations.

With the advancement and maturation of television and similar raster based systems and the development of medium and large scale integrated circuits, came the introduction of the video display terminal (VDT), and slightly later, the frame buffer based graphics system. The VDT made the old clunky TTY obsolete over night and now is the dominant user interface for alphanumeric computer interaction. The graphics system provided the capability to display graphics and text at moderate resolution; as well as true gray scale, pseudo-color, and full color images (pictures and photographs). These systems currently incorporate built in high performance processors for image and graphics generation, modification, and analysis.

A major limitation of frame buffer based raster scan systems are their relatively limited dynamic capabilities. The output buffer is designed to contain memory mapped information for the entire screen and thus requires extensive updating to modify the output presentation. In particular, to move an object requires both rewriting of the object at its new position as well as reconstruction of the what was uncovered at its old position. Furthermore, since the output buffer is basically a bitmap, all formats are handled in an identical manner rather than providing optimum processing for each one.

General Characteristics of Interactive Displays

Displays for computer output can be characterized by a variety of measures of performance including:

* Formats Supported - Pictures, Graphics, and Text
* Segmentation - Bitmap or Object Oriented.
* Interaction - Configuration, Geometric Transformations.
* Dimensionality - 2D, 2-1/2D, 3D, 4D.
* Resolution - Horizontal, Vertical, Depth, Time.
* Tone Scale - Binary, Grayscale, Pseudo-Color, Full Color.

The ultimate objective of a computer display system is to provide as realistic a presentation as possible for the class of applications for which it is designed. For the present and future this means the capability to display a variety of formats efficiently including images (pictures, radiographs, reconstructions), graphics (binary as well as shaded colored synthetic images), and text (both simple and high quality type fonts of multiple sizes and styles). The display should be object oriented dealing with each distinct segment of the output configuration as a separate object. Thus each picture, graphics construct, and each text paragraph should be independently and dynamically specified.

Some aspects of the display and manipulation of 2-D objects on a raster scan output device have been addressed with the development of the Generalized Segment Display Processor Architecture (SDP) [1], [2]. This system represents a unified approach to the specification of arbitrary output display configurations consisting of multiple independent image, graphics, or text regions which may be dynamically modified. The motivation for this work was provided by applications in the graphic arts including interactive full page layout and printing plate generation. Software simulations of the SDP have been developed [3], [4] and optimized versions of these are currently in commercial use for page composition applications. A hardware based implementation has been designed and is currently under construction.

The SDP uses separate data (Image Database, IDB) and control (Segment Descriptor Blocks, SDB) structures to provide for flexible display specification. Common attributes of a region or segment may be altered without changing the contents of the IDB. These include position, window size, cropping offset, and tonescale. Segments may be linked in a tree-like structure for efficient management of groups of related segments including combined movement, addition, deletion, and replication.

The spatial and temporal resolution of a display are primary characteristics in determining perceived quality. Current minimum acceptable spatial resolution would be 512 points and 512 lines for 2-D gray scale or color images and 1024 or more points for graphics applications. The total volume which must be represented in 3-D may be obtained by cubing these values. An additional factor of 60-100 frames per second to required to include refresh and motion. This is still far from the effective resolution of the human visual system which, in addition, varies as a function of the location in the visual field.

Tone scale resolution may be binary (two level) for crude graphics, 8-10 bits for monochrome or pseudo-color images, or from 24-30 bits (8-10 bits for each of Red, Green, and Blue) for high quality full color - and this does not even approximate the real world which would require an entire additional dimension for representation of the true total spectral distribution.

Current display technology is mostly two dimensional though perspective transformations can present the illusion of depth. Extensive work is being carried out on the display of shaded three-dimensional objects on a 2-D CRT (see PART II) which might be described as 2-1/2 D. The limiting factors for true 3-D displays are the output display device itself as well as the lack of required computation speed and storage capacity. We address some of these issues in PART III. The ultimate display could be 4-D: incorporating a true three dimensional presentation with real-time motion.

Part II - Interactive Display of Object Surfaces

We now discuss one approach to the generalized display of multiple configurable three dimensional objects. In this discussion, the output is a shaded image on a 2-D CRT providing for interactive display and manipulation in near real-time (10-30 frames/second) with hidden surface removal. Applications for interactive systems include industrial simulation, three dimensional modelling, and medical imaging for clinical diagnosis. Currently, systems that operate in real time (i.e., 15-30 frames/second or more) fall primarily into two classes: The first are based on random scan display generation and thus provide only wireframe images with little realism. The other techniques are based on polygons or other geometric primitives. Systems of this type are not entirely suitable for use with images derived from experimental data but are being increasingly utilized for synthesized computer graphics applications such as high performance aircraft simulators.

Software based systems which generate realistic images of natural structures are extremely slow. These include the DISPLAY software package developed by Herman et al [5], [6] for medical applications; others have been proposed independently [7], [8]. Even with hardware and firmware assist, the Lexidata SOLIDVIEW system [9] may take several minutes to generate a single view.

One important application of such a system is in the area of medical image processing using CAT, PET, or NMR scanning and reconstruction techniques. A system permitting a physician to visualize and interact with a shaded 3-D representation of an organ would greatly facilitate the examination of anatomical structures in conjunction with medical research, clinical diagnosis, and the planning of surgical procedures.

We present one possible architecture, still in an early stage of development, which permits the display and manipulation of multiple solid objects represented as a voxel (volume element) database with grayscale. Our objective is to provide certain capabilities such as 3-D rotation, scaling, and translation at or near video rates facilitating extensive real-time interaction. The architecture is highly modular permitting a cost tradeoff to be made to achieve a given level of performance. It also includes a great deal of regularity in its structure making it directly suitable for VLSI implementation. A key feature is that <u>no</u> computational operations more complex than adds, shifts, and comparisons are required in real time.

The DISPLAY Algorithm

The overall display processor architecture is based on the DISPLAY software package described in [5] and utilizes modified versions of those algorithms. The modified software generates surface views by mapping 3-D object space into 2-D image space using a time-ordered display procedure for hidden surface removal. For a given orientation of the object, pixels are written into the 2-D image (display) buffer in time-order corresponding to reading out voxels from the back to the front of the object. This simple "painter's algorithm" guarantees that any point that should be obscured by something in front of it will in fact be invisible in the final reconstruction.

Figure 1 illustrates a simple two dimensional analog of the back-to-front readout technique. It can be seen that for any orientation (rotation) of the object, there exists a readout sequence (and hence a processing time sequence) such that voxels early in the sequence (which should be hidden) will be overwritten by voxels later in the sequence. The required sequence is not unique and can be specified in a variety of ways. This architecture addresses the recursive decomposition of the sequence in such a way that (1) a near real-time update rate is possible, (2) common geometric modifications are instantaneous, and (3) a modular structure is created.

In order to reduce the problem of real-time display of 3-D objects to manageable proportions, it is necessary to partition either the input (object) space or output (image) space - or some combination of these. In a multiprocessor implementation, partitioning input space and assigning each partition to a separate processor will avoid object memory access conflicts, whereas partitioning output space will avoid image memory access conflicts. The former technique is clearly superior and will minimize conflict since a substantial amount of data reduction occurs in the projection from 3-D to 2-D space.

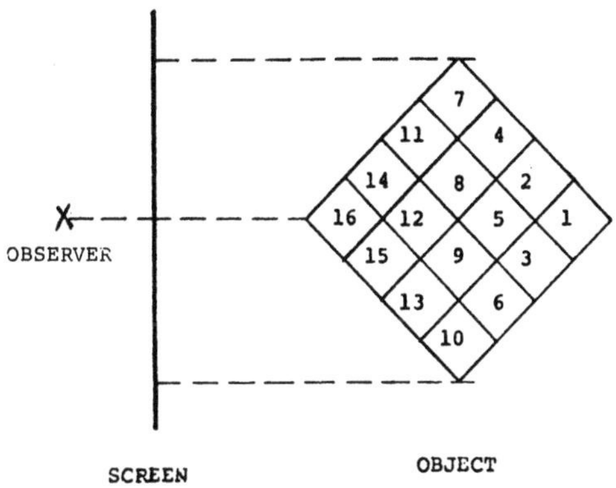

Figure 1 - 2-D Hidden Surface Removal.

Voxel readout in order shown

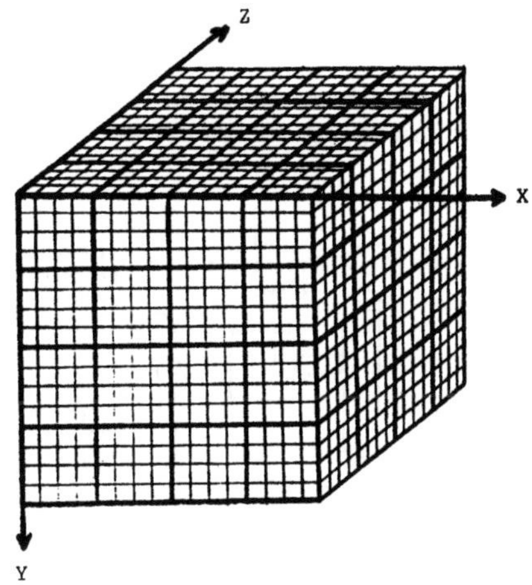

Figure 2 - Object Space Partitioning.

Small divisions represent 16-subcubes

Representation of 3-D Objects

We assume the input to the system (object space) is a 3-D scene subdivided by three sets of parallel planes into cube shaped volume elements or voxels as shown in Figure 2. Note that the voxel dissection is a special case of a general representation based on convex polyhedrons [10]. Associated with each voxel is a numeric quantity called the density which may correspond to color or brightness, or some other point property of the object. A natural data structure for such a scene is a 3-D array, indexed by X, Y, and Z where the value of each element is the density of the corresponding voxel. A binary (two level) object would require one bit per point. Typically, however, the storage format is one byte per point supporting up to 256 density levels.

Such a 3-D array is spatially presorted in the sense that for any viewpoint, voxels can be read out and displayed in a sequence which guarantees that voxels retrieved early in the sequence cannot obscure voxels retrieved later in the sequence. This property leads to the simple method of hidden surface removal described above. Using raw voxel data facilitates direct access and manipulation of object space by the host and minimizes the restrictions on the complexity of of structures that can be displayed. However, no data compression is achieved.

Two other possible data structures that can be used are octrees [11] and unsorted lists of voxels. The octree representation has the same spatial presorted property as the 3-D array. Octrees achieve excellent data compression when large regions of the scene contain the same density as, for example, in a binary scene. However, in our experience, the advantages for real world (particularly medical) objects are more than offset by the computational overhead associated with traversing the tree structure - especially for object analysis and contour extraction algorithms.

The second method is to store the voxels in random order, using 4 locations for each voxel (X, Y, Z, and density). This method is advantageous when a single small object has already been separated from the surroundings by means of thresholding or segmentation. However, a true Z-buffer is required for hidden surface removal. We have not found this technique appropriate for a real-time system capable of displaying entire scenes.

Display Processor Organization

The basic hardware realization of the DISPLAY algorithm consists of five components as illustrated by the block diagram in Figure 3:

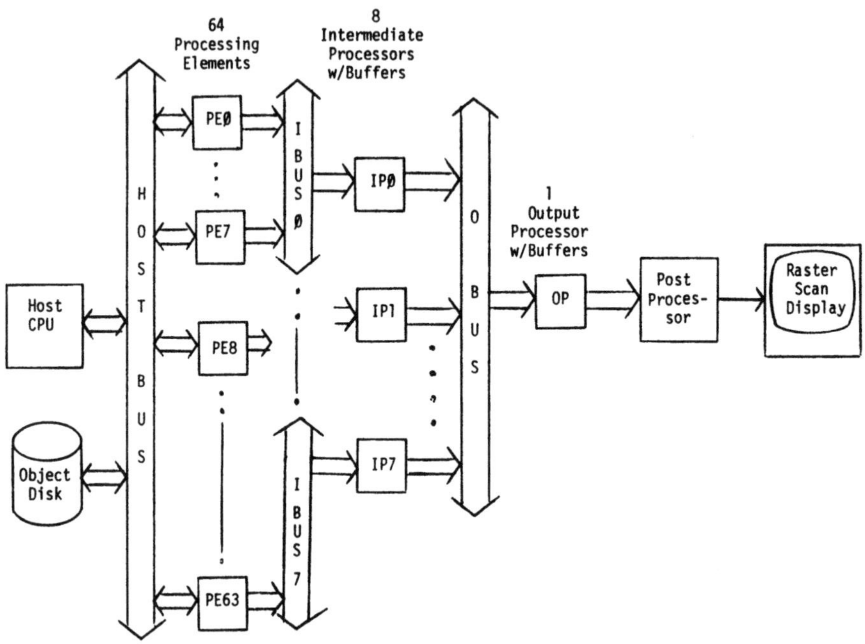

Figure 3 - Overall Display System Architecture

* Display processor array (64 PEs), each with associated object subcube memory module, and double 128x128 image buffer.
* Intermediate processors (for groups of 8 PEs) feeding double 256x256 intermediate image buffers.
* Output processor (for group of 8 intermediate buffers) feeding double 512x512 image buffer.
* Video postprocessor and video interface.
* Host computer interface and microprocessor based system controller.

Briefly, the processing strategy consists of the following. The processing elements (PEs) compute the 2-D subimages from each 64-subcube (64x64x64 voxels) of the overall 256-cube input object. Each PE contains a double buffer, each half of which is sufficient to hold the largest image that can be created from its associated 64x64x64 cube.

The reconstructed image will consist of two components. The first of these is the density of each active point in the object - those which have not been removed through thresholding, for example. Depth or Z coordinate - the distance from the point to the front end of object space - is buffered also for use by the shading postprocessor.

Each of the eight intermediate processors merges the 2-D subimages generated by its set of 8 PEs into the appropriate position in the eight intermediate double buffers following priority rules determined by the sequence control table (see below). Finally, the contents of the intermediate buffers are merged into the double 512x512 frame buffer, following the same priority rules. The two halves of the double frame buffer are filled alternately - one is computed while the other is displayed. Postprocessing consists of a global tone scale lookup table, shading algorithm implementation, and final brightness and/or pseudo-color lookup table.

A high speed interface permits communications with a host computer system for the purpose of image loading and readback. The host will also be responsible for archiving and retrieving appropriate data files, and converting formats to the internal object representation. The system controller is responsible for coordinating the activities of the 64 PEs by generating the sequence control tables for each desired object orientation. The control table includes X, Y, and Z position offsets for each of the subcubes making up object space. This information is used to recursively compute the absolute offsets for every point in the output image as well as the order of processing of voxels for the hidden surface removal algorithm.

Object Memory System

To display any set of objects with a scale factor of 1:1 within a 256-cube object space requires 16 M Bytes of high speed RAM (assuming 8 bit quantization for each point). While this may seem to be an extremely large amount of high speed memory, it should be recognized that the steep decline in MOS memory prices is expected to continue for some time. In addition, even at current prices, the cost of the overall display device (which is dominated by the cost of this memory) should be relatively small compared to the cost of a complete medical imaging system such as a CAT scanner.

Since the object space is divided into 64 equal subcubes, each PE requires 256 K Bytes of associated memory. In each memory module, data are organized into groups of eight voxels (a 2-cube) occupying a pair of 32 bit words. Each memory access (with an address derived from the Sequence Control Table) retrieves a word pair which is buffered between the memory and the processing element permitting an entire 2-cube to be traversed in any order. Suitable memory management hardware located between the host and the PE-memory system facilitates direct high speed access to restricted regions of object space such as X, Y, or Z planes or variable size rectangular volumes.

Display Processing Element (PE)

Each PE consists of a pipelined arithmetic processor, input density lookup table, its copy of the sequence control table, and a dual 128x128 image buffer memory. Figure 4 illustrates the overall organization of the PE and its associated 64-subcube object memory module. The density lookup table is used to preprocess the voxels retrieved from memory for various purposes including selective masking, thresholding, or image enhancement based on density value.

The arithmetic processor is responsible for computing X, Y, and Z offsets for each pixel of the image based upon the position of the corresponding input voxel. This is accomplished with no multiplies, divides, or other time consuming arithmetic or logical operations. As can be seen in Figure 5, the most complex operation is arithmetic addition. To obtain successively finer position offsets requires shifts but these are performed within the wiring of the pipelined system. Only

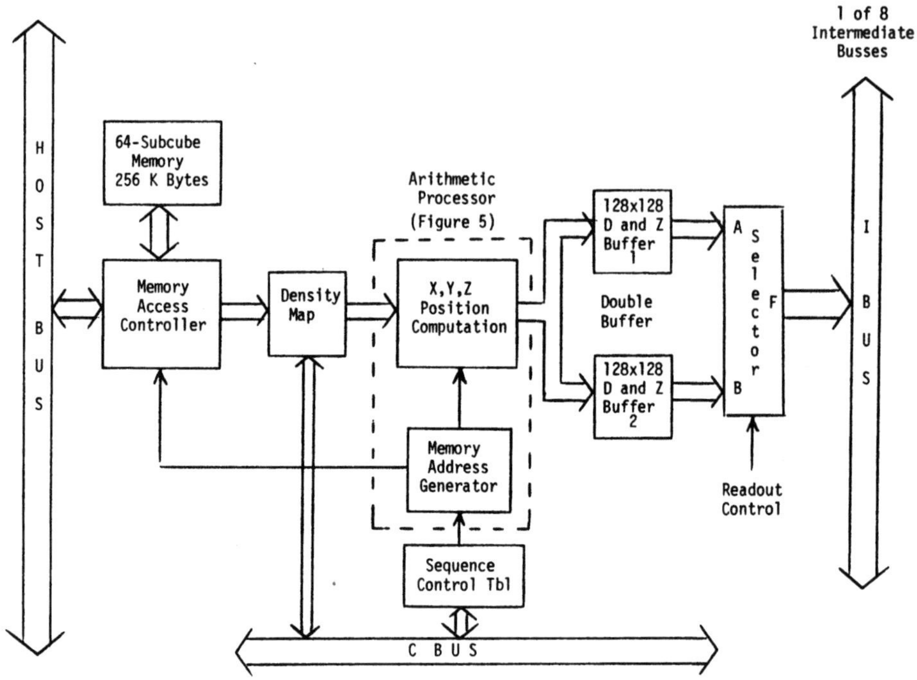

Figure 4 - Processing Element (PE) Organization

the data paths for position computation along one coordinate axis are shown - the other two are similar.

The operation of the arithmetic processor is based on the time-ordered display algorithm used for hidden surface removal. The fundamental concept which simplifies the hardware implementation is that regardless of object orientation, each subcube is entirely independent and all 64 subcubes may be processed in parallel since for any given subcube, every other subcube is either entirely in front of it or entirely behind it. The same characteristic also permits the overall computation of X and Y positions to be accomplished recursively, starting with the largest subcubes and working down to individual voxels, dividing by 2 at each step. For any particular voxel, the position offset along a given axis (X, Y, or Z) can be computed by simply adding the appropriately shifted control table entries. Thus, for a single orientation, only one control table of position offsets is sufficient for computation of <u>all</u> X, Y, and Z positions.

The precise X and Y destination coordinates in the 128x128 buffer are computed and converted to a memory address where the video (density and Z value) will be stored. A double buffer enables computation to proceed while the alternate buffer is being merged in subsequent stages of processing.

Anti-Aliasing

For magnifications from object space to image space greater than 1.732:1 ($1/\sqrt{3}$), holes would appear in the output image at certain orientations if anti-aliasing techniques were not utilized. Two methods have been investigated thus far: display of the centers of the visible faces of each voxel (1-cube) and double resolution interpolation with

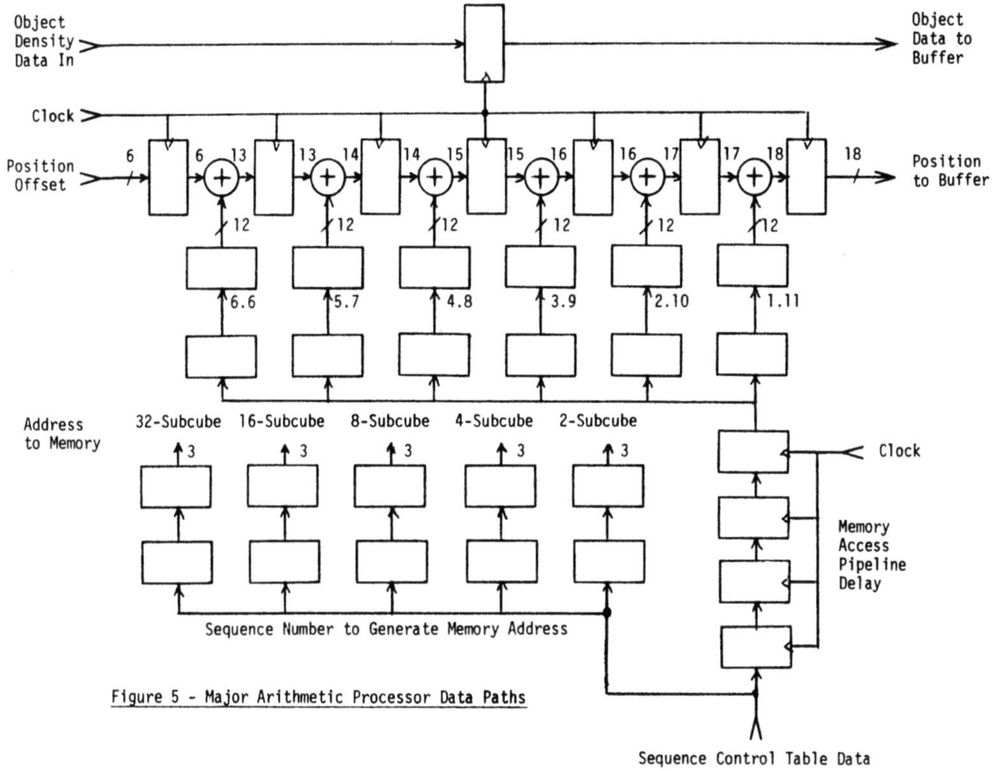

Figure 5 - Major Arithmetic Processor Data Paths

resampling. The first of these represents the singular case of the DISPLAY algorithm where the object cube faces have a size of exactly one pixel. At most, there will be three faces visible from any orientation. Interpolating out to a double resolution 3-D grid and resampling is similar to anti-aliasing techniques used in graphics display processors. Both of these require more sophisticated processing and additional buffer memory in each of the PEs, but can be accomplished within the pipelining time constraints.

Merge Processors and Buffers

Each of the images produced by the display processing elements consists of a two dimensional array of 112x112 points (in a 16384 word - 128x128 point memory - 1:1 scale factor) corresponding to the largest possible 2-D projection of the 64-subcube. These 64 images must eventually be merged into the output 512x512 frame buffer. This is accomplished in two steps. First the 64 images are combined 8-fold into the 256x256 point intermediate buffers, and then these are combined again 8-fold into the final output buffer. The first step is performed in parallel by the eight intermediate processors. Each of these merging processes requires the computation of position offsets as described for the individual PEs, above. Double buffers permit the merging and readout operations to be taking place concurrently. As described above, the same SCT determines both the order of computation within a PE and the order of combining for the merge operations. Figure 6 shows the second stage merge operation. The first stage data flow is similar.

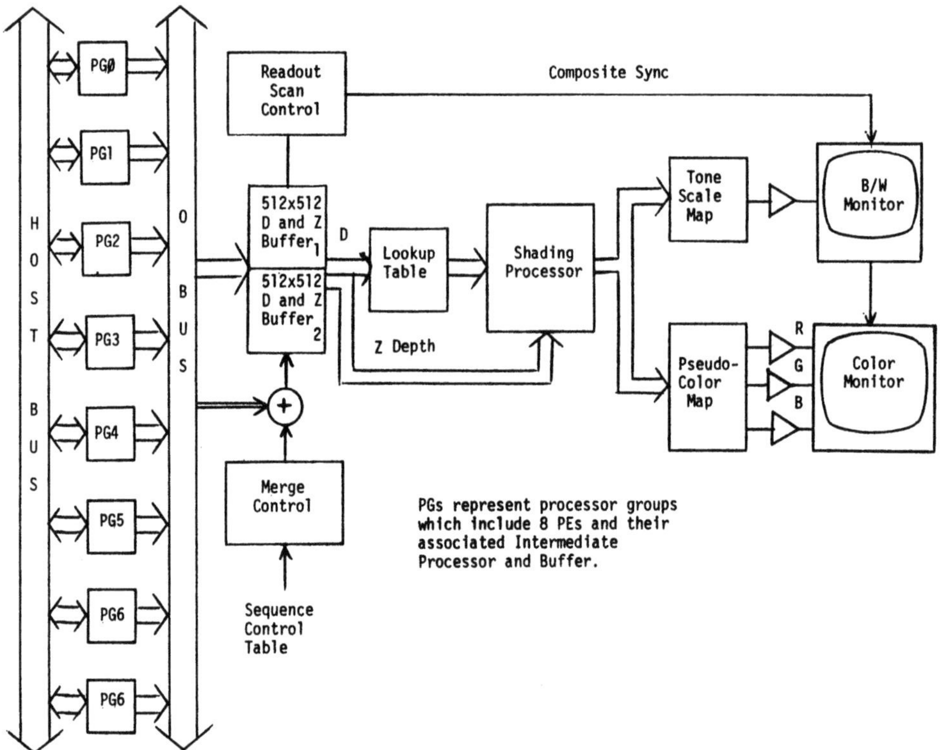

Figure 6 - Second Stage Merging - Intermediate Buffer to Output Buffer

The final buffer stores the output image and Z depth values for use by the shading hardware. The major function of this memory is to permit scan conversion to standard video format for display on a monochrome or color raster scan TV monitor. This memory is directly accessible by the host for image readback and display of auxiliary text or other information.

Sequence Control Table (SCT)

The SCT contains 8 entries sorted in the required time-order defining the X, Y, and Z offsets of the centers of the 8 largest subcubes with respect to the center of object space. Offsets for successively smaller subcubes are determined by shifting the table entries by an appropriate amount (between 0 and 7 places to the right).

In addition to 3-D rotation, many other interactive capabilities can be implemented through modifications of the entries in the sequence control table and simple additions to the display processor hardware. A few of these are described below. General anamorphic scaling is accomplished by simply multiplying the X, Y, and Z values stored in the table by the appropriate scaling factors with suitable interpolation of the input density data. Translation in 3-space is easily supported by adding X, Y, and Z offsets to the addresses of the output image buffer.

Display of Multiple Independent Objects

The display of up to 64 independently configurable objects can be achieved by loading object specific SCTs into each of the individual PEs or selected groups of PEs and modifying the implementation of the merge algorithms. This would permit complete control for objects within their own subcubes. These "sub-object spaces" could include any 3-D rectangular region comprising multiples of the basic 64-cube. Other display parameters can be associated with the individual PEs including a translation offset and the tone scale mapping to be used for the input data.

To extend the concepts of the Segment Display Processor [1] to 3-D we associate an Object Descriptor Block with each distinct object to be displayed. The ODB contains all of the parameters describing attributes unique to each object. These entries include:

* Position X,Y,Z of center of object within input object space.
* Orientation X,Y,Z of object for viewpoint control.
* Size X,Y,Z of bounding rectangular solid about object.
* Scale Factor X,Y,Z for reduction and magnification.
* Slice Plane Specifier - internal access.
* Tone Scale Lookup Table Specifier.
* Format Control - Bits/Voxel, Partitioning.
* Merge Control for overlap and transparency.
* Shading Direction X,Y,Z and Control.
* Object Linkage for hierarchical control structure.

A dedicated interface processor converts each of the ODBs into one or more Object Control Blocks (OCBs) which are the control structures required by each PE. An OCB is required for each instance of an object per processor. Thus an object which lies entirely within the memory of a single processor will require one OCB while an object which occupies 4 PE memories, for example, will require 4 related OCBs.

The Orientation and Scale Factor parameters are converted into a suitable SCT. Size and Slice Plane determine the bounds over which object accessing must take place. Note that there may be multiple accesses to a given region of object space. The Object Linkage permits groups of related objects to be manipulated as a single hierarchical structure for certain parameters including position, scale factor, and orientation.

Once the list of OCBs for each PE have been generated and loaded, processing in each PE is quite similar to that required for a single large object, though the sequencing is somewhat more involved. Restrictions on position require that all of the objects within a given PE memory must map into the projection of a 64-cube. However, this image may freely move about on the display screen as well as in depth as long as a true Z-buffer algorithm is used for the subsequent merge operations.

Computation Pipeline Timing

Using the architecture outlined above, we can calculate the expected performance and throughput of the system. We assume that the required processing time is 100 ns per primitive calculation. This represents a conservative design guideline for discrete TTL or high performance NMOS VLSI technology.

* The time required to generate a subimage (by the PE) from the 64-subcube is 256 K x 100 ns or ~25.6 ms.

* The time required to merge groups of 8 subimage buffers into a 256x256 intermediate buffer is 8 x 112 x 112 x 100 ns or ~11 ms.

* The time required to merge 8 intermediate buffers into the output buffer is 8 x 224 x 224 x 100 ns or ~40 ms.

Thus, the limiting time is the last - corresponding to a frame update rate of 1000/40 or approximately 25 frames/second. Note that because of the pipeline latency, however, a response to a change in orientation will require a total of three frame times to become visible. Assuming output to a standard NTSC compatible video monitor, the full 25 frame per second throughput rate can be exploited by switching buffers whenever a new frame has been completely loaded. Alternately, a dual port memory system may be used for the output buffer. However, visible image changes (breaks) may occur for fast changing objects during the frame display. An effective update rate of 20 frames per second can be easily achieved by displaying each frame generated by the display system 1-1/2 times corresponding to 3 video fields using 2:1 interlaced scanning.

Postprocessing

Two types of postprocessing are to be implemented in real time: tone scale lookup tables for the video intensity and other display parameters, and some form of shading to enhance the appearance and realism of the image. Tone scale transformation hardware will permit the entire class of point type image processing functions which are traditionally used with image processing systems to be implemented on the output image in real time. Examples of these operations include contrast enhancement, interactive thresholding, and pseudo-color processing.

Shading of the output image is essential to provide depth cues and other visual information about object structure. In distance-only shading, the intensity of a point of the image is determined by the distance of the corresponding point of the object from the light source. This is simple to compute and gives pleasing results. Other shading models take direction into account by computing the inner product of the normal to the surface with a unit vector along the light ray reaching thus providing curvature information. The distance-only shading algorithm simply uses the Z coordinate (depth) to modify the brightness of each output point. The other shading schemes are more difficult to implement since they are non-local operations requiring knowledge of neighboring voxels. One solution would use a gradient operator on the Z coordinates to obtain the surface normal at each point. Alternatively, local direction information can be stored in each voxel (along with the density) and passed to the shading postprocessor.

Relationship to Pyramid Architectures

Finally, it is interesting to point out some of the similarities between this hierarchical processor structure and pyramid architectures. Pyramids are traditionally thought of as being useful for image analysis where a full resolution image resides at the base of the pyramid and successive levels utilize reduced resolution images obtained through some averaging or other data reduction process.

The system described above could be classified as a 3-1/2 D pyramid not for analysis, but for synthesis. The base of this pyramid is the cubical input object space consisting of 16M individual voxels. The next level would be a cube of 2M 2-cubes and so forth as shown below:

Level -	1	2	3	4	5	6	7	8	9
Size -	Voxel	2-C	4-C	8-C	16-C	32-C	64-C	128-C	256-C
Number -	16 M	2 M	256 K	32 K	4 K	512	64	8	1

<---------------- PEs ----------------><-IPs-><-OP->

With the actual implementation, the physical pyramid consists of only three levels. However, conceptually, the entire processor hierarchy could be visualized as incorporating all 8 processing levels each performing similar merging operations on successively larger subimages.

Part III - Potential Impact of Emerging Technologies

While the primary emphasis in special purpose computer architecture has been toward exploitation of traditional digital systems implemented with increasingly sophisticated integrated circuits, it is important to consider the potential of alternative or emerging technologies. These may be used to implement conventional functions in novel ways, to implement devices not possible with traditional technology, or to implement totally new approaches to information processing.

The discussion below is somewhat speculative but is based on solid theory and in some cases, on actual implementation. Space limitation prevents the inclusion of an extensive bibliography. However, much of the material can be found in several recent special issues of the Proceedings of the IEEE. The following list (by no means exhaustive) provides some examples of technologies which have been demonstrated in the research laboratory but have, as yet, not made a significant impact for applications to spatially distributed data:

* Non-Boolean Logic, Multi-Valued Logic, Threshold Logic.
* High Performance Semiconductors - GaAs, VMOS, CMOS.
* Josephson Junction Devices.
* Three Dimensional Integrated Circuits.
* Molecular Integrated Circuits.
* Coherent Optical Systems.
* General Optical Computers.
* Electromagnetic Devices.
* Surface or Bulk Acoustic Wave Devices.
* Bulk Solid State Devices.
* Spatially Continuous Structures.

These may be broadly be divided into several classes dependent upon what impact they can have on computer organization:

1. Performance enhancements of current technology.
2. New structures using traditional devices.
3. New materials, primitive elements, and hybrid systems.

Some of these, such as Gallium Arsenide - GaAs, provide the mechanism for improving the performance of traditional architectures through the use of faster, higher density IC technology. Others, such as 3-D ICs, can be thought of as new organizations of currently available logic devices or future devices. However, the most interesting class, by far, for future exploitation makes use of fundamentally new materials effects, hybrid combinations of technology, and totally new basic logic primitives. Many of these are not widely known in the traditional architecture community and are thought to be too esoteric to be of current interest. However, it is only through the encouragement of the ultimate users of such technology that they will develop and mature.

Performance Enhancements of Current Technology

Integrated circuit technology has made enormous strides in the last 20 years in terms of improved switching speed, reduced power dissipation, and increased packing density. The current semiconductor 'art' can place 500,000 MOS transistors on a single chip representing an entire 32 bit CPU or more than 256K bits of dynamic memory. Bipolar logic elements with switching speeds of less than 1 nanosecond are used routinely in high performance computers. The power consumption of these devices has steadily decreased permitting relatively dense arrays of high speed devices to be increasingly utilized.

This trend is likely to continue for the forseeable future, which in this rapidly changing field means approximately 5 years. Extensive efforts are underway in industry as well as academia to develop higher performance integrated circuits using new semiconductor materials or structures. These include group III-V semiconductors such as Gallium Arsenide, as well as enhanced MOS and CMOS. The US government's VHSIC program is directed at these, among others, approaches to high speed ICs.

Device technologies such as these represent the smallest departure from main stream semiconductor production. They use the same basic manufacturing techniques and precision equipment. Some of these are already in commercial production.

<u>New Structures using Traditional Devices</u>

Digital technology, be it based on vacuum tubes or integrated circuits, has been predominantly a hierarchy of two-dimensional subsystems. Basic devices are arrayed on circuit boards or IC chips. These plug into the next successive interconnection level until the top or system level is reached. General three-dimensional systems constructed out of individual components are difficult to implement because of the problem of managing the interconnections. However, there is no basic reason why an entire 3-D structure could not be implemented within a Silicon (or GaAS) chip. Current IC fabrication techniques utilize only the top few percent of the chip. The remainder is for mechanical support.

Consider an entire image processing system which is self contained in such a structure. A scene is focused on the top of the chip by a lens. An array of photodiodes integrated as the first layer converts the optical image to a two dimensional digital image which is processed on successive levels as it propagates through the chip in parallel. The resulting information, either an answer to a question of pattern recognition, or an enhanced or otherwise modified image, is removed at the bottom. The output of an entire image could be transferred via an array of LEDs or even, perhaps, an integrated light valve formed on the bottom chip surface.

<u>New Materials, Primitive Elements, and Hybrid Systems</u>

This class of new technologies represents the most significant departure from the traditional. Current technology utilizes three terminal active devices with a passion. Essentially all traditional systems are based on logic primitives which are in turn based on spatially discrete structures of three terminal devices such as bipolar or MOS transistors. However, there is no basic law of nature requiring the use of these building blocks. These are only one instance of information processing elements. The world is essentially continuous at the scales of time and distance which are of interest for the processing of spatially distributed data. In addition, the term spatially distributed data does not need to imply spatially discrete division of object space. There is a wide class phenomena which could potentially be exploited to implement highly parallel systems which could have performances which would be many orders of magnitude greater then current technology <u>by any measure of performance one desires to employ</u>.

Such systems would almost certainly <u>not</u> be entirely based on integrated circuit technology (Silicon or otherwise). Such VLSI technology will be getting far too complex to be supported for any forseeable lithographer's art with the needed degree of yield and reliability. Rather, these systems will be hybrid in nature and will include various kinds of unconventional integrated circuits, and Electro-Magnetic and optical devices, among others. Brief descriptions of a few of these radically different technologies and some potential applications are given below.

Non-Boolean Logic, Multi-Valued Logic, Threshold Logic

Basic logic systems based on Binary Boolean Logic have had a monopoly on computer implementation almost since its origins. Given the technology of the time, such a logic had certain inherent advantages in terms of implementation, theoretical understanding, and reliability. However, this should not imply that this is the only logic which should be used. Biological systems appear to perform eminently well without ever having heard of George Boole. Threshold logic is inherently suitable for decision making processes such as are required in pattern analysis. Multivalued logic could alleviate the pin-out problems of modern ICs. Other forms of logic systems including Fuzzy logic, Temporal logic, and Stochastic or Statistical logic have never been considered seriously for use in hardware architecture. Is it not possible that there are superior logic systems to use?

Josephson Junction Devices

The Josephson effect provides for the tantalizing possibility of implementing switching circuits which operate at picosecond speeds, occupy minimal space, and dissipate almost no power. There are many significant obstacles to be overcome in achieving these capabilities. A temperature near absolute zero is necessary to maintain the required superconducting effects. To exploit the switching speeds possible with these devices requires the entire computing system to be packaged in a volume of a few cubic inches. Otherwise the propagation delays along the interconnection wires become significant. These systems cannot be tested at room temperature and cannot be repaired in the cryogenic operating environment.

The resulting performance to be obtained may be worth the effort. Typical gate speeds which have been achieved are in the range of 10 - 35 picoseconds. High speed random access memory is based on the storage of single quantas of magnetic flux. Packing densities are equivalent to traditional integrated circuit technology. The entire memory and CPU for a CRAY type computer could fit in a three inch cube and dissipate a total of 10 watts.

The International Business Machines Corporation (IBM) has had the major research effort in Josephson technology. Simple logic and memory devices have been fabricated and tested. Designs have been developed for the entire interconnection hierarchy of chips, chip carriers, and motherboard wiring panels which will operate at near absolute zero temperatures. Whether this effort pays off in the near future, or is decades ahead of its time remains to be seen.

Molecular Integrated Circuits

All current integrated circuits are manufactured by a top down approach - designing oversized photomasks and using a series of reducing steps to etch the circuit patterns on crystalline silicon or other semiconductor wafers. As these packing densities get finer and finer they are beginning to approach the molecular level in size.

Why not work from the bottom up? Generate structures by replicating groups of molecules in precisely defined patterns. This techniques could be especially effective for array type structures such as memory. Instead of simply growing crystals, grow the entire memory array as a single crystal. We could speculate on how this could be accomplished. Traditional chemical synthesis processes can be exploited to produce some of these structures. Techniques derived from genetic engineering may eventually provide us with processes for synthesizing arbitrary microstructures based on molecular programs.

Optical Systems

Optical systems using monochromatic coherent Laser illumination can be used to perform many of the required image processing and pattern analysis functions literally at the speed of light. The most important effect upon which such systems are based is the simple fact that an ordinary convex lens will generate the 2-D Fourier transform in real time. Simply place a spatial image 2f (where f is the focal length) in front of the lens, illuminate it with collimated Laser light, and the Fourier transform will be produced 2f behind the lens. Add another lens and you have the inverse Fourier transform. An amplitude only filter is simply realized by an intensity mask placed at the Fourier plane. General filtering, matched filtering, correlation, and other types of processing are possible but require the amplitude and phase control at the Fourier plane. Add programmable input (perhaps using liquid crystals) and output (using photodiodes) and such a system could be used as a super performance peripheral for a conventional computer.

Other types of optical system based computing devices are possible. For example, using optics to transmit information between levels of processing could eliminate untold numbers of wires. A large permutation network based on an array of LEDs with acousto-optic deflectors and another array of photodiodes would be possible. To interconnect 1024 processors would require 1024 LEDs and their associated deflectors and 1024 photodiodes. Think of an array of searchlights picking off distant targets. A true crossbar could be realized with the optical analogy of a broadcast system. Each processor would be assigned a unique carrier optical frequency channel. The bandwidth would be sufficient for the data rate desired. Each processor would also have an associated receiver which could tune in on any of the transmit frequencies. This could be implemented using an array of sharply tuned solid state Laser diodes which would illuminate an array of tunable receivers.

Electromagnetic Devices

Although the vacuum tube has utterly vanished from the face of the earth with respect to applications in information processing there is one area where this technology is thriving. This is of course image input and output. Solid state technology is only recently beginning to be successfully applied to video cameras and image displays - with only limited success. The basic reason is quite clear. Solid state devices require a discrete structure to be formed at each pixel location with well matched characteristics over the entire surface. Small imperfections in the material substrate or anywhere in the manufacturing process can have a disastrous effect on individual elements. Furthermore, current solid state imaging devices utilize spatially discrete structures necessitating complex scanning electronics to address individual elements.

Operations which can be implemented effectively with electromagnetic electron optical systems include: programmable image scaling, translation, and rotation; scanning and scan conversion; variable resolution and high speed image input; and individual and projection (light valve) display. Many of these functions are difficult or impossible to achieve with totally solid state technology and spatially discrete structures.

Conceptual Design for a True Three Dimensional Display

One of the problems in achieving a true three dimensional display presentation is in developing a suitable output device. In addition to their inherent lack of elegance, systems based on vibrating mirrors or rotating LED arrays are incapable of producing true solid views. There are no known devices or even principles which would permit the implementation of a volume type of display which would produce arbitrary solid images. However, holography may provide a solution. Figure 7 illustrates the overall approach that we propose for a true 3-D image processing system using a holographic output device.

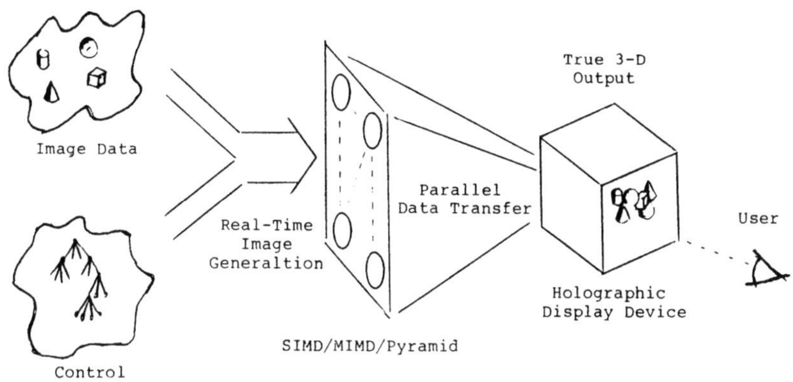

Figure 7 - Possible Future 3-D Display System Architecture

Holography is a collection of techniques which can generate a true three dimensional view from a 2-D image surface (the hologram) which may be seen by a group of people (as opposed to one individual). Holograms can be produced which provide a remarkably realistic 'window' onto a true three dimensional scene. Similar techniques could, in principle, be used to implement a true 3-D computer output display. Without going into the theory of holography, we now preset a possible design for such a system simply based on the required information bandwidth requirements.

Suppose we want a minimum output display space of 512x512x512x30Hz. This would be equivalent to adding a third dimension to conventional TV or computer graphics with a refresh rate of 30 frames per second. This represents a data rate of approximately 4 billion bytes per second. Assuming that the mapping from 2D to 3D via the holographic process is efficient (say only a 2:1 loss), we need to generate a 2D image (the hologram) of 16384x16384 elements every 1/30th of a second.

We can achieve this with a combination of technologies as outlined in Figure 8. The 3D object data itself can be generated with a pyramidal array of processors (called the hologram processor array or HPA) with a base size of 128x128 (the size of an augmented MPP array). We do not address the issues of the type of processing elements required. The output of this array, will be a sparse image representing a subsampling by a factor of 128 in the X and Y dimensions which will be scanned as a whole to produce the required hologram resolution. This output is taken from the HPA via a set of 16384 wires or a fiber optic bundle to an EM Image Converter Tube (ICT) which will perform the actual scanning. The input to the ICT is the spatially sparse image from the HPA. This falls on a photocathode which converts this optical image into an electron beam image. Coils surrounding the ICT scan this sparse image in synchrony with the generation by the HPA. In essence, each processor in the base of the HPA is responsible for generating a 128x128 raster scan mini hologram.

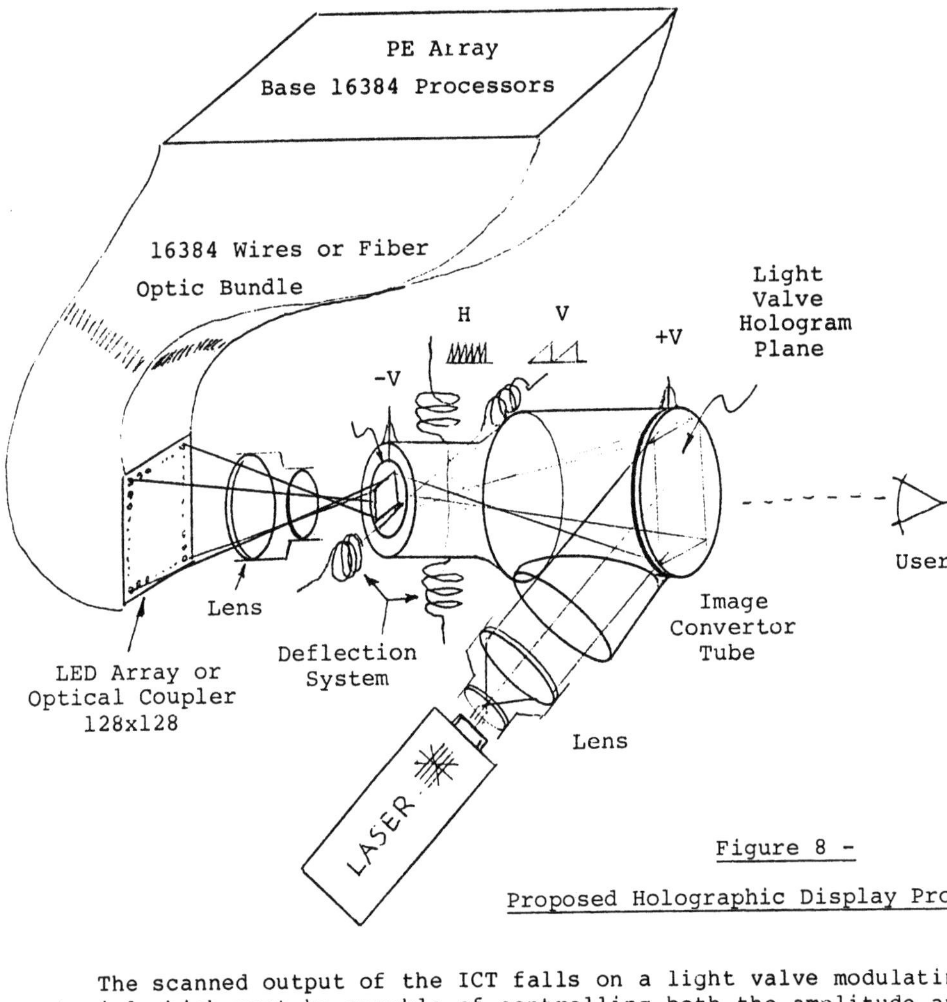

Figure 8 -

Proposed Holographic Display Processor

The scanned output of the ICT falls on a light valve modulating material which must be capable of controlling both the amplitude and phase of an incident Laser (or white light) beam. This resolution at this surface is the required 16384x16384 points refreshed at a 30Hz rate.

Note that the overall data rate here is of the same order of magnitude as the 6 billion 8 bit adds/second of the MPP. Admittedly, however, the processing required to generate a real time holographic image will be substantially greater. Furthermore, to achieve high quality of perhaps 4096x4096x4096x60Hz would require a data transmission rate of over 60 trillion bytes per second. So, while theoretically possible, the engineering has a way to go!

Comments on New Technologies

Some researchers would say that this kind of proposal is simply absurd and should not even be considered for serious investigation. Perhaps this is the case. Many prominent scientists and engineers had similar comments about new technologies in the past. On the other hand, without such possibilities to guide and stimulate the research direction, the overall engineering field would be very narrow indeed.

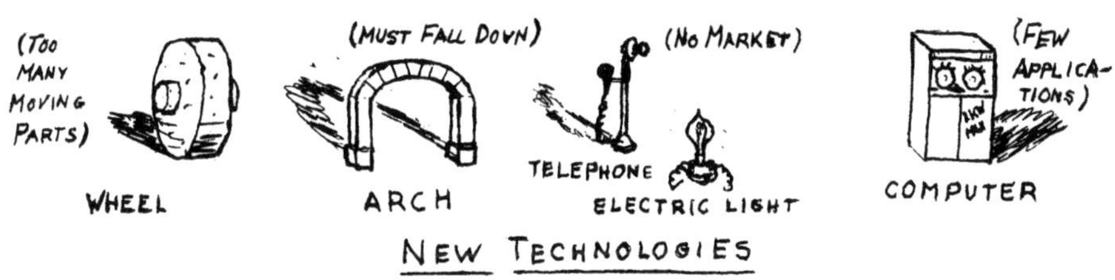

The purpose of the previous discussion was simply to make the basic statement: There are alternative technologies that should be at least considered for possible application to the processing of spatially distributed data. These may not be viable at the present time, or even 20 years from now. But, without the stimulation and encouragement of the computer architecture community, they could - and would - be delegated to the dusty shelves of the research laboratory storeroom and to obscurity in highly specilized technical publications. It is our responsibility to do our homework and give these potentially revolutionary techniques all possible consideration.

Summary and Conclusions

Several aspects of architecture for interactive display were addressed in this paper. First, the general requirements for advanced display systems were outlined including spatial, temporal, and tone scale resolution; desire for multiple formats; real-time and/or interactive response to changes; use of object oriented hardware and software; and the goal of realism in the presentation.

The hardware architecture for a high speed image display system which would permit the real-time manipulation of 3-D objects (surface display) obtained from real world data was then described. A key feature of this system is support for interactive manipulation of the object in 3-D space including rotation, translation, and scaling. Straightforward algorithms containing no complex arithmetic or logical operations are utilized throughout.

Functional simulations of the display processor have been performed and current efforts are directed toward development of effective 3-D anti-aliasing techniques and investigation of more sophisticated shading algorithms which are appropriate for hardware implementation. A prototype of the real-time hardware for one 64-subcube of the overall system using Schottky TTL devices and MOS dynamic RAMs will be constructed to gain experience from actual use. More complete information can be found in [12].

A somewhat speculative discussion followed on the potential of new, novel, emerging technologies for applications in spatial data processing. Several examples of such technologies were provided. Finally, a conceptual proposal for a true three dimensional holographic display was presented which utilized a hybrid combination of several of these technologies. The important point to be made in connection with these technologies is for the computer architecture designer or investigator to at least be 'technologically literate' about research outside his/her immediate area. Only with such awareness can the full potential of the vast amount of basic research ever be realized.

References

[1] S.M. Goldwasser, "A Generalized Segment Display Processor Architecture", Proceedings of the IEEE Computer Society Workshop on Computer Architecture for Pattern Analysis and Image Database Management, Hot Springs, Virginia, November 11 - 13, 1981.

[2] S.M. Goldwasser, "Hardware Considerations in the Implementation of a Segment Display Processor Architecture", Proceeding of Pattern Recognition and Image Processing, Las Vegas, Nevada, June 13 - 17, 1982.

[3] S.M. Goldwasser and D.E. Troxel, "Page Composition of Continuous Tone Imagery," Computer Graphics and Image Processing, to be published.

[4] D.E. Troxel, W.F. Schreiber, S.M. Goldwasser, M.M.A. Khan, L. Picard, M.A. Ide, and C.J. Turcio, "Automated Engraving of Gravure Cylinders", IEEE Transactions on Systems, Man, and Cybernetics, September, 1981.

[5] Herman, G.T., and Liu, H.K., "Three-Dimensional Display of Human Organs from Computed Tomograms", Computer Graphics and Image Processing 9 (1979), pp. 1-21.

[6] Herman, G.T., and Udupa, J.K., "Display of Three-Dimensional Discrete Surfaces", Proceedings SPIE 283 (1981), pp. 90-97.

[7] Batnitzky, S., Price, H.I., Lee, K.R., Cook, P.N., Cook, L.T., Fritz, S.L., Dwyer, S.J., and Watts, C., "Three-Dimensional Computer Reconstruction of Brain Lesions from Surface Contours provided by Computed Tomography", Neurosurgery 11 (1982), pp. 73-84.

[8] Sunguroff, A., and Greenberg, D., "Computer Generated Images for Medical Applications", Computer Graphics 12 (1978), pp. 196-202.

[9] SOLIDVIEW System, Lexidata Corporation, Billerica, Massachusetts.

[10] Meagher, D.J.R., "High Speed Display of 3D Medical Images using Octree Encoding", Rensselaer Polytechnic Institute Technical Report, September 1981.

[11] Fuchs, H., Keden, Z.M., Naylor, B.F., "On Visible Surface Generation by A Priori Tree Structures", Computer Graphics 14 (1980), pp. 124-133.

[12] Goldwasser, S.M. and Reynolds, R.A., "An Architecture for the Real-Time Display and Manipulation of Three Dimensional Objects", to be presented at the International Conference on Parallel Processing, Bellaire, Michigan, August 23-26, 1983.

THE PASM SYSTEM AND PARALLEL IMAGE PROCESSING

Howard Jay Siegel
School of Electrical Engineering
Purdeu University
West Lafayette, IN 47907 USA

1. Introduction

One way to do image processing faster is through the use of parallelism. Different modes of parallelism can be employed in a computer system. The SIMD (single instruction stream - multiple data stream) mode [9] typically uses a set of N processors, N memories, an interconnection network, and a control unit (e.g., Illiac IV [6], STARAN [5], CLIP4 [8], MPP [16]). The control unit broadcasts instructions to the processors and all active ("enabled") processors execute the same instruction at the same time. Each processor executes instructions using data taken from a memory with which only it is associated. The interconnection network allows interprocessor communication. An MSIMD (multiple-SIMD) system is a parallel processing system which can be structured as one or more independent SIMD machines (e.g., MAP [13]). The Illiac IV was originally designed as an MSIMD system [3]. The MIMD (multiple instruction stream - multiple data stream) mode [9] typically consists of N processors and N memories, where each processor can follow an independent instruction stream (e.g., C.mmp [27], Cm* [25]). As with SIMD architectures, there is a multiple data stream and an interconnection network. A partitionable SIMD/MIMD system is a parallel processing system which can be structured as one or more independent SIMD and/or MIMD machines (e.g., TRAC [17]).

This research was supported by the Defense Mapping Agency, monitored by the United States Air Force Command, Rome Air Development Center, under contract number F30602-C-0193; and by the Air Force Office of Scientific Research, Air Force Systems Command, USAF, under grant number AFOSR-78-3581. The United States Government is authorized to reproduce and distribute reprints for Governmental purposes notwithstanding any copyright notation hereon.

NATO ASI Series, Vol. F18
Computer Architectures for Spatially Distributed Data
Edited by H. Freeman and G. G. Pieroni

In this paper, the organization of PASM [20], a partitionable SIMD/MIMD system being designed at Purdue University, is overviewed. Example parallel image processing algorithms for use on PASM are given.

PASM is to be a large-scale dynamically reconfigurable multimicroprocessor system. It is a special-purpose system aimed at exploiting the parallelism of image processing and pattern recognition tasks. PASM can be partitioned so that it operates as many independent SIMD and/or MIMD machines of various sizes, and it is being developed using a variety of problems in image processing and pattern recognition to guide the design choices. It can also be applied to related areas such as speech processing and biomedical signal processing.

PASM is to serve as a research tool for experimenting with parallel processing. The design attempts to incorporate the needed flexibility for studying large-scale SIMD and MIMD parallelism, while keeping system costs "reasonable." Portions of PASM have been simulated and a prototype is planned for the near future.

In section 2, the PASM organization is overviewed. Section 3 describes the Parallel Computation Unit. The Micro Controllers are discussed in section 4. In section 5, the secondary memory system is explored. Parallel algorithms for computing global histograms and 2-D FFTs are given in sections 6 and 7, respectively.

2. PASM Organization

A block diagram of the basic components of PASM is shown in Fig. 1. The Parallel Computation Unit (PCU) contains $N=2^n$ processors, N memory modules, and an interconnection network. The PCU processors are microprocessors that perform the actual SIMD and MIMD computations. The PCU memory modules are used by the PCU processors for data storage in SIMD mode and both data and instruction storage in MIMD mode. Thus, each PCU processor can operate in both the SIMD and MIMD modes of parallelism. The interconnection network provides a means of communication among the PCU processors and memory modules.

The Micro Controllers (MCs) are a set of microprocessors which act as the control units for the PCU processors in SIMD mode and orchestrate the activities of the PCU processors in MIMD mode. There are $Q=2^q$ MCs. Each MC controls N/Q PCU processors. A virtual SIMD

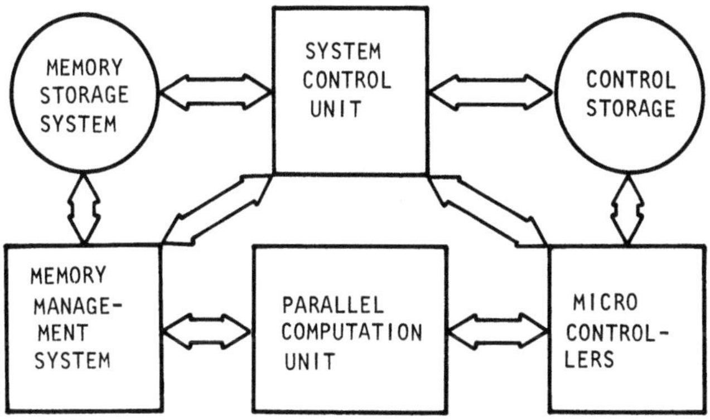

Fig. 1. Block diagram overview of PASM.

machine (partition) of size RN/Q where $R=2^r$ and $1 \leq r \leq q$, is obtained by loading R MC memory modules with the same instructions simultaneously. Similarly, a virtual MIMD machine of size RN/Q is obtained by combining the efforts of the PCU processors of R MCs. Q is therefore the maximum number of partitions allowable, and N/Q is the size of the smallest partition. Possible values for N and Q are 1024 and 32, respectively. Control Storage contains the programs for the MCs.

The Memory Storage System provides secondary storage space for the data files in SIMD mode, and for the data and program files in MIMD mode. Multiple storage devices are used in the Memory Storage System to allow parallel data transfers. The Memory Management System controls the transferring of files between the Memory Storage System and the PCU memory modules. It employs a set of cooperating dedicated microprocessors.

The System Control Unit is a conventional machine, such as a PDP-11, and is responsible for the overall coordination of the activities of the other components of PASM. The types of tasks the System Control Unit will perform include program development, job scheduling, and coordination of the loading of the PCU memory modules from the Memory Storage System with the loading of the MC memory modules from Control Storage. By carefully choosing which tasks should be assigned to the System Control Unit and which should be assigned to other system components, the System Control Unit can work effectively and not become a bottleneck.

Sections 3 through 5 provide more information about the PASM system. References for further reading about PASM appear at the end of this paper.

3. Parallel Computation Unit

The Parallel Computation Unit (PCU) is shown in Fig. 2. A memory module is connected to each processor to form a processor - memory pair called a Processing Element (PE). The N PEs are numbered from 0 to N-1 and each PE knows its number (address). The interconnection network is used for communications among PEs. A pair of memory units is used for each memory module. This double-buffering scheme allows data to be moved between one memory unit and secondary storage (the Memory Storage System) while the processor operates on data in the other memory unit.

The PCU processors will be specially designed for parallel image processing. A PASM prototype (for N=16, Q=4) has been designed based on Motorola MC68000 processors. The final (N=1024) system would most likely employ custom VLSI processors.

Two types of multistage interconnection networks are being considered for PASM: the Generalized Cube [19] and the Augmented Data Manipulator (ADM) [18]. Features of the Generalized Cube network will be described to familiarize the readers with the properties of multistage networks.

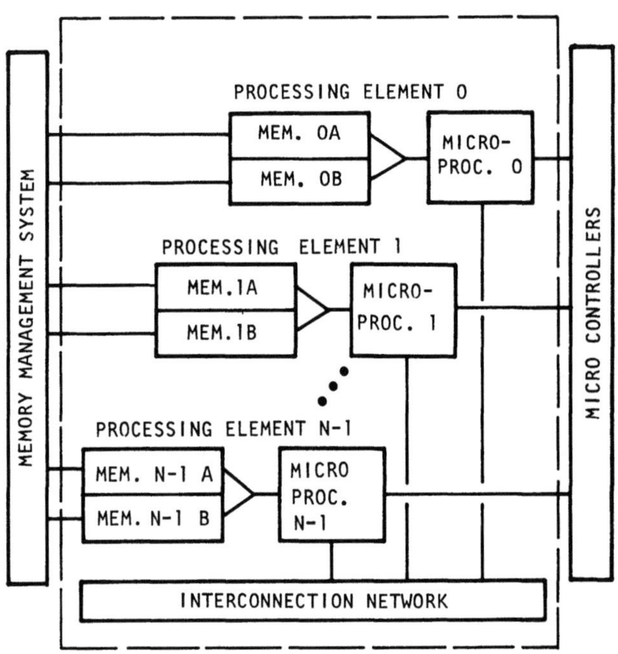

Fig. 2. Parallel Computation Unit (PCU).

The Generalized Cube network is a multistage cube-type network topology which was introduced as a standard for comparing network topologies. Other multistage cube-type networks include the baseline [26], delta [14], Extra Stage Cube [1], indirect binary n-cube [15], omega [12], STARAN flip [4], and SW-banyan (S=F=2) [10]. The Cube has N inputs and N outputs. It is shown in Fig. 3 for N=8. PE i, $0 \le i < N$, would be connected to input port i and output port i of the unidirectional network.

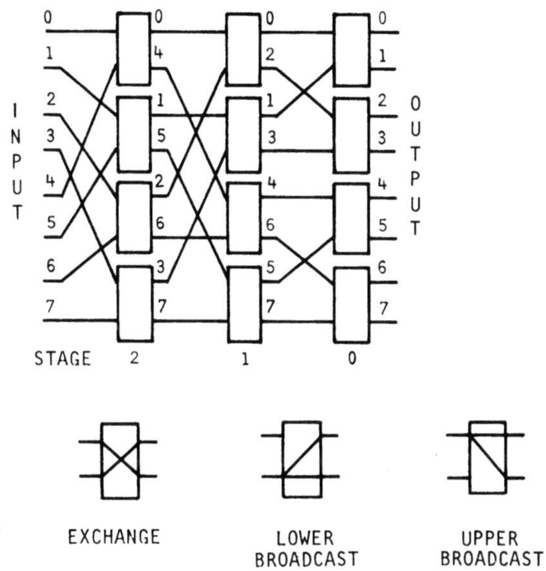

Fig. 3. Generalized Cube topology, shown for N=8.

The Generalized Cube topology has $n = \log_2 N$ stages, where each stage consists of a set of N lines connected to N/2 interchange boxes. Each interchange box is a two-input, two-output device. The labels of the input/output (I/O) lines entering the upper and lower inputs of an interchange box are used as the labels for the upper and lower outputs, respectively. Each interchange box can be set to one of the four legitimate states shown in Fig. 3.

The connections in this network are based on the cube interconnection functions [21, 22]. Let $P = p_{n-1} \cdots p_1 p_0$ be the binary representation of an arbitrary I/O line label. Then the n cube interconnection functions can be defined as:

$$\mathrm{cube}_i(p_{n-1} \cdots p_1 p_0) = p_{n-1} \cdots p_{i+1} \overline{p}_i p_{i-1} \cdots p_1 p_0$$

where $0 \le i < n$, $0 \le P < N$, and $\overline{p}_i$ denotes the complement of p_i. This means that the cube_i interconnection function connects P to $\mathrm{cube}_i(P)$, where $\mathrm{cube}_i(P)$ is the I/O line whose label differs from P in just the i-th

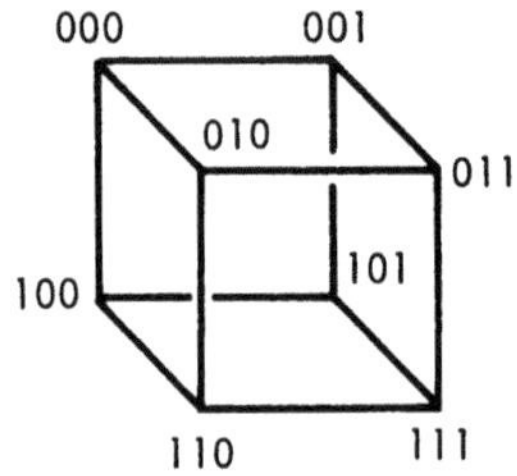

Fig. 4. Three-dimensional cube structure, with vertices labeled from 0 to 7 in binary.

bit position. Stage i of the Generalized Cube topology contains the $cube_i$ interconnection function, i.e., it pairs I/O lines that differ only in the i-th bit position.

The reason that these interconnections are referred to as cube connections can be seen by considering the case for N=8. This is shown in Fig. 4. The eight vertices can be labeled so each vertex is connected to the n=3 vertices that differ from it in just one bit position. The horizontal connections are $cube_0$, the diagonals are $cube_1$, and the verticals are $cube_2$.

Using routing tags (as headers on messages) allows network control to be distributed among the PEs. The routing tags for one-to-one data transfers consist of n bits. If certain broadcast capabilities are included, then 2n bits are used. The routing tags set the state of each interchange box individually.

The n-bit routing tag for one-to-one connections is computed from the input port number and desired output port number. Let S be the source address (input port number) and D be the destination address (output port number). Then the routing tag $T = S \oplus D$ (where "$\oplus$" means bitwise "exclusive-or"). Let $t_{n-1} \ldots t_1 t_0$ be the binary representation of T. An interchange box in the network at stage i need only examine t_i. If $t_i=1$, an exchange is performed, and if $t_i=0$, the straight connection is used. For example, if N=8, S=011, and D=110, then T=101. The corresponding stage settings are exchange, straight, exchange. Because the exclusive-or operation is commutative, the incoming routing tag is the same as the return tag. Since the destination PE has the routing tag to the source PE, it is easy to perform handshaking if desired. The address of the source PE can be computed by the destination PE using $S = D \oplus T$.

Routing tags that can be used for broadcasting data are an extension of the above scheme. They are described in [19].

The Cube network can be partitioned into independent subnetworks of varying sizes. The <u>partitionability</u> of a network is its ability to divide the system into independent subsystems of different sizes. Furthermore, in this case, each subnetwork of size $N' \leq N$ will have all of the connection properties of a Cube network built to be of size N'.

The key to partitioning the Cube network so that each subnetwork is independent is based on the choice of the I/O ports that belong to the subnetworks. The requirement is that the addresses of all of the I/O ports in a partition of size 2^i agree (have the same values) in n-i of their bit positions.

For example, Fig. 5 shows one way a network of size eight can be partitioned into two subnetworks, each of size four. Group A consists of ports 0, 2, 4, and 6. Group B consists of ports 1, 3, 5, and 7. All ports in group A agree in the low-order bit position (it is a 0). All ports in group B agree in the low-order bit position (it is a 1). By setting all of the interchange boxes in stage 0 to straight, the two groups are isolated. This is because stage 0 is the only stage which allows input ports which differ in their low-order bit to exchange data. As stated above, each subnetwork has the properties of a Cube network. Thus, each subnetwork can be separately further subdivided, resulting in subnetworks of various sizes. This network property allows the PASM PCU PEs to be partitioned into independent virtual machines of various sizes.

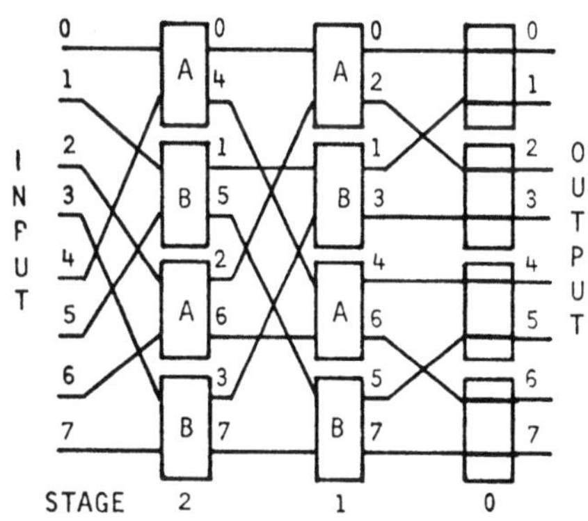

Fig. 5. Cube network of size eight partitioned into two subnetworks of size four based on the low-order bit position.

The routing tag scheme discussed previously can be used in conjunction with the partitioning concepts. Tags can be logically AND-ed with masks to force to 0 tag positions which correspond to interchange boxes which should be forced to the straight state.

The tradeoffs between the Cube and ADM multistage networks for PASM are currently under study. The ADM network is more flexible, but is more complex. The Cube may be more cost effective and sufficient for the system's needs. The Extra Stage Cube network [1] is a fault-tolerant variation of the Cube which is planned for inclusion in the PASM prototype.

In the following sections, it will be assumed that the PEs will be partitioned such that their addresses agree in the low-order bit positions. This constraint will allow either the Cube or ADM network to be used as the partitionable interconnection network in PASM.

4. Micro Controllers

In general, the possible advantages of a partitionable system include:

(a) fault tolerance - If a single PE fails, only those virtual machines (partitions) which must include the failed PE need to be disabled. The rest of the system can continue to function.

(b) multiple simultaneous users - Since there can be multiple independent virtual machines, there can be multiple simultaneous users of the system, each executing a different program.

(c) program development - Rather than trying to debug a program on, for example, 1024 PEs, it can be debugged on a smaller size virtual machine of 32 PEs.

(d) variable machine size for efficiency - If a task requires only N/2 of N available PEs, the other N/2 can be used for another task.

(e) subtask parallelism - Two independent subtasks that are part of the same job can be executed in parallel, sharing results if necessary.

Some form of multiple control units must be provided in order to have a partitionable SIMD/MIMD system. In PASM, this is done by having $Q=2^q$ MCs, physically addressed (numbered) from 0 to Q-1. Each MC controls N/Q PCU processors, as shown in Fig. 6.

Each MC is a microprocessor attached to a memory module. A memory module consists of a pair of memory units so that memory loading and computations can be overlapped. In SIMD mode, each MC fetches instructions from its memory module, executing the control flow instructions (e.g. branches) and broadcasting the data processing instruc-

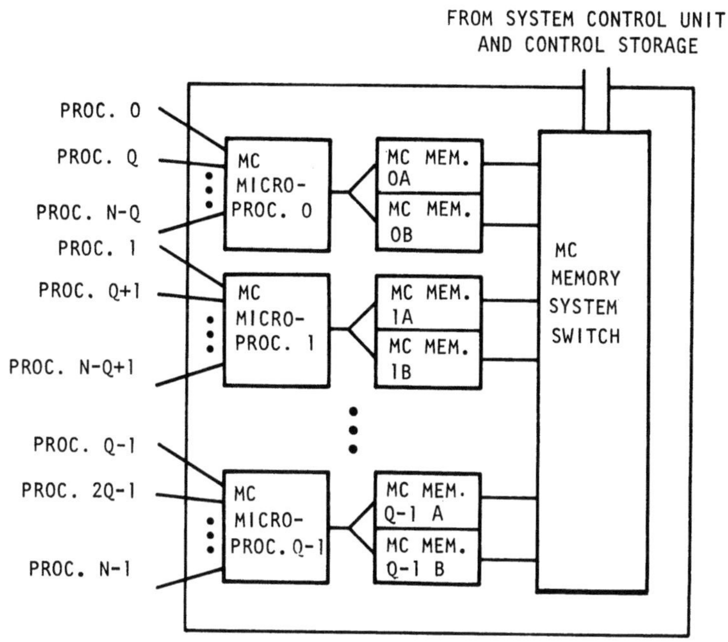

Fig. 6. PASM Micro Controllers (MCs).

tions to its PCU processors. The physical addresses of the N/Q processors which are connected to an MC must all have the same low-order q bits so that the network can be partitioned. The value of these low-order q bits is the physical address of the MC. A virtual SIMD machine of size RN/Q, where $R=2^r$ and $0\leq r\leq q$, is obtained by loading R MCs with the same instructions and synchronizing the MCs. The physical addresses of these MCs must have the same low-order q-r bits so that all of the PCU processors in the partition have the same low-order q-r physical address bits. Similarly, a virtual MIMD machine of size RN/Q is obtained by combining the efforts of the PCU PEs associated with R MCs which have the same low-order q-r physical address bits. In MIMD mode, the MCs may be used to help coordinate the activities of their PCU PEs.

Permanently assigning a fixed number of PCU PEs to each MC has several advantages over allowing a varying assignment, such as used in MAP. One advantage is that the operating system need only schedule (and monitor the "busy" status of) Q MCs, rather than N PCU PEs. When Q=32 and N=1024, this is a substantial savings. Another advantage is that no crossbar switch is needed for connecting processors and control units (such as proposed for MAP [13]). A third advantage is that it supports network partitioning. In addition, this fixed connection scheme allows the efficient use of multiple secondary storage devices, which is discussed below. The main disadvantage of this approach is that each virtual machine size must be a power of two, with a minimum value of N/Q. However, for PASM's intended experimental environment, flexibility at reasonable cost is the goal, not maximum processor utilization.

The loading of programs from Control Storage into the MC memory units is controlled by the System Control Unit. When large SIMD jobs are run, that is, jobs which require more than N/Q processors, more than one MC executes the same set of instructions. Each MC has its own memory, so that if more than one MC is to be used, several memories must be loaded with the same set of instructions. The fastest way to load several MC memories with the same set of instructions is to load all of the memories at the same time. A shared bus from Control Storage is used to do this parallel loading.

This basic MC organization can be enhanced to allow the sharing of memory modules by the MCs in a partition. The MCs can be connected by a shared reconfigurable ("shortable") bus [2, 11], as shown in Fig. 7. The MCs must be ordered on the bus in terms of the bit reverse of their addresses due to the partitioning rules. This enhanced MC connection scheme could provide more program space for jobs using multi-

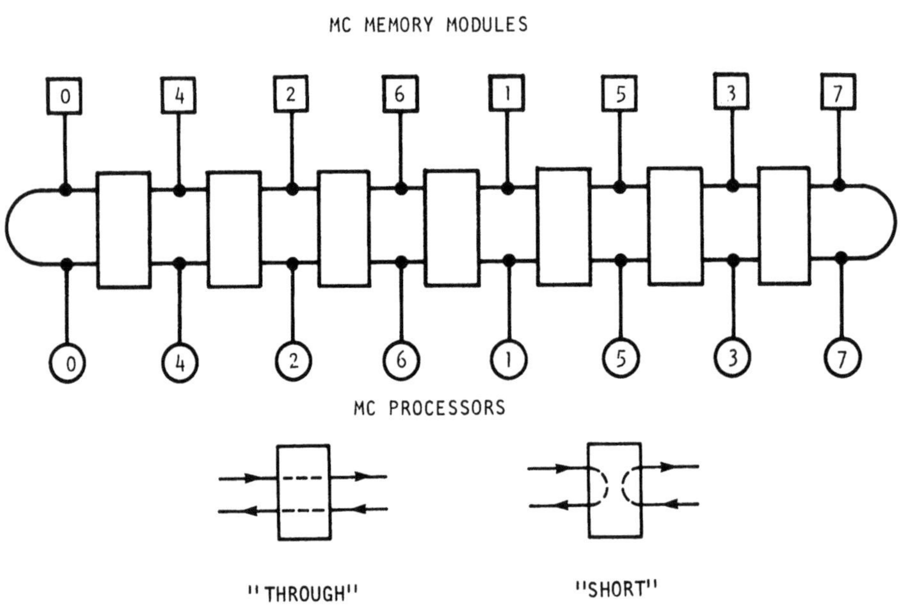

Fig. 7. Reconfigurable shared bus scheme for interconnecting MC processors and MC memory modules, shown for Q=8. Each box can be set to "through" or "short."

ple MCs and would also provide a degree of fault tolerance, since known-faulty MC memory modules could be ignored. These advantages come at the expense of additional system complexity, and the inclusion of the enhanced scheme in PASM will depend on cost constraints at implementation time.

Within each partition the PCU processors and memory modules are assigned logical addresses. Given a virtual machine of size RN/Q, the processors and memory modules for this partition have logical addresses (numbers) 0 to (RN/Q)-1, $R=2^r$, $0\leq r\leq q$. The logical number of a PCU PE is the high-order r+n-q bits of its physical number. Similarly, the MCs assigned to the partition are logically numbered (addressed) from 0 to R-1. For R>1, the logical number of an MC is the high-order r bits of its physical number. The PASM language compilers and operating system will be used to convert from logical to physical addresses, so a system user will deal only with logical addresses.

There are instructions which examine the collective status of all of the PEs of a virtual SIMD machine, such as "if any," "if all," and "if none." These instructions change the flow of control of the program at execution time depending on whether any or all processors in the virtual SIMD machine satisfy some condition. For example, if each PE is processing data from a different section of a radar unit, but all PEs are looking for enemy planes, it is desirable to know "if any" of the PEs has discovered a possible attack. This requires communication among the MCs comprising the virtual SIMD machine. There is a set of buses shared by MCs for this purpose.

When operating in SIMD mode, all of the active PCU PEs will execute instructions broadcast to them by their MC. A masking scheme is a method for determining which PCU PEs will be active at a given point in time. PASM will use PE address masks and data conditional masks.

The PE address masking scheme uses an n-position mask to specify which of the N PCU PEs are to be activated. Each position of the mask corresponds to a bit position in the addresses of the PEs. Each position of the mask will contain either a 0, 1, or X ("don't care") and the only PEs that will be active are those whose address matches the mask: 0 matches 0, 1 matches 1, and either 0 or 1 matches X. Square brackets denote a mask. Superscripts are used as repetition factors. For example: MASK $[X^{n-1}1]$ activates all odd-numbered PEs; MASK $[1^{n-i}X^i]$ activates PEs $N-2^i$ to N-1. PE address masks are specified in the SIMD program.

A negative PE address mask is similar to a regular PE address mask, except that it activates all those PEs which do not match the mask.

Negative PE address masks are prefixed with a minus sign to distinguish them from regular PE address masks. For example, for N=8, MASK [-01X] activates all PEs except 2 and 3. This type of mask can activate sets of PEs a single regular PE address mask cannot.

Data conditional masks will be implemented in PASM for use when the decision to enable and disable PEs is made at execution time. Data conditional masks are the implicit result of performing a conditional branch dependent on local data in an SIMD machine environment, where the result of different PEs' evaluations may differ. As a result of a conditional where statement of the form

where <data-condition> do ... elsewhere ...

each PE will set its own flag to activate itself for either the "do" or the "elsewhere," but not both. The execution of the "elsewhere" statements must follow the "do" statements; i.e., the "do" and "elsewhere" statements cannot be executed simultaneously. For example, as a result of executing the statement:

where A < B do C ← A elsewhere C ← B

each PE will load its C register with the minimum of its A and B registers, i.e., some PEs will execute "C ← A," and then the rest will execute "C ← B." This type of masking is used in such machines as the Illiac IV [3] and PEPE [7]. "Where" statements can be nested using a run-time control stack.

5. Secondary Memory System

The Memory Storage System will consist of N/Q independent Memory Storage Units, numbered from 0 to (N/Q)-1. These devices will allow fast loading and unloading of the N double-buffered PCU memory modules and will provide storage for system image data and MIMD programs.

Each Memory Storage Unit is connected to Q PCU memory modules. For $0 \leq i < N/Q$, Memory Storage Unit i is connected to those memory modules whose physical addresses are of the form (Q*i)+k, $0 \leq k < Q$. Recall that, for $0 \leq k < Q$, MC k is connected to those PEs whose physical addresses are of the form (Q*i)+k, $0 \leq i < N/Q$. This is shown for N=32 and Q=4 in Fig. 8.

For a partition of size N/Q, the two main advantages of this approach are that (1) all of the memory modules can be loaded in parallel and (2) the data is directly available no matter which partition (MC group) is chosen. This is done by storing in Memory Storage Unit

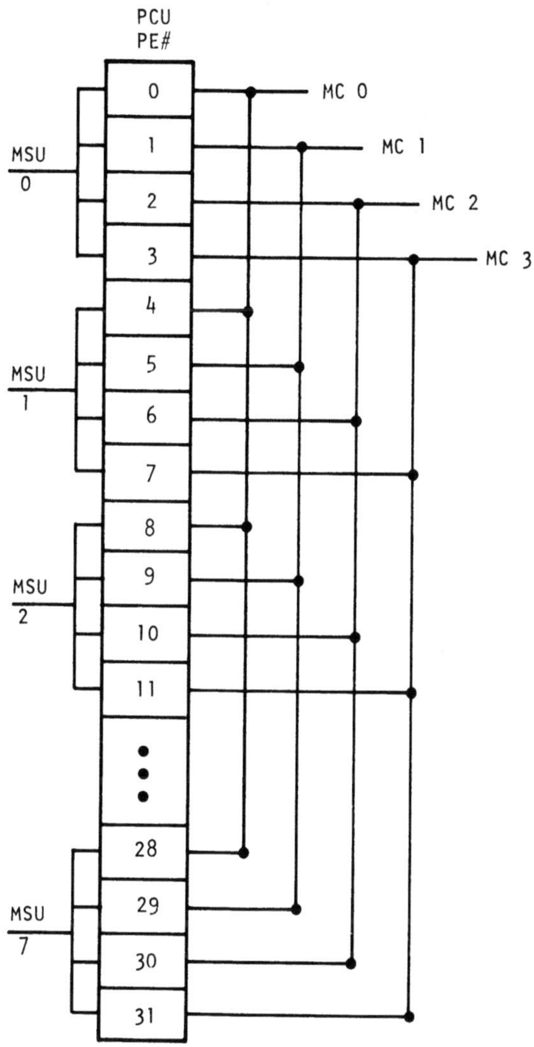

Fig. 8. Organization of the Memory Storage System, shown for N=32 and Q=4. "MSU" is Memory Storage Unit.

i the data for a task which is to be loaded into the i-th logical memory module of the virtual machine of size N/Q, $0 \leq i < N/Q$. Memory Storage Unit i is connected to the i-th memory module in each MC group so that no matter which MC group of N/Q processors is chosen, the data from the i-th Memory Storage unit can be loaded into the i-th logical memory module, $0 \leq i < N/Q$, simultaneously. Thus, for virtual machines of size N/Q, this secondary storage scheme allows all N/Q memory modules to be loaded in one parallel block transfer.

A virtual machine of RN/Q PEs, $1 \le R \le Q$, logically numbered from 0 to RN/Q-1, requires only R parallel block loads if the data for the memory module whose high-order n-q logical address bits equal i is loaded into Memory Storage Unit i. This is true no matter which group of R MCs (which agree in their low-order q-r address bits) is chosen.

As an example, consider Fig. 8, and assume a virtual machine of size 16 is desired. The data for the memory modules whose logical addresses are 0 and 1 is loaded into Memory Storage Unit 0, for memory modules 2 and 3 into unit 1, etc. Assume the partition of size 16 is chosen to consist of the processors connected to MCs 1 and 3. Given this assignment of MCs, the PCU memory module whose physical address is 2*i+1 has logical address i, $0 \le i < 16$. The Memory Storage Units first load memory modules physically addressed 1, 5, 9, 13, 17, 21, 25, and 29 (simultaneously), and then load memory modules 3, 7, 11, 15, 19, 23, 27, and 31 (simultaneously). No matter which pair of MCs is chosen, only two parallel block loads are needed. Thus, for a virtual machine of size RN/Q, this secondary storage scheme allows all RN/Q memory modules to be loaded in R parallel block transfers, $1 \le R \le Q$.

This same approach can be taken if only $(N/Q)/2^d$ distinct Memory Storage Units are available, where $0 \le d \le n-q$. In this case, however, $R2^d$ parallel block loads will be required instead of just R. The number and types of devices that will be used in PASM will depend upon speed requirements, cost constraints, and the state-of-the-art of storage technology at implementation time.

The _Memory Management System_ is composed of a separate set of microprocessors dedicated to performing tasks in a distributed fashion, i.e., one processor handles Memory Storage System bus control, one handles the peripheral device I/O, etc. This distributed processing approach is chosen in order to provide the Memory Management System with a large amount of processing power at low cost. The division of tasks chosen is based on the main functions which the Memory Management System must perform, including: (1) generating tasks based on PCU memory module load/unload requests from the System Control Unit; (2) scheduling of Memory Storage System data transfers; (3) control of input/output operations involving peripheral devices and the Memory Storage System; (4) maintenance of the Memory Management System file directory information; and (5) control of the Memory Storage System bus system.

6. Parallel Computation of a Global Histogram

In this section, an SIMD algorithm for computing the global histogram of an algorithm is given [20]. Assume there are $B=2^b$ bins in the histogram, $B \leq N$. An M by M image is represented by an array of M^2 pixels (picture elements), where the value of each pixel is assumed to be a b-bit unsigned integer representing one of B possible gray levels. The B-bin histogram of the image contains a j in bin i if exactly j of the pixels have a gray level of i, $0 \leq i < B$.

Assume the image is equally distributed among the N PEs in PASM, i.e., each PE has M^2/N pixels, and $B \leq M^2/N$. Since the image is distributed over N PEs, each PE will calculate a B-bin histogram based on its M^2/N segment of the image. Then these "local" histograms will be combined using the algorithm described below. This algorithm is demonstrated for N=16 and B=4 bins in Fig. 9.

Each block of B PEs performs B simultaneous recursive doublings [24] to compute the histogram for the portion of the image contained in the block in the first b steps. At the end of the b steps, each PE has one bin of this partial histogram. This is accomplished by first dividing the B PEs of a block into two groups. Each group accumulates

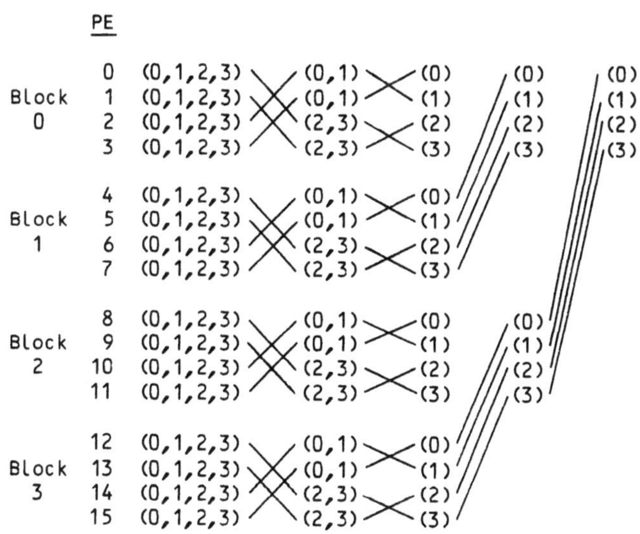

Fig. 9. Histogram calculation for N=16 PEs, B=4 bins. (w,...,z) denotes that bins w through z of the partial histogram are in the PE.

the sums for half of the bins, and sends the bins it is not accumulating to the group which is accumulating those bins. At each step of the algorithm, each group of PEs is divided in half such that the PEs with the lower addresses form one group, and the PEs with the higher addresses form another. The accumulated sums are similarly divided in half based on their indices in the histogram. The groups then exchange sums, so that each PE contains only sum terms which it is accumulating. The newly-received sums are added to the sums already in the PE. After b steps, each PE has the total value for one bin from the portion of the image contained in the B PEs in its block.

The results for these blocks can be combined in n-b steps to yield the histogram of the entire image distributed over B PEs, with the sum for bin i in PE i, $0 \leq i < B$. This is done by performing n-b steps of a recursive doubling [24] algorithm to sum the partial histograms from the N/B blocks, shown by the last two steps of Fig. 9. Note that B recursive doublings are being performed simultaneously, one for each bin. A general algorithm to compute the B-bin histogram for an image distributed over N PEs is given in [20].

Now consider relative speeds of sequential and parallel computation of the histogram. A sequential algorithm to compute the histogram of an M by M image requires M^2 additions. The SIMD algorithm uses M^2/N additions for each PE to compute its local histogram. At step i in the merging of the partial histograms, $0 \leq i < b$, the number of parallel data transfer/adds required is $B/2^{i+1}$. A total of B-1 transfer/adds are therefore performed in the first b steps of the algorithm. Then n-b parallel transfers and additions are needed to combine the block histograms. This technique therefore requires B-1+n-b parallel transfer/add operations, plus the M^2/N additions needed to compute the local PE histograms. For example, if N=1024, M=512, and B=128, the sequential algorithm would require 262,144 additions; the parallel algorithm uses 256 addition steps plus 130 transfer/add steps. The result of the algorithm, i.e., the histogram, is distributed over the first B PEs. This distribution may be efficient for further processing on the histogram, e.g., finding the maximum or minimum, or for smoothing the histogram. If it is necessary for the entire histogram to be in a single PE, B-1 additional parallel data transfers are required. Both the Cube and ADM multistage networks can perform all of the required inter-PE data transfers efficiently.

7. 2-D FFT Algorithms

In this section, an SIMD algorithm to compute the 2-D FFT of an image is given [23]. A standard approach to computing the 2D-DFT of an image S is to perform the 1-D DFT on the rows of S, giving an intermediate matrix G, and then perform the 1-D DFT on the columns of G. The resulting matrix F is the 2-D DFT of S. Suppose that an SIMD machine has N=M PEs, each of which has one row of an M by M input image S. An efficient method for obtaining F, the DFT of S, is to perform M 1-D FFTs in parallel on the rows of S to get G, "transpose" G, and then perform M 1-D FFTs in parallel on the columns of G to get F^T. This is shown in Fig. 10. (F^T can be transposed to give F, however, this may not be necessary depending on what further processing is done on F.)

To form the transpose of G, G^T, such that each row of G^T is in a different PE, the basic operation performed is the transfer of array

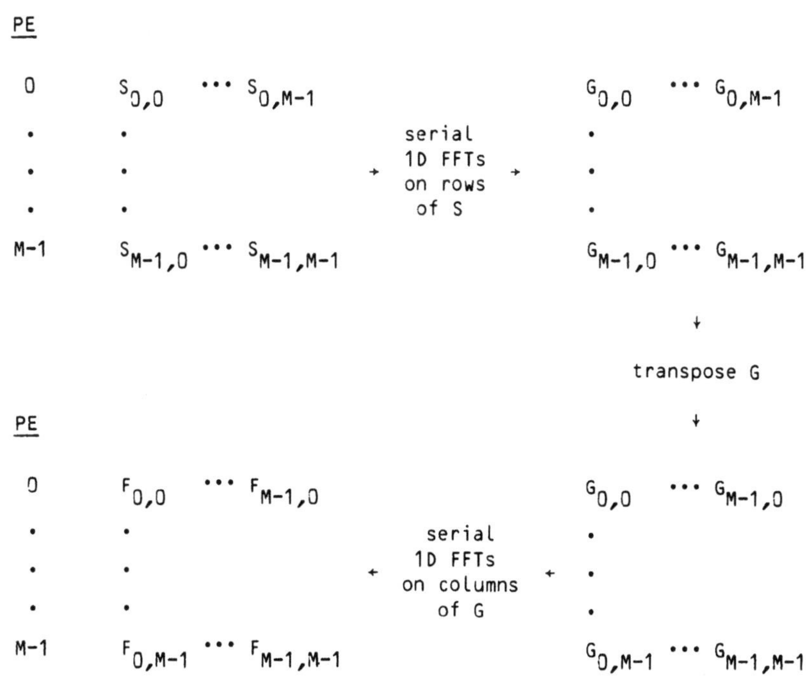

Fig. 10. Computation of 2-D FFT of M by M array S using M PEs.

element G(v,w) from PE v to PE w. This is done for M G(v,w)'s in parallel by sending data from PE v to PE (v+i) mod M for all of the G(v,w) for which (w-v) mod M = i. The parallel transfer operation is performed for $1 \leq i < M$. For each i value, the element which PE v sends is the w-th element of the row of G held in PE v, where w = (v+i) mod M. That element, received in PE w, is stored as the v-th element of the column of G being created in PE w, where v = (w-i) mod M. The elements on the diagonal G(v,w), where v=w, do not have to be transferred. Performing the transpose therefore requires M-1 parallel data transfers.

The serial complexity of 2M 1-D FFTs (i.e., an M by M 2-D DFT) is $M^2\log_2 M$ "butterflies." The above parallel implementation of the 2-D DFT executes two serial FFT algorithms and has a complexity of $M\log_2 M$ butterfly steps. Thus, an ideal speedup of M is achieved for butterfly operations with a cost of M-1 data transfers.

This approach can be generalized for N<M. For example, if N=M/2 each PE is given two rows of the input matrix S. The FFTs on the rows of S are performed by two serial FFTs, executed one after the other, on the two rows in each PE. This yields G, with each PE having two rows of G. The second step is to form the transpose of G, G^T, where each PE has two rows of G^T (i.e., each PE has two columns of G). If PE i contains rows 2i and 2i+1, then, in general, G(i,j) is transferred from PE $\lfloor i/2 \rfloor$ to PE $\lfloor j/2 \rfloor$, $0 \leq i, j < M$. The complexity associated with the transpose is 2M-4 parallel transfers. The -4 term appears because the diagonal and near-diagonal terms are already in the correct PE. The final step is to perform a 1-D DFT on the columns of G. This is done by two serial FFTs in each PE, as above. This gives F^T, with each PE having two rows of F^T. This implementation has a complexity of four serial FFT algorithms, or $2M\log_2 M$ butterfly steps. This is the maximum possible reduction in the number of butterfly steps, given M/2 PEs. The overhead associated with the transpose is 2M-4 transfers.

In general, when this method is implemented on N PEs, $N \leq M$, the complexity will be derived directly from the 1-D FFT algorithm used. If the complexity of the serial 1-D FFT algorithm is C, then the complexity of the 2-D FFT algorithm is 2(M/N)C plus the cost of computing the transpose. If $N = M/(2^r)$, the cost of the transpose is $2^r(M-2^r)$ data transfers. The -2^r term appears because before the transpose each PE holds 2^r rows, and after the transpose each PE holds 2^r columns. Thus, only $M-2^r$ elements of each row need to be transferred. In all cases, the necessary inter-PE data transfers can be done efficiently by the Cube and ADM multistage networks.

Table 1. The PASM design parameters, based on current plans.

	general	full PASM	PASM prototype
Number of PEs	N	1024	16
Number of network stages (Extra Stage Cube)	$\log_2 N+1$	11	5
Number of MCs	Q	32	4
Number of PEs per MC	N/Q	32	4
Number of Memory Storage Units	N/Q	32	4
Number of Memory Management System processors	fixed	5	5
Smallest size partition	N/Q	32	4
Maximum number of partitions	Q	32	4

8. Conclusions

This paper provided an overview of the PASM system and examples of its use. Table 1 summarizes the PASM design parameters. In order to contrast PASM to a different approach to parallel image processing, Table 2 compares the features of CLIP4 [8] to the planned features of PASM. A reading list for further information about PASM is provided at the end of this paper.

Table 2. A comparison of the features of CLIP4 and the planned features of PASM.

feature	CLIP4	PASM
Year built	1980	1983/4 ? (prototype)
Processor type	1-bit, simple	32-bit, complex (68000 prototype)
Memory size per processor	32 bits	64K words
Network type	8 nearest neighbors	multistage
Number of processors for computation	$96^2 = 9K$	1024 (16 prototype)
Image division	pixel/processor	subimage/PE
I/O	shift by column, rows in parallel	double-buffered PE memories, multiple secondary storage devices
Modes	SIMD	partitionable SIMD/MIMD

In conclusion, the objective of the PASM design is to achieve a system which attains a compromise between flexibility and cost-effectiveness for a specific problem domain. A dynamically reconfigurable system such as PASM should be a valuable tool for both image processing/pattern recognition and parallel processing research.

Acknowledgements

Portions of this overview of the PASM system and its use in parallel image processing are based on [19], [20], and [23]. The contributions of my co-authors on these papers are gratefully acknowledged. In addition, James T. Kuehn provided valuable comments and aid. I thank Mickey Krebs for typing the manuscript.

References

[1] G. B. Adams III and H. J. Siegel, "The extra stage cube: A fault-tolerant interconnection network for supersystems," IEEE Trans. Computers, Vol. C-31, May 1982, pp. 443-454.

[2] R. Arnold and E. Page, "A hierarchical, restructurable multimicroprocessor architecture," 3rd Symp. Computer Architecture, Jan. 1976, pp. 40-45.

[3] G. Barnes, et al., "The Illiac IV computer," IEEE Trans. Computers, Vol. C-17, Aug. 1968, pp. 746-757.

[4] K. E. Batcher, "The flip network in STARAN," 1976 Int'l. Conf. Parallel Processing, Aug. 1976, pp. 65-71.

[5] K. E. Batcher, "STARAN series E," 1977 Int'l. Conf. Parallel Processing, Aug. 1977, pp. 144-153.

[6] W. J. Bouknight, et al., "The Illiac IV system," Proc. IEEE, Vol. 60, Apr. 1972, pp. 369-388.

[7] B. A. Crane, et al., "PEPE computer architecture," COMPCON 1972, Sept. 1972, pp. 57-60.

[8] M. J. B. Duff, "Architectures of SIMD cellular logic image processing arrays," this volume.

[9] M. J. Flynn, "Very high-speed computing systems," Proc. IEEE, Vol. 54, Dec. 1966, pp. 1901-1909.

[10] L. R. Goke and G. J. Lipovski, "Banyan networks for partitioning multimicroprocessor systems," 1st Symp. Computer Architecture, Dec. 1973, pp. 21-28.

[11] S. I. Kartashev and S. P. Kartashev, "A multicomputer system with dynamic architecture," IEEE Trans. Computers, Vol. C-28, Oct. 1979, pp. 704-720.

[12] D. H. Lawrie, "Access and alignment of data in an array processor," IEEE Trans. Computers, Vol. C-24, Dec. 1975, pp. 1145-1155.

[13] G. J. Nutt, "Microprocessor implementation of a parallel processor," 4th Symp. Computer Architecture, Mar. 1977, pp. 147-152.

[14] J. H. Patel, "Performance of processor-memory interconnections for multiprocessors," IEEE Trans. Computers, Vol. C-30, Oct. 1981, pp. 771-780.

[15] M. C. Pease, III, "The indirect binary n-cube microprocessor array," IEEE Trans. Computers, Vol. C-26, May 1977, pp. 458-473.

[16] J. L. Potter, "MPP architecture and programming," in Multicomputers and Image Processing: Algorithms and Programs, K. Preston and L. Uhr, eds., Academic Press, New York, NY, 1982, pp. 275-290.

[17] M. C. Sejnowski, E. T. Upchurch, R. N. Kapur, D. P. S. Charlu, and G. J. Lipovski, "An overview of the Texas Reconfigurable Array Computer," AFIPS 1980 Nat'l. Computer Conf., June 1980, pp. 631-641.

[18] H. J. Siegel and R. J. McMillen, "Using the augmented data manipulator network in PASM," Computer, Vol. 14, Feb. 1981, pp. 25-33.

[19] H. J. Siegel and R. J. McMillen, "The multistage cube: a versatile interconnection network," Computer, Vol. 14, Dec. 1981, pp. 65-76.

[20] H. J. Siegel, L. J. Siegel, F. C. Kemmerer, P. T. Mueller, Jr., H. E. Smalley, and S. D. Smith, "PASM: a partitionable SIMD/MIMD system for image processing and pattern recognition," IEEE Trans. Computers, Vol. C-30, Dec. 1981, pp. 934-947.

[21] H. J. Siegel, "Analysis techniques for SIMD machine interconnection networks and the effects of processor address masks," IEEE Trans. Computers, Vol. C-26, Feb. 1977, pp. 153-161.

[22] H. J. Siegel, "A model of SIMD machines and a comparison of various interconnection networks," IEEE Trans. Computers, Vol. C-28, Dec. 1979, pp. 907-917.

[23] L. J. Siegel, P. T. Mueller, Jr., and H. J. Siegel, "FFT algorithms for SIMD machines," 17th Allerton Conf. Communication, Control, and Computing, Oct. 1979, pp. 1006-1015.

[24] H. S. Stone, "Parallel computers," in Introduction to Computer Architecture, 2nd edition, edited by H. S. Stone, Science Research Associates, Inc., Chicago, IL, 1980, pp. 363-425.

[25] R. J. Swan, S. H. Fuller, and D. P. Siewiorek, "Cm*: a modular, multi-microprocessor," Nat'l. Computer Conf., June 1977, pp. 637-644.

[26] C. L. Wu and T. Y. Feng, "On a class of multistage interconnection networks," IEEE Trans. Computers, Vol. C-29, Aug. 1980, pp. 694-702.

[27] W. A. Wulf and C. G. Bell, "C.mmp - a multi-miniprocessor," Fall Joint Computer Conf., Dec. 1972, pp. 765-777.

Further reading about PASM

reconfigurable organization:

H. J. Siegel, P. T. Mueller, Jr., and H. E. Smalley, Jr., "Control of a partitionable multimicroprocessor system," 1978 Int'l. Conf. Parallel Processing, Aug. 1978, pp. 9-17.

H. J. Siegel, L. J. Siegel, F. C. Kemmerer, P. T. Mueller, Jr., H. E. Smalley, and S. D. Smith, "PASM: a partitionable SIMD/MIMD system for image processing and pattern recognition," IEEE Trans. Computers, Vol. C-30, Dec. 1981, pp. 934-947.

parallel memory management system:

H. J. Siegel, F. Kemmerer, and M. Washburn, "Parallel memory system for a partitionable SIMD/MIMD machine," 1979 Int'l. Conf. Parallel Processing, Aug. 1979, pp. 212-221.

J. T. Kuehn, H. J. Siegel, and M. Grosz, "A distributed memory management system for PASM," IEEE Comp. Soc. Workshop Computer Architecture for Pattern Analysis and Image Database Management, Oct. 1983.

interconnection network - multistage cube:

R. J. McMillen and H. J. Siegel, "The hybrid cube network," Distributed Data Acquisition, Computing, and Control Symp., Dec. 1980, pp. 11-22.

R. J. McMillen, G. B. Adams III, and H. J. Siegel, "Performance and implementation of 4x4 switching nodes in an interconnection network for PASM," 1981 Int'l. Conf. Parallel Processing, Aug. 1981, pp. 229-233.

H. J. Siegel and R. J. McMillen, "The multistage cube: a versatile interconnection network," Computer, Vol. 14, Dec. 1981, pp. 65-76.

G. B. Adams III and H. J. Siegel, "The extra stage cube: a fault-tolerant interconnection network for supersystems," IEEE Trans. Computers, Vol. C-31, May 1982, pp. 443-454.

interconnection network - ADM:

S. D. Smith, H. J Siegel, R. J. McMillen, and G. B. Adams III, "Use of the augmented data manipulator multistage network for SIMD machines," *1980 Int'l. Conf. Parallel Processing*, Aug. 1980, pp. 75-78.

R. J. McMillen, G. B. Adams III, and H. J. Siegel, "Permuting with the augmented data manipulator network," *18th Allerton Conf. Communication, Control, and Computing*, Oct. 1980, pp. 544-553.

H. J. Siegel and R. J. McMillen, "Using the augmented data manipulator network in PASM," *Computer*, Vol. 14, Feb. 1981, pp. 25-33.

R. J. McMillen and H. J. Siegel, "Performance and fault tolerance improvements in the inverse augmented data manipulator network," *9th Int'l. Symp. Computer Architecture*, Apr. 1982, pp. 63-72.

G. B. Adams III and H. J. Siegel, "On the number of permutations performable by the augmented data manipulator network," *IEEE Trans. Computers*, Vol. C-31, Apr. 1982, pp. 270-277.

R. J. McMillen and H. J. Siegel, "Routing schemes for the augmented data manipulator network in an MIMD system," *IEEE Trans. Computers*, Dec. 1982, pp. 63-72.

interconnection network - comparisons:

H. J. Siegel and S. D. Smith, "Study of multistage SIMD interconnection networks," *5th Symp. Computer Architecture*, Apr. 1978, pp. 223-229.

H. J. Siegel, "Interconnection networks for SIMD machines," *Computer*, Vol. 12, June 1979, pp. 57-65.

H. J. Siegel, R. J. McMillen, and P. T. Mueller, Jr., "A survey of interconnection methods for reconfigurable parallel processing systems," *1979 Nat'l. Computer Conf.*, June 1979, pp. 529-542.

H. J. Siegel, "The theory underlying the partitioning of permutation networks," *IEEE Trans. Computers*, Vol. C-29, Sept. 1980, pp. 791-801.

R. J. McMillen and H. J. Siegel, "A comparison of cube type and data manipulator type networks," *3rd Int'l. Conf. Distributed Computing Systems*, Oct. 1982, pp. 614-621.

H. J. Siegel, *Interconnection Networks for Large-Scale Parallel Processing: Theory and Case Studies*, D.C. Heath and Co., Lexington, MA, 1983.

distributed operating system:

H. J. Siegel, L. J. Siegel, R. J. McMillen, P. T. Mueller, Jr., and S. D. Smith, "An SIMD/MIMD multimicroprocessor system for image processing and pattern recognition," *1979 IEEE Comp. Soc. Conf. Pattern Recognition and Image Processing*, Aug. 1979, pp. 214-224.

D. L. Tuomenoksa and H. J. Siegel, "Application of two-dimensional bin packing algorithms for task scheduling in the PASM multimicrocomputer system," *19th Allerton Conf. Communication, Control, and Computing*, Oct. 1981, pg. 542.

D. L. Tuomenoksa and H. J. Siegel, "Analysis of the PASM control system memory hierarchy," 1982 Int'l. Conf. Parallel Processing, Aug. 1982, pp. 363-370.

D. L. Tuomenoksa and H. J. Siegel, "Analysis of multiple-queue task scheduling algorithms for multiple-SIMD machines," 3rd Int'l. Conf. Distributed Computing Systems, Oct. 1982, pp. 114-121.

D. L. Tuomenoksa and H. J. Siegel, "Preloading schemes for the PASM parallel memory system," 1983 Int'l. Conf. Parallel Processing, Aug. 1983, pp. 407-415.

prototype design:

J. T. Kuehn and H. J. Siegel, "Simulation studies of PASM in SIMD mode," 1981 IEEE Comp. Soc. Workshop Computer Architecture for Pattern Analysis and Image Database Management, Nov. 1981, pp. 43-50.

J. T. Kuehn, H. J. Siegel, and P. D. Hallenbeck, "Design and simulation of an MC68000-based multimicroprocessor system," 1982 Int'l. Conf. Parallel Processing, Aug. 1982, pp. 353-362.

parallel programming language:

P. T. Mueller, Jr., L. J. Siegel, and H. J. Siegel, "A parallel language for image and speech processing," IEEE Comp. Soc. Fourth Int'l. Computer Software and Applications Conference (COMPSAC 80), Oct. 1980, pp. 476-483.

C. Cline and H. J. Siegel, "Extensions of Ada for SIMD parallel processing," IEEE Comp. Soc. Seventh Int'l. Computer Software and Applications Conf. (COMPSAC 83), Nov. 1983.

parallel image processing:

L. J. Siegel, P. T. Mueller, Jr., and H. J. Siegel, "FFT algorithms for SIMD machines," 17th Allerton Conf. Communication, Control, and Computing, Oct. 1979, pp. 1006-1015.

P. T. Mueller, Jr., L. J. Siegel, and H. J. Siegel, "Parallel algorithms for the two-dimensional FFT," 5th Int'l. Conf. Pattern Recognition, Dec. 1980, pp. 497-502.

P. H. Swain, H. J. Siegel, and J. El-Achkar, "Multiprocessor implementation of image pattern recognition: a general approach," 5th Int'l. Conf. Pattern Recognition, Dec. 1980, pp. 309-317.

H. J. Siegel and P. H. Swain, "Contextual classification on PASM," IEEE Comp. Soc. Conf. Pattern Recognition and Image Processing, Aug. 1981, pp. 320-325.

T. N. Mudge, E. J. Delp, L. J. Siegel, and H. J. Siegel, "Image coding using the multimicroprocessor system PASM," IEEE Comp. Soc. Conf. Pattern Recognition and Image Processing, June 1982, pp. 200-205.

L. J. Siegel, H. J. Siegel, and A. E. Feather, "Parallel processing approaches to image correlation," IEEE Trans. Computers, Vol. C-31, Mar. 1982, pp. 208-218.

L. J. Siegel, H. J. Siegel, and P. H. Swain, "Performance measures for evaluating algorithms for SIMD machines," IEEE Trans. Software Engineering, Vol. SE-8, July 1982, pp. 319-331.

M. R. Warpenburg and L. J. Siegel, "Image resampling in an SIMD environment, IEEE Trans. Computers, Oct. 1982, pp. 934-942.

H. J. Siegel, P. H. Swain, and B. W. Smith, "Remote sensing on PASM and CDC Flexible Processors," in Multicomputers and Image Processing: Algorithms and Programs, K. Preston and L. Uhr, eds. Academic Press, New York, NY, 1982, pp. 331-342.

D. L. Tuomenoksa, G. B. Adams III, H. J. Siegel, and O. R. Mitchell, "A parallel algorithm for contour extraction: advantages and architectural implications," 1983 IEEE Comp. Soc. Symp. Computer Vision and Pattern Recognition, June 1983, pp. 336-344.

THE CONVERSION VIA SOFTWARE OF A SIMD PROCESSOR

INTO A MIMD PROCESSOR.

PS-2000, AN ARRAY PROCESSOR, BECOMES AHR, A GENERAL PURPOSE LISP MACHINE

Adolfo Guzmán ∿ψ

Miguel Gerzso ∿

Kemer B. Norkin ρ

S. Y. Vilenkin ρ

ABSTRACT. In this paper a method is described which takes a (pure) Lisp program and automatically decomposes it (automatic parallelization) into several parts, one for each processor of a SIMD architecture. Each of these parts is a different execution flow--a different program--. The execution of these different programs by a SIMD architecture is the main theme of the paper.

The method has been developed in some detail for the PS-2000, a SIMD Soviet multiprocessor, making it behave like AHR, a Mexican MIMD multi-microprocessor. Both the PS-2000 and AHR execute a pure Lisp program in parallel; the user or programmer is not responsible for its decomposition into n pieces, their synchronization, scheduling, etc. All these chores are performed by the system (hardware and software) instead.

In order to achieve simultaneous execution of different programs in a SIMD processor, the method uses a scheme of node scheduling (a node is a primitive Lisp operation) and node exportation.

SUMMARY

The general goal: automatic parallelization of one program.

Let us define automatic parallelization as the automatic splitting (by the system, not by the programmer) of a program into n parts, one for each processor, such that this program executes efficiently in a multiprocessor with n processors. Automatic parallelization takes care not only of (1) the subdivision into n parts, but also of (2) their synchronization (3) scheduling, etc. Clearly, responsibilities

∿ψ Spending his sabbatical year (1983-84) at: Electrical Engineering Dept CIEA-IPN; National Polytechnic Institute. Apdo 14-740. 07000 México, D.F.

∿ Permanent address: Computing Systs. Dept., IIMAS-UNAM; Nat'l. University of Mexico. Apdo 20-726. 01000 México, D. F.

ρ Institute for Control Sciences. Academy of Sciences of the USSR. 65 Profsoyuznaya St. 117342 Moscow, USSR.

NATO ASI Series, Vol. F18
Computer Architectures for Spatially Distributed Data
Edited by H. Freeman and G. G. Pieroni

for chores (1), (2), (3), ..., can be placed upon the programmer, but this will reduce by much the efficiency of the programmer. Automatic parallelization is a good goal to achieve.

Achieving the goal using a MIMD architecture. Using pure Lisp (an applicative language), the AHR machine [3,4] shows how to achieve automatic decomposition (parallelization) for a MIMD architecture. Version 1 of AHR, built at the National Univ. of Mexico, uses up to 64 Z-80's to jointly execute a single Lisp program, each micro simultaneously executing some part of it, without the programmer worrying of parallelism-- in fact, the programmer or user needs not be aware that his program is running in a parallel machine--.

Achieving the goal using a SIMD architecture. A SIMD architecture can achieve automatic parallelization in the cases normally designed for it --namely, the same program is executed by all processors, each of them operating on different data--.

Can a SIMD architecture achieve automatic parallelization for cases where each processor executes a different task? That is, can we simultaneously run different programs in the different processors of a SIMD machine? NO, if we want to maintain full speed (full use) of all processors. Yes, with some degradation in the degree of parallelism.

This paper describes a method which performs automatic parallelization upon a (pure) Lisp program, breaking it into several parts, one for each processor of SIMD architecture. Each of these parts is a different program --a different execution flow--. These different programs are, nevertheless, executed in parallel in the SIMD machine. In order to achieve this, the method uses (a) node scheduling; (b) node exportation; (c) results exportation. The most important of these is node scheduling, where first all similar nodes of the same name or function type are collected, and later they are executed in the normal SIMD mode.

Software conversion of a SIMD into a MIMD architecture. Since we are able to make a SIMD machine behave like a MIMD AHR machine when executing arbitrary Lisp programs, it is clear that we can use a SIMD architecture for parallel execution of a single Lisp program. By this we do not mean that such Lisp program is replicated in the n processors of the SIMD machine and put to work simultaneously upon different data. We mean that such a Lisp program is automatically partitioned into different independent but interacting portions (n of them), and the nodes of each portion are executed in such a way that (generally) all the n processors are executing - necessarily the same node, although upon different data - simultaneously.

Possible defficiencies of the approach are

(a) the amount of overhead (book-keeping, system and administrative chores, and operating system overhead) versus the amount of effective computations;
(b) the amount of time that some of the n processors remain idle, while the remaining processors are executing some node. This may be the case if some of the n processors lack node "CONS", for instance, to execute; thus, they will remain idle while the rest proceed to CONS execution.

The different sections of this paper. While the first section explains what is automatic parallelization, the second tells us how to achieve it using a MIMD architecture, and gives some description of the AHR computer, built at the National University of Mexico in 1981 under these principles. The third section outlines the solution for applying the same approach to a SIMD machine. The last section gives account of the conversion (using only software) of "PS-2000", a SIMD processor, into a device capable of automatic parallelization, which also mimics the behavior of the AHR machine, in its capability to execute in parallel different parts of a single program.

WHAT IS AUTOMATIC PARALLELIZATION?

With the advent of cheap computing power, it is reasonable to produce architectures where several processors are running simultaneously, collaborating in the common execution of a program. On the other hand, software development is still expensive. For a multiprocessor having n processing elements (called processors), to have to write n different programs, plus n * (n-1)/2 synchronizations, plus scheduling,etc., is uneconomical from the point of view of programmer productivity. Thus, practical use of multiprocessors achieves one of the following forms:

(1) the programmer writes one program, and all the n processors execute this same program, although upon different data. At any given time, all the processors are executing exactly the same instruction (albeit some of them may skip the instruction, becoming idle during its execution). This solution has been popular for application to numeric matrices and vectors, and has caused the development of SIMD (single instruction, multiple data) architectures. To be efficient, all the n processors mus be active most of the time. This limits the algorithms for SIMD architectures to be data-independent; otherwise (as later explained) some or much parallelism--hence, efficiency-- is lost.

(2) the programmer writes one program, which is automatically decomposed (by the system) in small parts and given to a pipeline to execute [8]. This approach is fruitfull, but useful mainly when the same algorithm has to be applied to a large collection or vector of similar data.

(3) several small programs are given to a MIMD machine, and each processor executes one of them. This is possible when these programs interact nothing or little with each other, since the interactions must be explicitly considered by the programmers. This approach is useful specially when each program is independent (does not need to interact), but needs access to some common data or resource (special processor). As example, we have the Tandem multiprocessor [10] system.

(4) the user writes one program which is automatically decomposed (by the system) into n different parts, one for each processor; the system (and not the programmer) also takes care of synchronization, scheduling, etc., associated with these parts. The programmer may be unaware of the parallel environment. The parts are run in parallel by the multiprocessor.

To the tasks performed by the system in (4), we call <u>automatic parallelization</u>. It can be achieved using a MIMD architecture, because the n parts which result from the automatic decomposition will be different from each other, thus necessarily requiring (we thought at first) a MIMD architecture, where a plurality of instruction flows may be achieved.

As it turns out, it is also possible to execute these different parts using a SIMD architecture! How this is possible, will be explained later.

Use of applicative languages. Pure Lisp. If we remove from Lisp all the iterative parts (prog, goto, labels) and assignments (set, setq) we end us with pure Lisp, strictly applicative. Recursion is still there; iteration has dissapeared.

Applicative languages are specially useful for the task (4) above and for automatic parallelization, because evaluation (the replacement of an expression in Lisp by another having the same value; for instance (plus 3 5) gets replaced by 8) can then be performed in parallel. Data flow machines and applicative machines are then examples of (4) in automatic parallelization. The AHR machine [5] can be viewed as a kind of data flow machine.

AUTOMATIC PARALLELIZATION USING THE AHR MACHINE

Outline of our approach. Account is given of our approach using the AHR machine, of MIMD type.

(1) Somehow, the program to be evaluated is converted into node form and stored into the active memory (or grill) of the AHR machine (Figure 'The AHR Machine'). For instance,

```
(CONS (LIST X Y
            (CDR Z)
            W)
      (CAR X))
```

is to be stored in the grill as

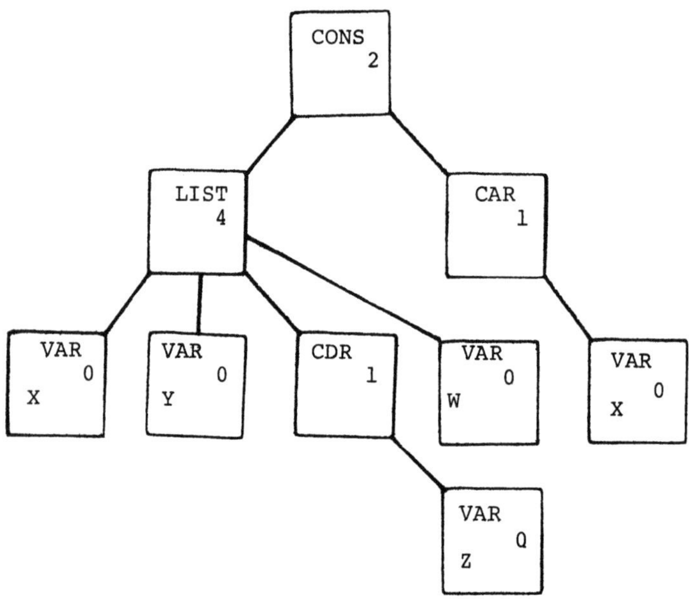

Each square box represents a node. Each node has, among others, fields for function name, space for arguments, field for "pointer to my father", and field "number of arguments not yet evaluated", or NANE. Those nodes with nane = 0 are ready for evaluation.

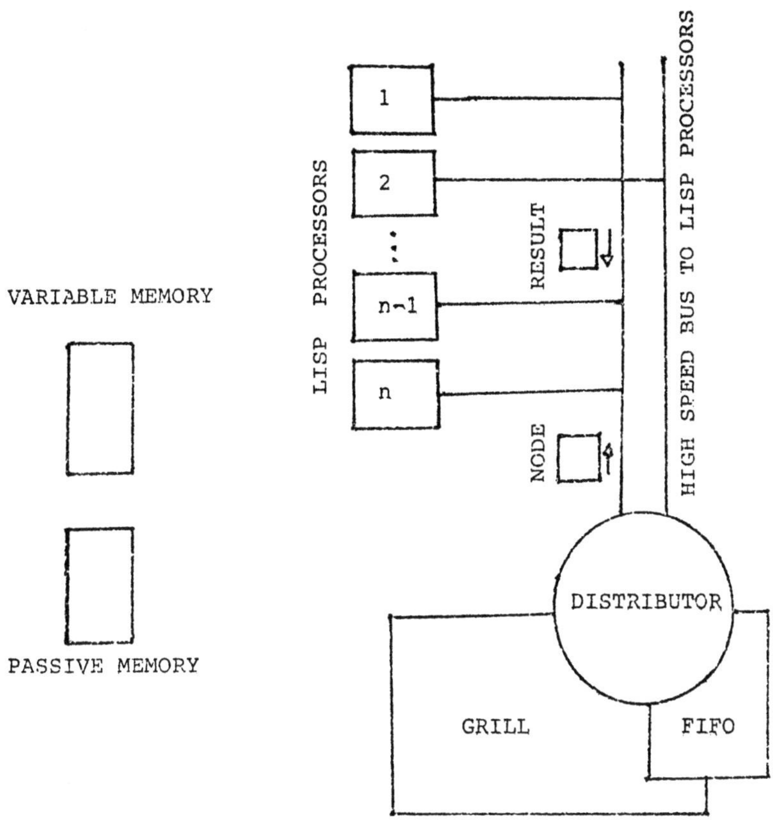

FIGURE "THE AHR MACHINE"

Lisp processor 2 is ready to accept more work. The distributor fetches a node (to be evaluated) from the fifo and sends it to processor 2, while accepting the results of the previous evaluation performed by such processor. That result is stored in the grill, in a place indicated in the destination address of the result.

Such exchange of new work--previous result is performed at each cycle of the distributor.

The Lisp processors also have access (connections not shown) to the variable and passive memories.

The AHR machine communicates with the host computer by linking the passive memory of AHR to the main memory of the host. This link is termed window [3].

(2) The AHR machine is a MIMD architecture formed by n (up to 64) processors. Each of them is called a Lisp processor, since it possesses in its local memory a Lisp interpreter written in Z-80 assembly language (3). Incidentally, note that all the processors have the same Z-80 program, namely the Lisp interpreter. But, in general, each will be executing (evaluating) a different Lisp node --a different part of the user program--.

(3) At the start of the execution (as well as in any other instant in time), the Lisp processors look into the grill for nodes ready for evaluation (those with nane = 0][11] . Each Lisp processor is either busy evaluating some previous node or looking for work (a new node with nane = 0) to do [12]. We can think that a Lisp processor "attaches" itself to a node with nane = 0, and begins to process it. First the node is marked "under process", to prevent other processors form wanting to execute it. Using the field "function name" of the node (actually, a number), a dispatch is done to the appropriate code that handles the Lisp primitive which the node represents. Nodes with nane = 0, being ready for evaluation, have all their arguments already evaluated, and inside the node.

While evaluation is in progress, another Lisp processors are simultaneously evaluating another nodes, no one being aware of what the others are doing. No message interchange takes place. No explicity synchronization is necessary; no semaphores, scheduling, etc., are placed upon the shoulders of the programmer.

After a processor completes evaluation of its node, it places its results into the corresponding slot of the node which is the father of the node just evaluated [13]. It also decrements the nane of the father (since the father has one less argument without evaluation). If such nane becomes 0, it also registers the father in the fifo (see figure 'The AHR Machine'), meaning that the father is now ready for evaluation.

Then, the processor requests additional work (a new node), thus initiating a new step (3).

(4) The machine gradually evaluates the tree from the leaves towards the root, or the Lisp expression form the inside to the outside, until the tree --the program-- has become a single result. Execution has finished. At this point,all processors are waiting, requesting 'more work to do', but there is none. The fifo (list of nodes ready for evaluation) is empty.

(5) Recursion is handled in a similar manner, substituting the name of the function by the lambda expression corresponding to it. This makes the tree grow. [3,4] give details.

(6) Input/output is handled through a window that maps part of the address space of the AHR machine into (part of) the address space of the host machine [4]. Thus, the AHR machine can be thought of as a memory-to-memory processor, as a back-end processor, or as an "intelligent peripheral device", into which Lisp programs are written and from which results or evaluations of such programs are read by the host machine.

(7) The (serial) conversion of a source Lisp program (with Ascii characters and lots of parentheses) into the tree of step (1) is performed by the host machine of step (6), through a loader from disk (in the host) into the memory of the host, and via the window, into the memory of AHR. Printing of the results, that

is, conversion of a list (stored in AHR memory as list cells) into a sequence of Ascii characters, is also performed (serially) by the host machine, which accesses AHR memory via the window.

(8) Everything that is placed in the grill is in the form of a tree of nodes, which will eventually disappear, because it will be transformed into a result. Thus, results can not be kept in the grill. They are kept in passive memory, another memory of the Lisp machine, which also contains programs (written in list notation, using list cells). These programs can be later placed in the grill, to be evaluated. Such copying is done by EVAL, which transforms programs in cell notation (in passive memory) into programs in node notation (in the grill). You can think of the programs residing in passive memory as "master copies", which are necessary since everything placed upon the grill is destroyed, converted into a result, evaluated, or "cooked"; hence the name "grill".

Who places the master copies in passive memory? The host machine, during input, as explained in step 6, converting from Ascii into cell (list) structure.

(9) And, who performs EVAL in step 8? The very Lisp processors, since EVAL is just another Lisp primitive, with the main duty of transporting a program (more likely, a piece of it) from list notation in passive memory into node notation in grill memory; leaving the program in grill assures evaluation (by the Lisp processors). Thus, EVAL can be performed in parallel: several processors can be executing EVAL at the same time, most probably on different data.

<u>The parts of the AHR machine</u>. Having explained in general the functioning of AHR, we now give a more detailed description of its parts. Refer to figure 'The AHR Machine'.

The memories of the AHR machine are the <u>grill</u> or active memory, where the programs to be executed reside in node notation; <u>the passive memory</u> where data (lists, atoms, numbers) and programs (master copies) reside in list (cell) notation; and the <u>variables memory</u>, holding different stacks (a tree of stacks, a cactus of stacks, a spaghetti stack) relating variable names to their values. Also, each Lisp processor has its <u>local</u> or private memory, holding some workspace as well as the Lisp interpreter, a collection of Lisp primitives written in Z-80 assembly language.

Also, we have mentioned the <u>fifo</u> or blackboard, a first-in first-out small memory associated to the grill, holding pointers to nodes in the grill with nane = 0.

The active elements of AHR are the <u>Lisp processors</u>. Each is an 8-bit microcomputer, with its own local memory. They perform the conversion from nodes in the grill into results in passive memory, evaluating nodes given to them by the <u>distributor</u>, another active element. There may be up to 64 (this number can be easily expanded) Lisp processors. The <u>distributor</u> is a piece of hardware (although in the first version of AHR, built in 1981, it was a micro with associated software) that takes nodes ready for evaluation from the fifo and handles them to the Lisp processors when they request additional work. It also takes results already computed by the Lisp processors, and stores them in the corresponding place in the node of the father. Footnotes [12] and [13] should now be clear.

The interconnection parts AHR are the high speed bus, linking the distributor with the Lisp processors, and carrying nodes (new work)and results (old results); the passive bus and variables bus (not shown in the figure), linking the Lisp processors to passive and variables memory; the window, connecting the passive memory to the memory of the host machine. Also, used for debugging and statistics gathering, AHR has the slow speed bus (not shown in the figure), linking the Lisp processors directly to the host machine.

Advantages of the AHR architecture. Among the advantages of AHR, we have:

* AHR achieves automatic parallelization for a MIMD architecture.
* User unaware of parallel environment/execution.
* User does not have to split his programs into parts.
* Synchronization and subtasking automatically done by the system --in fact, by the hardware--.
* No operating system is required for AHR.
* Incrementally expandible.
* If a Lisp processor stops, AHR continues running, showing only slight degradation.

Current status of AHR machine. Version 1, having five Lisp processors, was finished and operational by the end of 1981 [5]. It fulfilled all the premisses/expectations of the design [3]. The machine was taken apart early in 1983, to allow for additonal design and construction of Version 2. However, Version 2 still has not started to be built ($ shortage).

A sister of Version 1, built upor a PS-2000 SIMD machine [6], to be described in this paper, was designed [7] and is expected to be operational soon.

AUTOMATIC PARALLELIZATION USING A SIMD APPROACH

It is now desired to perform automatic parallelization in a SIMD architecture. By such architecture is meant a collection of n processors, called also processing elements (p.e.'s), which execute the same instruction upon different data. Each processor has its own private memory. A control unit (c.u.) outside the n processors has the following duties:

* To hold the program to be executed by all the processors.
* it fetches form c. u. memory the current instruction, decodes it and broadcasts it to all p.e.'s, for simultaneous execution.
* it also executes c.u.'s instructions (mainly scalar operation, as opposed to vector operations performed by the p.e.'s), which can be done in parallel with p.e.'s instructions.

Input/output is complicated, but parallel paths there exist to all p.e.'s. Generally a modified disk (head-per-track) is used. Usually, a SIMD architecture is slave to a host computer.

Connectivity (what processor is to the right of, or above which other) among processors can be modified by execution of special c.u. instructions. Once in a particular connection or configuration, the p.e.'s can simultaneously execute instructions such as "move data from your memory address x to your neighbor. The best example of a SIMD architecture is Illiac IV [1].

Algorithms best suited for SIMD machines. From the above description, it is easily seen that SIMD machines will attain full speed when executing programs

(a) that apply the same algorithm to different columns (vectors, matrices) of data. For instance, if a SIMD has 64 processors, then the same algorithm should be applied to 64 different collections of numbers; and

(b) that do not depend on the data being processed. The algorithms (although, of course, not the results) should be data-independent.

For instance, the average of n numbers can be expressed as an algorithm which does not depend on the values of the numbers being averaged. On the contrary, the square root of a number may be computed by an algorithm "a" that uses routine "b" to produce real numbers, when the input is positive or zero; but uses routine "c" to produce complex numbers when the input is negative. Thus, algorithm "a" is data-dependent.

Difficulties in a straightforward approach to parallelization. Data-dependent algorithms can be executed by a SIMD architecture, but with substantial loss of speed. For instance, suppose we apply algorithm "a" above to an input of 64 real numbers, one of each p.e. Many of them (half, in the average) will be positive or zero, so that branch "b" of the program has to be executed by the corresponding p.e.'s, while the others (those having negative inputs) wait. After "b" is completed, branch "c" of the program has to be executed by the other p.e.'s, while the former p.e.'s wait. Thus, in the average, parallelism is only n/2 instead of n. If we have two nested IF's, four possible branches (TT, TF, FT, FF) are needed, and parallelism decreases to n/4; and so forth.

There is another way to execute in parallel data-dependent (which essentially means, different) algorithms, which may possibly be more efficient. A general idea of it is now given.

General Idea of the Solution

STATIC PART OF DESIGN

The data structure. We are using in the PS-2000 all the standard data structures already in use in Version 1 of AHR [5]. Lists, arrays, fifo, stacks, trees of stacks, etc.

Continuity of address space. On the other hand, we had to make a careful design for pointers that go outside the memory space of a processor, into the memory space of another processor, of the control unit, or even of the host machine. This is because the data stored in one processor differs from the data stored in another processor. Not only the data differs but, unlike the normal SIMD case, the structure of the data is also different.. That is, in the typical SIMD case, every processor has the same array stored in the same place, beginning in the same local address, etc. The arrays possess different numerical values, when you visit the same cell in different processor memories. That is not the case of our design; in a processor memory, in locations xthrough x+y may be residing an array; in another processor memory, in the same location x through x+y some lists may be sitting.

The solution was to have pointers that span the whole set of memories; part of the pointer is interpreted as a number that indicates"processor number", control unit, host processor, etc. In addition, use is made of the fact that certain structures do not point towards the host processor, etc.

DYNAMIC PART OF DESIGN

The basic idea about how to place the AHR architecture inside the PS-2000 architecture, was to have the lists stored "globally" through all memories. That is, there was not going to be repetition of data. A given data resides in just one place of the PS-2000. This requires, as mentioned, global pointers.

Then, each processor "analyzes" its local memory, looking for nodes with nane = 0 and proceeds to their evaluation, substracts 1 from the nane of the father, etc. [3, 4, 5].

Basic difficulty. We soon hit the following difficulty: because it is a SIMD machine, one processor can not be taking CAR of some data, While another is making CONS of two Lisp expressions. Very strictly, the SIMD contruction requires that each and every processor perform exactly the same instruction.

The solution found was, roughly described, as follows: each processor will take notice (in a local list with as many entry groups as there are primitive Lisp operations) of what operations are ready to be done (what nodes have nane = 0). After this phase finishes, all the Lisp processors proceed to execute all the CAR's that need to be executed. Those processors having no CAR's or only a few of them, will soon go idle. Then, all the Lisp processors proceed to execute all the CONS'es that need to be executed. And so on.

This solution will be described in some detail below. Notice that this solution, together with a scheduler (a program that somehow decides what group of primitives to execute next, and how many of them: how many CAR's, how many CONS'es, etc.), effectively converts a SIMD machine into a MIMD architecture.

The different execution flows. Each p.e. (there are 64 of them in a PS-2000) runs a different user program. Thus, there are as many different Lisp programs as there are Lisp processors. Each atomic operation (a node) corresponds to a Lisp primitive. Each instruction flow is decomposed into its corresponding atomic operations, or nodes. Of these, some have nane = 0, being ready for evaluation. Those nodes with nane = 0 are inscribed into a list, during the first part of the scheduler: a list of CAR's ready for execution; a list of CDR's ready for execution,...

Distribution of a program into n subprograms. As the program is coming from the host machine, it is converted by the c.u. into node notation, and spread over the different local memories of the p.e.'s. This is possible,since global pointers are employed. Thus, each p.e. will have, initially, a few nodes with nane = 0 in its memory, where evaluation will begin.

The function that spreads a program among the memories of the p.e.'s has to have some careful design. For the function (F (G1 x) (G2 y) (G3 z)), it is better if its sons (G1 x), (G2 y), (G3 z) are placed in different processors, because then they can be evaluated in parallel. But, when the results are produced --let us call them r1, r2 and r3--, we have (F r1 r2 r3), but the results (the sons of F) are in different processors than the function F. Thus, the results have to be exported to the processor possessing F. Hence, spreading the arguments across the p.e.'s increases the parallelism, but also increases the exportation of results.

In the current implementation, the spreading function places the first son in the same processor as the father; each of the other sons are placed in different processors. In the example, F, G1 and x are placed in the same processor, while (G2 y) goes in the second p.e., and (G3 z) in a third.

The scheduler. The first part of the scheduler simply takes note of how many CAR's, how many CDR's, etc., each Lisp processor has ready to execute, and where they are located in local memory. This information is collected in local lists held in local memory of the p.e.'s. This collection of information is done by the p.e.'s, in parallel. Thus, each p.e. maintains a CAR-fifo, a CDR-fifo, a CONS-fifo, etc. One fifo for each primitive funtion.

Then, the scheduler proceeds to ascertain the best order of evaluation among the Lisp primitives. Should it be first the CONS, then the CDR's, then the CAR's, to be executed? Or should the order be CAR-CONS-CDR, or what? This is not easy to determine, we think. The execution first of CAR's, for instance, could give rise to many more CONSes (ready for evaluation) to appear. Then, the order should be CAR-CONS. On the other hand, to be looking for the optimal ordering may consume more machine time than the time saved. In the current implementation [7], the most popular primitives are executed first. This is to exploit the idea that the most popular nodes will "free" additional nodes for evaluation, which then will be evaluated gratis, keeping all or most of the p.e.'s busy. [14].

Then, the scheduler determines how many nodes of each type to evaluate. How many CAR's, how many CDR's, etc. For instance, suppose that after phase 1, the distribution of the number of CAR nodes ready for evaluation is 0, 0, 20, 9, 11, 10, 10, 20, assuming only eight processing elements. To order 20 executions of CAR will keep only two processors busy; two will never have work to do (because they have no CARs) and four of them will become idle at the middle in time. Perhaps would have been better to order only 10 or 11 executions. In this manner, the processors having 20 CARs would have to wait for the next "CAR execution cycle", leaving some CAR nodes unexecuted in this cycle.

The scheduler makes the above determination based in the count of phase 1, which is a static count. For instance, knowing that a processor has 11 CAR's ready for execution really means that it has al least 11, since during execution of another primitives --and even of the CAR's themselves--, more CAR's ready for evaluation are likely to appear.

Then, the scheduler proceeds to the execution (done by the p.e.'s) of the determined number of primitive 1, then the determined number of primitive 2, etc. That is, "execute 11 CARS's, then 23 CDR's, then 15 CONS'es,..." In this phase, the scheduler asks all the Lisp processors to execute the same primitive function (or to remain idle), although, of course, over different data.

After finishing the above, the scheduler looks for more nodes with nane = 0, starting the first part of another cycle. In general, the execution of nodes with nane = 0 tends to make zero the nanes of their parents; in this way more nodes with nane = 0 are produced.

The execution ends when the scheduler finds (in its phase 1) no nodes with nane = 0.

Node exportation. It often occurs that a processor needs to perform a primitive operation over data which resides in another processor. Certain primitive operations are capable of being performed even if data resides elsewhere (for instance, if the needed information is inside the global pointer). Nevertheless, most primitive operations need to be done "locally", that is, the processor than owns the data should execute it. In order to accomplish this, a node is exported to the processor owning the data, if it ever happens that such node is tried for execution, only to find that its data is elsewhere. This is easier than bringing the data to reside together with the node that wants to manipulate it.

Exportation takes place in two phases:

* In phase e1, a node to be exported is placed in a "list of nodes which desire to be exported". Phase e1 occurs all the time, When it is impossible to perform an operation signaled by a node, because its data is not locally available, then "Phase e1" is called, which annotates this node into the list, and the node is considered "formally exported". (The node is still waiting for execution).

* In phase e2, exportation actually takes place. All the p.e.'s use the inter-processor communication facilities, and all proceed to exchange nodes.

  After phase e2, nodes imported are considered to "belong" to the importer processor, and we are sure that it can handle them.

  The main idea is: when you have a node, try to do as much work as it is possible to perform locally; when you can't do any further work, export it. But do not export it to any processor; export it precisely to the processor that owns the data that is "causing the problem". In this way, we try to guarantee that there are no nodes "perpetually circulating around processors" and getting no attention from any of them. More details in [7].

What happens if there is a function, (PLUS r1 r2 ...rn) that wants to add all its arguments (already evaluated; shown as results r_i), but every argument resides in different p.e.'s, so that, no matter to whom you export the nodes PLUS, it can not do anything about it? We believe that this should not happen, if the following steps or precautions are taken:

* provide space in the node for fixed and real numbers. This will solve the problem with PLUS above.

* carefully design the primitives of the language, so that no one of them depends on more that one "non-present" arguments (an argument is not present if it needs more information than that carried in the pointer).

* If necessary, decompose the primitives into another primitives having dependency in at most one "non-present" argument. This decomposition can be done by a macro expansor at loading time (performed by c.u. or by the host computer). For instance, suppose that the language has a primitive (PLUSCAR x1 x2) that adds the CAR of list x1 to the CAR of list x2. That is (PLUSCAR A B), when A is (3 4) and B is (5 6), gives a result of 8. Then A and B are "non-present" arguments because, even if they are already evaluated --their values being (3 4) and (5 6) respectively-- the pointer to (3 4) does not contain information about "3", and the pointer to (5 6) does not contain information about "5". Then PLUSCAR should be deleted as a primitive expanding it at loading time into

something like (PLUS (CAR A) (CAR B)), or (PLUSS(CAR A)B). In this last case, PLUSS has B as the only "non-present" argument, and thus is still safe.

Exportation of results. Once a node is evaluated, its result is sent to the node higher up (to its father) in the tree. If the node of the function which is to receive the result is not in the same processor as the result node [that is, if the father of a given result is in another processor], then the result is exported (as a "results node", something similar to QUOTE) to the processor which has the function node (the father).

HOW TO REPROGRAM A SIMD MACHINE TO MAKE IT BEHAVE LIKE A MIMD

Reasons to change the philosophy of operation of PS-2000. Although the way of working of a SIMD machine is simple and well understood, we want to change it to a MIMD machine "mode of operation", due to the following reasons:

* In the MIMD case, we can have algorithms that depend on the data and even in this case full parallelism is sustained.

* It is desired to do other operations, such as symbol manipulation, instead of simple numerical operations.

In addition, we have reasons for chosing the PS-2000:

* It is the multicomputer designed, built and available at the Institute of Control Sciences, where this work was done.

* This computer is widely available, commercially, in the Soviet Union.

* It is a powerful computer. Each of its 64 processors is a minicomputer both in speed, in word size (24 b) and in memory size (64 K words).

In addition, we have reasons for chosing the AHR computer as the target architecture:

* The AHR machine works, and it has a proven and sound design.

* The AHR machine is easy to program, differing in this from more conventional MIMD machines.

* The AHR machine was built and existed at IIMAS-UNAM (Mexico) and there was a great deal of familiarity and experience with its design, its architecture and its functioning.

* While doing design and construction of AHR, some improvements came to mind, that were postponed to a later version. There was some desire to bring these improvements and variations into existence.

Only software was used to accomplish the change. During the design and construction of AHR it was soon learned that, if we have both the ability to specify the hardware and the software (that is, if the design engineers are allowed to change both hardware and software), the resulting structure is more easily tuned to requirements than if we can specify or change only hardware (or only software). Thus, it was our original idea to modify both software and hardware of the PS-2000, in our efforts to convert it into an AHR-like machine. Nevertheless, this was not done. In fact, we did not do any hardware change. We accomplished the conversion using only programs --software, that is--. The reasons for doing this rather contrived design were:

* Time. We had only two months to learn about the PS-2000, to design the changes and to begin implementing them. To have gone into the detailed circuits of the machine, and through the extensive documentation it possesses, would have meant additional efforts. Although this, in return, would have produced a more efficient result (a new PS-2000 running in AHR mode more efficiently, faster than the current machine).

* Portability. If we do any hardware changes to our PS-2000, it ceases to be a PS-2000, in the sense that it no longer behaves as its PS-2000 sisters intalled elsewhere. To these sisters, the same hardware changes would have to be done in order to run in AHR-mode. Also, our PS-2000 may even stop running programs that were previously running in an unmodified PS-2000. Thus, it was decided not to touch the hardware, so as to

    * Allow our installed changes to run in any PS-2000 machine;
    * Allow the PS-2000 to continue running old PS-2000 programs.

General characteristics of the design. The general organization of the PS-2000 Lisp is such that the input and the output routines reside in the host machine, and the evaluation routines reside in the PS-2000. The consequences of this organization are several. To begin with, the host machine always retains the oblist (object list); that is, the literal atoms. The PS-2000 has an indirect reference (not to be confused with indirect addressing) to the elements of the oblist by the fact that the first cells of the property list in the PS-2000 reside at the same addresses as the literal atoms in the host machine. Next, the Lisp evaluation system, which includes EVAL, resides completely in the PS-2000, and in particular in the memories of the c.u. Parallel execution of the Lisp primitives is achieved by the p.e.'s. Other modules also reside in the memories of the c.u., such as the interprocessors communication routines among the p.e.'s, the memory management of the entire system, etc.

How a Lisp expression is evaluated. The process for evaluating a Lisp expression is begun by a user typing a Lisp expression. The input routine that reads this expression (the Reader) in the host, converts the character string representation of the expression into an internal representation consisting of nodes and pointers. Some syntactic verification of the expression is performed by the reader, such as balanced parentheses and the like.

Then, the expression (in internal form) is sent to the PS-2000 for evaluation. Upon arrival in the PS-2000, the expression is spread over several p.e.'s. The number of processors that are required for evaluating the expression depends upon the size of the expression and the total number of processors that the PS-2000 configuration has. The expression is then evaluated in the PS-2000. Finally, the result of the evaluation is sent back to the host machine. In it, the result (a Lisp expression) is converted back into a character string by the output system (Printer).

Both the reader and printer are standard Lisp input/output routines as found in sequential machines. However, the evaluation process in the PS-2000 is not standard. It works as follows:

The system continuously maintains a table of the nodes to be processed. The table is ordered according to the so-called popularity of the node function type. This means that the table is a representation of the demand for nodes to be processed; the nodes that have the most entries in the table are considered first, the nodes with next-to-the-most entries in the table are considered second, and so on. The table is updated at certain times during the processing, but not after each node is processed. The table resides in c.u.'s memory.

The popularity table is used by the system to decide what node to process. Once this decision has been made, the system transfers control to the routine that evaluates such node. The consequence of this evaluation may be more nodes, which may or may not be registered in their respective fifos. Independently of whether new nodes are created or not, the evaluation of the original node is finished, possibly temporarily, and control is returned to the system. Then the process begins over again by selecting a new node to evaluate according to the popularity table.

It should be emphasized that much of the process of getting the node out of the Grill and evaluating it is done in parallel. However, if a node is selected but a given p.e. does not have such a node, then the p.e. waits until another node function type, which the p.e. may have, is to be processed.

It has been mentioned before that an expression is loaded by spreading it over several processors. The consequence of this action is that at the time a node is evaluated, the node may require one or more of its parameters to be accessed but these parameters can not be accessed because they reside outside of the processor of the node being evaluated. Therefore, the system suspends the evaluation on the node temporarily and registers the node to be exported to the processor where the parameter resides. At some time later, the node is exported, the parameter is accessed and its value is used to help to evaluate the node. If there are other parameters in other processors, then the node is re-exported to the processors of the parameters, and subsequently evaluated. In the end, the node is evaluated, and its result is sent to the father node (the node above the evaluated node in the tree). And as in the case of the parameters, if the father resides in another processor, the result is exported to the location of the father node.

As in the case of standard Lisps, the PS-2000 Lisp maintains its various memories by garbage collection in parallel. This is done when the cell lists are exhausted. Processing of Lisp expressions is suspended until the free lists are reconstructed again.

Other related work. Strong [9] analyzes the problem of how to sequence (schedule) different programs (flow graphs) residing in the processors of a SIMD machine, so as the be optimally executed by it. His solution has theoretical insights, while ours is a "practical" bridge between two existing machines.

CONCLUSIONS

* It is possible to attain automatic parallelization in a MIMD machine, as the AHR machine shows.

* It is possible to attain automatic parallelization in a SIMD machine, as the emulation of AHR by the PS-2000 shows. More over, this emulation requires no hardware modification.

* In the above emulation, the whole memory of the SIMD is considered "a single memory". No data needs to be replicated.

* The paper describes a procedure which enables a SIMD architecture to execute (in parallel) different programs, each one residing (as nodes) in each processing elements. Thus, it is possible to mimic the behavior of a MIMD machine using a SIMD architecture.

* The above execution seems to be rather efficient, because we can

know and control (with the scheduler) how many processors are going to be idle, during the execution of a given type of node.

Recommendations for further work.

* Finish the ongoing implementation of the scheduler [7] , and the parallelgarbage collector.

* Measure the efficiency of some critical parts:
  * The % of time that some p.e.'s wait because they lack the type of node being currently executed;
  * The % of time that the scheduler takes. That is overhead due to the scheduler and to handling the queues of nodes --one queue for each Lisp primitive function--.

* Diminish, if needed, the overhead due to the scheduler, by
  * improving it through software changes and theoretical considerations;
  * transfering some time-consuming part of it to hardware, inventing suitable machine instructions for p.e.'s and c.u.

ACKNOWLEDGMENTS. We want to thank Professors Herbert Freeman (USA) and Goffredo Pieroni (Italy) for the opportunity to present this material at the NATO Advanced Study Institute.

This paper is based on the work done [6,7] under the Joint Research Agreement between the USSR Academy of Sciencies and CONACYT, the National Council for Science and Technology (Mexico).

Work herein described has been partially supported by CONACYT (Grants PVT EE NAL 81 1211 and 14112H22-044).

We acknowledge our institutions,the Institute for Control Sciences and IIMAS-UNAM; specially the members of the AHR project [5].

Finally, A. Guzmán acknowledges the fruitful research environment provided at the Electrical Engineering Department of CIEA-IPN by Profs. Juan Garduño (Dept. Head), Héctor Nava Jaimes (Director of CIEA-IPN) and Dr. Manuel Ortega (Undersecretary of Public Education for Technological Research, Federal Govt. of Mexico).

REFERENCES

1 Bouknight, W. J., et al. The Illiac IV System. Proc. IEEE 60 4 April 72 369-388.

2 Glushkov, V. M., et al Recursive machines and computing technology. Proc. IFIP 1974, North Holland, 65-70.

3 Guzmán A. A parallel heterarchical machine for high level language processing. In Languages and Architectures for Image Processing, M. J. B. Duff and S. Levialdi (eds). 1981 Academic Press, 230-244. Also in: Proc. 1981 Int'l conf. on Parallel Processing, 64-71.

4 Guzmán A. A heterarchical multi-microprocessor Lisp machine. Proc. 1981 IEEE Workshop on Computer Architecture for Pattern Analysis and Image Database Management. IEEE Publication 81CH-1697-2, pages 309-317.

5 Guzmán, A., and Norkin, K. The design and construction of a parallel heterarchical machine; final report of phase 1 of the AHR Project. Technical Report AHR-82-21, AHR Lab, IIMAS, Nat'l Univ. of Mexico 1982.

6 Guzmán, A., Gerzso, M., Norkin, K., and Kuprianov, B. The PS-2000 SIMD computer; technical description and instruction set. Tech. Report AHR-82-23, AHR laboratory, IIMAS, Nat'l Univ. of Mexico, 1982.

7 Guzmán, A., Gerzso, M., Norkin, K., and Vilenkin, S. Y. Functional design of Lisp interpreter for the PS-2000 SIMD computer. Technical Report AHR-83-24, IIMAS, Nat'l University of Mexico, 1983.
8 Russell, R.M. The Cray-1 computer system C ACM 21 1 Jan 78, 63-72.
9 Strong, H. R. Vector execution of flow graphs J ACM 31 1 Jan 83 186-196.
10 Tandem Nonstop II sytem description manual, Vols 1 and 2. P/N 82077 Tandem Computers Inc. Cupertino, C , USA. April 1981.
11 Glushkiv [2] postulated this search. To avoid it, AHR uses a fifo holding nodes ready for evaluation;they are handed out by the distributor.
12 The Lisp processor does not actually look for more work to do; instead,it just"signals" to the distributor that it wants more work; the distributor accesses the fifo and provides a new node to the processor.
13 Actually, the Lisp processor just request that thing to the distributor, which actually does the placement of the result into the father, as well as the decrementing of the nane of the father and its optional inscription in the fifo.
14 To give an example, let us suppose that the scheduler has just run its first part and it counted 12, 14, 7, 9, 10, ... CAR's and 5, 8, 2, 4, 6,... CONS'es, in processors 1, 2, 3, 4, 5, ... Using this information, it decides to go through 10 (parallel) executions of CAR's and 6 (parallel) evaluation of CONS'es, in that order. Let us supposse that the evaluation of the CAR's has generated 2, 1, 3, 2, 0,... additional CONS'es ready for evaluation. That is, there are now 7, 9, 5, 6, 6,...CONS'es ready. When coming to the evaluation of the CONS'es which was already decided to be 6, each processor evaluates 6 CONS'es (or less, if it had fewer ready). Efficiency was lost only in processor 3 (who evaluated 5 CONS'es and wasted one CONS evaluation cycle), as oppossed to the case when no additional CONSES were made ready. In this last hypothetical case, since the CONS count remained at 5, 8, 2, 4, 6,...,processors 1, 3, 4,... would be below 100% efficiency. The example shows that, without spending additional computing time, the additional CONS'es made ready by the CAR evaluations, improved the efficiency of every processor who had fewer CONS'es that the number(six, in our example) of executions chosen by the scheduler.

Those processors with 6 or more CONS'es did not improve their efficiency; it deteriorated neither; all of them remained busy during the 6 executions of CONS'es, and efficiency was 100% whether more CONS'es appeared or not for those processors.

Between a scheduler intervention and the next, what is said for CAR's with respect to CONS'es is also true of CAR's for any other Lisp primitives: the execution of primitive i will improve the efficiency of execution of primitive j, if j is executed at any time (between two consecutive scheduler interventions) after i. Thus, the popular primitives should be executed first.

VLSI MULTIPROCESSOR FOR IMAGE PROCESSING*

K. S. Fu, K. Hwang, and B. W. Wah
School of Electrical Engineering
PURDUE UNIVERSITY
West Lafayette, Indiana 47907 USA

I. INTRODUCTION

Image analysis refers to the use of digital computers for Pattern Recognition and Image Processing (PRIP). On-line imagery data needs to be stored on disks and quickly retrieved for PRIP applications. This article presents a systematic approach to developing a special-purpose computer for processing pictorial information. This approach integrates both pattern-analysis and image-database-management capabilities into a unified design to meet the challenges. The integrated design is aimed at the development of a real-time and interactive computer system for both high-level pattern recognition and low-level image processing.

We shall examine special database machines suggested for handling imagery data. Recent efforts on VLSI hardware approaches to implementing PRIP algorithms and to language recognition will be discussed. The integrated architectural approach is initiated by the PUMPS architecture currently under development at Purdue University. We shall identify the desired architectural features, processing languages, image database systems, and underlying VLSI computing structures for developing intelligent computer imaging systems.

II. INTEGRATED IMAGE PROCESSING

A typical computer imaging system consists of four stages as depicted in Fig.1. The preprocessing stage includes image operations

* This research was supported by the U. S. National Science Foundation under grant ECS-80-16580.

NATO ASI Series, Vol. F18
Computer Architectures for Spatially Distributed Data
Edited by H. Freeman and G. G. Pieroni

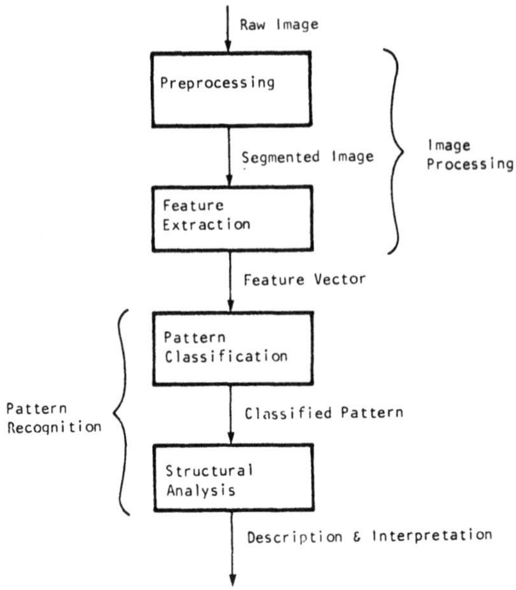

Fig. 1 Processing stages of a pattern-analysis computer system

like smoothing, enhancement, restoration, edge detection, and segmentation, etc. Raw images are reduced to segmented patterns by this initial stage. The next stage is for image segmentation and _feature extraction_, which further reduces the segmented image to a small set of feature vectors. Clustering techniques may be applied at this stage. The third stage is for _pattern classification_, which recognizes the membership of extracted features among known pattern classes. The fourth stage is for _structural analysis and interpretation_, to produce a concise description and interpretation of the pattern information.

Conventional computers are primarily designed to process one-dimensional strings of alphanumeric data. To process multi-dimensional information on SISD computers requires image coding and picture transformation (such as projection, registration, etc.). Sequential machines cannot efficiently exploit parallelism embedded in most PRIP operations. On the other hand, large parallel computers, such as (SIMD) array processors and (MIMD) multiprocessors, may not be necessarily cost-effective in implementing simple and repetitive image operations over very large and, sometimes, dynamically changing image databases.

An adequate pattern-analysis computer is expected to perform at least 100 megaflops with a memory bandwidth of at least 256 megabytes for applications in the 1980's, and many require a processing power of 1000 megaflops or higher for those applications in the 1990's. Two earlier surveys on special computer architectures for PRIP have been given by Danielsson and Levialdi [6] and Hwang and Fu [22].

Computer Image Analysis

Identified below are desired architectural and functional features in an image processing computer. We focus on the interplay between computer architectures and PRIP applications. In general, a PRIP computer should be featured with as many of the following capabilities as possible:

(a) To explore spatial parallelism, a pattern-analysis computer may be equipped with replicated arithmetic/logic units operating synchronously in SIMD mode. Moreover, high degree of pipelining (temporal parallelism) is desired for overlapped instruction execution and pipelined vector arithmetic.

(b) Some PRIP computers choose a multiprocessor configuration to support asynchronous computations in MIMD mode. Data flow multiprocessor systems also been also suggested for PRIP or Artificial Intelligence computations.

(c) Hierarchical memory system is needed for image storage and manipulation. Large main memory with fast image cache must be employed to alleviate the problem of image data overflow. Fast and intelligent I/O and sensing devices are needed for interactive pattern analysis and image query processing.

(d) Special image database management systems or image database machines are demanded for fast image information retrieval. Toward this end, some high-level picture description/manipulation languages need to be developed, in addition to developing image query languages.

(e) PRIP computers should fully utilize state-of-the-art hardware componentsand available software packages. Dedicated VLSI devices are needed for PRIP at signal-processing level and at symbol-manipulation level. Special VLSI pattern recognizers and image filtering chips are needed for fast image construction, thresholding, FFT, histogram analysis, feature selection, and syntax analysis.

Image Database Management

An image database system provides a large collection of structured imagery data (digitized pictures) for easy access by a large number of users. It provides both high level query support and low level image access. Most of these image database systems are implemented with specially developed software packages upon dedicated pattern analysis systems. It is highly desirable to develop a dedicated backend database machine for image database management. So far, several hardware attempts were suggested. But none of them has yet been implemented for image database management.

Image database management functions and peripheral supports are depicted in Fig. 2. First, we need faster and intelligent image input devices. The image features and structures (shape, texture, and spatial relationships) extracted by the host image processor should be converted into symbolic image sketches stored in a logical image database. For those unconverted raw images, the system must convert them into efficient codes stored in the physical image database.

Flexible image manipulation and retrieval functions must be established using high-level image manipulation languages and image description languages. The logical database is used for image reconstruction from relational sketches. The compressed raw images must be

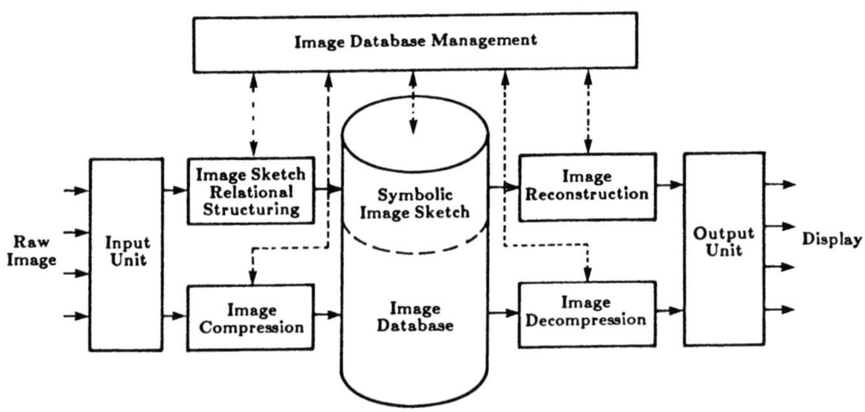

Fig. 2 An intelligent image database system and its management functions

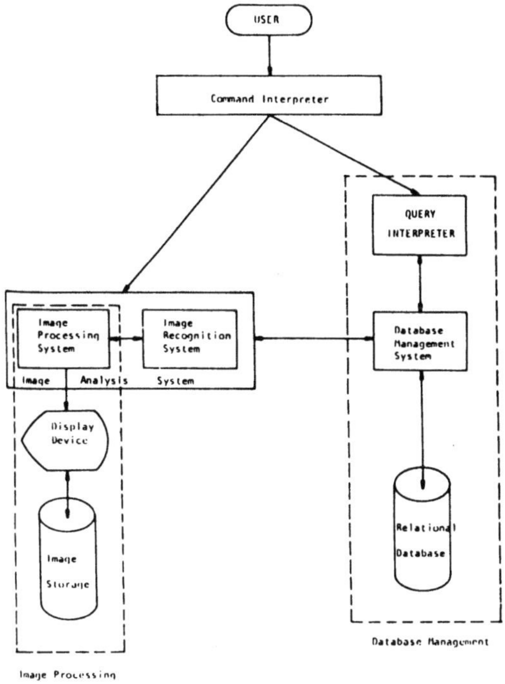

Fig. 3 Integrated image analysis and database management system

decompressed for high-resolution console display. The output unit is responsible for extracting results to be sent to the host computer. The above image database management functions should be supported with specially designed hardware units that constitute an image database machine.

The Integrated System

The three functions, image processing, pattern recognition, and image database management, must be integrated into an efficient pictorial information system. A data-flow block diagram of such an integrated system is shown Fig. 3. Three subsystems in the diagram correspond to the three addressed functions. These subsystems must interact and cooperate with each other to achieve the said objectives. The user communicates with the system through pictorial query language. The raw images are physically stored on disks (or tapes). A relational image database is established by mapping the physical images into the logically structured database. The image processing subsystem performs image preprocessing and feature extraction. The

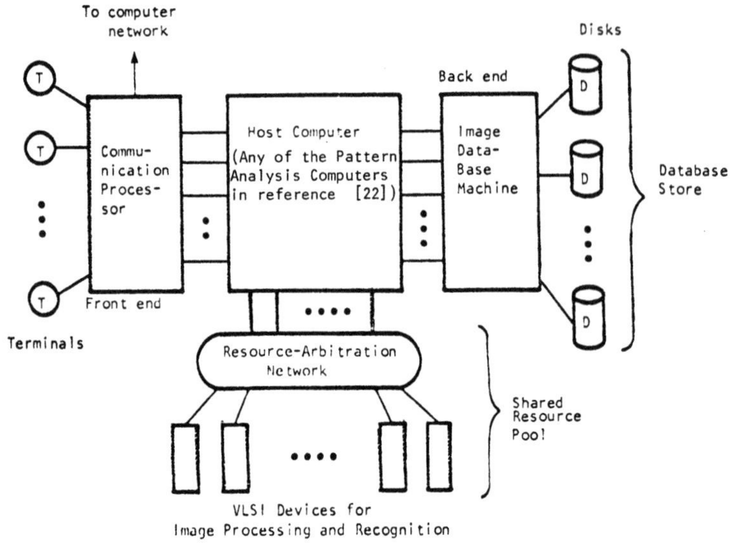

Fig. 4 Architecture of an integrated computer system for pattern analysis and image database management

pattern recognition subsystem performs pattern classification and picture interpretation operations. The image data management subsystem handles query processing and image database operations.

The system architecture of such an integrated image analysis computer is conceptually illustrated in Fig. 4. The system consists of four major subsystems, as shown by the four blocks in the drawing. The host computer can be any one of those existing pattern-analysis computers [22]. The backend database machine is specially developed for image database management. Either software or hardware approaches can be adopted in developing image database management systems. The front-end communication processor is used to handle terminal activities or to be connected to a computer network for remote users. The shared resource pool contains VLSI functional units or attached special processors for fast PRIP operations. A resource sharing network is needed between the host processors and the shared resource pool.

III. THE PUMPS ARCHITECTURE

PUMPS is a high-performance multiprocessor computer with a shared resource pool of VLSI devices. A block diagram showing the major components in PUMPs is given in Fig. 5. There are p processors in the system, each of which is multiprogrammed. The processors can operate

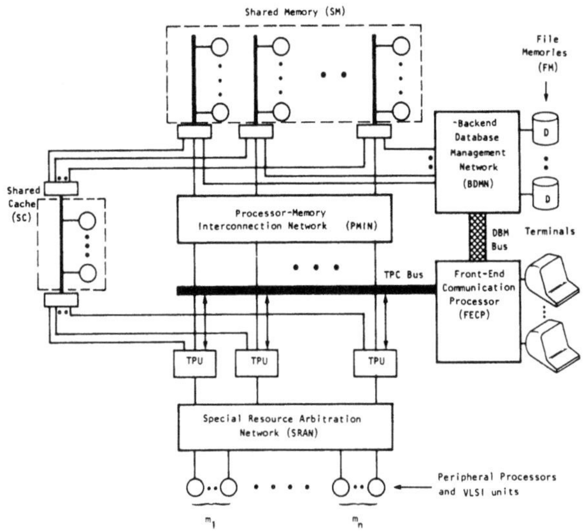

Fig. 5 System architecture of PUMPS

in an interactive fashion through the shared resource pool and shared memory system. They can communicate with each other via an interrupt bus. This intercommunication medium is very effective in passing interrupts, synchronization and other control signals.

All the processors are connected to the shared-resource pool via a Resource Sharing Network. This network provides connections between each processor and the desired peripheral processor or VLSI functional unit. As VLSI technology develops, modular switches will become more cost-effective because of their regular and local connections. In case several processors reference the same functional unit, some priority must be established to resolve the conflicts.

The allocation of the shared resources in the pool to the processors depends on the computational requirements of the active processes. The allocation is considered dynamic. Furthermore, the selection of the resource types in the pool is tailored to special application requirements. For example, one may wish to include an FFT processor, a histogram analyzer, and some VLSI array or pipeline processors in the pool for image analysis applications. In this sense, PUMPS has a dynamically reconfigurable structure. Different applicative environments may be equipped with different functional units. The remaining system resources such as processors and shared memories, are designed for MIMD computations needed in high-level pattern recognition applications.

The processors perform three basic functions: (i) dispatching and initiating tasks for the shared peripheral processors and VLSI units; (ii) executing purely sequential tasks; (iii) participating in MIMD

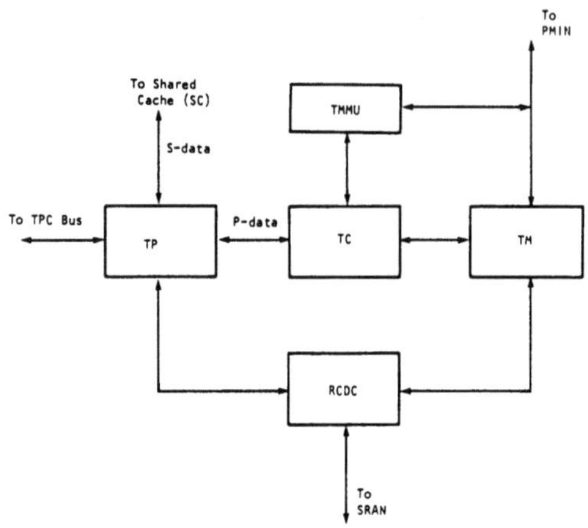

Fig. 6 Architecture of a task processing unit (TPU)

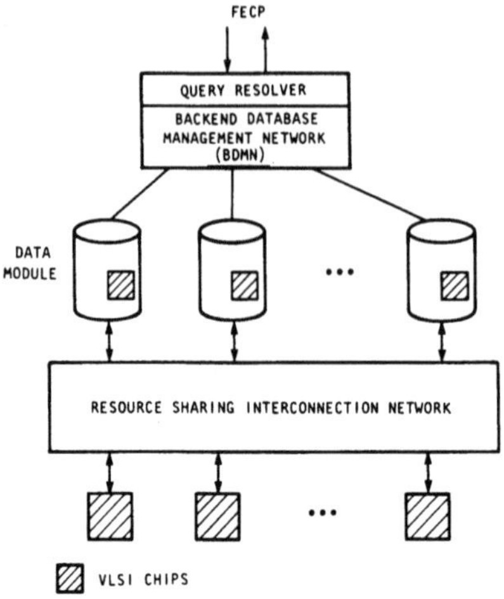

Fig. 7 A Conceptual view of an image database machine.

processes and running the operating system. In order to perform the first type of function, a local Memory is provided within each processor as depicted in Fig. 6. The local memory is partitioned into several segments. These consist of the unmapped memory, which is used for the operating system kernel and device drivers, the local image buffers and the local scratch-pad. The local image buffers are shared between the Task Processor and the resource pool. The processor, acting as a controller, must provide the peripheral devices with a continuous flow of data. A resource controller and data channels are used to format and channel the data between the task memory and peripheral units.

The PUMPS has a distributed memory organization using virtual memory addressing based on paged segments. Within the task cache, misses are serviced by initiating block transfer from the task memory. If a block does not reside in the task memory but is known to the process, a page fault occurs which is also serviced by the page-fault handler. The occurrence of a page fault causes the current active process in the task processor to be blocked, whereupon a task switch is made to a runnable process also residing in the processor. By distributing the memory management functions the task processors are relieved of performing memory management functions and thereby increase their effectiveness in performing useful computations.

The interleaved task memory serves as a high-spaced buffer between the processor and the Shared Memories, which are semiconductor memories organized to permit efficient block transfers of information. A block-transfer oriented Interconnection Network such as the delta network, is used between the processors and the shared memories. The shared memories are also connected to the disk memories via an image database management network, which is designed to handle data transfers from multiple disks. The file memories, together with a backend computer and the backend network, comprise the database machine for image processing.

The architectural design of the database machine for image processing consists of three parts: a set of data modules, each of which includes a disk with the associated cellular logic for processing picture queries, a backend computer, and the backend database management network (Fig. 7). The necessity of providing a high-level language interface to the users complicates the design issues. However, the design of the database machine is based on various image data manipulation and retrieval operators. These operators are interpretable via a language interface which permits a logical representation of the images.

IV. VLSI IMAGE PROCESSORS

Recent advances in VLSI micro-electronic technology have triggered the thought of implementing some PRIP algorithms directly in hardware. VLSI image recognizers offer high speed and accuracy which are useful in real-time, on-line, pictorial information processing. This is the first step towards advanced automation and machine intelligence. Recently, many attempts have been made in developing special VLSI devices for signal/image processing and pattern recognition. Some of these approaches involve large-scale matrix computations and some syntactic parsing operations. We list in Table 1 some candidate PRIP algorithms that are suitable for VLSI implementation.

Statistical Pattern Recognition

Partitioned matrix algorithms can be used in L-U decomposition, matrix multiplication, matrix inversion, and solution of triangular systems of equations [9]. Pipelined VLSI networks have been developed to realize these partitioned matrix algorithms [10].

Table 1 Candidate image algorithms for VLSI

Image Processing	Enhancement, Filtering, Thinning, Edge Detection, Segmentation, Registration. Restoration, Clustering, Texture Analysis, Convolution, Fourier Analysis, etc.
Pattern Recognition	Feature Extraction, Template Matching, Statistical Classification, Graph Algorithms, Syntax Analysis, Change Detection, Language Recognition, Scene Analysis and Synthesis, etc.
Image Query Processing	Query Decomposition, Query Optimization, Attribute Manipulation, Picture Reconstruction, Search/Sorting Algorithms, Query-by-Picture-Example Implementation, etc.
Image Database Processng	Relational Operators (JOIN, UNION, INTERSECTION, PROJECTION, COMPLEMENT), Image-Sketch-Relation Conversion, Similarity Retrieval, Data Structures, Priority Queues, Dynamic Programming, Spatial Operators, etc.

Consider the following example. Given a triangular matrix U, we want to compute its inverse matrix $V = U^{-1}$

$$U^{-1} = \begin{bmatrix} U_{11} & U_{12} & U_{13} & U_{14} \\ 0 & U_{22} & U_{23} & U_{24} \\ 0 & 0 & U_{33} & U_{34} \\ 0 & 0 & 0 & U_{44} \end{bmatrix}^{-1} = \begin{bmatrix} V_{11} & V_{12} & V_{13} & V_{14} \\ 0 & V_{22} & V_{23} & V_{24} \\ 0 & 0 & V_{33} & V_{34} \\ 0 & 0 & 0 & V_{44} \end{bmatrix} = V$$

Each square box in Fig. 8 corresponds to a VLSI matrix arithmetic device for handling submatrix computations. The input to the pipeline is an n x n upper triangular matrix U partitioned into k^2 submatrices each of dimension m x m, where $n = k \cdot m$. Listed below are required submatrix computations in four sequential steps to generate the inverse matrix V in a partitioned fashion. Note that U_{ij} and V_{ij} are m x m submatrices and U_{ii} and V_{ii} are both upper triangular m x m submatrices.

The partitioned matrix inversion for $k = n/m = 4$ consists of the following steps:

Step 1. $V_{ii} = U_{ii}^{-1}$ for i=1,2,3,4

Step 2. $V_{i,i+1} = -V_{ii}(U_{i,i+1} \cdot V_{i+1,i+1})$ for i=1,2,3

Step 3. $V_{i,i+2} = -V_{ii}(U_{i,i+1} \cdot V_{i+1,i+3} + U_{i,i+2} \cdot V_{i+2,i+2})$; for i=1,2

Step 4. $V_{14} = -V_{11}(U_{12} \cdot V_{24} + U_{13} \cdot V_{34} + U_{14} \cdot V_{44})$

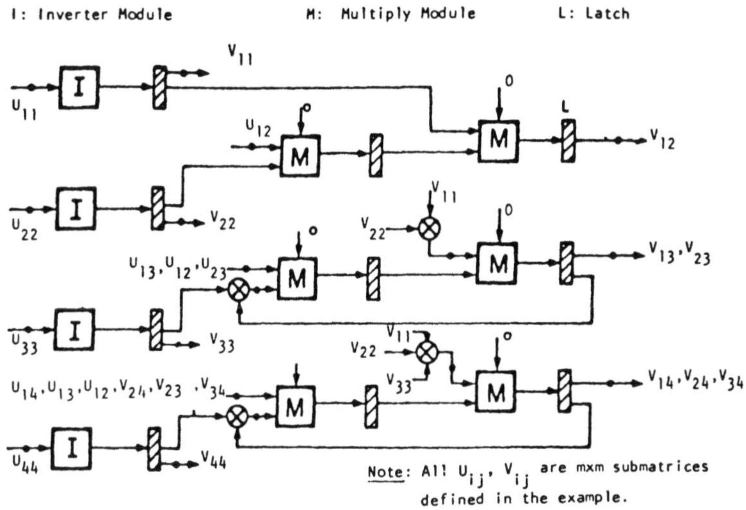

Fig. 8 A pipelined VLSI matrix inverter for partitioned matrix inversion with $k^2 = (n/m)^2 = 4^2 = 16$ submatrix computations.

The I-modules in Fig. 8 are used to perform the inversion of the m x m upper-triangular submatrices at step 1. The M modules are used to perform the cumulative matrix multiplications specified in Steps 2 through 4. The inputs and outputs at four successive computation steps are indicated at the I/O terminals. In general, to invert an n x n triangular matrix with this VLSI pipeline, k I-modules and 2(k - 1) M-modules must be used. Thus, the total VLSI module count equals $O(k) = O(n/m)$ for $n >> m$. The total time delay to generate $V = U^{-1}$ equals $O(n^2/m)$ for $n >> m$.

An application of these VLSI matrix manipulation networks is shown in Fig. 9 for the construction of a hardware feature extractor based on Foley and Sammon's algorithm. Arithmetic pipelines can be similarly constructed for matrix multiply, L-U decomposition, and training sample manipulation using these VLSI arithmetic modules. Details of these VLSI matrix solvers can be found in [9,10].

Context-Free Language Recognition

A VLSI systolic array for high-speech recognition of context-free languages is shown in Fig. 10. The recognition process is based on

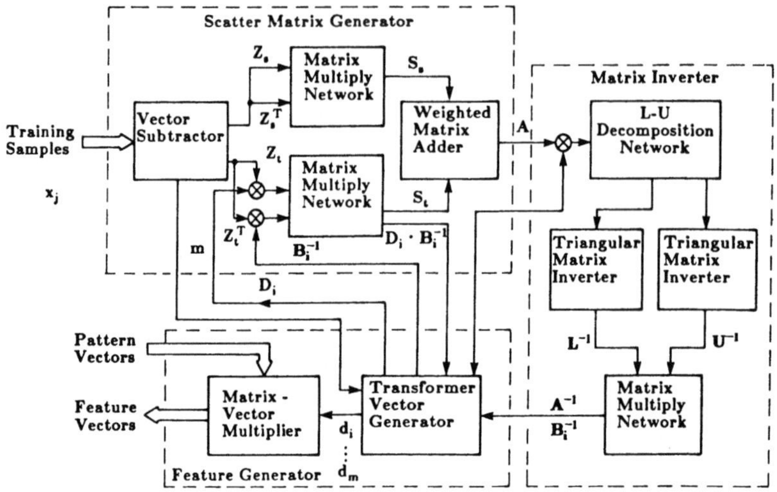

Fig. 9 Functional block diagram of a VLSI feature extractor

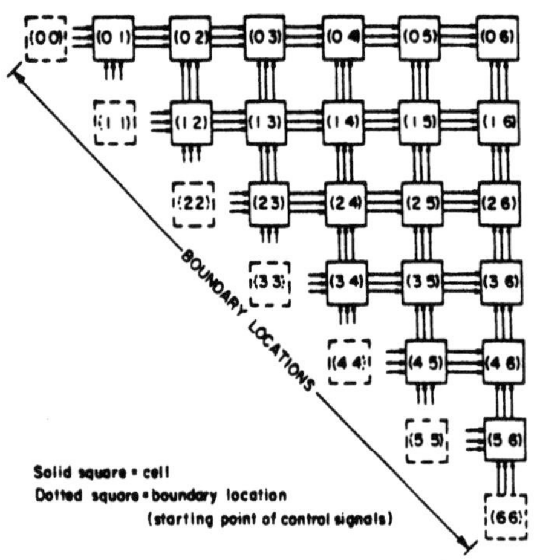

Fig. 10 Systolic array for context-free language recognition

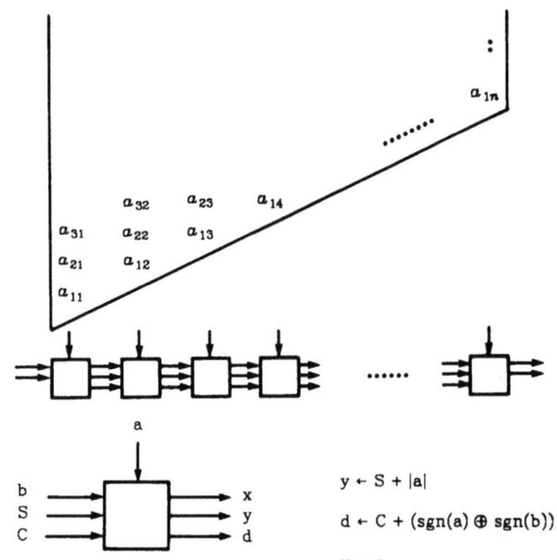

Fig. 11 Processor array, data movement and operations of each processor for feature extraction

the Cocke-Kasami-Younger algorithm. This pipelined triangular array, constructed of n(n+1)/2 processing cells, can be applied in syntactic pattern recognition. Each cell has two unidirectional data channels and one control line along each direction. Data appear as strings of symbols flowing through the recognition matrix from left to right and bottom to top. This two-dimensional array can recognize any input string of length n in 2n time units. This context-free language recognizer and its extension to recognize finite-state languages are described in more detail in [5]. A VLSI architecture for high-speed recognition of context-free languages using Earley's algorithm has recently been proposed [4].

VLSI Seismic Classification

A special-purpose VLSI processor is presented below for fast classification of seismic waveforms [24]. This special-purpose processor which contains three systolic arrays can be attached to a host computer. Each systolic array has time complexity O(1) provided that input data can be properly supplied. The systolic array for feature extraction contains linearly connected processing elements as shown in Fig. 11. The input data, which are the digitized and quantized seismic waveform coded in binary form, are stored in separate memory modules in a skewed format. Two features, zero-crossing count and sum of absolute magnitudes, are computed. All the n PE's compute the two features simultaneously and pass the partial results to the next PE's.

It is well-known that the Levenshtein distance between two strings can be computed by a dynamic programming procedure. We have developed a processor array for this string matching computation in Fig. 12. The proposed string matcher can be used for any problem where the

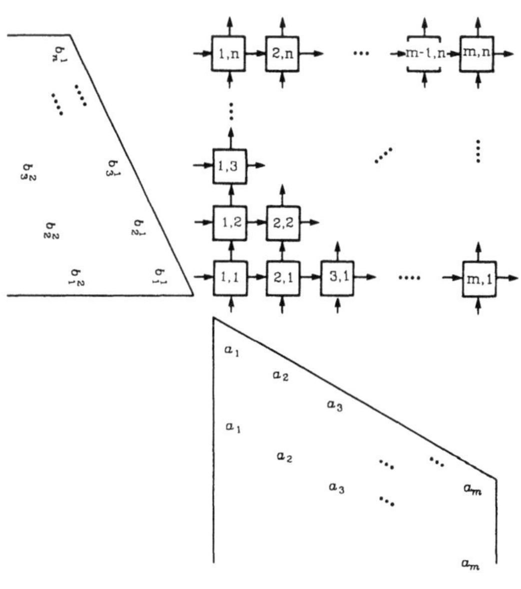

Fig. 12 Processor array and data movement for computing Levenshtein distance

Levenshtein distance computation is required. It can be used for string matching in our seismic recognition, for character string matching in information retrieval or for pattern matching in shape analysis if the object can be represented by a string. The primitive recognizer can also be applied to any minimum-distance recognition problem and vector pattern matching. Simulations have been performed for three systolic arrays: feature extraction array, primitive recognition array and string matching array.

V. DISTRIBUTED SCHEDULING OF VLSI RESOURCES

In general, an interconnection network routes requests from a set of source points to a set of destination points (they may coincide with each other). In a resource sharing mode, the destination points are identical (or sets of identical) resources such as special purpose VLSI chips for which requests or tasks can be delegated to. In this respect, jobs initiated at source processors can be sent to any one of the free resources of a given type at the destination. This is the important point that differentiates resource sharing from address mapping.

Since the system operates continuously, requests from source processors can be initiated at random times. At any time, a set of processors may be making requests and a set of resources are free. It is the function of a scheduler to route the requests in order to connect the maximum number of resources to the processors, that is, to have the maximum resource utilization.

The earliest study of networks for resource sharing has been realized with centralized control. A uni-bus is used in a time shared fashion for connecting peripheral I/O devices to the CPU. Multiple time-shared buses have been used in the PLURIBUS minicomputer multiprocessor. A cross-bar switch has been used in C.mmp although the network is mostly used in address mapping mode. The single or multiple bus approach is a source of bottleneck, and is the least expensive design.

The cross-bar switch is the most expensive network but has the least degree of blocking. A compromise is to use a less expensive network than the cross-bar switch and has less blocking probability than the single bus systems. This has been studied with respect to the Banyan network. A tree network is proposed to aid the scheduler in choosing a resource to allocate. The tree network has a delay of $O(\log_2 n)$ in selecting a free resource (n is the total number of resources).

A solution which avoids the sequential scheduling of requests is to allow requests to be sent without any destination tags and it is the responsibility of the network to route the maximum number of requests to the free resources. In this way, the scheduling intelligence is distributed in the interconnection network. This approach permits multiple requests to be routed simultaneously. We termed this network a resource sharing network [25,26].

The distributed algorithm is implemented by distributing the routing intelligence into the interconnection network so that there is no centralized control. Each exchange box can resolve conflicts and route requests to the appropriate destinations. If a request is blocked, it will be sent back to the originating exchange box in the previous stage. Request routing is, thus, dynamic and all the exchange boxes operate independently.

The distributed algorithm is illustrated in Figure 13 on an 8 by 8 Omega network. Suppose resources R_0, R_1, R_4 and R_5 are available and status information are passed to the processors. The number on the output/input ports represent the status information received/sent. Assuming that P_0, P_3, P_4, and P_5 are requesting one resource each, the

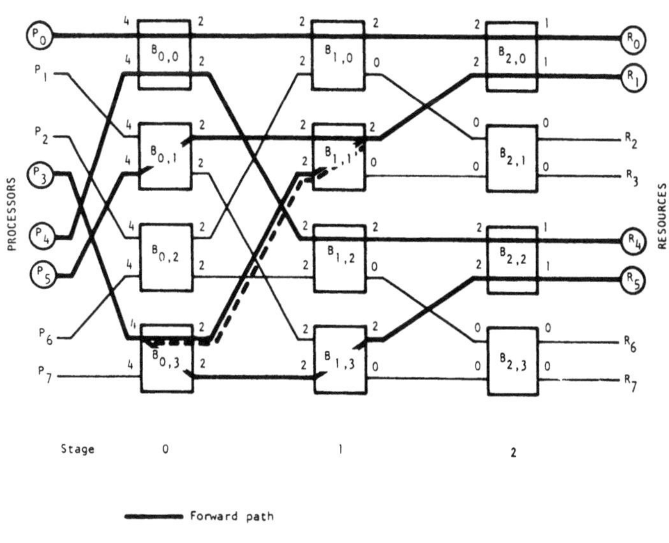

Fig. 13 Example of Omega network with four requesting processors and four free resources, (25% of requests are blocked and backtracked; 100% resource allocation; average delay = 3.50 units)

requests are sent simultaneously to the network after new status information arrives. In stage 0, no conflict is encountered. $B_{1,1}$ and stage 1 receives two requests. Since only one output terminal leads to free resources, the request originating from $B_{0,3}$ is rejected. This request, subsequently, finds another route via $B_{1,3}$ and $B_{2,2}$ to R_5. In this example, each request has to pass through 3.5 exchange boxes on the average before it finds a free resource.

VI. IMAGE DATABASE MACHINE

A database machine for image processing can be identified to have the following functional features. High level database functions such as selection, projection, and join are implemented. These operations are useful for manipulating the image database. On the other hand, low level image processing operations such as histogramming and edge detection are also implemented. An image database machine is, therefore, a conventional database machine enhanced with low level image processing hardware.

We have previously studied the design of a relational database system for images--IMAID [3]--and a relational database machine--DIALOG [16]. IMAID is designed as an integrated database system interfaced with an image understanding system for the efficient storage and retrieval of image and pictures. By using image processing and pattern recognition manipulation functions, structures and features of images are extracted and integrated into relational databases. A relational query language, query-by-pictorial example (QPE) is introduced for manipulating queries regarding spatial relations as well as conventional queries.

A general assumption about VLSI chips are that they are inexpensive. For complex operations, this is not really true due to the fact that external control, timing, memory, and software must be provided. Furthermore, as the types of VLSI chips increase and the degree of replication is large, the system becomes expensive. A solution to this problem is to use a resource sharing network so that a pool of common resources can be used. VLSI chips are distributed into each storage module. They can be used for real-time off-the-track processing. A pool of common resources is also shared among the storage modules. The resource-sharing interconnection network connects these resources to the storage medium.

VII. CONCLUSIONS

Towards the eventual realization of a VLSI multiprocessor system for the said purposes, we identify below a number of research topics. Some of the listed topics have been investigated for years at various research institutions. Before the technology can be applied for practical applications, still many problems need rigorous research efforts. Related previous researches are identified with the listed tasks. These tasks are not meant to be exhaustive, as the subject matter covers almost all disciplines in computer engineering.

- Develop image description languages, image manipulation language, and pictorial query languages [5].
- Study memory hierarchy for on-line image processing, in particular, fast cache memory for imagery data [12].
- Develop backend image database machines, including both image database structures and management policies [16].
- Compression/decompression techniques for image data communication, storage, and display [13,14].
- Develop specialized VLSI functional chips for image processing (see Table 1).
- Investigate dynamic image processing, change detection, and scene analysis towards computer vision and related applications [13].
- Develop resource arbitration networks for resource sharing in a multiprocessor system with shared VLSI resource pool [26].
- Study reconfigurable architectural controls, partitionable interconnection network design, and macropipelining requirements [12].
- Develop effective resource allocation schemes for multiple pipelining, multiple-SIMD array processing, and asynchronous multiprocessing [26].
- Investigate possible use of data flow concept in designing computers for PRIP and artificial intelligence computations [28].
- Integrate image analysis techniques with natural language and speech processing techniques in designing intelligent robots [12].

REFERENCES

[1] F. A. Briggs, K. S. Fu, K. Hwang, and B. W. Wah, "PUMPS Architecture for Pattern Analysis and Image Database Management," IEEE Trans. Computer, October 1982, pp. 969-982.

[2] F. A. Briggs, M. Dubois, and K. Hwang, "Throughput Analysis and Configuration Design of a Shared-Resource Multiprocessor System: PUMPS," Proc. of 8th Annual Symposium on Computer Architecture, May 1981, pp. 67-80.

[3] N. S. Chang and K. S. Fu, "Picture Query Languages for Pictorial Database Systems," IEEE Computer, Nov. 1981, pp. 23-33.

[4] Y. T. Chiang and K. S. Fu, "A VLSI Architecture for Fast Context-Free Language Recognition (Earley's ALgorithm)," Proc. 3rd International Conference on Distributed Computing Systems, Oct. 18-22, 1982.

[5] K. H. Chu and K. S. Fu, "VLSI Architectures for High-Speed Recognition of General Context-Free Languages and Finite-State Languages," Proc. 9th Int'l. Symp. on Computer Arch., Austin, Texas, April 1982, pp. 43-49.

[6] P. E. Danielsson and S. Levialdi, "Computer Architectures for Pictorial Information Systems," IEEE Computer, November 1981, pp. 53-67.

[7] M. J. Duff and S. Levialdi (Editors), Languages and Architectures for Image Processing, Academic Press, N.Y., 1981.

[8] K. S. Fu and T. Ichikawa (Editors), Special Computer Architecture for Pattern Processing, CRC Press, 1982.

[9] K. Hwang and Y. H. Cheng, "Partitioned Matrix Algorithms for VLSI Arithmetic Systems," IEEE Transactions on Computer, December 1982, pp. 1215-1224.

[10] K. Hwang and S. P. Su, "VLSI Architectures for Feature Extraction and Pattern Classification," Journal of Computer Vision, Graphics, and Image Processing, Vol. 24, No. 2, November 1983.

[11] K. Hwang, S. P. Su, and L. M. Ni, "Vector Computer Architecture and Processing Techniques," in Advances in Computers, Vol. 20 (Yovits, Ed.) Academic Press, 1981, pp. 115-197.

[12] K. Hwang and F. A. Briggs, Computer Architectures for Parallel Processing, McGraw-Hill Book Co., N.Y. March 1984.

[13] M. Onoe, K. Preston, and A. Rosenfeld (Editors), Real-Time/Parallel Computing: Image Analysis, Plenum Press, N.Y. 1981.

[14] K. Preston, Jr. and L. Uhr (Editors), Multicomputers and Image Processing, Academic Press, N.Y. 1982.

[15] J. Sklansky and G. N. Wassel, Pattern Classifiers and Trainable Machines, Springer-Verlag, N.Y. 1981.

[16] B. W. Wah and S. B. Yao, "DIALOG - A Distributed Processor Organization for Database Machine," Proc. of NCC, Vol. 49, AFIPS Press, 1980, pp. 243-253.

[17] F. A. Briggs, K. S. Fu, K. Hwang, and J. H. Patel, "PM^4 - A Reconfigurable Multiprocessor System for Pattern Recognition and Image Processing," Proc. of NCC, 1979, pp. 255-265.

[18] R. Hon and D. R. Reddy, "The Effect of Computer Architecture on Algorithm Decomposition and Performance," in High-Speed Computers and Algorithm Organization (Kuck, et al. editors), Academic Press, 1977, pp. 411-421.

[19] J. H. Patel, "Performance of Processor-Memory Interconnection for Multiprocessors," IEEE Trans. on Computers, Vol. C-30, No. 10, pp. 771-780, Oct. 1981.

[20] C. V. Ramamoorthy, J. L. Turner, and B. W. Wah, "A Design of a Cellular Associative Memory for Ordered Retrieval," IEEE Trans. on Computers, Vol. C-27, No. 9, Sept. 1978.

[21] B. D. Rathi, A. R. Tripathi and G. J. Lipovski, "Hardwired Resource Allocators for Reconfigurable Architectures," Proc. of 1980 International Conference on Parallel Processing, pp. 109-117, Aug. 1980.

[22] K. Hwang and K. S. Fu, "Integrated Computer Architectures for Image Processing and Database Management," IEEE Computer, Jan. 1983, pp. 51-61.

[24] H. H. Liu and K. S. Fu, "VLSI Systolic Processor for Fast Seismic Classification," Proc. of 1983 Int'l. Symp. on VLSI Tech., Systems, and Appl., Taipei, Taiwan, March 31, 1983.

[25] B. W. Wah and A. Hicks, "Distributed Scheduling of Resources on Interconnection Networks," Proc. of NCC, AFIPS Press, June 1982.

[26] B. W. Wah, A Comparative Study of Resource Sharing on Multiprocessors," Proc. of 10th Annual Symposium on Computer Architecture, June 1983, pp. 301-308.

[27] K. S. Fu, Syntactic Pattern Recognition and Applications, Prentice Hall, 1982.

[28] S. Hanaki, and T. Temma, "Template Controlled Image Processor (TIP) Project" in Multicomputers and Image Processing, (Preston and Uhr, Editors), Academic Press, New York, 1982, pp. 343-352.

ONE, TWO,...MANY PROCESSORS FOR IMAGE PROCESSING

S. Levialdi
Institute of Information Sciences
University of Bari, Italy

1. Computation with a sequential uniprocessor

We are witnessing a great number of modifications in the computing systems that are designed, built and available to the community. Not all of these changes are radical and some are only technical, yet it may be important to trace back the origins of these changes and, if possible, predict the future trends, particularly within the field domain of this Institute: spatially distributed data analysis.

Let us start from the first computer: conceptually the one based on the Von Neumann architecture, commercially called the Univac 1, available on the market in 1951. As we all know, this machine was oriented to business applications and even if it was a remarkable engine at that time, it may make us smile to-day when our children play videogames on microprocessor-based machines.

For reasons of computational efficiency but also because a better understanding of the classical sequential computer is now achieved, this structure has been severely criticized. As clearly pointed out in (1), the main problems that directly follow from that architectural design are: a) a one word-at-a-time processing of information and b) a store-to-store mapping performed in the actual computation.

In fact, the main activity of the processing unit of this computer is to fetch the data (or the instruction) whilst a very small time is dedicated to perform the real computation. The address calculation may consume a large amount of time, specially when an indirect or indexed mode is employed.

The second point, b) refers to the fact that programs always map stores into stores, i.e. the information coming from a set of named cells will be transformed in some way so as to be placed in a, perhaps different, set of cells. On the contrary, the purpose of a program is to map objects into objects (for instance a set of simultaneous equations into their roots) so that a great burden is put on the programmer who must translate the scope of the program into a mapping of stores where, for instance, the equations with their constants will occupy an initial set of cells and their roots another, final, set. This fact has a number of consequences on the difficulties of writing natural, (error prone) programs, but this particular subject does not belong to the theme of this talk.

In conclusion, it has been firmly established by a number of authors that the Von Neumann architecture, although being extremely general purpose (hence its name) is not adequate for fast and efficient computation.

2. Architectonics

2.1 Definitions

At this point it seems appropriate to introduce the concept of computer ar-

NATO ASI Series, Vol. F18
Computer Architectures for Spatially Distributed Data
Edited by H. Freeman and G. G. Pieroni

chitecture in a modern way, as done by G.J. Myers (2) where he considers the different possible implications that this word may have.

If we now refer to the drawing of figure 1, we may see a number of areas with labels that represent the different typical functions a processing system must have. Each architecture is defined by the positions of the borders between the different functional areas. The first kind of architecture, called system architecture, will determine which data processing functions will be provided by the system and which by the user; two different interfaces are available to the outside world: the programming language and the system application.

The borders labelled 2,3 and 4 do not correspond to specific architectures; logical resource management and physical resource management regard data base management, virtual-storage management etc. and teleprocessing-network management respectively. These three last levels fall under software architecture.

The next level, 5, is the frontier between the system's software and firmware and hardware. More precisely, this level represents the abstraction of the system's physical representation as seen by the software: it corresponds to the computer architecture.

The levels 7, 9 and 10 represent the distribution of the input/output processors with regards to the input/output controllers. This section falls under the input/output architecture.

Level 8 is the interface between the processor and the main memory, whilst level 6 is connected to the microprogram architecture: levels 6 and 8 may be called processor architecture.

If we now consider the block diagram along a vertical direction (a horizontal direction was chosen before) we may discuss how to distribute the system functions by means of a number of processors: this kind of architecture is called configuration architecture.

The main task of a computer architect is to decide which functions must be performed by the hardware and which by the software so as to define and design the interface between them.

A main point towards the clarification of the computer architecture, as defined here, is that the purpose of the new architecture must be to increase the efficiency of the problem solution more than just speeding up the calculations.

The efficiency referred to above, involves the interrelationships between the programming language, the compiler and the machine. In the new computer architectures less bits will be transmitted between the CPU and the main memory and the instruction set will be more powerful (more can be accomplished with the same instruction). The speed is obviously important, but the number of instructions required for a specific problem solution is the significant issue.

All these ideas regarding definition and features of the role of computer architecture in a modern framework refer to general purpose computers and touch on problems of reliability of programs, automatic fault handling, arithmetical and logical speedup, decrease of compiler complexity, unified view of memory, main memory management, etc. The difference between the high level language concepts and their version at machine level is called semantic gap: the new architectures are aimed towards the reduction of such a gap.

Now that we have a definition of computer architecture and that we also have recalled the main negative aspects of the conventional stored program computer, we may ask ourselves: which are the suggested solutions for designing and building better computers. There are many answers to this question, in fact there are many projects regarding new computer architectures and, as we will see in another lecture, even the problem of classifying the new suggested architectures is not an easy one.

2.2 Speed-up factors

From what has already been mentioned, to increase the power of the single processor making it faster will not improve the efficiency very much since only a relatively small amount of time is dedicated by the processor to perform computing. Moreover, the breakthrough that we are expecting to accomplish, is related to the processing of spatial data, a very particular structured set of data composed of a collection of picture elements: the "pixels".

It might turn useful to quote (3) where a table is presented, showing the different speedups that may be obtained by different means. Refer to fig.2. As can easily be seen, the major increase in speed can be gained by architectural changes, although the interest in the other factors, belonging to related disciplines, is still strong and important. As a confirmation that the artificial intelligence techniques will be applied in practice, we may see from the table that both knowledge sources (to-day used in expert systems) and heuristics, may provide from 10 to 1000 speed increase.

All what has been mentioned pushes towards the remodelling of what a computer system should be like.

In fact, the first idea which came into the mind of the architects was to use more than one processor, i.e. a multiprocessor system. Since microprocessors are already built in large quantities and their price is rapidly decreasing (although we are near the limit), they are the candidate processing elements for the new computing systems.

In this way if most (or even better all) processors of the system are active, the concurrent execution of the tasks will, theoretically, enhance the performance by a factor which is at most, of the order of the number of processors.

2.3 Expected performance gains

Unfortunately it is not so easy to ensure that all the processors remain active during all the time. Moreover, according to Grosch's Law (see (4)) the processors performance is proportional to the square root of its cost. In other words, with a cost of a single processor given by two we improve the system so that the performance gain is of root two. Yet,with the advances in microprocessor technology, we are approaching a "no cost" processing power with respect to the cost of the other parts of the system, we may therefore straighten the curve originally suggested by Grosch. (See figure 3).

If Grosch's law is extended in the upper region the speed-up is limited by technological reasons (influence of the speed of light and the maximum density at which processors may be integrated) so that the performance does not increase indefinitely. (Trans-Grosch range on figure 3).

Some authors have suggested that the computer manufacturers have used Grosch's model for their pricing policy; so as to encourage sales of their most powerful systems the pricing curve becomes steeper so that their price does no reflect their real performance value. (See figure 4).

The problem of evaluating the cost, with respect to the performance, of a multiprocessor system, is still an open one since cost is largely influenced by the quantity of systems which are produced and sold and performance values depend on the chosen benchmarks.

The performance is also dependent on the operating system which assigns the tasks but, above all, on the well-matchedness of the algorithms which are implemented on the machine, (See (6)).

Since processors must communicate, a number of paths must be provided between each processor and all the remaining ones, this number grows quadratically with the number of processors, $O(n^2)$. A measure of global complexity, G (introduced in ref.5) can be given using the total number of paths:

$$G \text{ (global complexity)} = n(n-1)/2$$

so that for a system having 5 processors G= 5.(5-1)/2=10, for 7 processors G = 7(7-1)/2 = 21. (Refer to fig.5).

If the number of processors increases, and we have 50, 100 or so processors, the traffic of information becomes very heavy, a common bus is not able to support the system and other communication structures are required.

In the first place it becomes mandatory that each processor has its own memory regardless of the existence of a common memory of the system. In a simplified manner we may consider four basic types of interconnection schemes: common bus, star, ring and fully connected (which is the one on which the G factor was computed), see figure 6.

2.4 Interconnection schemes

As is often the case in the computing structures applied to the image processing field, the "restricted neighborhood" has substituted the "fully connected" pattern of connectivity.

Two reasons are the driving forces behind this scheme: a) the reduction in hardware complexity and b) the adaptation of this structure to the typical kind of local operations that are usually performed on images.

In a manner analogous to the influence a programming language has on the way a program is written, the system structure guides the kind of operations that will be optimally performed on the machine; neighborhood connectivity will enhance the performance of local operations and will assist in coding them naturally in a high level language.

In general terms, the problems of interconnecting processors and memory, independently from the application, can be solved by a number of networks which are called banyan and reduce the complexity of the connections from n^2 to nlogn. If we refer to figures 6,7 from ref.7, we may see the first interconnection pattern which is known as the crossbar switch and which has in matrix form, one connection from each processor to each memory bank bringing therefore the total number of interconnections to exactly n^2.

It is clearly very expensive to use such a network for a number of processors which exceed 50 since the typical number of processors for the multiprocessor system is generally above 100. The second network, a banyan one, has a spread of 2 (two lines entering each switching node) and also a fanout of 2 (two lines leaving each node) and three levels from apex to base. In this case we have only nlogn connections, each processor may communicate with any memory module.

Another banyan network, known as the omega network, is built with "perfect shuffle" connections, i.e. each element has the possibility of being exchanged with a symmetrical element around an axis which divides the number of elements exactly in half, like in a card deck when a shuffle in performed.

Again, in the omega network, the number of connections is nlogn and, furthermore, the switching arrangement can be binary coded according to which final memory module is required to be connected.

2.5. Reliability

In a very recent paper (8), a number of issues have been raised to motivate and understand the importance and implications of multimicroprocessor systems. For instance one important factor involved in these systems is reliability which is described in slightly different terms than those usually referred to in conventional uni-processor systems where meantime-between-failure (MTBF) is the standard parameter.

Generally, multiprocessing systems use redundancy in two ways: they do have a number of identical units operating together to protect against errors (massive redundancy) and in other systems when a fault is detected, a procedure will switch from a faulty element to a spare one operating correctly, (selective redundancy).

Fault-tolerance can be obtained if some jobs are transferred from some units to other available ones possibly without impairing the performance; another important point is to ensure a continuity of operation even when some units are malfunctioning, this is usually referred to as graceful degradation or soft-fail mode.

In some systems there is even the possibility of reconfiguring the processing units and of reallocating job responsibilities among other system elements: this provides flexibility that may ease further expansion of the system.

In the concluding remarks of the quoted paper some hints are given as to when it is appropriate to choose a multiprocessor system: in elaborate process control applications with different computational requirements, in applications with extensive input-output processing and in applications which require a high degree of reliability but due to cost considerations cannot make use of massive redundancy.

If we now refer to the specific field of image processing as termed in this Institute, the analysis of spatially distributed data, I believe that the last two points are pertinent. In fact the large amount of information to be input to a machine to be stored, processed, displayed and output plus the need to ensure a correct result on all the elements of the image (since the error may propagate along the image from a pixel to its surrounding pixels) correspond to the two points previously mentioned.

In short, during the last five years a relatively wide number of different architectures for image processing have been suggested and built (see 9, 10 and 11), some of them will be discussed during this Institute.

3. Some recent systems

3.1 Spatial Information System

We must now explore some of the newly suggested architectures so as to understand which are the different approaches to the general problem of designing better computing structures for image processing. Let us firstly refer to the project of a Spatial Information System (refer to (12)) which is based on an entity oriented approach of a spatial relational data base system. Since the main goal of the system is to fastly retrieve data from secondary memory, two facts influence the design of the system: a) the use of a predicate (like join, select and division) and b) the hypothesis that most of the tasks require sequential analysis of all the tuples of a relation in order to obtain an answer.

The general operation looks for all the tuples satisfying a given condition, either a constant one or one depending on the tuples currently examined in a related relation. In this last case some concurrent processing may be performed by subdividing the tuples in the relation into mutually exclusive subsets so as to have one processor dealing with the tuples in the subset assigned to it. Finally, all results are collected and output when available. To increase speed, the mass storage device can be preliminarly read and this information stored in the memory of an input processor which acts as a queue ensuring that it has the tuples to be requested.

The main idea on which this system is based is the emphasis on representations of the spatial data and of the organization of geographic data in a relational data base.

For their particular application, stream data and road data were the specific pictorial information to be stored. The basic entities were regions, described by polygons with closed boundary, water streams, streams; roads network represented by chains of ordered lists of points, roads, labels which were given by a point with coordinates.

The relational approach is independent from the way in which the image is given, either in raster on in vector form, so that in order to obtain the wanted information a high level query language may be used. Very briefly, the relational base uses a unified approach to store the geographical information in a universal structure. Basically, couples of attribute-value are written having the form A/V = ((a,v)) like Age, 23 as a crude example. Each entity (in our case we have spatial entities) has global properties, component parts and related spatial entities; each spatial data structure has one distinguished binary relation containing the global properties of the entity that the structure represents.

Each spatial data structure of type REGION has four relations: 1) the A/V relation, A/V REGION, 2) SUBREGION ADJACENCY, 3) STREAM NETWORK and 4) LABELS. The A/V relation has four attributes: NAME (its value is a character string with the name): AREA whose value is a number corresponding to the area; BOUNDARY, whose value is a spatial data structure of type POLYGON representing the boundary, and PARENT which is a spatial structure of type REGION representing the next immediate region which contains the region under study.

The kind of queries which they expect to answer with the system are: how many rivers are there in region X? or how many streams of any kind are in region X? down to what points do stream X and Y have in common? etc.

Three different kinds of operations are involved in answering the queries: low-level access (quick look-up), high level relational operators and geometric operations.

The high level relational operations must extract information from the Spatial Information System referenced by each tuple of a given relation, select tuples of a relation that satisfy a constraint, join pairs of tuples from two relations, project a relation onto certain columns and select tuples of a relation that satisfy a constraint with respect to every tuple of a second relation. As it may now be seen, a generalized form of the relational database operators will prove adequate for the spatial information system.

Although this system is still on an experimental stage some tests were already performed by simulation on a Vax machine using the VMS file system.

A general spatial data structure is the core of this system and demonstrates the possibility of storing and retrieving a wide number of entities that are in a certain well defined relation with other entities, i.e. it allows queries on arbitrary predicates. Relations could be stored by column instead of by tuple and some parallel processors would help in speeding up the mechanism of generalized queries.

3.2 The PICCOLO

Along similar lines to the ones described before, a project named PICCOLO, (see ref. (13)), may provide us with a greater insight regarding the pictorial database approach to an operational image processing system.

The two main issues which have been addressed in this project are the representation problem and the high speed which is required from the system to be a practically usable one.

Representation implies the possibility of storing both logical and physical images, the relationships between the objects belonging to each kind of images and the relations between such relations. Physical images refer to the classic pixel format (arrays of picture elements each one having a grey level value) and logical images refer to a more abstract representation like a quadtree (see 14) or a minimum spanning tree (see 15), shortly named MST.

The authors also coin a term, "architecture engineering" which refers to inclusion of four separate sequential steps in the design of an overall system: a) the requirement specifications, b) the logical framework decisions, c) the architectural decisions and d) the design interfacing. This kind of engineering, contrasts the more typical process of using the available hardware (computer system) and adapting it to the application by means of special software and tailored interfaces.

Another important point when considering physical and logical images in a unified manner is that one may go from each one of these images to the other with the same ease: from a physical to a logical one is the direction used in pattern recognition applications whilst from the logical one to a physical one concerns the computer graphics field where a synthesis of the image is required on the display once a preliminary description has been given (the logical image).

In conclusion, the three main goals that were set for PICCOLO are:

1) Uniformity of representation
2) Concurrency of execution (as much as possible)
3) Representations and their relationships should be treated within the same framework.

PICCOLO uses a relational model to embed the pictorial data structure and the relationships between the objects contained in the images (physical and logical). For instance, an array of pixels is represented by little circles (objects) and arrows (direction relationship), if the arrow points rightwards the relation is "on the right of", if the arrow points downwards the relation is "below", refer to figure 8.

The extension of the relational model refers to the concept of "generic tuple" which substitutes a set of tuples by the rules they obey so compacting the information.

Let us show with some examples how is an image represented in PICCOLO. The figure 9 (from (13)) illustrates the quadtree, the MST and region representations to see whether an object belongs to a region or not.

To show how the physical image can be manipulated to provide the MST (in this example, two objects are connected if their grey value difference is smaller than a threshold); refer to figure 10 (always from ref. (13)).

The process of finding objects, computing predicates and obtaining answers is performed by an abstract machine called "EVAL" which evaluates the extended relational calculus of PICCOLO. The machine is defined recursively, an association list is also defined in order to associate a; [variable] with a [value] [list]::=empty| [list]([variable][value]).

The rightmost pair is the most recent one, when two pairs appear with the identical variable in the list, the value associated with the variable is the rightmost one.

To use the list, a function which returns a value associated with a variable v is defined as follows

```
assoc(v,list):=
      if list = empty then return undef
      else if list = [list]nlist( [variable]x[value]y) then
             if v = x then return y
             else return assoc (v,nlist)
      else error
```

The interesting part of the process performed by EVAL is that many lists may be processed concurrently, they are enclosed in a control structure COBEGIN-COEND.

The term to be evaluated (by EVAL) may be of type constant, or of type variable or of the type function which is the case for concurrent processing of the different arguments, processing resumes when all the arguments are evaluated.

Programs terminate if, for the parallel evaluation of different arguments there is one or more which returns value undefined after a second try in a modified list.

Since there are many similarities between the architecture envisaged for PICCOLO and the AHR machine proposed and built by Guzmàn (see ref. 16) a slight modification of the AHR is suggested so as to include a processor to take charge of the data base. Such a processor is added to the common bus where all the other processors are in charge of evaluating the nodes (LISP functions) stored in the Active Memory of the machine. A Distributor is responsible for assigning the nodes (in FIFO style) to the processors. This project is now oriented towards the selection of strategies for processor allocation (in order to increase the computation speed) and also to the design of an interface for a secondary storage memory to contain the data base.

The uniformity of the data structure is the main feature of this system which allows the access of different kinds of images and the processing of a logical image or a physical one and their relations within the same framework; moreover, concurrent execution and the concept of generic tuple speed up the processing and save storage memory.

3.3 Task-oriented architectures

Another, rather different approach, is the one followed by (17) in which most of the effort is dedicated to the reformulation of the algorithms and the design of the architecture and systems programming whilst only a small amount of effort is dedicated to the hardware design.

The authors claim that three points are the essential guiding principles for developing task-oriented architectures:

1) consider the hardware developed as a piece which may be discarded even after a short amount of time; i.e. throwaway hardware!
2) two activities must be correctly planned (in terms of man-years) custom architectures and tools for producing software (operating systems, run-time environments, diagnostic aids, etc); the first one should take a relatively short time, the second one is certainly more expensive and therefore longer.
3) The problem must be a real one not a toy case so that the parallel architecture is really mapped from the class of problems and not viceversa.

The algorithm analysis generally proceeds along the lines of an evaluation of the total computational effort and the memory occupation, but it rarely produces the information which is relevant to establish which architecture is most suited, i.e., the characterization of the basic computation. In other words, the architect is interested in the interaction between the class of algorithms and the class of architectures (having something in common, for instance array processors, pipeline machines, etc).

Once an algorithm has been evaluated, it may be restructured so as to isolate the computational part from the rest. For instance in an algorithm regarding the evaluation of a search in a speech recognition system, the greater part of the time is spent accessing large and complex data structures (more than 50%), whilst 5% of the time is spent in arithmetic operations and 10% of the time is spent on comparisons (IF statements). The result of this analysis is to change the access mode to the information (avoiding packing and unpacking, for instance), perhaps using some special hardware implementation and, on the same issue, the data management which was done by Hash codes proved to be time consuming so that another algorithm must be employed.

In order to design the architecture a number of parameters are required: number of operations per second, amount of data to be stored and program size.

Since the search algorithm to be implemented was the most significant part as found in the analysis of the algorithm behaviour, the authors indicate the main features of the search that affect the architecture:

a) a large amount of data has to be accessed in an unpredictable manner
b) the data structures are complex and their access is slow
c) synchronization overhead and delay may become high burdens if many processors are used
d) for more than one processor, the load must be equally distributed in time so as to have task and input independence
e) the algorithm behaviour depends on the input data (speech in this case)
f) some of the data access operations are indivisible; the algorithm requires operations that temporarily invalidate the correctness of the data structure on which it operates
g) the search process can be parallelized since the evaluation of a node only depends on the result of the evaluation of the nodes directly preceeding it.

Since all these features have a relevance on the architecture, the conclusions arrived indicate that the overhead due to synchronization must be minimal, the synchronization delays should be avoided when possible, the load should be dynamically partitioned between processors and the solution should be independent of the language and vocabulary used in the recognition process.

The first two conclusions interact in the sense that decreasing the delay, the overhead increases; in any case by reducing the granularity, in other words breaking down the algorithm into smaller steps, the overhead will be reduced.

In the machine used by these authors (the Harpy Machine, see 18), the synchronization overhead can be kept as low as the time it takes to access one memory location.

The fact of partitioning the load dynamically is necessary because the algorithm will behave differently according to the input. In this algorithm a beam search is performed and the number of expanded nodes depend from case to case, certain times some nodes will be pruned so that it is difficult to predict an equal computing weight on all the available processors. One possibility is to divide the algorithm in small steps letting the first free processor handle the first available task in the queue ("producer-consumer queue"); it works well with the beam search because the paths can be parallel-expanded without much information sharing.

To make the solution task-size independent, fail-soft and also independent from the number of processors a partition of the algrithm is required, the producer-consumer queues are stored in global memory but this may lead to memory contention problems.

The suggested solution, containing all the suggestions brought forward from the algorithm study is a multiprocessor structure (with five processors each having and 8k memory of 16 bit words), a host computer (PDP11/40) and a Data Structure Machine (DSM) containing a shared memory of 4 million bits. This memory is fast and will be addressed by the Data Structure Machine as the requests from the processors arrive, this Machine is responsible for synchronization and load sharing.

Since 50% of the computation is involved in calculating the addresses of the information in the network data structure, the DSM (Data Structure Machine) is designed to perform this task in a much smaller time.

The implementation of the Harpy system is such that the input data (speech) comes from an analog source (the microphone) and the output (recognized words) is visualized on a display. Some parts are in hardware (like the input signal processing stage) and others are in software, as new hardware pieces are finished they substitute the software components. In this way, the parts may be tested, then translated into the microcode, so that errors are cornered and easier to correct.

The hardware development for task-oriented architectures is performed by gradual migration from the simulation on the host computer to the target system, so designing, testing and building one component at a time.

The software development cannot be made in a modular way (think about operating systems, for instance). Within this development a programming environment is required so that debugging, language and operating system support, device control and application program development may be available.

If all these tools are required, an enormous amount of time must be spent on them, therefore all these tools must be obtained from other environments. In task-oriented architectures there is a strong interdependency between hardware and software design and this influences the decomposition of the application software. For bare hardware and an unconventional system, no existing operating system is available and a diverse set of nonconventional debugging functions are required.

Finally the problem of evaluation of the designed architecture crops up and a number of parameters have been indicated like: the execution time of a software module, the utilization of a hardware functional unit or the traffic on a communication link.

In general, no adequate tools are available to perform evaluation of multiprocessor architectures. But on task-oriented architectures it is the tasks themselves that become the tools (see 19). Moreover, in these architectures a number of processes cooperate to solve the task so that security and protection are not important. Sometimes there is an interaction between the measurement and the measure in a program, yet the overhead due to the modification of the program to perform measurements on it is easily determined.

The authors have suggested a Performance Evaluation Machine which, starting from the definition of an "event" (a change of state in the machine that marks a salient change in processing, like a procedure call, a communication of a message, etc.) counts events. It has a number of processing cells, each one specialized in counting specific events with given sampling rate, quite high (every 50nsecs,s for instance) so that the PEM cannot be implemented by a general purpose processor (it would be too slow). The same concept, i.e. a special machine for measuring events, can be applied to debugging VLSI chips (see 20).

For an artificial intelligence task ("When was the last paper by Holland published?") we may see in figure 11 (from ref.17) that the Harpy machine reaches real time recognition with only four processors.

In closing with this work, we may conclude by saying that some general criteria have been established to design task-oriented architectures based on the algorithm analysis, its mapping to the architecture and the introduction of a performance evaluation methodology by means of special hardware.

3.4. A Pseudo-parallel System

This work (ref.21) considers the problem of analyzing moving images and applying an algorithm for image segmentation which forms the key point in the processing of a dynamic scene.

The general scheme of the system is divided into three main stages called peripheral, attentive and cognitive. Each phase has its own knowledge source or knowledge base, according to the stage. The algorithm assumes one stationary telecamera and uniform illumination of the scene but a direct use of parallelism is not possible since data belonging to the various parts of the picture frame interact. In other words, the problem in speeding up the computation is not the one of incrementing the resources (putting more processors to work) but the one of determining the concurrency either by decomposition of the problem or by using a data driven system with decentralized control. The main idea here is to use parallelism within each subtask so as to ease the interprocessor cooperation and coordination. Since the algorithm is divided into sequential steps, the process may be called "pseudo-parallel". The main goal is to ensure that the forward/backward branching is confined within each partitioned step.

The pseudoparallel algorithm converts the serial algorithm into a suitable form to run on a multiprocessor system.

The algorithm for segmenting images containing moving objects may be briefly summarized as a seven-step process: 1) condensed frame generation, 2) difference picture generation, 3) labelling of the picture, 4) detection of motion on the picture, 5) classification of the region 6) extraction of the object and 7) analysis of the motion.

In short, the condensed frame generation compacts the image from 570x512 pixels (each having one of 256 possible grey levels) into 95x128 pixels; each new element is obtained averaging the intensities of the corresponding pixels and also their variance. The difference picture is obtained by comparing two consecutive pictures (previous and current frames) and then computing R (see below) and comparing it with a threshold, if above such threshold a 1 will be put in DP (the difference picture).

R = ((Sp+Sc)/2+((Mp-Mc)/2))**2/(Sp*Sc) where M and S are the mean and the variance, respectively, for a pixel of the condensed frame.

Labelling is obtained by an algorithm which evaluates the presence of edges in three frames: in DP, and in the previous and current frame, called ED, EP, EC respectively. Two operators are used, one for binary images and the other for grey level images. The attribution of labels (1,2,3,4,5) corresponds to the presence of 1 elements in DP which are ($\overline{ED}$, $\overline{EP}$, $\overline{EC}$), (ED,$\overline{EP}$,$\overline{EC}$), (ED, EP,$\overline{EC}$), (ED,$\overline{EP}$,EC) and (ED,EP,EC). The detection of motion is based on the information contained in DP where noise is supposed to generate only isolated dissimilarities and the connected components with more than N elements are considered to be the result of motion. The classification of regions (in a DP) separates occlusion from disocclussion (or both) from the background when a moving object is present. A factor, called CURPRE, gives an indication as to which situation occurs:

CURPRE = # of points labeled 4 in the region/ # of points labeled 3 in the region; occlusion is for CURPRE $\geqslant 1$, disocclusion for CURPRE $\leqslant 1$ and nearly 1 for the remaining case.

By means of region growing for the occlusion and disocclusion types classified above, object masks are generated, they are further improved by refinement techniques; finally the motion is analyzed by measuring velocity and acceleration from the displacement of the image.

Referring to figure 12, a sequential dataflow of the first two stages peripheral and attentive, can be seen. The corresponding computational analysis can be seen on the table of figure 13 where a number of significant parameters like, required processing time, computation mode and required data have been assessed for each functional block.

Since the total process is sequential, there is no possibility of parallelizing it as a whole, parallelism may be introduced within each step so as to pipeline the computation. Moreover, data for each step may be needed not only from the previous step but also from preliminary steps along the process, furthermore the number of useful processors for each step must be determined.

In scanning the table we may see that in the first three blocks we may operate in SIMD mode by partitioning the frame into 20 sections where each section is stored in 20 different memory blocks so as to allow 20 processors to work concurrently. The difference picture requires only 10 processors so that data must be distributed over 10 memory blocks considering two logically adjacent memory modules of the first level as a single macro memory block; multiple-port memory blocks may also be used. By analogy, the third step uses 5 processors for the labelled difference picture generation.

The region growing and refinement steps require three time steps yet only one processor has been allocated to each step, otherwise copies of the data must be supplied to each processor. In motion image analysis a large amount of data is redundant so that it is better not to process all the regions for each frame.

Without entering into details, it may be appropriate to look at the table where the pipelined process may be seen along 10 successive frames, (with the size of each module) as well as the correspondence between the processing step and its storage requirements can be observed.

An important feature of the proposed system is the absence of synchronization problems since each processor has its own program to accomplish the task and a distributed operating system may be adequate to manage all the computing elements.

To increase reliability, some redundant hardware modules could be added at all steps of the processing, extra processors and memory blocks could be the best candidates.

As the authors point out, the main advantage of this scheme is the generality of the procedure: breaking down the algorithm in the sequential steps, parallelizing each step, timing each step and balancing the computational requirements so as to have just the maximum number of required processors and memory blocks. As is well known, the important part of the analysis is the discovery of the independent operations to be performed on the image, this ensures the correct parallelization of the process.

4. Computational power of different systems

4.1 Time evaluation

In (19) a tentative approach to the evaluation of existing architectures for image processing has been attempted. Although a number of important questions must be answered before trying to score the merits of existing architectures, like the "well matchedness"' between the algorithm to be implemented and the architecture on which such an algorithm will be mapped, a cautious approach selects a number of benchmarks and tries them on well defined architectures. In the referenced paper the chosen architectures are four: a) the sequential machine, b) the SIMD machine, c) the pipeline machine and d) the paracomputer or Schwarz machine.

The chosen tasks were the point operations, the local operations, histogramming, co-occurrence matrix computation and the 2D Fourier transform.

The analysis was performed in terms of time dependency of each task from the chosen architecture split into two components: execution time and communication time (time required to load the data and the instructions into the processors memories).

The conclusions of this analysis were that only the SIMD architecture requires more communication time than computation time in general whilst the sequential computer is the slowest (an easily predictable result) and the paracomputer (a theoretical machine that, by definition, does not have memory contention problems) is the fastest. The pipeline architecture performs well as long as the algorithm is perfectly broken down into the processors along the pipe.

According to the selected benchmark there are spans of two orders of magnitude in the obtained time figures: this shows the strong dependency of the architecture from the task. For instance the availability of data to the active processors-so as to have a good utilization of the active resources of the system-is strongly influenced by the system organization, i.e. the architecture of the computing system.

4.2 Active resources evaluation

In sequential computing systems, the traditional measurement for system efficiency is the percentage of CPU utilization time during the execution of a program. In general, a system will be rated as a poor one if this percentage is lower than 30% whilst it will be considered an efficient one if the percentage is higher than 70%. The problems which influence the correct appraisal of the system utilization as a whole (as compared to the utilization of its processing unit) are those concerning the specific tasks that the processor is executing: are they all relevant to the program execution? or even better, are they necessary at all? In fact, as seen at the beginning of this paper, and largely discussed in many different places, the processor activity is mostly dedicated to the instruction and data fetch ad only marginally dedicated to the actual computation; this is a consequence of the Von Neumann architecture. Turning now to some of the systems that have been suggested for image processing applications, the usage of processors is dependent on the chosen architecture and on the task. For instance, in array processors each computing unit only works for executing "useful" instructions on the image data.

In (22) some interesting considerations are made as to the detection of "active resources" to introduce a criteria to compare different architectures and their efficiency in performing image processing tasks.

Active resources can be gates, connecting wires, memories, or switches but can be normalized in the sense that 1 bitgates are assumed throughout as a unit. If we refer to figure 15 (from 23) we may see an interesting comparison between the ways in which active resources are deployed in serial computers (small, medium, large and super) and in the 1-bit SIMD arrays.

Some real machines are considered and analized like the CLIP4 (23) the DAP (24) and the MPP, (25).

We may deduce from the table that in the traditional computers about 99% of the gates regard the memory whilst in an extreme case only 9% of the gates in a SIMD machine are used for the memory (the CLIP4 machine), the DAP has still 98% in memory and MPP 63% in memory.

As mentioned before, the activity of the processor does not imply "useful activity" so that we must monitor it to deduce the relevance of such activity. As previously discussed, some activity of the processor must be dedicated to data communication to resolve memory contention, to load its program (in cases where the programs come from a host computer), etc. All this produces overhead and a waste (from the point of view of the computation) of processor's time.

Pipeline architectures (26) use specialized tasks to be implemented on simple processors having small memories, one single controller (generally the host computer) is employed.

Finally, systolic computers (27) use a two dimensional pipeline to map, in hardware, an algorithm so increasing efficiency at the expense of flexibility.

5. Summing up

A number of concepts concerning parallel architectures have been reviewed in connection with some recent projects aiming at the implementation of an efficient image processing system.

The need to increase throughput, computational efficiency and reliability of the existing systems is dictated by modern applications which are always more demanding.

The use of parallel processing to achieve the above aims has been developed pragmatically and experimentally in the past with a number of theoretical papers which concentrated on the formal description of computational models (28).

Such models considered the communication and synchronization problems, the data access to ensure and adequate use of the existing processors and also suggested a notation and primitives to be incorporated to high level languages for improving the description and understanding of concurrency at the computational level.

There is no doubt that the progress in this field is strongly dependent upon the new technologies, particularly the VLSI one; yet no real progress can be achieved if a methodology for "parallel thinking" is not defined so as to allow the natural formulation of algorithms in parallel terms so that the architecture can exploit such algorithm re-formulation. As shown in 3.3 a deep analysis of the algorithm is required in order to achieve this result.

Factors influencing the architectural design are: the choice of the instruction set, the control structure that will allow a branch in a concurrent execution situation, the data representation and compression in the machine, the extension of an existing high level language to match the image processing requirements, and the formal description (which allows the simulation) of a candidate architecture (29).

6. Acknowledgements

I want to express my sincere gratitute to Miss E. Lampugnani for typing the manuscript and Mr. B. Bia for drawing the figures.

REFERENCES

1. J. Backus, "Function-level computing", IEEE Spectrum, 1982, August, pp.22-27.

2. G.J. Myers, Advances in Computer Architecture, John Wiley & Sons, 1978.

3. D. Reddy, A. Newell, "A multiplicative speed-up of systems", in Perspectives on Computer Science, ed A.K. Jones, Academic Press, New York, 1978.

4. A. Baum, D. Senzing, "Hardware considerations in a Microcomputer Multiprocessor system", Digest of Papers Compcon Spring 75, San Francisco, Calif. Feb. 1975, pp.27-30.

5. W. Händler, "Innovative computer architecture" in Parallel Processing Systems, edit. D.J. Evans, Cambridge University Press, 1982, pp.1-42.

6. V. Cantoni, S. Levialdi, "Matching the task to an Image Processing Architecture", to appear on Image Processing, Vision and Computer Graphics, 1983.

7. R. Bernhard, "Computing at the speed limit", IEEE Spectrum, July 1982, pp.26-31.

8. E.T. Fathi, M. Krieger, "Multiple Microprocessor systems: What, Why and When", IEEE Computer, 1983 March, pp.23-32.

9. Real-time/parallel computing, edit. M. Onoe, K. Preston Jr., A. Rosenfeld, Plenum Press, 1981.

10. M.J.B. Duff, S. Levialdi, edits. Language and Architectures for Image Processing, Academic Press, London, 1981.

11. K. Preston Jr., L. Uhr, Multicomputers and Image Processing, Academic Press, London, 1982.

12. P.D. Vaidya, L.G. Shapiro, R.M. Haralick, G.J. Minden, "Design and architectural Implications of a Spatial Information System" IEEE Trans. on Comp., Vol. C-31, N°10, 1982, pp.1025-1031.

13. K. Yamaguchi, T.L. Kunii, "PICCOLO Logic for a Picture Database Computer and Its Implementation", IEEE Trans. on Computers, Vol. C-31, N°10,

1982, pp.983-996.

14. A. Rosenfeld, "Multiresolution Image Representation" in Digital Image Analysis, edit. S. Levialdi, Pitman Books Ltd., London, 1983 (in press).

15. C. Zahn, "Graph-theoretical methods for detecting and describing Gestalt clusters", IEEE Trans. on Comp., C-20, 1971, pp.68-86.

16. A. Guzmàn, "A heterarchical multi-microprocessor lisp machine", in Proc. IEEE Workshop Comp. Architecture Pattern Anal. Image Data Management (CAPAIDMA), Hot Springs, VA, 1981, pp.309-317.

17. R. Bisiani, H. Mauersberg, R. Reddy, "Task-Oriented Architectures", invited paper on the IEEE Proc. of July, 1983, to appear.

18. R. Bisiani, "The Harpy Machine: A Data Structure Architecture", 5th Workshop on Computer Architecture for Non Numeric Processing, ACM SIGARCH, SIGIR and SIGMOD, 1980.

19. V. Cantoni, C. Guerra, S. Levialdi, "Towards and evaluation of an image processing system", in Computing Structures for Image Processing, edit. M.J.B. Duff, Academic Press, London, 1983.

20. R. Bisiani, "An Architecture for Real Time Debugging of Custom VLSI Chips", in 1983 Int. Symp. on VLSI Technology, Systems and Applications, March 1983.

21. D.P. Agrawal, R. Jain, "A pipelined pseudoparallel system architecture for real-time dynamic scene analysis", IEEE Trans. on Comp., C-31, N°10, 1982, pp.952-962.

22. L. Uhr, "Comparing serial computers, arrays and networks using measures of active resources', IEEE Trans. on Comp., vol. C-31, N°10, 1982, pp. 1022-1025.

23. M.J.B. Duff, "Review of the CLIP image processing system", in Proc. Nat. Comput. Conf., 1978, pp.1055-1060.

24. P.M. Flanders, D.J. Hunt, S.F. Reddaway, D. Parkinson, "Efficient High Speed Computing with the Distributed Array Processor", High Speed computer and algorithm Organization, D.J. Kuck, D.H. Lawrie, and A.H. Sameh, eds., Academic Press, New York, 1977, pp.113-127.

25. K.E. Batcher, "Design of a Massively Parallel Processor", IEEE Trans. on Comp., Vol. C-29, N°9, 1980, pp.836-840.

26. R.M. Lougheed, D.L. McCubbrey, S.R. Sternberg, "Cytocomputers: Architectures for Parallel Image Processing", Proc. Workshop Picture Data Desc. and Management, Pacific Grove, Calif., 1980, pp.281-286.

27. H.T. Kung, "Let's design algorithms for VLSI systems", in Proc. of Conf. on VLSI: Architecture, Desing, Fabrication, pp.65-90, California Institute of Technology, 1979.

28. C. Guerra, S. Levialdi, "Computational Models for Image Processing, to appear in Progress in Pattern Recognition edits. L. Kanal, A. Rosenfeld, Springer-Verlag, Berlin, 1983.

29. P. Quinton, "Conception d'Architectures parallèles", Bulletin de Liaison de la Recherche en Informatique et Automatique, N°83, 1983, pp.27-28.

A DEFINITION OF COMPUTER ARCHITECTURE

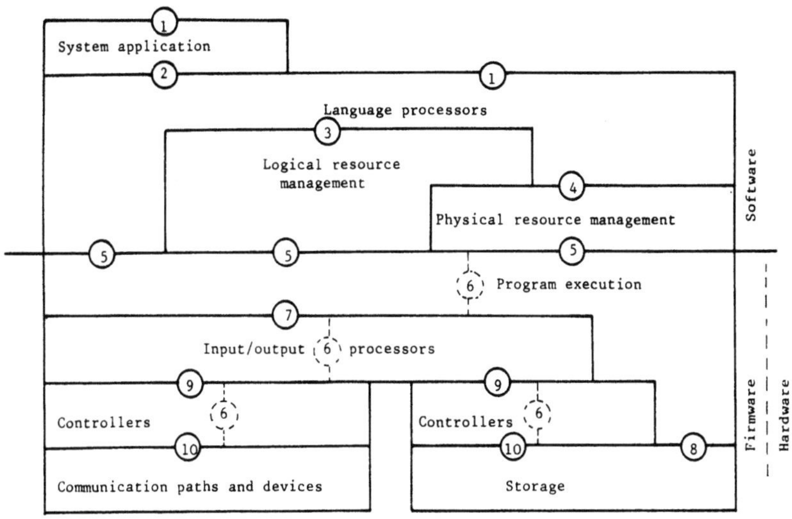

Fig.1 Levels of architecture within a computing system.

Speedup		Level
10^3	10^5	Architecture and Technology
2	10	Software
2	10	System Organization
10	100	Algorithm analysis
10	1000	Knowledge sources
10	1000	Heuristics
2	5	Program Optimization

Fig.2 Speed-up factors.

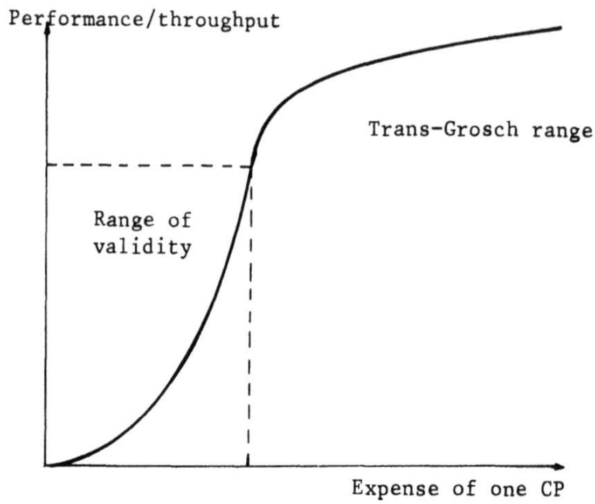

Fig.3 Grosch's law extended.

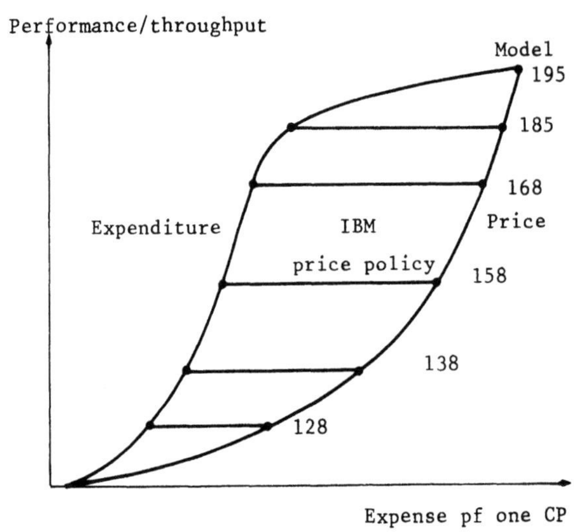

Fig.4 Price/expenditure policy
for computer family.

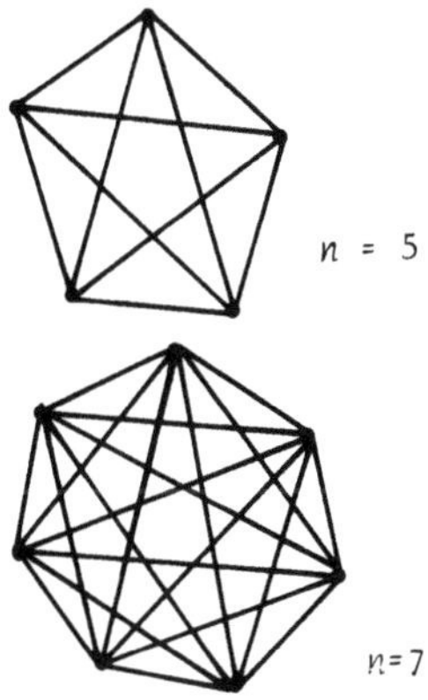

Global Complexity
(number of edges)

$$K = \frac{n(n-1)}{2} = 10$$

Global complexity

$K = 21$

Fig.5 Global complexity increases with the square of the number of units.

Fig.6

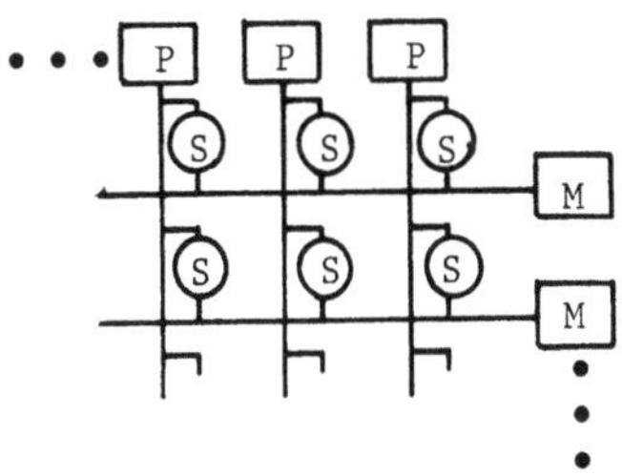

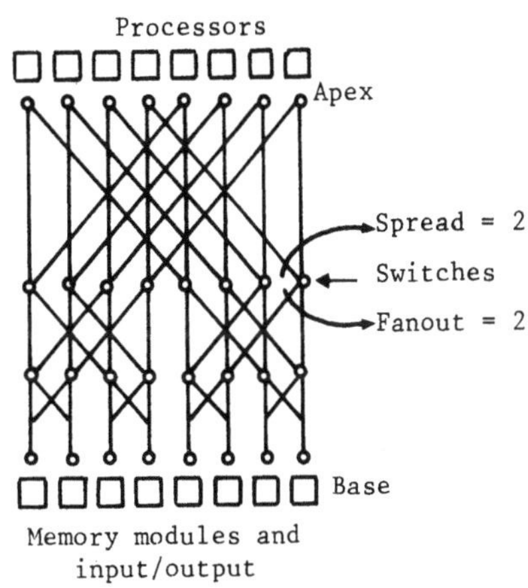

Fig.7

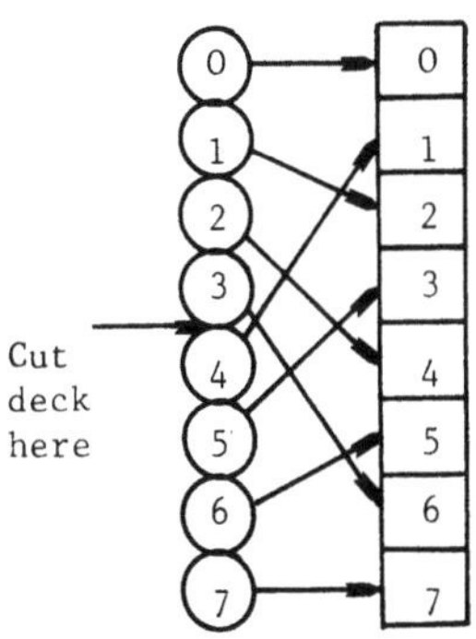

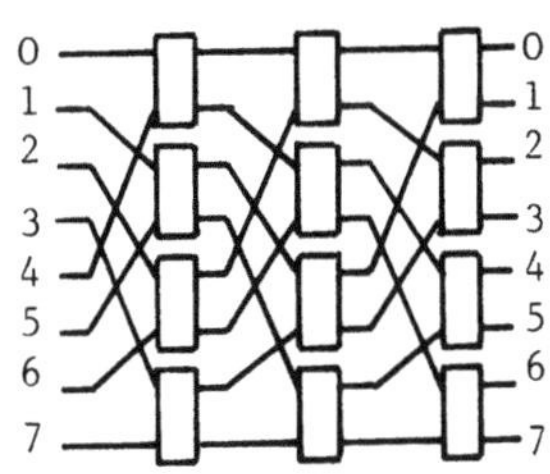

Different interconnection schemes:
Banyan networks.

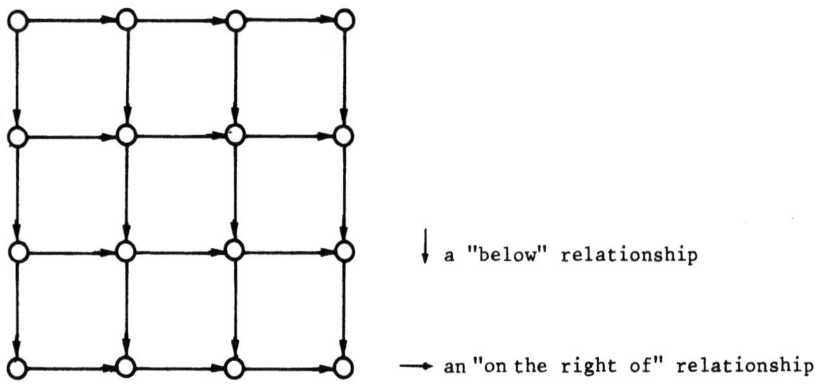

Fig.8 A two dimensional array of pixels represented by objects "O" and relationship "→", "↓".

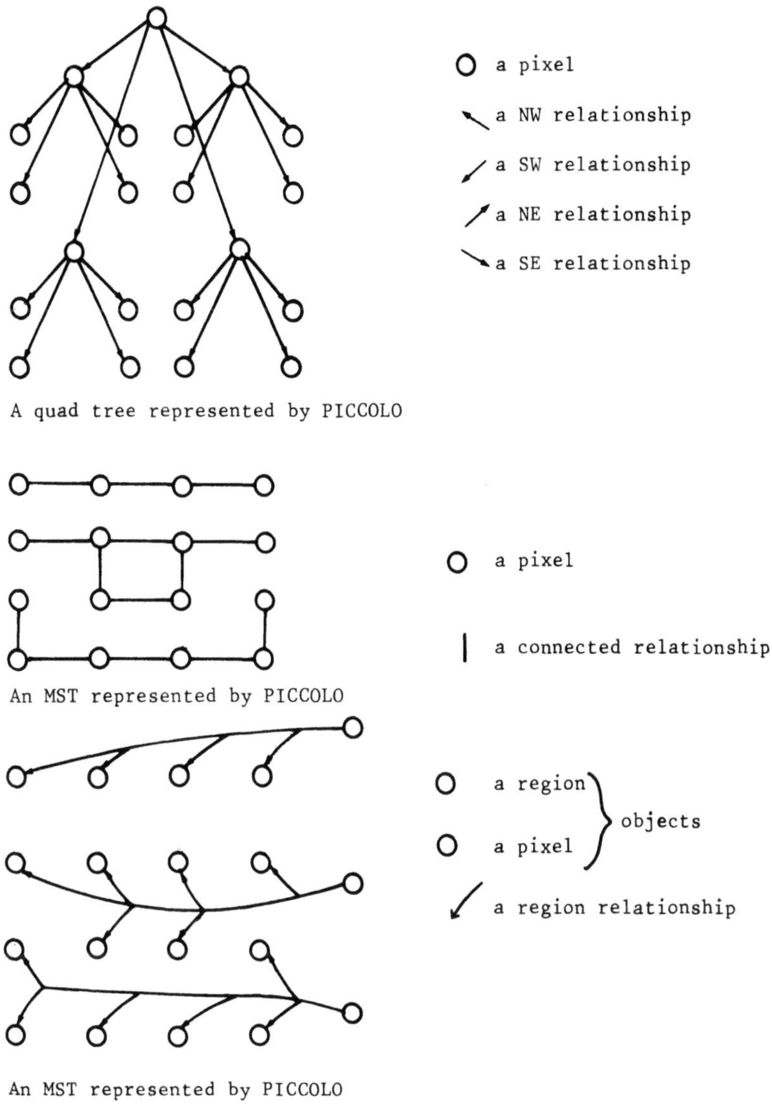

Fig.9 MST representation in PICCOLO.

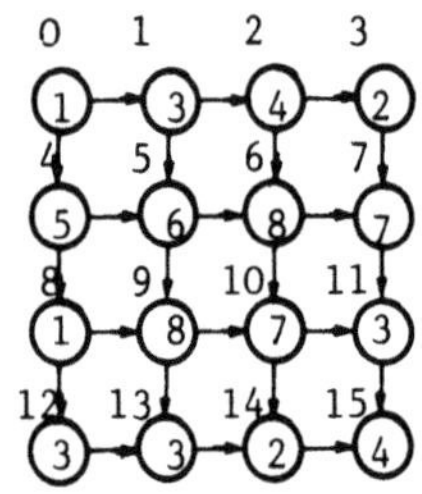

An original picture representation in PICCOLO.
A number on the left shoulder of each circle is a pixel id and that in a pixel is a gray level.

nid	value
0	1
1	3
2	4
3	2
4	5
5	6
6	8
7	7
8	1
9	8
10	7
11	3
12	3
13	3
14	2
15	4

Picture relation

nid 1	nid 2
0	1
1	2
2	3
4	5
5	6
6	7
8	9
9	10
10	11
12	13
13	14
14	15

On the right of relation
(Relation names are omitted.)

nid 1	nid 2
0	4
4	8
8	12
1	5
5	9
9	13
2	6
6	10
10	14
3	7
7	11
11	15

Below relation
(Relation names are omitted.)

An MST operation in Figure 9.

nid 1	nid 2
0	1
1	2
2	3
4	5
5	6
6	7
9	10
12	13
13	14
14	15
5	6
6	10
8	12
11	15

Connected relation
(Relation names are omitted)

Fig.10 A sample application of the MST operation.

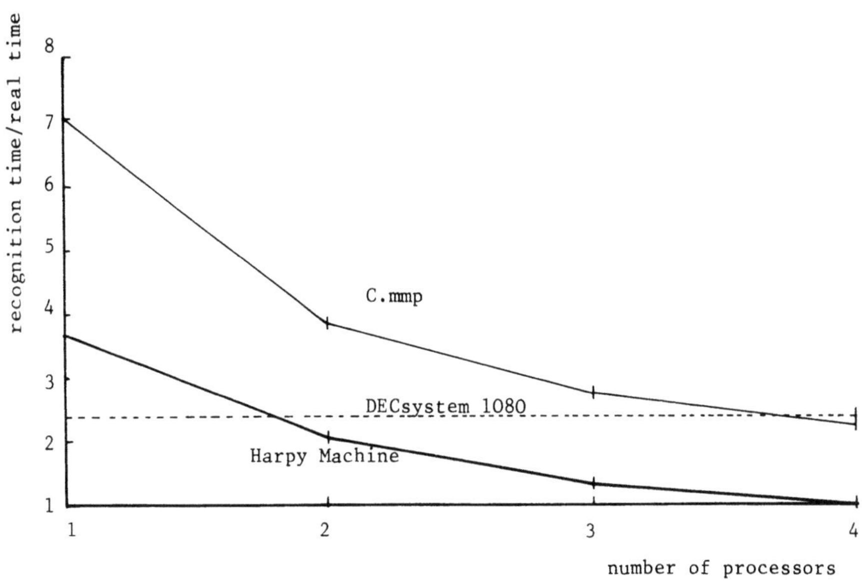

Fig.11 Speed of the Harpy Machine for the 1000 word artifical intelligence retrieval task.

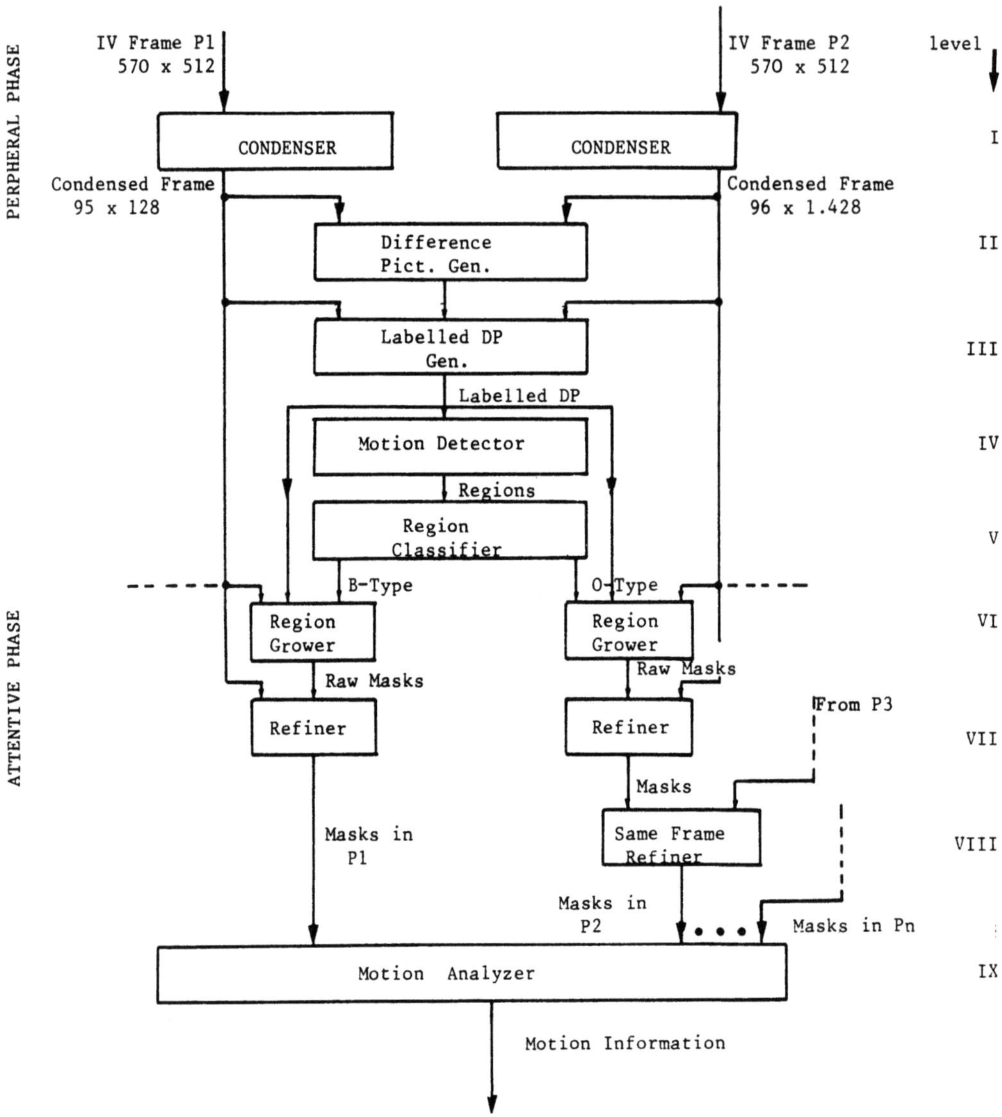

Fig.12 Sequential data flow and motion analyzer.

TABLE I

Characteristics of Various Functional Blocks for Motion Analysis

Level No.	Functional Block	Required Processing Time*	No.of Processors Allocated for the Block	Data Needed Through Level Numbers	Computation Mode	Computation Time With Distributed Processing
I	Condenser	20	20	I - VII	SIMD	1
II	Difference Picture Generator	10	10	II - III	SIMD	1
III	Labelled Difference Picture	5	5	III - VI	SIMD	1
IV	Motion Detector	5	5	IV - V	MIMD	1
V	Region Classifier	0.5	1	V - VI	SISD	0.5
VI	Region Growing	3	1**	VI - VII	SISD	1
VII	Refinement	3	1**	VII - VIII	SISD	1
VIII	Same Frame Reference	1	1	VIII - IX	SISD	1
IX	Motion Analyzer	1	1	IX	SISD	1
	Total no. when not Pipelined	48.5 for uniprocessor	20		SISD/SIMD/MIMD	8.5
	Total no. when Pipelined	48.5 for uniprocessor	45		SISD/SIMD/MIMD	1

* Integer indicate their relative values
** Only one region to the processed for a frame pair.

Fig.13 Analysis of functional blocks.

TABLE II

Information Contents of Various Memory Blocks in the Proposed Pipelined Pseudoparallel System for Frame Size of 570x512(At the *i*th Instant)

Storage Step	Total No. of Memory Modules	Size of Each Memory Module in Words	Number of Memory Modules for Frame Number									
			i	(i-1)	(i-2)	(i-3)	(i-4)	(i-5)	(i-6)	(i-7)	(i-8)	(i-9)
Original Picture	40	14592	20	20								
Condensed Picture	80	1216		10	10	10	10	10	10	10	10	
Difference P.G.	10	2432			5	5						
Labelled D.P.	20	12160				5	5	5	5			
Motion Detector	2	12160					1	1				
Region Classifier	2	12160						1	1			
Region Growing	2	12160							1	1		
Refinement	3	12160								1	1	1
Same Frame Refinement	2	12160									1	1
Motion Analyzer	1	12160										1
TOTAL	162											

Fig.14 Information contents of the memory blocks.

TABLE I

Gate Counts of Resources in Different Types of Computers

(Assume 1 Bit/Gate)

Computer	Proc(a)	Memory(s)
Serial:		
small (8bit)	3,000	64,000
medium	10,000	6,400,000
large	30,000	64,000,000
super	100,000	256,000,000
1-bit SIMD Arrays:		
small	50	32
medium	100	256
large	300	1,000
super	600	4,000
Examples:		
CLIP4	300	32
DAP	100	4,000
MPP (planned)	600	1,000

TABLE II

Total Gates in Arrays

Total	Computers	Proc-Gates	Mem-Bits
CLIP	9,216	3,000,000	320,000
DAP	4,096	400,000	16,000,000
MPP	16,384	9,600,000	16,000,000

Fig.15 Active resources in the sequential computer and in the SIMD Architectures.

MICROCOMPUTER AND SOFTWARE ARCHITECTURE FOR PROCESSING SEQUENCES OF MAPS: ASSOCIATION OF SUCCESSIVE FRAMES.

G.G. Pieroni
Department of Computer Science
University of Houston
Houston, TX 77004

M.F. Costabile and G. Gaglianese
Dipartimento di Matematica
Universita' della Calabria
Cosenza, Italy

ABSTRACT

This work regards a specific module of a software-hardware system designed in order to analyze sequences of frames representing a curve slightly modifying during the time. The software procedure is formed by a set of modules each one of which executes a well defined task of a process characterized by the following activities. 1) Considering a sequence of frames each one containing a closed curve (map), a decomposition of each curve into meaningful segments is carried out. 2) Given a pair of maps laying on contiguous frames, a correspondence among the segments of the first map and the segments of the second one is found. The technique is based on the assignment to the segments of the first map, of labels which correspond to well defined geometrical properties. Using the same set of labels, a similar assignment is carried out for the second map (slightly modified in comparison with the previous one) using a probability vector referred to the labels. A relaxation process is then accomplished in order to reinforce the probability of a specific label for each given segment. At the end of the process a reorganization of the labels belonging to both maps is carried out and a correspondence one to one among the segments reorganized in such a way is found. 3) A successive match among the geometrical properties which characterize the segments obtained as above, leads to the extraction of transfer operators which map the first frame onto the second. By iterating the activities described in the previous points, it is possible

NATO ASI Series, Vol. F18
Computer Architectures for Spatially Distributed Data
Edited by H. Freeman and G. G. Pieroni

to produce a sequence of transfer operators which describe the entire sequence. The software system is implemented on a multimicro computer formed by a sequence of processors sharing a given area on a disk unit. Each software module is addressed to accomplish a specific step of the procedure working on a specific processor. The partial result obtained by a given module is stored on a disk file and constitutes the input of the following module working on the successive processor. The last module of the system furnishes the sequence of transfer operators. In this paper the problem regarding the association of two successive frames of a sequence is presented; the algorithm used is described and some results are shown.

I. INTRODUCTION

The idea of tracking objects moving in a three-dimensional or two-dimensional reference system, has been investigated by many authors during the last ten years (1,3,4,5,7,8,15,16,24,27). This class of problems arises mainly when dealing with radar targets, traffic control or, more generally, when a moving object must be recognized and its trajectory classified. Another class of problems is connected with the recognition of two-dimensional moving shapes or two-dimensional moving shapes representing projections on a plane of three-dimensional objects which slightly modify their position during the time. In this class of problems no trajectory must be generally classified and the task of the automatic observer should consist of describing the modifications of shapes in terms of variations of the boundary structure. There are many fields in which the application of such an approach seems to have a special interest. Some of these are biomedical applications, territorial monitoring or, sometimes, military applications.

The information which constitues the input of the system is generally represented by a sequence of frames each one that represents a shape boundary at a given time. Considering a sequence of frames representing the slight variation of a curve, the aim of the approach presented here consists of extracting the structural differences existing between a frame and the following one, in order to classify the sequence.

Let us consider two contiguous curves M_i and M_{i+1} belonging to the sequence as represented in Fig.1.

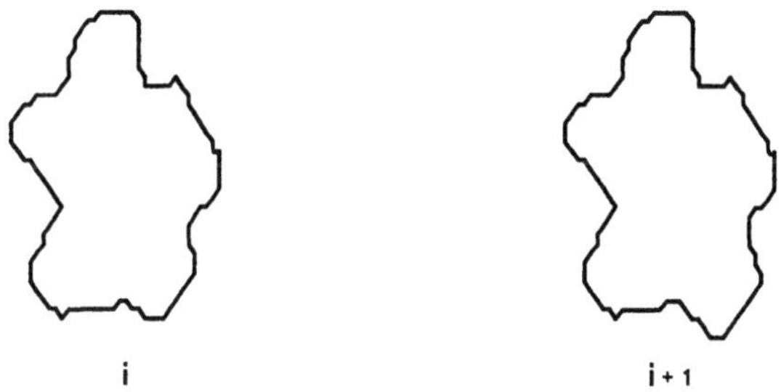

Figure 1.

The two curves are stored by the eight links Freeman encoding. In order to evaluate the degree of similarity among curves, a certain number of methods are at present available. Several authors have used Freeman chains, medial axis transforms, decomposition into primary convex subsets, polar coordinates (20), decomposition at concave vertices; decomposition by clustering, mirroring axes (28) and stroke detectors.

The chain correlation function method compares two curves extracting a global evaluation of the similarity existing between the configurations (9). Given two curves $M_1 = a_1a_2 \ldots a_n$ and $M_2 = b_1b_2 \ldots b_m$ expressed by chains of links as defined by Freeman (9) and $n \leq m$, it is possible to define a chain crosscorrelation function for chain M_1 with chain M_2 by

$$\Phi_{M_1, M_2}(j) = \frac{1}{n} \sum_{i=1}^{n} \cos(a_i - b_{i+j}) \pi/4$$

This function provides a measure of the average pair-wise alignment between the links of M_1 and M_2 and gives an indication of the degree of shape congruence for different shifts of M_2 relative to M_1. Note that $|\Phi_{M_1, M_2}(j)| \leq 1$ for all j and if n=m $\Phi_{M_1, M_2}(j) = \Phi_{M_2, M_1}(-j)$. If we let $M_1 = M_2$, we obtain the chain autocorrelation function, $\Phi_{M_1, M_1}(j)$, which characterizes the chain and can be used for contour classification purposes. It must be noted that the chain crosscorrelation function is sensitive both to the relative shapes of the contours as well as to their relative orientation.

Considering a segmentation of a contour and their representation by chainlets, a classification can be accomplished according to some rotation-invariant geometric features. The features suggested by Freeman (9) are: 1) the length of the chainlet; 2) the length of the chainlet chord; 3) the net positive area of the piece lying between the chainlet and its chord; 4) the maximum separation between chainlet and chord to the left side of the chord (maximum peninsula) and 5) the maximum separation between chainlet and chord to the right of the chord (maximum bay).

Bibriesca and Guzman (2) proposed to extract shape numbers from chainlets encoded by a four links Freeman encoding. Considering a grid of arbitrary cell size, it is overlaied on top of a region where a given closed curve exists. A "black" region is formed with all the cells that fall 50 per cent or more inside the region. The boundary of such a block region forms a chain that is denoted by the derivatives of the standard four links Freeman encoding. These numbers, which are formed by the digits 1,2,3 are then collected travelling clockwise. Given a chain there are several strings of such digits corresponding to the chain depending on the start point (Fig.2).

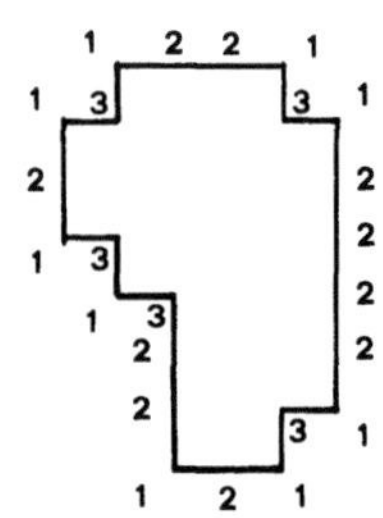

F: 121312213122221312122313

Figure 2.

Moreover only one of them is a minimum when regarded as a number in base 3; considering the fact that the orientation of the grid is not arbitrary but it does coincide with the major axis of the region, the number obtained in such a way can be considered rotation invariant. The number of ternary digits that the shape number contains is called the "order" of the shape number. It is always even because the boundary is closed. It is clear that the same shape gives rise to several shape numbers. But given n, the shape number of order n of that shape is unique.

The construction procedure is based on the following steps.

1. Find the basic rectangle of the region.
2. From the family of discrete shapes of order n, find the rectangle of order n with eccentricity closest to that of the region.
3. Make "black" all those cells falling more than 50% inside the region; leave white all others.

The boundary of this black region, expressed in the derivative notation, is the desired shape number. The more interesting properties are expressed by the fact that this number is insensitive to orientation of the region, to its position, to its size and to the origin of the chain. Moreover the precision of the resulting shape number can be varied in function of the chosen order. A comparison between two shape numbers at given degree can furnish a measure of the similarity existing between the curves.

A third method, strictly connected with the problem of evaluating similarities among frames representing a curve that slightly varies during the time, is presented in (21). In that work a procedure for extracting the structural features of each curve belonging to a sequence is presented. A set of basic primitives represented in the following Fig.3 are introduced.

The elements 1, 2, 3 are characterized by four attributes: sign, position, length and angle; the fourth element (circle) is characterized by sign, position, length and eccentricity. The sign (+,-) represents a conventional mark in order to identify a curve between two possible families. The position (values 1,2,3,...,12) represents the place occupied by a given curve in the reference system. The length means the length of the curve. The angle represents the value of the angle existing between the chord of the curve and the x axis of the reference system. The eccentricity is the ratio between max and min diameters of the "circle". The structure of the procedure is expressed by the following operations. The first operation computes the length of the curve; then a test is carried out on the condition of the curve (closed or open). For a closed curve the code is "circle" (code number 4) and the attributes are then computed. The evaluation of the ratio of the distances existing between the chord and the curve, in case of ele-

ELEMENT		ATTRIBUTE				
		Sign	Pos.	Length	Angle	Ecc.
1	l	Y	Y	Y	Y	N
2	c	Y	Y	Y	Y	N
3	s	Y	Y	Y	Y	N
4	o	Y	Y	Y	N	Y

ATTRIBUTE	VALUES AND RANGES
Sign	+ , -
Position	1 , 2 , ..., 12
Length	$1 < L < 144$
Angle	Mult. of 45 degrees
Eccentric.	$1 \leq e \leq 12$

Figure 3.

ments 1,2,3, similarly provides the possibility to assign a specific code. An evolution scheme, completed by a given number of comparisons among the geometrical characteristics of the elments, gives the possibility to associate the element on the frame i with the corresponding element on the frame i+1 considered to be the evolution of the previous one in the sequence (21).

In the context described above much work has been made in the last years mainly in order to find an efficient method for decomposing lines into meaningful parts and combining such parts from frame to frame.Some results of that work are presented in the following sections.

II. SEGMENTATION OF LINES BELONGING TO A SEQUENCE

Let us consider a sequence of closed lines representing the boundary of a shape which slightly changes its structure during the time. In order to analyze this variation, a model which describes the evolution can be based on the evaluation of the dissimilarity detected between two contiguous frames.By encoding such a dissimilarity, a sequence of transfer operators T_i which map a line onto the following one in the sequence can be built. The sequence obtained in such a way encodes a meaningful part of the information regarding the dynamics of the line sequence and can be used in order to classify movements. A tentative approach has been presented in (22). In that work a very simple method of articulation is analyzed. Given a point P(x,y) which remains fixed in a reference system, the experiment consisted in generating a sequence of closed lines which slightly modify from frame to frame and where the P point is always contained inside the line. Such a special technique allows to decompose the lines in a fixed number of segments that exactly correspond from frame to frame.In such a way the association of corresponding segments and the following extraction of structural dissimilarities can be carried out easily (22). But this method of decomposition strongly depends on the position of the line in the reference system (translations and rotations). A first improvement can be reached by considering as P point the centroid of each line. But, by definition,the position of the centroid can also move due to the structural modifications of the line passing from frame to frame; in such a way the decomposition of a line M_{i+1} belonging to the frame i+1 of the sequence is very frequently different from the decomposition of line M_i even in the parts where no modification occurred.

Some experiments have been made in order to point out a method of decomposition which can give a certain degree of independence from the structural modifications which occur when the lines are subjected to small variations from frame to frame. A method which seems to work better is presented in the following section.

III. DECOMPOSITION OF LINES AND ASSOCIATION PROCEDURE

Our procedure for decomposing a shape boundary into convex parts uses a polygonal approximation of the boundary. Methods for piecewise approximation are reviewed by Pavlidis in (18) where an algorithm is proposed for segmenting waveforms by dividing their domain into intervals where the data can be approximated by simple functions. For the problem of piecewise approximation, several methods require that the function to be approximated has certain continuity and smoothness properties. These requirements do not appear to be essential for pattern recognition applications where discontinuities are inherent in the nature of the data, and Pavlidis describes a discrete optimization method for segmenting waveforms that does not require any smoothness assumptions about the waveforms for its convergency (18). Piecewise approximation is still described in (19) as a way of feature **extraction**, data compaction and noise filtering of boundaries of regions of pictures and waveforms. Our technique for obtaining a polygonal approximation of a shape boundary is described in (4).

Let $P = P_1, P_2, \ldots, P_n$ be a polygonal approximation of a shape boundary; our method for decomposing the shape boundary into simple parts, described in (11), uses a binary relation L_I between points of the set P. Precisely, L_I consists of all pairs of points of P whose line segment is entirely within the shape. The L_I relation may be represented by a binary matrix ML_I where $ML_I(i,j)=1$ if $(P_i, P_j) \in L_I$(i.e. P_iP_j is an interior line segment), $ML_I(i,j)=0$ otherwise (i.e. P_iP_j is an exterior or intersecting line segment). The relation L_I determines a set of maximal parts on the polygonal approximation of the shape. More precisely each part consists of points which are in L_I relation (pairwise in L_I relation). A simple way for determining such a set consists in extracting from the ML_I matrix, in a sequence going from the left top to the right bottom, triangular submatrices having the main diagonal lying on the main diagonal of ML_I and having only 1 as elements. Because this decomposition can strongly be **influenced by** the presence of points of noise on the boundary line, a procedure for merging successive parts in some cases, is discussed in (11). Then a matching procedure which works on lines decomposed with that algorithm was developed and it is based on the considerations below (4).

Let $M_i = M_i^1, M_i^2, \ldots, M_i^s$ be a curve decomposed into $M_i^1, M_i^2, \ldots, M_i^s$ convex parts; in the following we will refer to convex parts as segments; to each segment M_i^r is attached a list $\left\{M_{i,m}^r\right\}_{m=1,\overline{m}}$ of $\overline{m}$ attributes. Let $M_j = M_j^1, M_j^2, \ldots, M_j^t$ be the representation of another shape that we wish to match against M_i. Based on the chosen attributes a measure of dissimilarity $d(M_i^r, M_j^u)$ between segments M_i^r and M_j^u of two different lines can be defined as follows. For each attribute the absolute value of the difference between the corresponding values of the two segments is evaluated and the sum of these differences over all the attributes is considered; in order to take care of the different nature of magnitude of the attributes (for example attributes based on area and perimeter) this sum is weighted with real positive numbers W_m. Thus

$$d(M_i^r, M_j^u) = \sum_{m=1}^{\bar{m}} \left| M_{i,m}^r - M_{j,m}^u \right| * W_m \qquad (1)$$

and $d(M_i^r, M_j^u) \geq 0$ with $d(M_i^r, M_j^u) = 0$ if M_i^r and M_j^u have the same attributes. Let δ be a non negative real number; we will define two segments M_i^r and M_j^u to be "similar" if $d(M_i^r, M_j^u) < \delta$. An algorithm for the segment matching problem, which is rotation invariant,is now described. A matching procedure must find some correspondences between segments of the polygonal decomposition of M_i and segments of M_j. Such correspondences,(association), must preserve the sequencing of segments on each curve. The association may be described as follows: if we consider the relation R consisting of all pairs of contiguous segments, an association is a mapping f between segments of M_i and segments of M_j

$$f : M_i \dashrightarrow M_j$$

such that segments map into similar segments and the relation R is preserved, that is

$$f(M_i^r) = M_j^u \quad \text{and} \quad f(M_i^{r+1}) = M_j^k \qquad \text{imply } k=u+1.$$

The relation preserving mappings, homomorphisms, of which the above association is a particular case, have been extensively studied by Haralick (12). The problem of finding an homomorphism is a NP-complete problem;procedures have been proposed to solve this problem which often in practice yield interesting results.Since it is possible for two similar shapes to be decomposed into a different number of elements, an association should consider the possibility for one segment of M_i to map into several segments of M_j and viceversa; so a merging or splitting operation on segments must be considered. For semplicity the merging of only two contiguous segments is considered. Furthermore, the mapping should be able to associate two segments on M_i with two segments of M_j, in order to obtain a better fitting of segments that otherwise could not correspond due to the difference among attributes. In other words, in associating segments the matching procedure must take into account the possibilities expressed in Scheme 1.

shape M_i	shape M_j
M_i^r	M_j^u
M_i^r	$M_j^u \oplus M_j^{u+1}$
$M_i^r \oplus M_i^{r+1}$	M_j^u
$M_i^r \oplus M_i^{r+1}$	$M_j^u \oplus M_j^{u+1}$

Scheme 1.

The symbol $\oplus$ denotes the merging operation of segments.

IV. A DEPTH-FIRST SEARCH FOR DETERMINING THE ASSOCIATION

The technique we used for determining an association between segments of two curves is a depth-first search (4). The search procedure fixes a segment on the first curve and a segment on the second curve which are similar on the basis of chosen attributes; that is it fixes an initial association: $M_i^r \dashrightarrow M_{i+1}^u$; then the procedure chooses successive correspondences of segments among the four possible alternatives indicated in Scheme 1. Each time the value expressed in Formula (1) is computed for the considered segments and the correspondence is accepted if that value is less than the fixed threshold. Whenever the procedure cannot find a pairing for successive elements because of dissimilarity between them, it backtracks to the previous correspondence and looks for a different solution. If the procedure finds an association for all segments on the curves, it has found a solution of the problem. Otherwise, if the procedure backs up to the initial association without finding any correspondence between segments and there are no more choices for the starting association, the procedure halts with failure (4). It could be useful not only to find a solution for the shape matching problem, but to find a good solution. In fact a measure of goodness of an association can be easily defined since a cost can be attached to each single correspondence between segments. As a cost of a single correspondence we will assume the measure of dissimilarity between segments previously introduced. The measure of goodness of an association f will be the sum of the costs over all the single correspondences of an association.

The above algorithm can now be modified to consider the problem of determining the association of minimal cost among the associations with a fixed initial correspondence: whenever the procedure finds a solution better than the best solution previously found, it replaces the old solution with the new one and goes on looking for other different solutions (i.e. it backtracks) (4). This procedure can be improved using a branch and bound method. At each step of the search a test is made between the cost of the actual best solution and that one of a partial solution being considered. If this last value exceeds the first one, the procedure backtracks after discarding the partial solution.

V. ASSOCIATION BY RELAXATION

It is quite plain that the efficiency of the algorithm presented in the previous section strongly depends on the starting segment pair. This condition is very limiting. In order to overcome this difficulty a technique to have a controlled starting pair for the association procedure has been carried out (5). Let $M_1 = M_1^1, M_1^2 \ldots M_1^s$ be a closed line represented in the first frame of a sequence, decomposed into $M_1^1, M_1^2, \ldots$ $\ldots, M_1^s$ convex parts following the method presented in section III. Considering the attributes (geometrical properties) used in the previous section which characterize each segment, let us assign a label $l_1^r (r=1,2,$

...,s) to each segment of this frame. Let $M_2 = M_2^1, M_2^2 \dots M_2^t$ be the second line of the same sequence. Considering the labels of the first line as primitives, let us assign to each segment M_2^u (u=1,2,...,t), the whole set of labels l_1^r(r=1,2,...,s) where a probability coefficient $p_{r,u}$ is linked to each one of these labels giving a measure of the match between the attributes of the segment M_2^u and the attributes characterizing the label l_1^r.

A relaxation process is then accomplished in order to reinforce the evaluation of the labels that fit better on the segments M_2^u (6,14,25, 26). This process takes into account the fact that a correct label assignment of the segments of M_2 must consider the labels in the same order they appear along the line M_1 . For this reason we have some particular compatibility functions among labels which contribute to a faster convergence of the relaxation process. In case of equal number of segments between M_2 and M_1 (s=t) and when the segments are similar in the structure, the application of the relaxation method converges fast to a perfect correspondence between the segments of the two lines, segment by segment. In case that two contiguous lines are decomposed in a different number of segments ($s \neq t$) or even when s=t but the structure of some segment differs greatly from the structure of the potential correspondent, the convergency is obtained at least for one pair of segments, because we suppose that only slow variations can occur between a frame and the following one.

At that moment we apply the tree-search procedure in order to adjust the correspondences regarding the residual segments, which are generally a small number; this means that the complete procedure ends faster. Moreover, introducing the relaxation process, it is drastically overcomes the degree of uncertainty that is in relation to the choice of the first pair of segments if we use only the tree-search method.

VI. EXPERIMENTAL RESULTS AND CONCLUSIONS

Let us consider the frames given in Fig. 1. The algorithm given in section III decomposes the lines as illustrated in Fig. 4.

Figure 4.

The following Table 1. shows the initial assignment of the probability coefficients.

number of segments	labels l_1^1	l_1^2	l_1^3	l_1^4
1.	0.303	0.279	0.247	0.171
2.	0.242	0.311	0.273	0.174
3.	0.236	0.284	0.317	0.163
4.	0.306	0.267	0.230	0.197
5.	0.250	0.284	0.306	0.160

Table 1.

The following Table 2. shows the configuration of the probability coefficients after 9 iterations of the relaxation pocess.

1.0	0.0	0.0	0.0
0.0	1.0	0.0	0.0
0.0	0.0	1.0	0.0
0.0	0.0	0.0	0.0
0.0	0.0	0.0	0.0

Table 2.

The resulting association is expressed by the following Scheme 2.

1 -----→ 1

2 -----→ 2

3 -----→ 3

Scheme 2.

By applying the tree-search procedure at this moment, considering as fixed the associations given in Scheme 2., the algorithm gives the result which is expressed in Scheme 3.

1 -----→ 1

2 -----→ 2

3 -----→ 3

4 -----→ 4 ⊕ 5

Scheme 3.

The problem of connecting parts of lines belonging to successive frames of a sequence seems at present to have positive approach. A syntactic model which can be used to evaluate structural dissimilarities between segments of two lines is, at present, under experimentation.

REFERENCES

1. Aggarwal, J.K., and Duda, R.O., IEEE Trans. on Computers, C24, 966, (1975).
2. Bibriesca, E., and Guzman, A., Pattern Recognition, 12, 101,(1980).
3. Chow, W.K., and Aggarwal, J.K., IEEE Trans. on Computers, C26, 179, (1977).
4. Costabile, M.F., et al., Tech. Rep., 03-82, Istituto di Automatica, Universita' di Roma, Italy, (1982).
5. Costabile, M.F., and Pieroni, G.G., Tech. Rep., 02-83, Depart. of Mathematics, University of Calabria, Cosenza, Italy, (1983).

6. Davis, L.S., and Rosenfeld, A., TR-448, Computer Science Center, U.O.M., College Park, March, (1976).
7. Eiho, S., and Kuwahara, M., 4th IJCPR, Kyoto, Japan, 740, (1978).
8. Endlick, R.M., et al., J. of Appl. Meteorol., 10, 105, (1971).
9. Freeman, H., Computing Surveys, 6, 57-97, (1974).
10. Fu, K.S., Syntactic Methods in Pattern Recognition, New York, Academic, (1974).
11. Guerra, C., and Pieroni, G.G., IEEE Trans. on PAMI, 3, 405-408, (1981).
12. Haralick, R.M.,and Kartus, J.,IEEE Trans. on SMC,8, 600-612,(1978).
13. Haralick, R.M., and Shapiro, L.G., IEEE Trans. on PAMI, 1,173-184, (1979).
14. Hummel, R.A., and Rosenfeld, A., TR-562, Computer Science Center, U.O.M., College Park, August, (1977).
15. Martin, W.N., and Aggarwal, J.K., C.G.I.P., 7, 356, (1978).
16. Nagel, H.H., 4th IJCPR, Kyoto, Japan, 186, (1978).
17. Pavlidis, T., Structural Pattern Recognition, New York, Springer, (1977).
18. Pavlidis, T., IEEE Trans. on Computers, 22, 689-697, (1973).
19. Pavlidis, T., and Horowitz, S.L., IEEE Trans. on Computers, 23, 860-870, (1974).
20. Perkins, W., IEEE Trans. on Computers, 27, 126, (1978).
21. Pieroni, G.G., C.G.I.P. 10, 375, (1979).
22. Pieroni, G.G., et al., Map Data Processing,309-329,Academic,(1980).
23. Pieroni, G.G., et al., 5th IJCPR, Miami, USA, 618-623, (1980).
24. Potter, J., C.G.I.P., 6, 558, (1977).
25. Rosenfeld, A., et al., Tech. Rep., TR-379, Computer Science Center, U.O.M., College Park, May, (1975).
26. Rutkowski, W.S., et al., TR-762, Computer Science Center, U.O.M., College Park, May, (1979).
27. Takagi, M., and Sakane, K., 4th IJCPR, Kyoto, Japan, 735,(1978).
28. Wechsler, H., C.G.I.P., 9, 246, (1979).

DISPARITY BASED SCENE ANALYSIS

J. L. Potter
Mathematical Sciences Department
Kent State University
Kent, Ohio 44242 USA

ABSTRACT

A large image processing computer capable of billions of operations per second is not sufficient to accomplish effective scene analysis. A complete system based on a comprehensive theory of scene analysis is needed. In designing hardware for scene analysis, first an overall processing approach must be established and then the hardware can be designed to efficiently implement the various components of the approach. A complete scene analysis system can be designed using an image processing computer, a mobile sensor and an intelligent control module based on the premise that frame-to-frame disparity in the sensor's imagery is the most important source of scene analysis information, that the world is the best repository of image information, and that an intelligent control module can interactively position sensors so that the image processing subsystem can effectively extract information from the scene as it is needed. The discussion will focus on the image processing and control subsystems. The description of these two major subsystems will provide a basis for the design of a disparity based scene analysis computer architecture.

INTRODUCTION

Before an architecture for a specific set of tasks can be designed, it is necessary to define the tasks. The proposed system is intended to be capable of real time interactive scene analysis. In this mode of operation, there is no need to save raw imagery for more than a few seconds. If a previous image is required to be processed again, the

NATO ASI Series, Vol. F18
Computer Architectures for Spatially Distributed Data
Edited by H. Freeman and G. G. Pieroni

system executive can simply direct the sensor system to rescan the scene. The real time nature of the sensor system allows the scene analysis process to be based on information rich time varying imagery instead of isolated static frames. The analysis of scenes based on time varying imagery depends on the ability to detect and analyze the disparities between frames. These disparities may be due to object motion, sensor motion or both. Optical flow concepts can be used in analyzing these data. Certainly other cues such as color, texture, etc. will be used, but the primary basic feature will be motion and depth information obtained from the analysis of frame-to-frame disparity data.

The overwhelming computational requirements of sophisticated image analysis algorithms can not simply be met by building larger SIMD processors given todays technology. One alternative approach is to reduce the raw computational requirement by a selective application of computing power. This implies sophisticated hardware and software in the form of a scene analysis control mechanism.

While the ultimate source of information is the raw imagery itself, information which has been extracted will be saved in any of several data bases. Due to the amorphous nature of the imagery and recognition grammars, it is likely that this information will be stored in a flexible data structure such as nested strings of attribute value pairs. Thus the basic storage cell for both grammars and information is likely to be lists. It is clear then that efficient control of scene analysis functions involves the ability to effectively search and match list structures.

FRAME-TO-FRAME DISPARITY ANALYSIS

The basic approach of frame-to-frame disparity analysis is to convert sequences of 2d spatially distributed data into 4d spatially distributed data by analyzing the disparities between successive frames of imagery assuming that the image data is approximately continuous in time but not in x, y or z.

Considerable research has been conducted on time varying imagery analysis over the past several years, but a robust approach for computer based analysis which can be applied to all naturally occurring imagery has yet to be developed. A number of researchers have developed algorithms which assign motion values to objects and object components by analyzing their various positions in sequences of frames. The positional disparity of the object features in the two scenes can be analyzed to determine depth and motion information about the object (for example, Aggarwal, Davis and Martin 1981). In these efforts, the disparity information is a secondary feature. It can only be determined late in the scene analysis process after intermediate feature detection in all cases and only after complete object recognition in others. Consequently in systems which use these algorithms, this information can only be used to assign a motion attribute value or 3d (depth) information to an already identified object or subobject. It can not be used to delineate, define or recognize objects directly.

The concept of ecological optics described by Gibson, 1966, and perspective decoding theory described by Johansson, 1974, both emphasize the primacy of pattern motion on the retina. These theories state that time varying disparity information in natural visual systems is a powerful, fundamental feature useful in the scene analysis/object recognition process itself not just for describing previously recognized objects. Several researchers have proposed algorithms which allow the calculation of velocity vector fields for certain areas of the focal plane (Horn and Schunk, 1980, Fennema, 1979, Thompson, 1981, and Ullman, 1981). However, these techniques can not be applied to the entire image plane. If a visual system is to be based on the theories proposed by Gibson and/or Johansson, then it must use robust algorithms which operate under all natural conditions and must not impose artificial restrictions on the scenes to be analyzed. The algorithms should be based on a single technique which can detect motion at all points in a focal plane regardless of the number of objects, the type of object motion and the cause of the frame to frame variance.

Potter, 1975, described how the disparity information of a sequence of frames could be extracted at each point of an image plane without any a priori knowledge of the image contents or any need to preprocess the imagery to detect objects or subobjects. The approach was applied to a stationary sensor observing moving objects only and was robust in that it accommodated scenes with multiple whole and occluded objects each with its own velocity. The technique was to define a template about each point in the focal plane which characterized that point's position relative to primitive near-by features. The template's position was then located in subsequent frames by matching. The displacement of the template provided a measurement of the movement of the associated central point.

Disparity Detection

The basic approach of template definition and searching is proposed as the primary frame disparity detection and measurement mechanism because: 1) It does not impose unnatural restrictions on the scene such as: a) continuous intensity levels, or b) a limited number of objects. 2) It can be used to detect both local and global motion values. 3) It operates effectively on scenes with objects of all sizes (i.e. from a few pixels up to the entire focal plane). 4) It is easily implemented on parallel computers for rapid computation. 5) The motion information is extracted at a low level and thus can be integrated with other elementary features for more effective scene analysis.

The disparity detection algorithm can be implemented using the simple image processing functions shown in Table 1. The implementations of these functions are described in detail elsewhere (Potter, 1981). The programming is straight forward because the lock-step synchronism of SIMD processors means that you program the function for just one pixel and the entire processor array executes the same algorithm in parallel on all the pixels in the array. Due to the DMA interface into the array memory, there is virtually no I/O overhead associated with these algorithms.

TABLE 1 MPP THROUGHPUT RATES FOR SELECTED ALGORITHMS

FEATURE DETECTION (3x3 convolution)	621m bits per second
THRESHOLDING	56,988m bits per second
TEMPLATE MATCHING (7X7)	14,266m bits per second
PSEUDOMEDIAN FILTER (3X3)	7,400m bits per second
TWO-DIMENSIONAL CROSS CORRELATION	16,364m bits per second

The disparity detection algorithm begins by using convolution and similar functions to detect edges, texture and other primitive features at each point in the image. The feature values are saved and associated with each pixel (See Figure 1). Each feature type is normalized across the entire image and then thresholded. The strongest feature values are retained while the weaker ones are cleared. The most prominent of the remaining features is identified, the prominent feature flag is set and the type and value of the feature are saved in the prominent feature fields. Not all pixels will have sufficiently strong features to warrant a prominent feature selection.

X	Y	GRAY VALUE	....

a Pixel Location and Value

FEATURE 1	...	FEATURE n	... ...	PROMINENT FEATURE FLAG	PROMINENT FEATURE TYPE	PROMINENT FEATURE VALUE	..

b Feature Fields

X DISTANCE 1	Y DISTANCE 1	...	X DISTANCE 16	Y DISTANCE 16

c Template Vector

DIFFERENCE SQUARED (0,0)	DIFFERENCE SQUARED (0,1)	...	DIFFERENCE SQUARED (5,4)	DIFFERENCE SQUARED (5,5)

d Difference Squared Values

Figure 1 - Layout of Related Pixel Values

Next, a template for every point in the image is generated by calculating the direction and distances from the point to all points with prominent features. The closest feature point in each of 16 directions is determined and saved as the template vector. Figure 2a illustrates the 16 directions. Figure 2b illustrates the corresponding template. Figure 1c shows the template vector organization.

After the template vectors have been generated, the prominent feature points in frame one are searched for in frame 2. The search consists of a difference squared operation with each of the feature's neighboring pixel within a specified window size. The window size can be kept small (5x5 or 7x7) because the assumption is that the imagery is processed in real time and that object and sensor motion is "slow" compared to the frame rate. The difference-squared value is calculated only if the prominent feature types match. The values for all neighboring pixels are saved (See Figure 1d).

The analysis of the difference-squared data to estimate pixel displacement can be quite complex and still is being investigated for such motion as object rotation, occluded objects, etc. However, the analysis of simple linear displacement will serve as an example of the process. Since the overall approach is to estimate the displacement of an object point by matching a template centered on that point it is important to obtain the best fit. The best template fit is obtained by calculating the sums of the template's feature points difference-squared values. In order to simplify the illustration, a 4 direction template instead of a 16 direction template is shown in Figure 3. The four corresponding difference square values are summed as shown in Figure 3 to find the best over all fit. The displacement of the best fit is an estimate of the displacement of the original image point. Figure 4 is a PDL description of the disparity detection algorithm.

Disparity Analysis

Once the disparity for each point has been calculated, it can be analyzed to obtain 1) object motion and 2) object depth information. The determination of this information depends on the geometry of the sensor system. Recently, several researchers (Hadani, et al. 1980) have developed mathematical models of the human eye which permit calculations based on Gibson's and Johansson's concepts of the priority of motion in visual perception. However, their intent is to model the human visual system and therefore their techniques are not directly applicable to computerized visual systems. For example, Hadani assumes that information about movement of the eye is extracted by the visual system from retinal information. In a computerized system , the movement of the sensor would be known by feedback from the sensor positioning mechanism and would not need to be calculated. The result

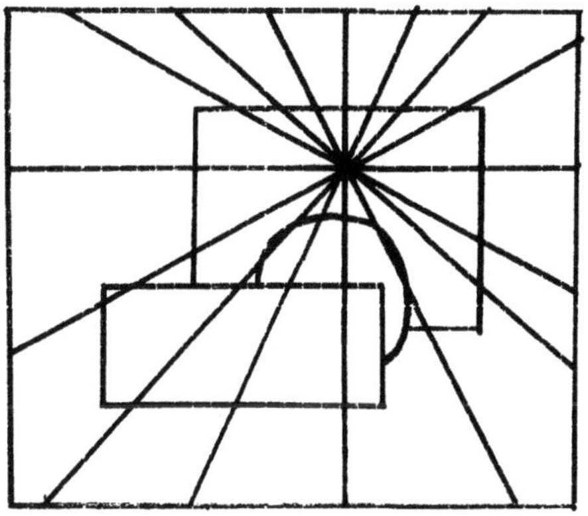

Figure 2a - 16 Template Sections

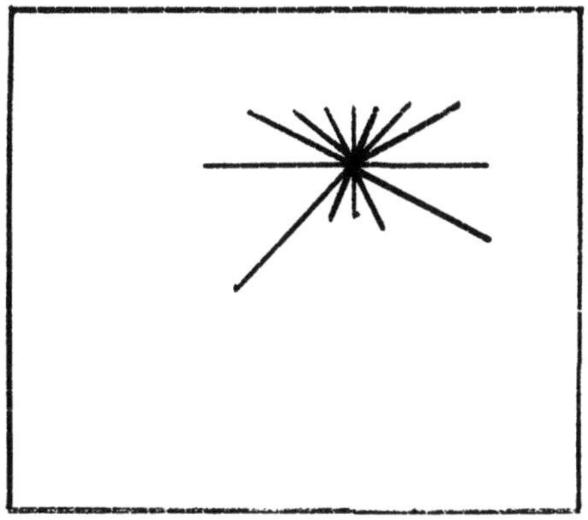

Figure 2b - A Template

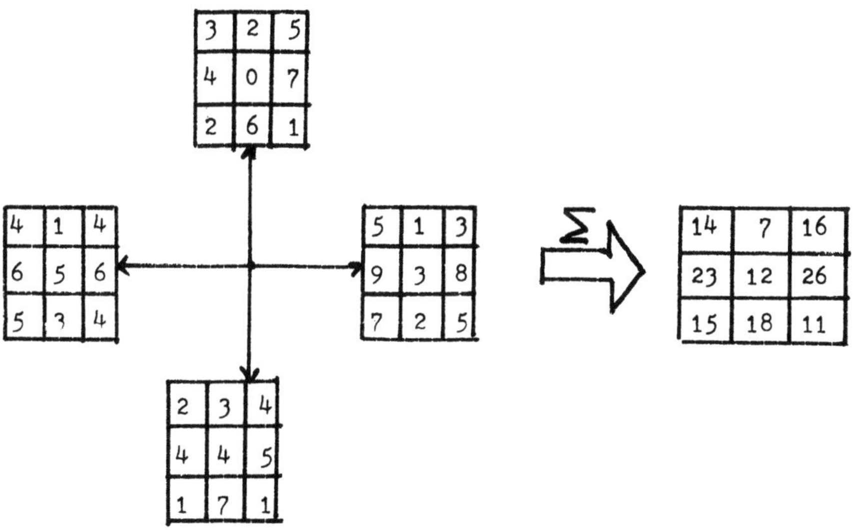

Figure 3 - Least Squares Fit

```
: DETECT FEATURES
    CALL FEATURE1 . . .  CALL FEATUREn
: GENERATE TEMPLATE  -  * index implies parallel calculations
: The TAG function returns a pointer used with ASSOCIATEDWITH
    FOR I = 1 TO 512: J = 1 TO 512
    DISTANCE(*,*) = SQRT((X(*,*)-X(I,J))**2+(Y(*,*)-Y(I,J))**2)
    RATIO(*,*) = (Y(*,*)-Y(I,J))/(X(*,*)-X(I,J))
    FOR M = 1 TO 16
    S1 = (2*PI*(M-1))/16
    S2 = (2*PI*M)/16
    IF TANGENT(S1) LE RATIO(*,*) LE TANGENT(S2) AND PFF(*,*) EQ TRUE
        THEN
        CLOSEST = TAG(MINIMUM(DISTANCE(*,*)))
        XDISTANCE(I,J,M) = X ASSOCIATEDWITH CLOSEST
        YDISTANCE(I,J,M) = Y ASSOCIATEDWITH CLOSEST
    ENDFOR  M,J,I
: GENERATE DIFFERENCE-SQUARED VALUES (DSV)
: PFVn = PROMINENT FEATURE VALUE IN FRAME n
: PFTn = PROMINENT FEATURE TYPE IN FRAME n
: DSV = DIFFERENCE SQUARED VALUE
    FOR K = 1 TO 5: L = 1 TO 5
    IF PFT1(*+K-3,*+L-3) EQ PFT2(*,*) THEN
      DSV(*,*,K,L) = (PFV2(*,*)-PFV1(*+K-3,*+L-3))**2
    ENDFOR L,K
: CALCULATE BEST TEMPLATE FIT AND DISPARITY MEASUREMENT
: LSF = LEAST SQUARES FIT
    FOR I = 1 TO 512: J = 1 TO 512
    FOR K = 1 TO 5: L = 1 TO 5
    LSF(K,L) = 0
    ENDFOR L,K
    FOR M = 1 TO 16: K = 1 TO 5: L = 1 TO 5
    LSF(K,L) = LSF(K,L) + DSV(XDISTANCE(I,J,M),YDISTANCE(I,J,M),K,L)
    ENDFOR L,K,M
    MIN = MAXIMUM
    FOR K = 1 TO 5: L = 1 TO 5
    IF LSF(K,L) LT MIN THEN MIN = LSF(K,L): MINK = K:  MINL = L
    ENDFOR K,L
    DISPARITYX(I,J) = K
    DISPARITYY(I,J) = L
    ENDFOR I,J
```

Figure 4 - PDL of the Disparity Detection Algorithm

is that the computer system may use a much different, perhaps simpler, geometry.

As an example of the use of the sensor geometry in a computerized system, consider the process of calculating the depth of a stationary object. (For simplicity, a 2d world will be assumed). The edges of the object can be made to move on the image plane by rotating the sensor system about a point behind the center of the image plane. In figure 5 a real world scene consisting of a single object is depicted. In Figure 5a, the sensor is oriented such that a point P of the object is focused on the center of the focal plane. In Figure 5b, the sensor has been rotated. As a result, P is now focused to the left of center.

If the sensor system is designed such that the center of rotation is taken as the origin of the reference coordinate system and the optical axis is the abscissa, then the equation of the line from the point P to its image point P' on the focal plane is easily generated since the distance from the origin to the focal point and the location of P' on the focal plane are known.

After rotation, a second equation can be similarly generated in the rotated coordinate system. This second equation can be easily transformed into the coordinate of the first coordinate system since the amount of rotation is known. The equations can then be solved simultaneously to obtain the position of P in x from the two y values obtained from the focal plane (See Figure 6).

The analysis of object motion with a stationary camera is straight forward from the point displacement data and is described in Potter, 1975. The more difficult problem of combined object motion and sensor motion analysis is still under investigation.

LIST STORAGE

A fundamental property of SIMD processors is that they are organized into 'words' of memory which can be accessed in parallel. That is, the same field of all words can be processed in one memory access. Thus the entire memory can be searched as fast as a single word. If one record of a file is stored in each word, then the entire

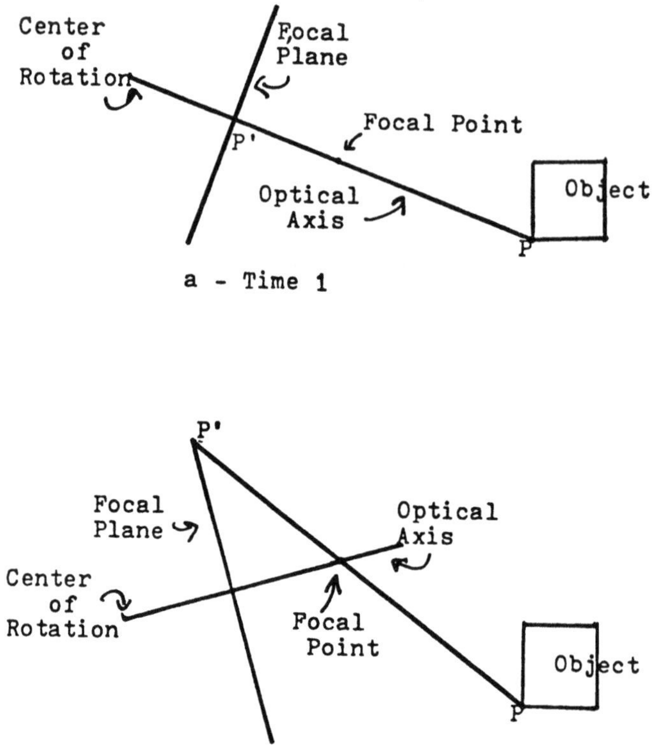

b - Time 2

Figure 5 - Depth Perception by Sensor Movement

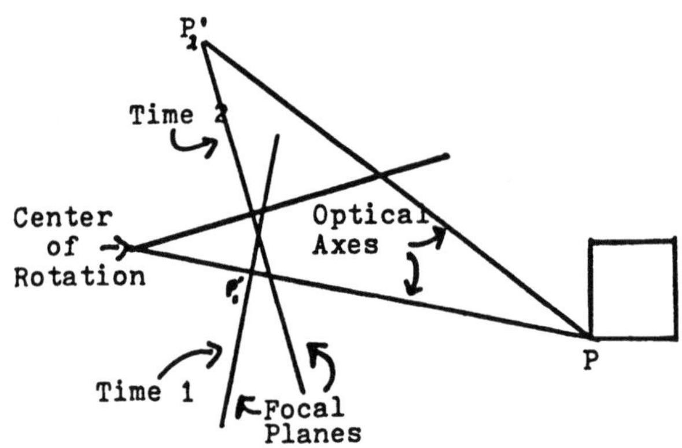

Figure 6 - Position of P

Let 0=CAR, 1=CDR,left justify with 1 fill, then
LIST = ((A B (C D) (((E) F))) G) can be stored as:

	LIST NAME FIELD	CDAR CODE FIELD	ATOM FIELD
	----	----------------	-----
WORD 0	LIST	0011111111111111	A
WORD 1	LIST	0101111111111111	B
WORD 2	LIST	0110011111111111	C
WORD 3	LIST	0110101111111111	D
WORD 4	LIST	0111000011111111	E
WORD 5	LIST	0111001011111111	F
WORD 6	LIST	1011111111111111	G

Figure 7 - CDAR Encoding

file can be searched and processed in one step.

Conventional storage techniques using linked lists require that chains of CAR and CDR functions (henceforth abbreviated CDAR functions) be executed sequentially. However, if the data representation shown in Figure 7 is stored with each record in a word, then any sublist which can be defined by a CDAR function string can be searched for directly and in parallel.

The storage technique illustrated in Figure 7 is designed so that numeric range searches can be used to search for sublists. Thus if the list ((A B (C D) (((E) F))) G) is to be processed by the function CDDAR, the function string is first converted into the CDAR code 011. Then, the lower bound of the search is obtained by adding zero fill, the upper bound by adding one fill. Thus in this example, the CDDAR of the list shown in Figure 7 is obtained by selecting all elements greater than or equal to 0110000000000000 and less than or equal to 0111111111111111. These elements, C, D, E, and F, form the sublist ((C D) (((E) F))). Details of this and other techniques for storing and processing lists in SIMD processors are given in Potter, 1983.

HARDWARE

Image Processing Aspects

The two dimensional aspect of imagery is often felt to be best exploited by two dimensional arrays of processors such as the MPP. However, experience with SIMD processors such as the STARAN and MPP indicate that the important consideration for processing two dimensional image data is the mapping between the pixels in the image memory and the individual processors in the processor array.

Figure 8 shows a diagram of the type of SIMD computers being considered. They have a single global memory accessed in parallel by all the processors in the array. The processors may be interconnected but do not have any internal memory. SIMD architectures of this type are easy to program in such a manner that each processor produces one complete result in parallel with the other processors. For example, if one of the processors in the array is to calculate a convolution or other areal function then it must have access to a two dimensional area of pixels. However, as far as the processor is concerned, it makes no difference if the data comes from memory or from neighboring processors. Consequently, overall, direct two dimensional access to the memory is more efficient, since in order for a processor to obtain data from his neighbor, the neighbor must have fetched it first himself and then passed it on (two cycles versus one).

A two dimensional global memory is not difficult to construct. Conventional memory addressing structure provides one dimension of access. A simple shifting operation between the memory and the processor array provides the other dimension of access. The shifting operation can be performed by shift circuitry, a network, memory address manipulation or a combination of these. Thus the model shown in Figure 8 includes an x and y address component. In an m processor machine, the y component accesses main memory as a traditional random address and causes m elements of row y to be fetched. The x component controls the shifting circuitry causing the column element desired by processor j to be aligned with it.

A two dimensional memory design also substantially reduces the semantic gap between software and hardware resulting in easier, more

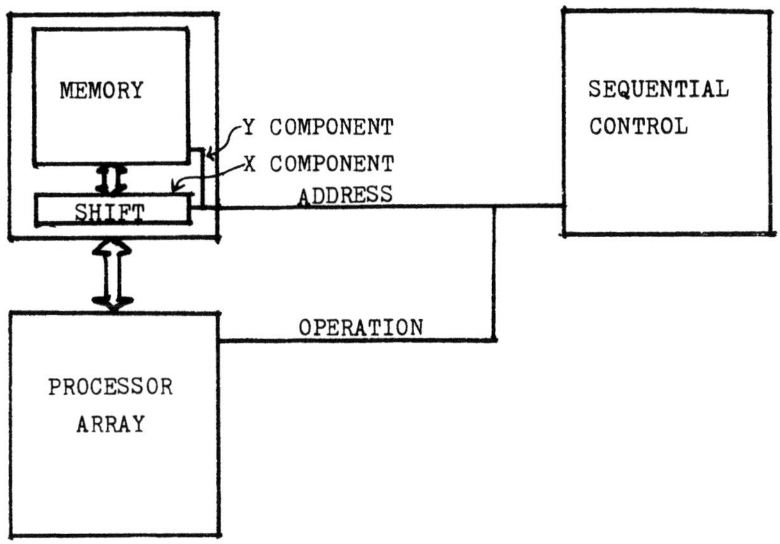

Figure 8 - Generic SIMD Processor with X and Y Address Components

efficient software design and implementation. For example, assuming a linear array of processors, during the alignment process, processor i's neighbors, i-1 and i+1 in the negative and positive x direction respectively, are aligned with pixels to the left and right of the pixel aligned with i. This is the exact desired result. To see this, consider convolution where:

$$p(i,j) = \underset{m,n = -1,0,1}{\mathrm{SUM}}[w(m,n)*p(i+m,j+n)]$$

If processor i is calculating the output for pixel p(i,j), then processors i-1 and i+1 are calculating the outputs for pixels p(i-1,j) and p(i+1,j) respectively. If the instruction sequence is at the point where m=1 and n=-1 for example, then processor i will multiply weight w(1,-1) times p(i+1,j-1) while processors i-1 and i+1 are multiplying p(i-1+1,j-1) and p(i+1+1,j-1) respectively by the same weight. That is, when one processor is operating on data from its upper right neighbor, all processors are operating on data from their respective upper right neighbors, etc.

It can easily be seen then that with a two dimensional memory access capability, a one dimensional processor array is sufficient to effectively process two dimensional data. Whether a two dimensional or one dimensional array of processors is used is primarily one of practicality. For example, if a SIMD machine has 512 processors, then a linear array is best since it matches well with the expected image size of 512 elements per row. If however, a SIMD machine such as the MPP has 16k processors, then a two dimensional array is best since images with rows of 16k elements are rare but images with 128x128 subimages are common. Of course, an array of 32x512 would be a good arrangement also. Note that with a two dimensional array of processors, the memory access mechanism is identical except that multiple rows (128 or 32) are retrieved instead of just one.

A brief analysis of the disparity detection algorithm reveals that it requires approximately 554 parallel adds, 172 parallel multiplies and 400 parallel shifts per pixel, where one parallel operation is effective on all elements of the image array (512x512). This results in about 300 MOPS per pixel processed with about 50% of the operations being addition and subtraction, 15% being multiplication and the remaining 35% being shift operations. These statistics would imply that the shifting and multiply operations are an important part of the overall computational requirements and should be efficiently implemented in the design.

Figure 9 shows the logical organization of a SIMD processor based on the frame-to-frame disparity analysis algorithm. The processing elements(PEs) need to be 8 bits wide with parallel add and multiply circuitry. They have 16 general purpose registers which can be used in address formation (i.e. as index registers - thus each memory must have an independent address bus). The y (random access) portion of the addresses are calculated in the individual PE's and delivered to the associated memories. The data is fetched and passed through the interconnection network where the x (shift) portion of the address is delivered by the program control unit resulting in the correct shift to align the data with the processor. Each PE also contains a set of 16 status registers. In many algorithms it is desirable to save the state of a logical condition to avoid having to recalculate it. Up to 16 different logical results can be saved in the status registers. Since, conditional instructions specify the status register to use, up to 16 different logical paths can be maintained simultaneously.

The memory is dual ported to allow I/O access without going through the processor array. I/O for image processing is a very regular (synchronous) process where each memory receives a fixed amount of data

(1 or 2 bytes per pixel for example) in a fixed order. During this mode of operation, the I/O control first broadcasts the number of bytes in a pixel to the I/O buffers. It then sends data in the proper order so that the first pixel is accepted by I/O buffer 1. When the first buffer has received the specified number of bytes of data, it sets an internal flag and subsequent data are passed on to buffer two. Buffer 2 then accepts data until it has received the specified number of bytes, then it sets its flag and the data is passed on to the next buffer, etc. When the entire row of pixels has been input, the I/O control broadcasts

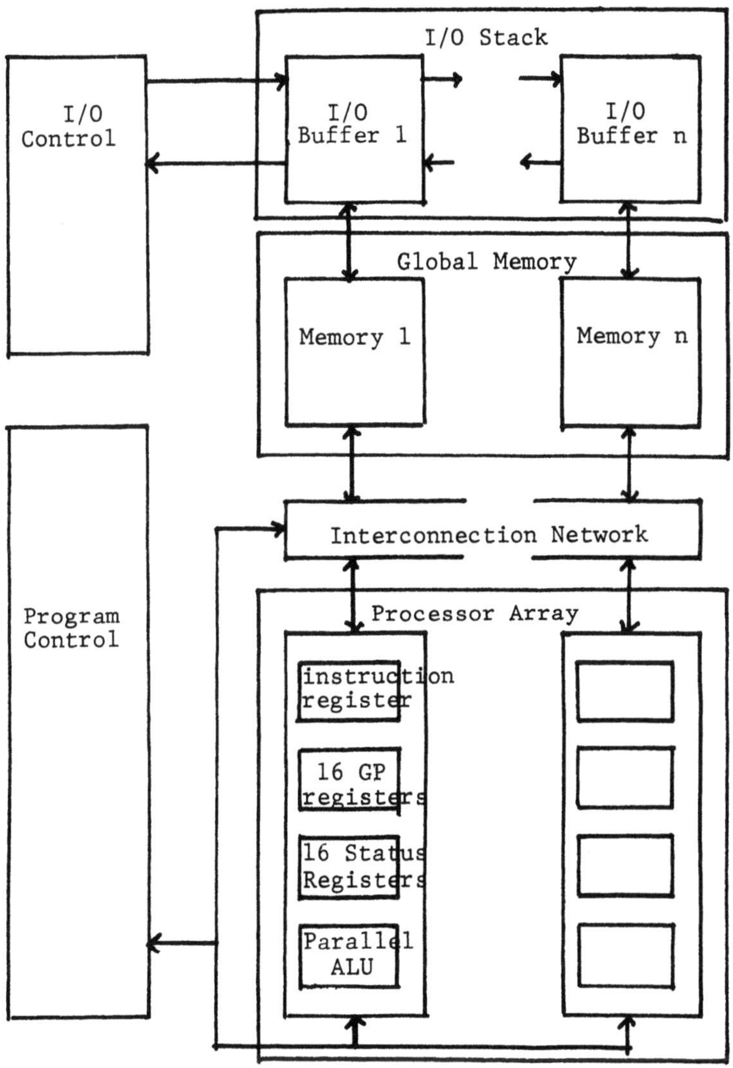

Figure 9 - Disparity Analysis Based SIMD Processor

the memory address, the program is interrupted and the data is transferred to memory.

On output, the process is reversed, the I/O control specifies the number of bytes and the address of the pixels, interrupts the program and the data is transferred from memory to the output buffers. The I/O control then starts to read the first I/O buffer. As it reads the data, data from the other buffers 'trickle down' until all buffers are emptied. Thus the I/O process is functionally similar to a FIFO stack instead of a bus. Note in particular, that there is no unit addressing only data is transferred.

Control Aspects

Raw image processing functions are characterized by the large amounts of arithmetic calculations that need to be performed due to the large amount of data to be processed. For example, convolution is not done on simply one pixel but on all pixels in an image. However, the object recognition functions are frequently based on non-arithmetic calculations such as linguistic pattern recognition or similar techniques. And while there are a relatively small number of objects (a few hundred versus millions of pixels), there will not simply be one grammar to recognize one object, but hundreds if not thousands of grammars to recognize an equal or larger number of objects. The problem is not simply identifying features in a raw image to match the terminal states of a grammar, but determining which of the thousands of grammars are pertinent and therefore to be processed. The combinatorial explosion and the non-arithmetic nature of linguistic recognition techniques will make this process as computationally intensive in real world applications as simple raw image processing problems. Thus a complete scene analysis system must have a major component dedicated to pattern recognition and control.

The Disparity Analysis Based SIMD architecture not only can perform raw image processing functions efficiently, it holds the potential for parallel execution of searching and matching processes fundamental to rule based recognition schemes. However, there is a major difference in the design of the I/O component of SIMD processors for image processing and scene analysis. In image processing algorithms, large volumes of spatially regular data must be input to the machine. In scene analysis, once the grammars have been input, they and the associated data bases tend to require random updating. Thus I/O servicing will require accessing the global memory for a few processors at a time.

Scene analysis I/O needs can be characterized in two ways. First if the data organization described in Figure 7 is used, data is 'relocatable'. That is, during a parallel search, it makes no difference which processor memory contains which datum. Second, complex searches are such that only a portion of the processors are busy at any one time. These two aspects can be combined to achieve an effective I/O scheme. The I/O stack described earlier can be easily modified for random I/O operation. As for image data, when data is input in the Scene Analysis Control (SAC) mode, it trickles down the stack until an empty input buffer is found. When the complete record has been input to the buffer, it is marked full and subsequent records pass over the buffer until an idle one is found.

When a SIMD processing element is not busy, if the machine is in the SAC mode, control is passed to the I/O processor which empties the input buffer (if full) and fills the output buffer (if empty). Note that in general, the processors become idle in a random order, thus data will not be stored in memory in the same order as it was input. However, the relocatable aspect of the data makes this acceptable. Thus by fitting the I/O in during otherwise unused idle processor time, the random I/O characteristic of grammar control processing requires very little overhead. The I/O control shown in Figure 9, retrieves files from disks and assigns storage locations in the processor memories (but does not specify which processor). On output, as the control reads data from the first I/O buffer, data automatically trickles down from the other buffers. The I/O processor formats the data into blocks and writes it out on the disks.

CONCLUSIONS

It was shown that a one dimensional array of processors with a two dimensional memory configuration can easily process 2d data. A two dimensional array of processors is not needed . While the attempt to match the machine's configuration to the distribution of the data is an interesting concept, it distorts the computational problem of image analysis since it emphasizes local mathematical neighborhood operations such as 3x3 convolution for edge detection, noise reduction, etc. at the expense of the equally complex problem of object recognition and scene analysis.

The final question is whether one single computer architecture can effectively perform both the image processing and scene analysis tasks. It would appear that the parallelism in a SIMD computer can be used to great advantage in both situations and that by scaling the computer for the total computing requirements, the architecture presented would be able to accomplish both tasks in real time.

BIBLIOGRAPHY

Aggarwal, J. K., L. S. Davis and W. N. Martin, 'Correspondence Processes in Dynamic Scene Analysis', PROCEEDINGS OF THE IEEE, vol. 69, no. 5, pp. 562-572, May 1981.

Aho, A. V. and M. J. Corasick, 'Efficient String Matching: An Aid to Bibliographic Search,' COMMUNICATIONS OF THE ACM, 18, 1975, pp. 333-340.

Baker, Henry G.,'List Processing in Real Time on a Serial Computer,' COMMUNICATIONS OF THE ACM, April, 1978, pp. 280-294.

Bobrow, Daniel G. and Douglas W. Clark, 'Compact Encodings of List Structure,' ACM TRANSACTIONS ON PROGRAMMING LANGUAGES AND SYSTEMS, October, 1979, pp. 266-703.

Bonar, Jeffrey G. and Steven P. Levitan, 'Real-time LISP Using Content Addressable Memory,' IEEE, 1981, pp. 112-117.

Fennema, C. L. and W. B. Thompson, 'Velocity Determination in Scenes Containing Several Moving Objects,' COMPUTER GRAPHICS AND IMAGE PROCESSING, 9, 1979, pp.301-315.

Gibson, J. J., 'The senses considered as perceptual systems,' Houghton Mifflin, Boston, 1966.

Hadani, I., G. Ishai and M. Gur, 'Visual Stability and Space Perception in Monocular Vision: Mathematical Model,' JOURNAL OF THE OPTICAL SOCIETY OF AMERICA, vol. 70, no. 1, January 1980, pp.60-65.

Horn, B. K., and B. G. Schunk, 'Determining Optical Flow,' ARTIFICIAL INTELLIGENCE, vol. 17, 1980, pp.185-203.

Johansson, G. 'Spatio-temporal differentiation and integration in visual motion perception,' Research Report No 160, University of Uppsala, Dept. of Psychology, 1974.

Potter, J., 'Scene Segmentation by Velocity Measurements Obtained with a Cross-Shaped Template,' PROCEEDINGS IV INTERNATIONAL JOINT CONFERENCE ON ARTIFICIAL INTELLIGENCE, 1975, pp. 803-810.

Potter, J. L., 'Continuous Image Processing on the MPP,' PROCEEDINGS OF THE 1981 IEEE COMPUTER SOCIETY WORKSHOP ON COMPUTER ARCHITECTURE FOR PATTERN ANALYSIS AND IMAGE DATABASE MANAGEMENT, Hot Springs, Virginia, Nov. 11-13, 1981.

Potter, J. L., 'Alternative Data Structures for Lists in Parallel Associative Computers,' To be published in the PROCEEDINGS OF THE 1983 INTERNATIONAL CONFERENCE ON PARALLEL PROCESSING, August 23-26, 1983.

Simmons, R. F. and D. Chester, 'Relating Sentences and Semantic Networks with Procedural Logic,' COMMUNICATIONS OF THE ACM, vol. 25, no. 8, August 1982, pp. 527-547.

Thompson, W. B., 'Lower-Level Estimation and Interpretation of Visual-Motion,' COMPUTER, vol. 14, August 1981, pp.20-28.

Ullman, S., 'Analysis of Visual Motion by Biological and Computer Systems,' COMPUTER, August 1981, pp. 57-69.

PYRAMID ARCHITECTURES FOR IMAGE ANALYSIS

Azriel Rosenfeld
Center for Automation Research
University of Maryland
College Park, MD 20742

1. Introduction

This paper discusses some methods of image analysis that make use of a "pyramid" of reduced-scale representations of the information in the given image. Section 2 discusses "intensity pyramids" that consist of reduced-resolution versions of the image, and indicates how such pyramids provide an efficient means of performing "coarse" feature detection operations on the image. Section 3 describes "feature pyramids" based on the approximate representations of edges or curves, and shows that such pyramids can be used to efficiently detect simple shapes such as blobs and ribbons in an image. Section 4 suggests that pyramids provide a vehicle for "pixel-region cooperation" in which global properties of regions are able to influence the segmentation processes that give rise to these regions.

There is a rapidly growing literature on "pyramid" methods in image analysis; for two collections of papers on the subject, see [1,2].

2. Intensity pyramids and coarse feature detection

The simplest type of image pyramid is constructed by repeatedly averaging the image intensities in nonoverlapping 2-by-2 blocks of pixels. Given an input image of size 2^n by 2^n, applying this process yields a reduced image of size 2^{n-1} by 2^{n-1}. Applying the process again to the reduced image yields a still smaller image of size 2^{n-2} by 2^{n-2}; and so on. We thus obtain a sequence of images of exponentially decreasing size: 2^n by 2^n, 2^{n-1} by 2^{n-1},..., 2 by 2, 1 by 1. If we imagine these images stacked on top of one another, they constitute an exponentially tapering "pyramid" of images. Note that the total number of pixels in the pyramid is $4^n(1+\frac{1}{4}+\frac{1}{16}+\ldots)<4^{n+1}/3$, i.e., less than 1/3 more than in the original image.

In this simple method of pyramid construction, each node in the pyramid, say k levels above the base, represents the average of a square block of the base of size 2^k by 2^k. For most purposes, it would

NATO ASI Series, Vol. F18
Computer Architectures for Spatially Distributed Data
Edited by H. Freeman and G. G. Pieroni

be preferable to use averages over regions that were more isotropic, i.e. (approximately) circular rather than square. The sharp cutoff characteristic of unweighted averaging would also usually be undesirable; weighted averages, peaked at the center of the averaging region and falling off to zero at its border, would be preferable, and the regions represented by adjacent nodes should overlap. On methods of defining pyramids using overlapped weighted averaging, with isotropically varying weights, see [3,4]. These ideas can be straightforwardly extended to multispectral images, where the pyramids are constructed by componentwise averaging. Pyramids based on textural properties can also be constructed, but we will not discuss them here.

Intensity pyramids provide an economical method of performing "coarse" feature detection (e.g., edge, spot, or bar detection) operations on an image at a range of resolutions. Sets of feature detection operations whose sizes grow by powers of 2 have been studied by several investigators [5-8]. We can compute such operators by building a pyramid and applying fine operators at each level; this yields results based on differences of block average gray levels rather than single-pixel gray levels, just as if we had applied scaled-up operators to the original image. By building the pyramid first, we have done the block averaging once and for all, and can now compute each coarse operator by performing only a few arithmetic operations on these averages. Note that the larger the operator, the fewer the positions in which we are computing it, but this is reasonable since values based on overlapping blocks would be redundant.

3. Feature pyramids and primitive region detection

The pixels in a pyramid need not represent averages of the gray levels (etc.) in blocks of the input image; they can also represent other types of information about these blocks. For example, we can apply edge (or curve) detection operators to an image, and then build a pyramid in which each pixel contains information about the edges that cross its block of the image. This information can be computed by combining information about sub-blocks, which is available from the pixels on the next lower level. The information about each edge might consist of the positions of its endpoints (and other critical points such as curvature maxima or inflections), the equation of an approximating polynomial, etc. This information can be stored in a pixel as long as the number of edges crossing its block does not exceed some allowable maximum. On such methods of pyramid representation of edges and curves see [9,10].

The use of pyramids to encode edges (or curves) makes it possible for the edges to interact locally at higher levels of the pyramid, even though they are far apart in the original image. For example, we can bridge the gaps in broken edges; even if two fragments of an edge are far apart, they will eventually be encoded by adjacent pixels, and a pixel on the next higher level will then merge them if they are in alignment [10]. Angles can be detected at any scale without the need for extensive searches along the edge. Edges of major significance (having simple representations at high levels of the pyramid) can be extracted and displayed at full resolution by "tracking" their representations down to the base of the pyramid [11]. A "blob" (compact region) in the image eventually gives rise to a pixel at some level in the pyramid that is locally surrounded by edges, so that it can be detected by local search [12]; this is more economical than the "spoke filter" approach of Sklansky, in which we must search for edges out to a distance that depends on the maximum expected blob size. Similarly, a "ribbon" in the image eventually gives rise to pixels having edges near it on opposite sides, so that it too can be detected by local search; the resulting detections can then be combined into approximations at higher levels of the pyramid, where we can encode the ribbon's shape (as we did for curves) as well as its width.

4. Pyramids and local-global cooperation

When pyramids are used to encode global features of an image (edges, blobs, etc.), pixels at high levels of the pyramid contain information about global properties of these features. We can transmit this information back down the pyramid and use it to modify the encoding criteria (e.g., the criterion for merging two pieces of curve into a single curve) and thus refine the features; the process can be iterated, if necessary. This allows global information about an image feature to influence the segmentation process that gives rise to that feature (e.g., eliminate curve segments that do not conform to the overall shape of the curve). Local/global cooperation in feature detection is also used in [13].

Local-global cooperation processes can also be defined in intensity-based pyramids. Here the pixels initially represent block average gray levels. We can modify these averages by giving less weight to pixels on the level below if their values (subblock averages) differ from that of the given pixel. By iterating this process, we can reach a situation where the pixels at the higher levels of the pyramid represent averages of homogeneous pieces of the image. A number of variations on this type of intensity-based local-global cooperation process are described in [14-19].

By using such local-global cooperation schemes we can construct links in the pyramid between pixels at adjacent levels that represent pieces of the same feature or region in the image. These links define trees whose leaves are the pixels (of the original image) belonging to the given feature (or region), and whose roots can be regarded as nodes representing the feature as a whole. Such trees can be thought of as bridging the gap between the pixel-array representation of the image and its relational-structure representation, in which global features of the image are represented by single nodes.

5. Concluding remarks

The process of pyramid construction is an application of the divide-and-conquer principle. The information at a given pixel is computed from the information at a small number of pixels on the level below; each of these in turn computes its information from that at a small number of pixels on the next lower level; and so on. If we could assign a processor to each pixel, and provide it with inputs from the appropriate pixels on the level below, the pixels on each level could compute their information in parallel. The total number of time steps required to compute the information at all levels of the pyramid would then be proportional to the pyramid height, which is the logarithm of the image diameter. Note that the algorithms described in this paper involved only "vertical" flow of information from level to level of the pyramid, together with local information flow within levels.

We have seen that pyrmaids provide computationally inexpensive methods of detecting coarse features and primitive types of regions in an image. In the latter application they take advantage of the fact that simple types of region shape information become local at some level of the pyramid, thus allowing "action at a distance" (interaction among widely separated features) to be performed using local operations only. Perhaps even more important, pyramids provide a possible mechanism for bridging the classical "pixel-region gap" by allowing direct feedback of global information about regions to the pixels comprising these regions, so that the process of region extraction can be modified or refined.

References

1. S. Tanimoto and A. Klinger, eds., Structured Computer Vision: Machine Perception through Hierarchical Computation Structures, Academic Press, NY, 1980.

2. A. Rosenfeld, ed., Multiresolution image processing and analysis, Springer, Berlin, 1983.

3. P. J. Burt, Fast filter transforms for image processing, Computer Graphics Image Processing 16, 1981, 20-51.

4. P. J. Burt, Fast algorithms for estimating local image properties, Computer Vision, Graphics, Image Processing 21, 1983, 368-382.

5. A. Rosenfeld and M. Thurston, Edge and curve detection for visual scene analysis, IEEE Trans. Computers 20, 562-569.

6. D. Marr and E. Hildreth, Theory of edge detection, Proc. Royal Soc. B207, 1980, 187-217.

7. M. Shneier, Extracting linear features from images using pyramids, IEEE Trans. Systems, Man, Cybernetics 12, 1982, 569-572.

8. M. Shneier, Using pyramids to define local thresholds for blob detection, IEEE Trans. Pattern Analysis Machine Intelligence 5, 1983, 345-349.

9. M. Shneier, Two hierarchical linear feature representations: edge pyramids and edge quadtrees, Computer Graphics Image Processing 17, 1981, 211-224.

10. T. H. Hong, M. Shneier, R. Hartley, and A. Rosenfeld, Using pyramids to detect good continuation, IEEE Trans. Systems, Man, Cybernetics, to appear.

11. T. H. Hong, M. Shneier, and A. Rosenfeld, Border extraction using linked edge pyramids, IEEE Trans. Systems, Man, Cybernetics 12, 1982, 660-668.

12. T. H. Hong and M. Shneier, Extracting compact objects using linked pyramids, IEEE Trans. Pattern Analysis Machine Intelligence, to appear.

13. M. Hedlund, G. H. Granlund, and H. Knutson, A consistency operation for line and curve enhancement, in Proc. IEEE Conf. Pattern Recognition Image Processing, 1982, 93-96.

14. P. Burt, T. H. Hong, and A. Rosenfeld, Segmentation and estimation of image region properties through cooperative hierarchical computation, IEEE Trans. Systems, Man, Cybernetics 11, 1981, 802-809.

15. T. H. Hong, K. A. Narayanan, S. Peleg, A. Rosenfeld, and T. Silberberg, Image smoothing and segmentation by multiresolution

pixel linking: further experiments and extensions, IEEE Trans. Systems, Man, Cybernetics 12, 1982, 611-622.

16. H. J. Antonisse, Image segmentation in pyramids, Computer Graphics Image Processing 19, 1982, 367-383.

17. M. Pietikäinen, A. Rosenfeld, and I. Walter, Split-and-link algorithms for image segmentation, Pattern Recognition 15, 1982, 287-298.

18. S. Kasif and A. Rosenfeld, Pyramid linking is a special case of ISODATA, IEEE Trans. Systems, Man, Cybernetics 13, 1983, 84-85.

19. T. H. Hong and A. Rosenfeld, Unforced image partitioning by weighted pyramid linking, IEEE Trans. Pattern Analysis Machine Intelligence, to appear.

USING QUADTREES TO REPRESENT SPATIAL DATA

Hanan Samet*
Computer Science Department
University of Maryland
College Park, MD 20742
USA

ABSTRACT

Use of the quadtree data structure in representing spatial data is reviewed. The focus is on its properties that make it appropriate for applications in image processing. A number of operations in which the quadtree finds use are discussed.

1. INTRODUCTION

The quadtree is a term used to describe a class of hierarchical data structures whose common property is that they are based on the principle of regular decomposition. Such data structures are becoming increasingly important as representations in the fields of image processing, computer graphics, and geographic information systems [1]. The numerous variants of quadtrees can be differentiated on the basis of the type of data that they are used to represent, and on the principle guiding the decomposition process. Presently, quadtrees are used for point data, regions, curves, and volumes. The decomposition may be into equal-sized parts (termed a regular decomposition), or it may be governed by the input. In this chapter we focus on quadtree representations of two-dimensional binary regions and to a minor extent on point and curvilinear data. The chapters by Freeman and Rosenfeld discuss the related octree and pyramid representations respectively.

In order to illustrate the quadtree data structure, consider the region shown in Figure 1a which is represented by a 2**3 by 2**3 binary array in Figure 1b. 1's correspond to picture elements (termed pixels) which are in the region and 0's correspond to picture elements that are outside the region. Quadtrees represent regions by successively subdividing their array representation into four equal-size quadrants. When the array does not consist entirely of 1's or 0's

*The support of the Engineering Topographic Laboratories (under Contract DAAK-70-31-C0059) is gratefully acknowledged, as is the help of Janet Salzman in preparing this paper.

NATO ASI Series, Vol. F18
Computer Architectures for Spatially Distributed Data
Edited by H. Freeman and G.G. Pieroni

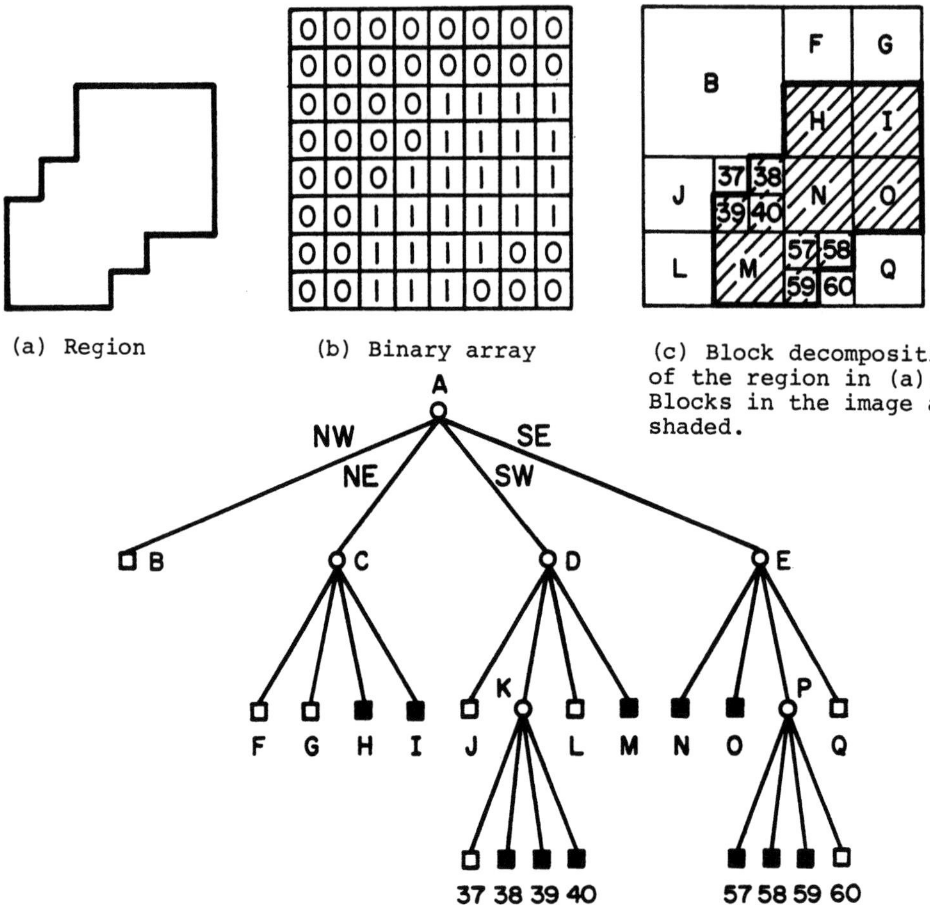

(a) Region

(b) Binary array

(c) Block decomposition of the region in (a). Blocks in the image are shaded.

(d) Quadtree representation of the blocks in (c).

Figure 1. A region, its binary array, its maximal blocks, and the corresponding quadtree.

(i.e., the region does not cover the entire array), we subdivide it further into quadrants, subquadrants, ... until we obtain blocks (possibly single pixels) that consist of 1's or 0's; i.e., they are entirely contained in the region or entirely disjoint from it. For example, the resulting blocks for the binary array of Figure 1b are shown in Figure 1c. This process is represented by a tree of out degree 4 (i.e., each non-leaf node has four sons) in which the root node corresponds to the entire array. The four sons of the root node represent the quadrants (labeled in order NW, NE, SW, SE), and the leaf nodes correspond to those blocks for which no further subdivision is necessary. Leaf nodes are said to be BLACK or WHITE depending on whether their corresponding blocks are entirely within or outside of the region respectively. All non-leaf nodes are said to be GRAY. The quadtree representation for Figure 1c is shown in Figure 1d.

As described above, the region quadtree is a partition of space into a set of squares whose sides are all a power of two long. This formulation is due to Klinger [2,3] who used the term Q-tree whereas Hunter [4] was the first to use the term quadtree in such a context. A similar partition of space into rectangular quadrants, also termed a quadtree, is due to Finkel and Bentley [5]. It is an adaptation of the binary search tree [6] to two dimensions (and can be easily extended to an arbitrary number of dimensions). It is primarily of use for representing multidimensional point data and we refer to it as a point quadtree. As an example, consider the tree in Figure 2 which is built for the sequence Chicago, Mobile, Toronto, Buffalo, Denver, Omaha, Atlanta, and Miami. Note that its shape is highly dependent on the order in which the points are added to the tree. For an improvement on the point quadtree see the k-d tree of Bentley [7]. The survey of Bentley and Friedman [8] describes related data structures.

The principle of recursive decomposition has been frequently used. Warnock [9] implemented a hidden surface elimination algorithm using a recursive decomposition of the picture area. It is repeatedly subdivided into successively smaller rectangles while searching for areas sufficiently simple to be output. Other early uses include robotics [10], space planning in an architectural context [11], and edge detection [12]. Related developments in the image processing domain include the recognition cone [13], the preprocessing cone [14], and the pyramid [15].

2. MAXIMAL BLOCK REPRESENTATIONS

A number of region representations are characterized as being a collection of maximal blocks that are contained in a given region. The simplest such representation is the run length where the blocks are 1 by m rectangles [16]. A more general representation treats the region as a union of maximal square blocks (or blocks of any desired shape) that it contains. The region is determined by specifying the centers and radii of these blocks. This representation is called the medial axis transformation (MAT) [17,18]. The quadtree is a variant on the maximal block representation where the blocks are disjoint,

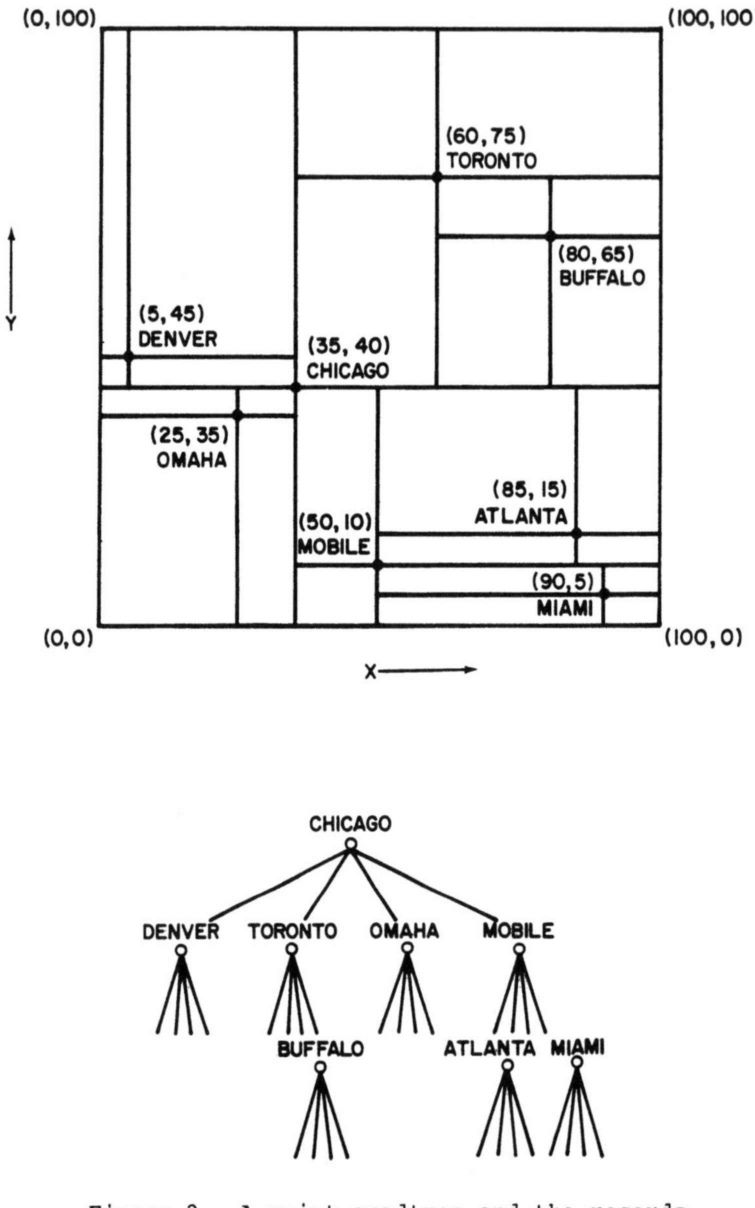

Figure 2. A point quadtree and the records it represents.

square, and have standard sizes (i.e., sides of lengths that are powers of two) and positions.

It should be clear that the quadtree is not a unique image representation. Representations based on triangular and hexagonal tessellations are also appropriate. In general, a planar decomposition should be an infinitely repetitive pattern and also should be infinitely decomposable into increasingly finer patterns [19]. The latter requirement is not satisfied by the hexagonal tessellation since a hexagon cannot be decomposed into smaller hexagons although hexagon-based systems do exist [20]. The choice between square and triangle quadtrees depends on the grid (i.e., the result of a sampling process). Our discussion is limited to the square quadtree.

3. NEIGHBOR FINDING TECHNIQUES

Most of the operations that we wish to perform on quadtrees are implemented as tree traversals. The difference between them is in the nature of the computation that is performed at the node. Often, these computations involve the examination of some nodes that are adjacent to the node being processed (i.e., the blocks corresponding to the nodes are touching along a common side). We call such nodes, corresponding to blocks of greater than or equal size, neighbors (the neighbor may be GRAY). In order for the operations to be performed in the most general manner, we must be able to locate neighbors in a way that is independent of both position (i.e., the coordinates) and size of the node. We also do not want to use any additional links to adjacent nodes. In other words, we only use the structure of the tree and no pointers in excess of the four links from a node to its four sons and one link to its father for a non-root node. This is in contrast with the methods of Klinger and Rhodes [21] which make use of size and position information, and those of Hunter and Steiglitz [4, 22,23] which locate neighbors through the use of explicit links (termed ropes and nets).

It is quite easy to locate adjacent neighbors in the horizontal or vertical directions. The basic idea is to ascend the tree until a common ancestor is located, and then descend back down the tree in search of the neighboring node. For example, suppose we wish to find the western neighbor of node N in Figure 1. The nearest common ancestor is the first ancestor node which is reached via its NE or SE son (i.e., the first ancestor node of which N is not a western descendant). Next, we retrace the path used to locate the common ancestor, except that we make mirror image moves about an axis formed by the common boundary between the nodes. In the case of a western neighbor, the mirror images of NW and SW are NE and SE respectively. Therefore, the western neighbor of node N in Figure 1 is node K. It is located by ascending the tree until the nearest common ancestor, A, has been located. This requires going through a NW link to reach node E, and a SE link to reach node A. Node K is subsequently located by back-tracking along the previous path with the appropriate mirror image moves (i.e., following a SW link to reach node D, and a NE link to reach node K).

It should be clear that neighbors need not be of the same size. If the neighbor is larger, then only part of the path from the common ancestor is retraced. Note that similar techniques can be used to locate diagonal neighbors (i.e., nodes corresponding to blocks that touch a given node's block at a corner). For example, node 57 in Figure 1 is the SE neighbor of node 40. For more details see [24].

4. CONVERSION

The quadtree is a useful representation for binary images because its hierarchical nature facilitates the performance of a large number of operations. Nevertheless, images are traditionally represented using binary arrays, rasters (i.e., run lengths), chain codes (i.e., borders), or polygons (vectors). Some of these representations are chosen due to hardware reasons (e.g., run lengths are particularly useful for raster-like devices such as television). Thus we need techniques to efficiently switch between these various representations.

The most common image representation is the binary array. There are a number of ways of constructing a quadtree from a binary array. The simplest approach is one that converts the array to a complete quadtree (i.e., for a 2**n by 2**n image, a tree of height n with one node per pixel). The resulting quadtree is subsequently reduced in size by repeatedly attempting to merge groups of four pixels or four blocks of a uniform color that are appropriately aligned. This approach is simple but is extremely wasteful of storage since many nodes may be needlessly created. In fact, it is not inconceivable to exhaust available memory when an algorithm employing this approach is used while the resulting tree fits in the available memory.

We can avoid the needless creation of nodes by visiting the elements of the binary array in the order defined by the labels on the

Figure 3. Binary array representation of the region in Figure 1a.

array in Figure 3 which corresponds to the image of Figure 1. Using such a method we never create a leaf node until it is known to be maximal. Equivalently, we never need to merge four leaves of the same color and change the color of their parent from GRAY to BLACK or WHITE as is appropriate. For example, we note that since pixels 25,26,27, and 28 are all BLACK, no quadtree nodes were created for them - i.e., node H corresponds to the part of the image spanned by them. This algorithm is shown in [25] to have an execution time proportional to the number of pixels in the image.

When a raster representation is used, we have to scan the array in a row by row manner as we build the quadtree. Such an algorithm, having an execution time proportional to the number of pixels in the image, is described in [26]. The reverse process is also useful since output is usually done on a raster device. The most obvious method is to generate an array corresponding to the quadtree. However, this method may require more memory than is available and we do not consider it further. In [27] a number of quadtree to raster algorithms are described. All of the algorithms traverse the quadtree by rows and visit each quadtree node once for each row that intersects it. These algorithms have execution times that only depend on the number of blocks in the image (irrespective of their color) and not on their particular configuration.

Another very common representation used in cartographic applications is the chain code (also known as a boundary code). It can be specified, relative to a given starting point, as a sequence of unit vectors (i.e., one pixel long) in the principal directions. We can represent the directions by numbers, e.g., let i, an integer quantity ranging from 0 to 3, represent a unit vector having a direction of 90*i degrees. For example, the chain code for the boundary of the region in Figure 1, moving clockwise starting from the left of the uppermost border points, is

$0^4 3^4 2^2 3^1 2^1 1^1 2^3 1^3 0^1 1^1 0^1 1^2$.

An algorithm for the conversion of quadtrees to chain codes is given in [29] and the algorithm for the reverse process of converting chain codes to quadtrees is given in [30].

Use of the chain code corresponds to approximating a polygon by unit vectors. It is also common to represent polygonal data by a set of vertices, or even a point and a sequence of vectors consisting of (magnitude, direction) pairs. Hunter and Steiglitz [4,22,23] address the problem of representing simple polygons (i.e., polygons with non-intersecting edges) using quadtrees. A polygon is represented by a three-color variant of the quadtree. In essence, there are three types of nodes - interior, boundary, and exterior. A node is said to be of type boundary if an edge of the polygon passes through it. Boundary nodes are not subject to merging. Interior and exterior nodes correspond to areas within, and outside of, respectively, the polygon and can be merged to yield larger nodes. Figure 4 illustrates a sample polygon and its quadtree corresponding to the definition of [22]. The disadvantage of such a representation for polygonal lines is that a width is associated with them whereas in a purely technical sense these lines have a width of zero. Algorithms for building a quadtree from a polygon are presented in [4,22].

5. SET OPERATIONS

Perhaps the most useful application of the quadtree is the performance of set operations such as union (i.e., overlay) and intersection

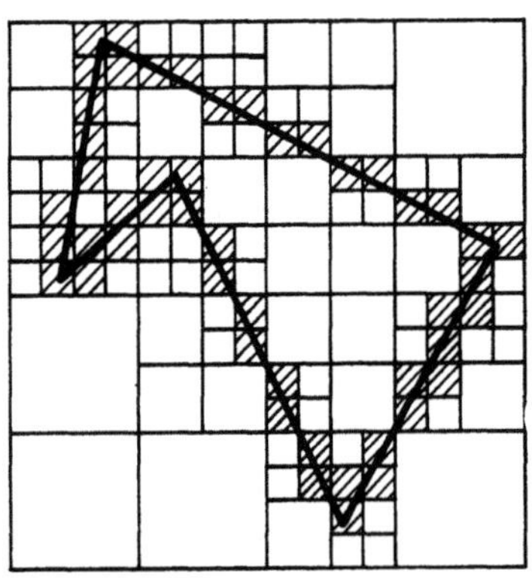

Figure 4. Hunter and Steiglitz's quadtree representation of a polygon.

of several images. This is described in greater detail in [4,22,31]. For example, to obtain the quadtree corresponding to the union of S and T we merely traverse the two trees in parallel while constructing the resulting tree, say U. If either of the two nodes is BLACK, then the corresponding node in U is BLACK. If one node is WHITE, say S, then the corresponding node in U is set to the other node, i.e., T. If both nodes are GRAY, then U is set to GRAY and the algorithm is applied recursively to the sons of S and T. However, when both nodes are GRAY, once the sons have been processed, we must check if a merger is to take place since all four sons could be BLACK. Computing the intersection of two quadtrees is analogous to computing the union with the roles of BLACK and WHITE interchanged.

6. TRANSFORMATIONS

The impetus for the development of the quadtree concept was a desire to provide an efficient data structure for computer graphics. Warnock [9] used recursive decomposition as the basis for the hidden surface elimination algorithm. Hunter's Ph.D. thesis [4] was a significant extension of the quadtree concept from both a theoretical and practical standpoint. Hunter's goal was to provide a framework for performing computer animation efficiently. In order to do this, a capability is necessary to perform a number of basic transformations. Scaling by a power of two is trivial when using quadtrees since it corresponds to a reduction in resolution. Rotation by multiples of 90 degrees is equally simple - i.e., a recursive rotation of sons at each level of the tree. The transformation of one quadtree into another by applying a linear operator is also feasible [22].

The linear transformation algorithm, and the scaling and rotation operations have a common shortcoming. With the exception of scaling or translations by a power of two and transformations involving rotations in multiples of 90 degrees, the results are approximations. Straight lines are not necessarily transformed into straight lines. This shortcoming is often mistakenly attributed to the quadtree representation where in fact it is a direct result of the underlying digitization process. It should be clear that it manifests itself no matter what underlying representation is used when doing raster graphics. For a quadtree-based representation that is free of such a problem see the PM quadtree [32].

Quadtrees have also been used for image processing operations which involve gray-scale images rather than binary images. Some examples include image segmentation [33], edge enhancement [34], image smoothing [35], and threshold selection [36].

7. GEOMETRIC PROPERTIES

Areas and moments for images represented by quadtrees are easy to compute. To find the area we only need to traverse the quadtree in postorder and accumulate the sizes of the BLACK blocks. For a BLACK block at level k, the contribution to the area is 2**(2*k). Moments can be computed with equal ease - i.e., we simply sum the moments of the BLACK blocks. The position of each BLACK block is easy to ascertain because we know the path that was taken to reach the block when we start processing at the root of the tree. With knowledge of the area and the first moments, we can compute the coordinates of the centroid and now central moments relative to the centroid can be obtained [31].

One of the basic operations in any image processing system is connected component labeling. In graph-theoretical terms, it is analogous to finding the connected components of a graph. For example, the image of Figure 5 has two components. Given a binary array representation, the traditional method of performing this operation is to scan the image row by row from left to right and assign the same label to adjacent BLACK pixels that are found to the right and in the downward direction. During this process pairs of equivalences may be generated and thus two more steps are needed. The first merges the equivalences and the second updates the labels associated with the various pixels to reflect the merger of the equivalences.

When an image is represented by a quadtree, we perform an analogous three-step process [37]. The first step is a postorder tree traversal where for each BLACK node that is encountered, say A, we find all adjacent BLACK nodes on the southern and eastern sides of A and assign them the same label as A. Adjacency exploration is done using the neighbor finding techniques described in [24]. At times, the adjacent node may already have been assigned a label in which case we note the equivalence. The second step merges all the equivalent pairs that were generated during step one. The third step performs another traversal of the quadtree and updates the labels on the nodes to reflect the equivalences generated by the first two steps of the algorithm.

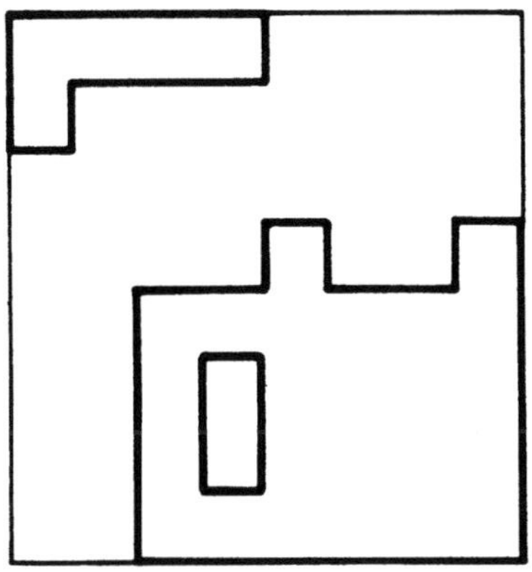

(a) Image

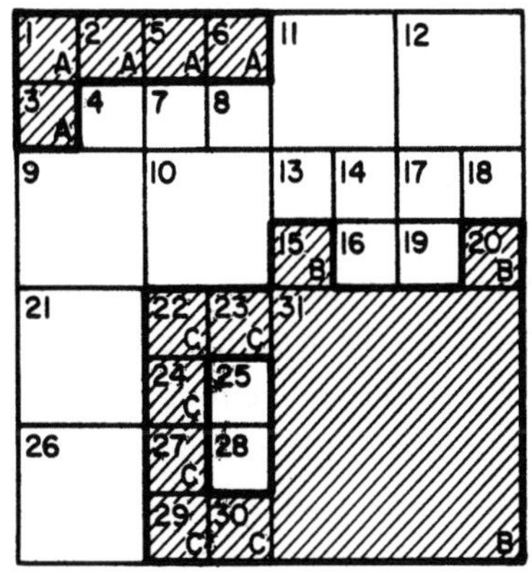

(b) Block decomposition of the image in (a).

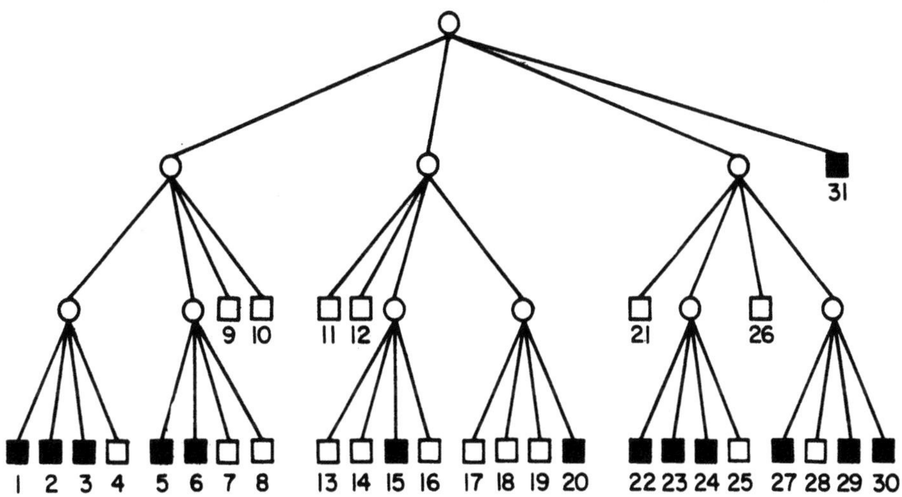

(c) Quadtree representation of the blocks in (b).

Figure 5. An image, its maximal blocks, and the corresponding quadtree. Blocks in the image are shaded, background blocks are blank.

The execution time for labeling the connected components can be obtained by examining the three steps of the algorithm. Let B be the number of BLACK nodes in the quadtree. Steps 1 and 3 are of O(B) while step 2, the merger of equivalence classes, is known to be of O(B*log B) [38] and thus the algorithm is of O(B*log B). This is a very important result because it is dependent only on the number of blocks in the image and not on their size. In contrast, the analogous algorithm for the binary array has an execution time that is proportional to the number of pixels and hence to the size of the blocks. Thus we see that the hierarchical structure of the quadtree data structure not only saves space but also saves time. A somewhat analogous result is shown in [39] as a byproduct of an algorithm for the computation of the Euler number (i.e., genus) [40] of an image represented by a quadtree.

Perimeter computation of an image represented by a quadtree [41] can be done in a manner analogous to step one of the connected component labeling process described earlier. The only difference is that when labeling connected components we looked for adjacent BLACK neighbors whereas for the purpose of computing the perimeter we must look for adjacent WHITE neighbors. In other words, we perform a postorder tree traversal and for each BLACK node that is encountered, we explore its four adjacent sides looking for WHITE neighbors. For each WHITE neighbor that is found, the length of the corresponding shared side is included in the perimeter. For an alternative perimeter computation algorithm that transmits neighbors as parameters rather than having to rely on neighbor exploration, see [42].

8. SPACE REQUIREMENTS

The development of the quadtree was motivated by a desire to aggregate homogeneous blocks of space in the hope of realizing savings in space. As we have seen in the previous discussion, an important byproduct of this aggregation has been the speeding up in execution time of a number of basic operations. Nevertheless, the quadtree is not always the ideal representation. Clearly, the worst case in terms of storage requirements occurs when the region corresponds to a checkerboard pattern. The amount of space required is a function of the resolution (i.e., the number of levels in the tree). Hunter [4] has proved that the quadtree grows linearly in the number of nodes as the resolution is doubled whereas when using a binary array representation, each doubling of the resolution leads to a quadrupling of the number of pixels.

The space required by a quadtree is very sensitive to its orientation. Dyer [43] has shown that the amount of space necessary when arbitrarily placing a square of size 2**m by 2**m at any position in a 2**n by 2**n image is o(p+n) when p is the perimeter (in pixel widths) of the block. Clearly, shifting the image within the space in which it is embedded can reduce the total number of nodes. Grosky and Jain [44] have shown that for a region such that d is the maximum of its horizontal and vertical extent (measured in pixel widths) and 2**(n-1)< d<2**n, then the optimal grid resolution is either n or n+1. In other words, embedding the region in an area larger than 2**(n+1) by 2**(n+1) and shifting it around will not lead to fewer nodes being required. This result is used by Li, Grosky, and Jain [45] to obtain an algorithm which finds the optimal configuration of the quadtree in the sense of requiring a minimum number of nodes. The shift sensitivity of the quadtree data structure can be reduced, at times, by using the Quadtree Medial Axis Transform (QMAT) [46] which is based on a partition of space into square blocks, possibly non-disjoint, of side lengths which are sums of powers of two rather than disjoint square blocks of side lengths that are powers of two as is the case for the quadtree.

The fact that the quadtree data structure requires pointers leads to a considerable amount of overhead. Recently, there has been an increasing amount of interest in pointer-less quadtree representations. They can be grouped into two categories. The first represents the image in the form of a preorder traversal of the nodes of its quadtree [47]. The second treats the image as a collection of leaves. Each leaf is encoded by a base 4 number termed a locational code, corresponding to a sequence of directional codes that locate the leaf along a path from the root of the tree. It is difficult to attribute the origin of this technique. It was used as a means of organizing quadtrees on external storage by Klinger and Rhodes [21]. A base 5 variant of it which has an additional code as a don't care is used by Gargantini [48] and Abel and Smith [49] (see also [50,51,52,53,54]) to yield an encoding where each leaf in a 2**n by 2**n image is n digits long. A leaf corresponding to a 2**k by 2**k block (k<n) will have n-k don't care digits.

9. BOUNDARY REPRESENTATIONS

The region quadtree is an approach to region representation that is based on describing its interior. There also exist representations that specify borders of regions. One of the most common representations is the chain code [28]. Other popular representations include polygons in the form of vectors [55]. Recently, there has also been a considerable amount of interest in hierarchical representations. These are primarily based on rectangular approximations to the data [56,57, 58]. In particular, Burton [57] uses upright rectangles, Ballard [56] uses rectangular strips of arbitrary orientation, and Peucker [58] uses sets of bands. There also exist methods that are based on a regular decomposition in two dimensions as reported by Hunter and Steiglitz [22], Shneier [59], Martin [60], and Samet and Webber [32,61].

The edge quadtree of Shneier [59] is an example of a quadtree-based boundary representation. It is an attempt to store linear feature information (e.g., curves) for an image (binary and gray-scale) in a manner analogous to that used for storing region information. A region containing a linear feature or part thereof is subdivided into four squares repeatedly until a square is obtained that contains a single curve that can be approximated by a single straight line. Each leaf node contains the following information about the edge passing through it: magnitude (i.e., 1 in the case of a binary image or the intensity in case it is a gray-scale image), direction, intercept, and a directional error term (i.e., the error induced by approximating the curve by a straight line using a measure such as least squares). If an edge terminates within a node, then a special flag is set and the intercept denotes the point at which the edge terminates. Applying this process leads to quadtrees in which long edges are represented by large leaves or a sequence of large leaves. However, small leaves are required in the vicinity of corners or intersecting edges. Of course, many leaves will contain no edge information at all. Note that the edge quadtree is pixel-based and thus the accuracy of the resulting approximation is constrained, in part, by the resolution of the data being represented. For a representation that does not suffer from this problem, see the PM quadtree [32]. As an example of the decomposition that is imposed by the edge quadtree, consider Figure 6 which is the edge quadtree corresponding to the polygon of Figure 4 when represented on a 2**4 by 2**4 grid. What is desired is a regular decomposition

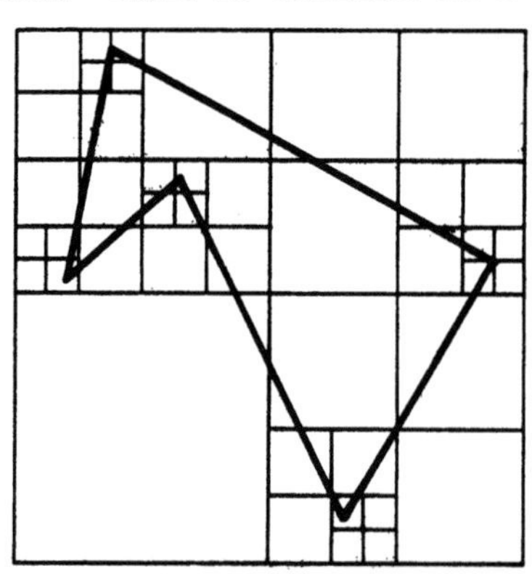

Figure 6. The edge quadtree corresponding to the polygon of Figure 4.

strip tree or variant thereof.

10. CONCLUDING REMARKS

In this chapter, we have attempted to review the use of the quadtree data structure for representing spatial data. We have seen that the quadtree is a representation that can be applied in many traditional image processing operations. Its value is not merely in the saving of space but more importantly in the speeding up of the execution times of these operations. As time passes, alternative representations to the pointer-based quadtree will undoubtedly be developed (e.g., [62]). However, conceptually speaking, the principle of recursive decomposition, of which the quadtree is an embodiment, will continue to be of utility.

REFERENCES

1. A. Rosenfeld, H. Samet, C. Shaffer, and R. E. Webber, Application of hierarchical data structures to geographical information systems, Computer Science TR-1197, University of Maryland, College Park, MD, June 1982.

2. A. Klinger, Patterns and search statistics, in Optimizing Methods in Statistics, J. S. Rustagi, Ed., Academic Press, New York, 1971.

3. A. Klinger and C. R. Dyer, Experiments in picture representations using regular decomposition, Computer Graphics and Image Processing 5, 1976, 68-105.

4. G. M. Hunter, Efficient computation and data structures for graphics, Ph.D. dissertation, Department of Electrical Engineering and Computer Science, Princeton University, Princeton, NJ, 1978.

5. R. A. Finkel and J. L. Bentley, Quad trees: a data structure for retrieval on composite keys, Acta Informatica 4, 1974, 1-9.

6. D. E. Knuth, The Art of Computer Programming, vol. 1, Fundamental Algorithms, Second Edition, Addison-Wesley, Reading, MA, 1975.

7. J. L. Bentley, Multidimensional binary search trees used for associative searching, Communications of the ACM 18, September 1975, 509-517.

8. J. L. Bentley and J. H. Friedman, Data structures for range searching, ACM Computing Surveys 11, December 1979, 397-409.

9. J. L. Warnock, A hidden surface algorithm for computer generated half tone pictures, Computer Science Department TR 4-15, University of Utah, Salt Lake City, June 1969.

10. N. J. Nilsson, A mobile automaton: an application of artificial intelligence techniques, Proceedings of the First International Joint Conference on Artificial Intelligence, Washington, DC, 1969, 509-520.

11. C. M. Eastman, Representations for space planning, Communications of the ACM 13, April 1970, 242-250.

12. M. D. Kelly, Edge detection in pictures by computer using planning, Machine Intelligence 6, 1971, 397-409.

13. L. Uhr, Layered "recognition cone" networks that preprocess, classify, and describe, IEEE Transactions on Computers 21, 1972, 758-768.

14. E. M. Riseman and M. A. Arbib, Computational techniques in the visual segmentation of static scenes, Computer Graphics and Image Processing 6, 1977, 221-276.

15. S. Tanimoto and T. Pavlidis, A hierarchical data structure for picture processing, Computer Graphics and Image Processing 4, 1975, 104-119.

16. D. Rutovitz, Data structures for operations on digital images, in Pictorial Pattern Recognition, G. C. Cheng et al.,Eds., Thompson Book Co., Washington, DC, 1968, 105-133.

17. H. Blum, A transformation for extracting new descriptors of shape, in Models for the Perception of Speech and Visual Form, W. Wathen-Dunn, Ed., M.I.T. Press, Cambridge, MA, 1967, 362-380.

18. A. Rosenfeld and J. L. Pfaltz, Sequential operations in digital image processing, Journal of the ACM 13, October 1966, 471-494.

19. N. Ahuja, On approaches to polygonal decomposition for hierarchical image representation, to appear in Computer Vision,Graphics and Image Processing, 1983 (see also Proceedings of the IEEE Conference on Pattern Recognition and Image Processing, Dallas, 1981, 75-80).

20. L. Gibson and D. Lucas, Vectorization of raster images using hierarchical methods, Computer Graphics and Image Processing 20, 1982, 82-89.

21. A. Klinger and M. L. Rhodes, Organization and access of image data by areas, IEEE Transactions on Pattern Analysis and Machine Intelligence 1, 1979, 50-60.

22. G. M. Hunter and K. Steiglitz, Operations on images using quadtrees, IEEE Transactions on Pattern Analysis and Machine Intelligence 1, 1979, 145-153.

23. G. M. Hunter and K. Steiglitz, Linear transformation of pictures represented by quadtrees, Computer Graphics and Image Processing 10, 1979, 289-296.

24. H. Samet, Neighbor finding techniques for images represented by quadtrees, Computer Graphics and Image Processing 18, 1982, 37-57.

25. H. Samet, Region representation: quadtrees from binary arrays, Computer Graphics and Image Processing 18, 1980, 88-93.

26. H. Samet, An algorithm for converting rasters to quadtrees, IEEE Transactions on Pattern Analysis and Machine Intelligence 3, 1981, 487-501.

27. H. Samet, Algorithms for the conversion of quadtrees to rasters, to appear in Computer Vision, Graphics, and Image Processing, 1933 (also University of Maryland Computer Science TR-979).

28. H. Freeman, Computer processing of line-drawing images, ACM Computing Surveys 6, March 1974, 57-97.

29. C. R. Dyer, A. Rosenfeld, and H. Samet, Region representation: boundary codes from quadtrees, Communications of the ACM 23, March 1980, 171-179.

30. H. Samet, Region representation: quadtrees from boundary codes, Communications of the ACM 23, March 1980, 163-170.

31. M. Shneier, Calculations of geometric properties using quadtrees, Computer Graphics and Image Processing 16, 1981, 296-302.

32. H. Samet and R. E. Webber, Using quadtrees to represent polygonal maps, Proceedings of the IEEE Conference on Computer Vision and Pattern Recognition, Washington, DC, 1983, 127-132.

33. S. Ranade, A. Rosenfeld, and J. M. S. Prewitt, Use of quadtrees for image segmentation, Computer Science TR-878, University of Maryland, College Park, MD, February 1980.

34. S. Ranade, Use of quadtrees for edge enhancement, IEEE Transactions on Systems, Man, and Cybernetics 11, 1981, 370-373.

35. S. Ranade and M. Shneier, Using quadtrees to smooth images, IEEE Transactions on Systems, Man, and Cybernetics 11, 1981, 373-376.

36. A. Y. Wu, T. H. Hong, and A. Rosenfeld, Threshold selection using quadtrees, IEEE Transactions on Pattern Analysis and Machine Intelligence 4, 1982, 90-94.

37. H. Samet, Connected component labeling using quadtrees, Journal of the ACM 28, July 1981, 487-501.

38. R. E. Tarjan, On the efficiency of a good but not linear set union algorithm, Technical Report 72-148, Computer Science Department, Cornell University, Ithaca, New York, November 1972.

39. C. R. Dyer, A. Rosenfeld, and H. Samet, Region representation: boundary codes from quadtrees, Communications of the ACM 23, March 1980, 171-179.

40. M. Minsky and S. Papert, Perceptrons: An Introduction to Computional Geometry, MIT Press, Cambridge, MA, 1969.

41. H. Samet, Computing perimeters of images represented by quadtrees, IEEE Transactions on Pattern Analysis and Machine Intelligence 3, 1981, 683-687.

42. C. Jackins and S. L. Tanimoto, Quad-trees, oct-trees, and k-trees - a generalized approach to recursive decomposition of Euclidean space, Department of Computer Science Technical Report 82-02-02, University of Washington, Seattle, 1982.

43. C. R. Dyer, The space efficiency of quadtrees, Computer Graphics and Image Processing 19, 1982, 335-348.

44. W. I. Grosky and R. Jain, Optimal quadtrees for image segments, IEEE Transactions on Pattern Analysis and Machine Intelligence 5, 1983, 77-83.

45. M. Li, W. I. Grosky, and R. Jain, Normalized quadtrees with respect to translations, Computer Graphics and Image Processing 20, 1982, 72-81.

46. H. Samet, A quadtree medial axis transform, Communications of the ACM, 26, November 1983, 680-693.

47. E. Kawaguchi and T. Endo, On a method of binary picture representation and its application to data compression, IEEE Transactions on Pattern Analysis and Machine Intelligence 2, 1980, 27-35.

48. I. Gargantini, An effective way to represent quadtrees, Communications of the ACM 25, December 1982, 905-910.

49. D. J. Abel and J. L. Smith, A data structure and algorithm based on a linear key for a rectangle retrieval problem, to appear in Computer Vision, Graphics and Image Processing, 1983.

50. G. M. Morton, A computer oriented geodetic data base and a new technique in file sequencing, IBM Canada, 1966.

51. B. G. Cook, The structural and algorithmic basis of a geographic data base, in Proceedings of the First International Advanced Study Symposium on Topological Data Structures for Geographic Information Systems, G. Dutton, Ed., Harvard Papers on Geographic Information Systems, 1978.

52. W. Weber, Three types of map data structures, their ANDs and NOTs, and a possible OR, in Proceedings of the First International Advanced Study Symposium on Topological Data Structures for Geographic Information Systems, G. Dutton, Ed., Harvard Papers on Geographic Information Systems, 1978.

53. J. R. Woodwark, The explicit quadtree as a structure for computer graphics, Computer Journal 25, 1982, 235-238.

54. M. A. Oliver and N. E. Wiseman, Operations on quadtree-encoded images, Computer Journal 26, 1983, 83-91.

55. G. Nagy and S. Wagle, Geographic data processing, ACM Computing Surveys 11, June 1979, 139-181.

56. D. H. Ballard, Strip trees: A hierarchical representation for curves, Communications of the ACM 24, May 1981, 310-321 (see also corrigendum, Communications of the ACM 25, March 1982, 213).

57. W. Burton, Representation of many-sided polygons and polygonal lines for rapid processing, Communications of the ACM 20, March 1977, 166-171.

58. T. Peucker, A theory of the cartographic line, International Yearbook of Cartography, 1976.

59. M. Shneier, Two hierarchical linear feature representations: edge pyramids and edge quadtrees, Computer Graphics and Image Processing 17, 1981, 211-224.

60. J. J. Martin, Organization of geographical data with quad trees and least square approximation, Proceedings of the IEEE Conference on Pattern Recognition and Image Processing, Las Vegas, 1982, 458-463.

61. H. Samet and R. E. Webber, Line quadtrees: a hierarchical data structure for encoding boundaries, Proceedings of the IEEE Conference on Pattern Recognition and Image Processing, Las Vegas, 1982, 90-92 (also University of Maryland Computer Science TR-1162).

62. M. Tamminen, Encoding pixel trees, Laboratory of Information Processing Science, Helsinki University of Technology, Espoo, Finland, 1983.

OCTREES: A DATA STRUCTURE FOR SOLID-OBJECT MODELING

H. Freeman
Computer Engineering Program
Rensselaer Polytechnic Institute
Troy, New York (USA)

Donald J. Meagher
Phoenix Data Systems, Inc.
80 Wolf Road
Albany, New York (USA)

Abstract

This paper describes a novel data structure for modeling solid objects. The new data structure, called the octree modeling scheme, can be regarded as an extension to three dimensions of the familiar quadtree method for modeling two-dimensional images. The method is hierarchical and permits the user precisely to select the amount of resolution that is required by his application (and thereby to control the amount of storage space and computation time consumed). Algorithms for processing objects represented with the octree data structure require only simple arithmetic and logic operations, thus making the data structure an ideal candidate for processing using highly parallel VLSI technology.

Introduction

For the past five years an effort has been under way in the RPI Image Processing Laboratory to develop a scheme for modeling three-dimensional solid objects. Primary motivation was the need to model objects for robotics applications and for computer-aided design. As the work progressed, additional application areas were identified, of which the modeling of 3D medical objects from computed tomography data is one of the more important.

A number of solid modeling schemes have evolved in the past two decades[1]. The most common of these are constructive solid geometry[2] and boundary representation[3]. All of them tend to be complex and to require elaborate computations for object modeling,

NATO ASI Series, Vol. F18
Computer Architectures for Spatially Distributed Data
Edited by H. Freeman and G.G. Pieroni

object manipulation, and object analysis. None seem to lend themselves conveniently to parallel processing approaches. What was sought here was a hierarchical modeling scheme that in addition to providing a valid solid object description would have a resolution capability that could be precisely tailored to the requirements of the task at hand, and that would be suitable for implementation using parallel processing techniques. The scheme also had to be "general"; that is, it was not to be limited to (or to favor) any particular class of 3D objects.

The modeling scheme sought was one that would facilitate the design of fast algorithms for the generation, manipulation, analysis, and display of solid objects. It was considered especially desirable that the algorithms used for such processing would grow at most linearly with object size or resolution. This clearly indicated use of a hierarchical data structure and presorting[4]. The modeling scheme selected represents solid objects in a spatially presorted data structure that never requires additional sorting. It can be regarded as an extension to three dimensions of the quadtree method for modeling images in two dimensions[5]. The scheme was given the name of <u>octree modeling</u>[6,7].

An additional objective for an effective modeling scheme is the desirability that it lend itself to processing using highly parallel VLSI technology. This in turn implies that the algorithms use only simple arithmetic, comparison, and shift operations. As will be shown, the octree scheme satisfies this objective to a high degree.

Octree Encoding

In the octree scheme, the object domain - also referred to as the <u>universe</u> - is taken to be a cube of such dimension that the object to be modeled will be totally contained within it. The modeling process is then begun by subdividing the cube using planes parallel to the cube's sides into 8 equal-volume subcubes, as shown in Fig. 1. These subcubes are tested against the object to be modeled to determine whether (a) they lie entirely inside the object (FULL cubes), (b) they lie entirely outside the object (EMPTY cubes), or (c) they lie partially inside and partially outside the object (PARTIAL cubes). Only the PARTIAL subcubes are then subdivided into sub-subcubes and the latter again tested as to whether they are FULL, EMPTY, or PARTIAL.

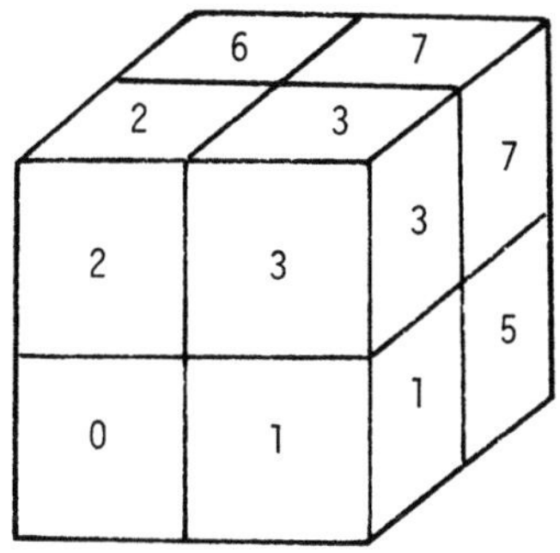

Fig. 1. Subdivision of "universe" octree into 8 subcubes.

This process of successive subdividing and testing continues until a cube size is reached that is of the resolution fineness desired for the modeling.

The hierarchical PARTIAL-cube subdivision process can be represented by an 8-ary tree structure in which each node represents a cube, the root of the tree corresponds to the universe, the terminal nodes correspond to the FULL or EMPTY subcubes, and at each non-terminal (i.e., PARTIAL) node there is an 8-fold branching until a depth limit - corresponding to the desired resolution fineness (precision) - is reached. It is this 8-fold branching that has given the scheme the name octree modeling. The scheme is illustrated in Fig. 2.

The actual generation of an octree for a given object is relatively straightforward. The decision as to the value of a node depends on whether a particular vertex point is interior or exterior to the object. Child vertex coordinates are then computed from parent coordinates by simple addition and shift (divide by 2) operations.

There was an initial concern that the octree scheme would lead to prohibitively large memory requirements. Although for high-resolution representations, the memory requirements are substantial, they are not excessive for today's computers. It was shown[8] that the number of nodes required for representing a 3D object with an octree is proportional to the product of the area of the object and the square of the resolution ratio. (The latter is the ratio of the length of an edge of the universe to that of an edge of the cube at the depth limit of the tree.)

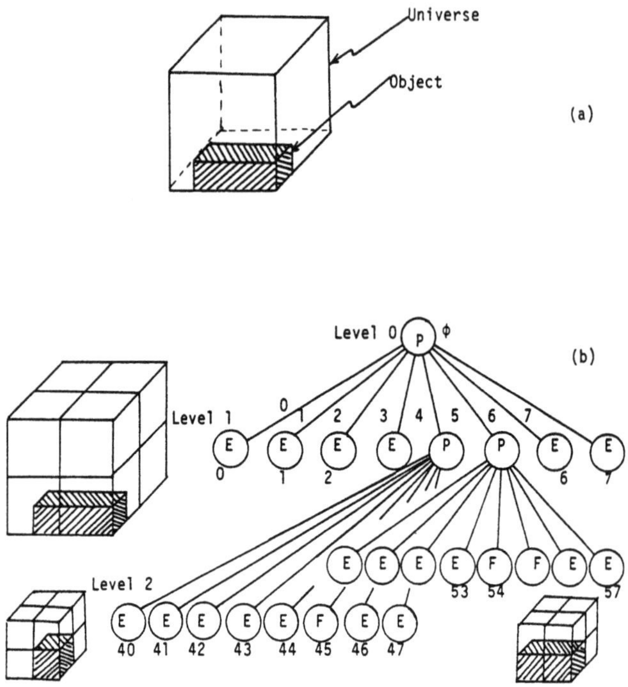

Fig. 2. Octree representation: (a) a 3D object, (b) octree representation of 3D object.

Storage of an octree in computer memory can be done fairly efficiently by placing all the children of one node in a fixed-length block of 8 4-byte words and using a pointer to relate each node to its children. An octal number addressing scheme is then easily devised for the nodes. This is illustrated in Fig. 3. A two-bit field contains the FULL (F), EMPTY (E), or PARTIAL (P) value of each node. A null pointer is used for terminal nodes.

Algorithms for Octree Processing

Simple algorithms exist for determining object properties from their octree models. The methods are straightforward 3D extensions of techniques developed for 2D quadtrees[9]. Thus for volume, one needs only to sum over all levels of the tree the products of the number of F nodes and the cube volume at that level. (Cube volumes at successive level are, of course, in the ratio of 8:1 to each other.) Analogous techniques exist for computing first and second moments[8].

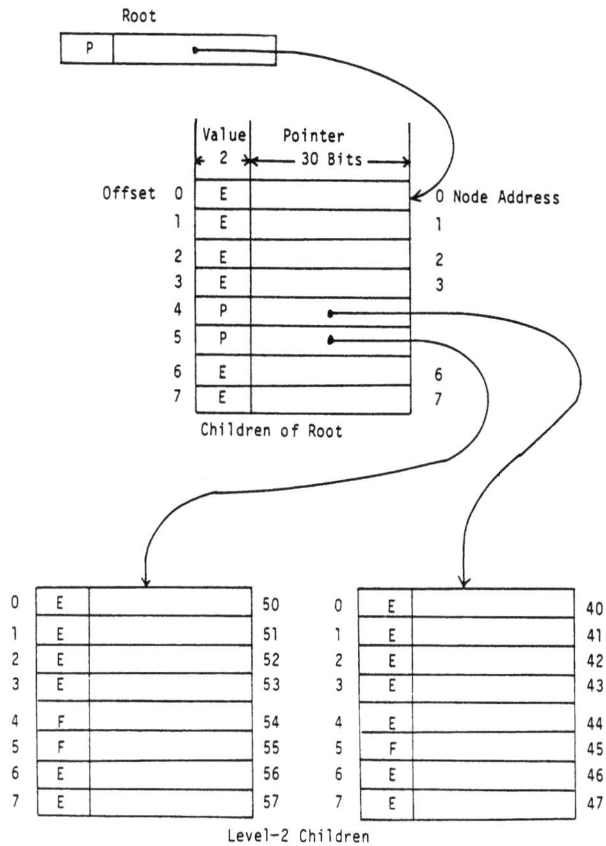

Fig. 3. Octree storage scheme using 4 bytes per node.

For surface area, one sums the surface areas of all exterior F cubes, that is, those F-cube faces that border on an E node. In a similar vein, one can easily formulate techniques for the basic set operations (a AND b, a OR b, and a BUT-NOT b). This is illustrated in Fig. 4.

The most basic operations encountered when processing octree-modeled objects are translation, scaling, rotation, perspective projection, and hidden-surface elimination. For translation, scaling and rotation, an algorithm is required which will convert the given object tree (source object tree) to a new tree, corresponding to the translated, scaled, and rotated object (the target object tree).

The algorithms for each of these transformations require that the universe for the target object lie within the universe for the source object. To insure this, the original source universe is first expan-

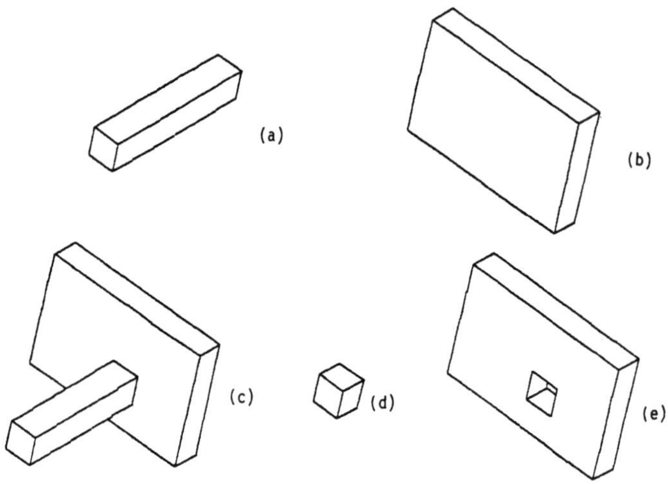

Fig. 4. Illustration of the set operations on the two objects (a) and (b): (c) a OR b, (d) a AND b, (e) b BUT-NOT a.

ded by augmenting it with a set of empty universes until it is of the size required to enclose also the target universe. (This is illustrated in Fig. 5 for the analogous 2D case using a quadtree.) The target octree is then generated by beginning at the root of its universe and successively generating the nodes of the tree by simultaneously traversing the tree of the source object. When a FULL or EMPTY node is generated for the new tree, it is a terminal node and no descendants need be considered. The actual node generation is achieved through the use of overlays. The value of a subcube in the target universe is completely determined by its overlay position in the source universe. The overlay subcubes represent the portion of the old universe that encloses the new object subcubes. The finer the resolution of the overlay subcubes, the more precisely they will describe the object. In a sense, the source object, described by its octree, is transformed and then re-digitized to yield the target octree.

The foregoing scheme lends itself particularly well to hidden-surface elimination. Let us first take a look at the 2D projection shown in

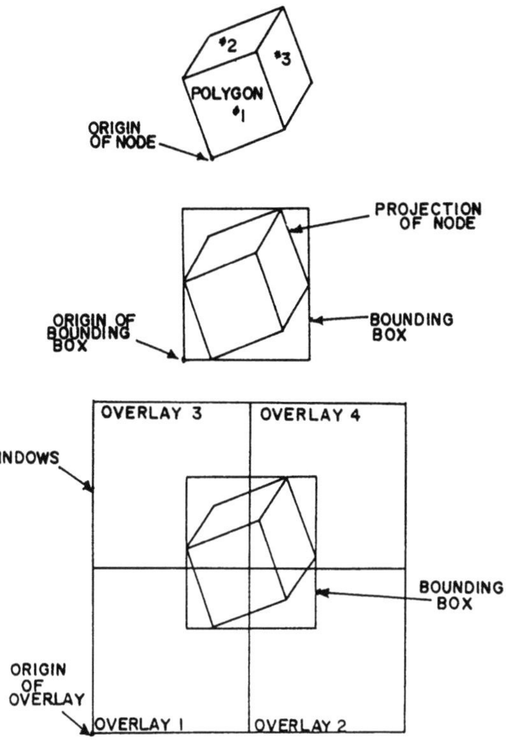

Fig. 5. Quadtree view of octree node projection. Quadtree level is normalized so that bounding box of projection will lie within 4 quadtree windows of overlay.

Fig. 6(a). The subcubes are labeled in the manner indicated. It is clear that nothing in squares 0 through 2 can obscure any portion of square 3. Similarly, nothing in squares 0 and 1 can obscure any part of square 2, etc.

Now let us consider the 3D case illustrated in Fig. 6(b). For the position of the observer shown, nothing in subcubes 0 through 6 can obscure anything in in subcube 7; nothing in subcubes 0 through 5 can obscure anything in subcube 6, etc.

This ordered-priority property provides a convenient basis for visible-surface display (or, what is equivalent, hidden-surface removal). One sets up a quadtree to represent the display screen and then projects all FULL (F) and PARTIAL (P) subcubes on to this quadtree, using a recursive front-to-back traversal order (i.e., 7-to-0 order in Fig. 7) . If a particular quadtree location has not been already marked, we now mark it with the attribute (i.e., color shading) of the subcube being examined. If the traversal order shows an octree node to be

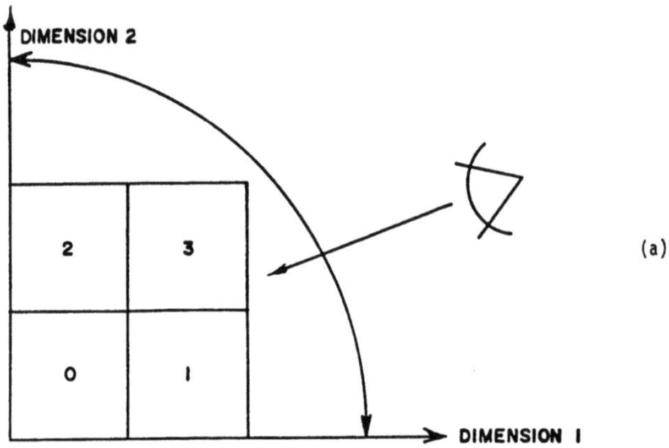

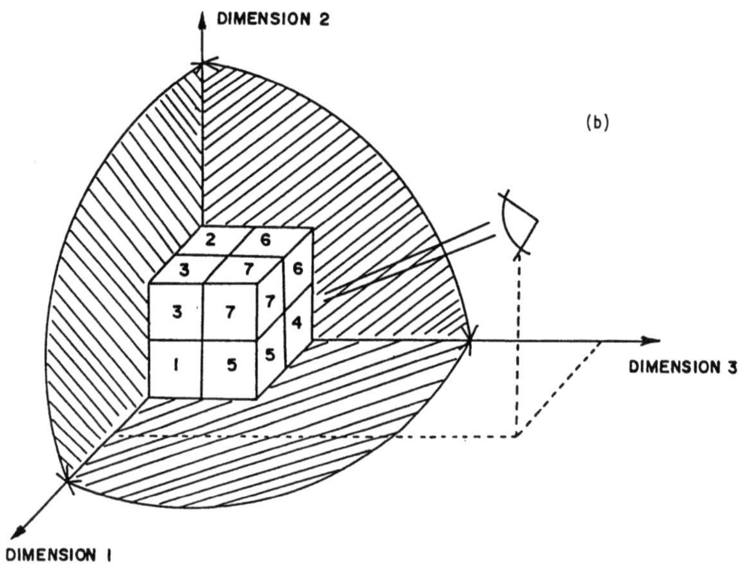

Fig. 6. Ilustration of the presorted hidden-line property of the octree data structure. (a) two-dimensional case, (b) three-dimensional case.

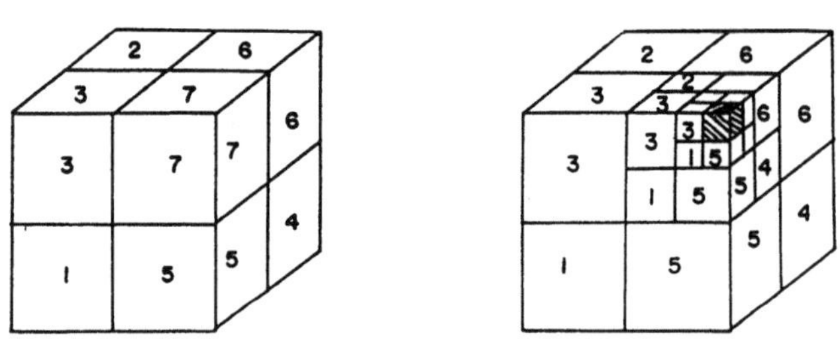

Fig. 7. Recursive 7-to-0 traversal sequence to take advantage of octree's ordered-priority property.

completely obscured, it is not further considered (and, of course, neither are any of its descendants). The process is illustrated in Fig. 8.

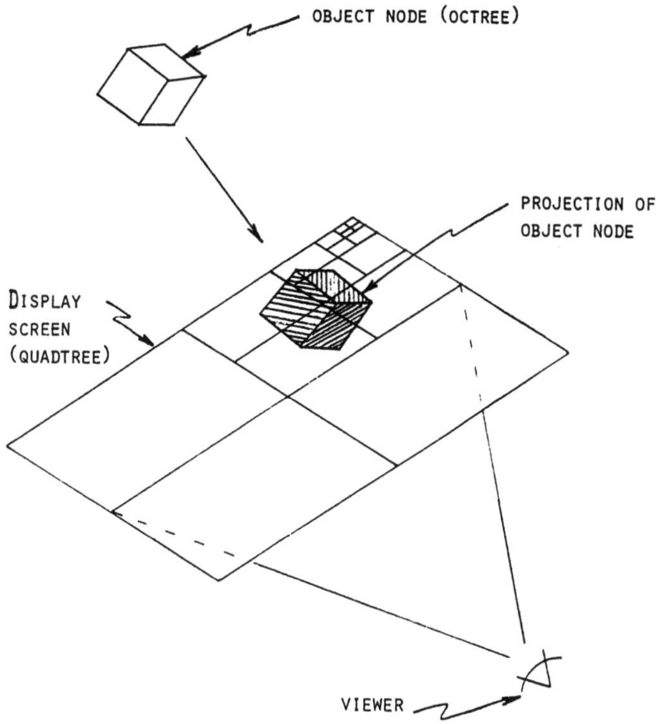

Fig. 8. The process of generating a visible-image quadtree for an octree-modeled 3D object.

The actual intensity/color value of the quadtree square will be derived from the faces of the subcube being projected. For the subcube we can use simple block shading by assigning to the three visible faces of the subcube uniform intensity values that are related to their orientation relative to the light sources. For more realistic-looking displays, the intensity on the faces of the subcube can be computed by using the dot product between the surface normal and the line-of-sight vector to the observer. Both cases are illustrated in Fig. 9. The procedure is the same whether there is a single point source of light or a multiplicity of light sources.

Conclusions

The octree method of modeling 3D objects derives its primary advantages from its hierarchical nature, which lets the user choose just the amount of precision needed for the application at hand, and from the inherent simplicity of its primitives, which makes it an ideal candidate for implementation with VLSI technology. The memory requirements, though substantial, are not excessive, and a large set of fast algorithms already exists for generating, manipulating, and analyzing solids modeled in this manner. Virtually all of the standard graphics and CAD tasks can be readily implemented in terms of simple algorithms, involving only primitive arithmetic operations. The method appears to be particularly well-suited for applications in robotics (path planning and interference determination), medical imagery reconstruction (tomography), and those applications in computer-aided design where a hierarchical approach to modeling is considered advantageous.

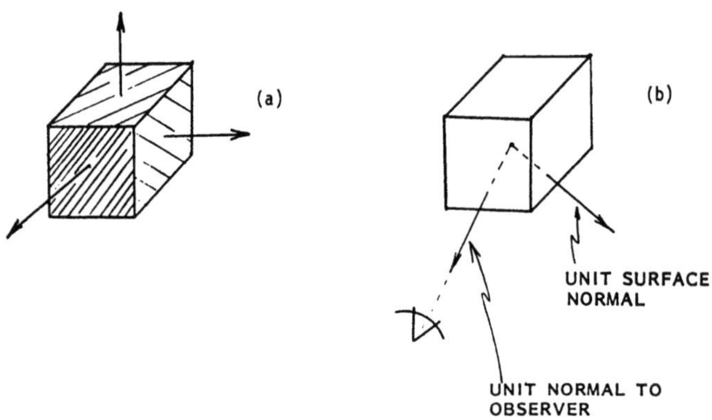

Fig. 9. Illumination models. (a) simple block shading, (b) surface-normal shading.

References

1. A. Requicha, "Representations for rigid solids: theory, methods, and systems," *Computing Surveys, 12*, (4), Dec. 1980.

2. W. Fitzgerald, F. Gracer, and R. Wolfe, "GRIN: Interactive graphics for modeling solids," *IBM Jour. of R&D, 25*, (4), July 1981.

3. J. W. Boyse and J.E. Gilchrist, "GMSolid: Interactive modeling for design and analysis of solids," *IEEE Computer Graphics and Applications, 2*, (2), March 1982.

4. W.R. Franklin, "A linear-time exact hidden-surface algorithm," *Computer Graphics, 14*, (3), July 1980.

5. G.M. Hunter and K. Steiglitz, "Operations on images using quad trees," *IEEE Trans. Pattern Anal. and Machine Intell., PAMI-1*, (2), April 1979.

6. D. Meagher, *Octree encoding: A new technique for the representation, manipulation and display of arbitrary 3-D objects by computer*, Tech. rept. IPL-TR-111, Image Process. Lab., Rensselaer Polytechnic Institute, Troy, NY 12181, October 1980.

7. D. Meagher, "Geometric modeling using octree encoding", *Computer Graphics and Image Proc., 19*, (2), June 1982.

8. D. Meagher, *The octree encoding method for efficient solid modeling*, doctoral dissertation, Electrical, Computer and Systems Eng'g. Dept., Rensselaer Polytechnic Institute, Troy, NY 12181, August 1982.

9. H. Samet, *Computing perimeters of images represented by quadtrees,* TR-755, Computer Science Center, University of Maryland, College Park, MD, April 197 9.

EFFICIENT STORAGE OF QUADTREES AND OCTREES

Markku Tamminen
Helsinki University of Technology
Laboratory of Information Processing Science
02150 Espoo 15, Finland

ABSTRACT

We study a method of representing space efficiently quadtrees, octrees and related pixel trees. Its efficiency of encoding two-dimensional black-and-white and multicolour images is compared to that of established methods such as chain encoding. For both two- and three-dimensional images we show that beside quad- and octrees it is relevant to consider also pixel trees based on a binary division of space. A paged storage scheme is proposed for accessing encoded pixel trees by spatial location.

INTRODUCTION

The quadtree[7,10] as a representation of a two-dimensional image and the similar octree[15] for representing a discrete model (here also called image) of a solid are receiving widespread attention. The two methods complement each other nicely and specialized processors are being built for both. For simplicity we shall use the term pixel tree for both quad- and octrees and employ two-dimensional terminology.

From the point-of-view of algorithms the explicit tree structure with pointers is most convenient for representing a pixel tree. However, it often consumes more space than the pixel matrix and is not well suited for secondary storage. More compact linear representations are required for long term storage and transmission of pixel trees. They may also be necessary for utilizing effectively the i/o-bandwidth of specialized processors.

NATO ASI Series, Vol. F18
Computer Architectures for Spatially Distributed Data
Edited by H. Freeman and G. G. Pieroni

One linear representation of quad- and octrees proposed by Gargantini[5] is based on storing a linear array of the "black" leaves of a pixel tree. Another method proposed by Kawaguchi and Endo[10] and used by Meagher[15] for octrees is based on encoding the whole structure of a pixel tree in the sequence of preorder traversal. We will study extensions to this method providing very compact storage.

The encoding of black-and-white (B/W) images is quite well understood[8,17] and the compaction of images typical of faximile transmission has reached a level where little improvement seems possible with general purpose codes. However, often more important than maximal compaction is compatibility with algorithms for operations on the images. From this viewpoint it is relevant to study encodings of pixel trees.

The best compaction ratios achieved for gray-scale images are typically much lower than for B/W images. The most efficient methods known either encode the difference of succeeding gray-scales with one code word per pixel or apply efficient B/W techniques separately to each bit plane of the gray-scale code. There seems to exist some room for improvement in these schemes but it is not easy to envision reversible methods achieving a much higher efficiency if the amount of detail or noise is high with respect to resolution.

However, there is a class of "colour coded" images for which higher compaction is possible using other kinds of methods. This is the case when the colour code has a nominal scale so that the difference of two codes has no meaning. At the same time areas of uniform code value are rather large and represent a polygonal partition of the image. In this article we use the attribute "multicolour" to denote such images and also call them maps[17]. The characteristics of the thresholded images and solid models, to which quad- and octrees are applied, often present similar spatial coherence.

Pavlidis[17] has shown how maps may be encoded using run length or chain codes. At high resolution a chain code would require on the average 2-3 bits per boundary pixel. The best run-length scheme that he presents would typically utilize somewhat less than $(n + \log_2 m - 1)/2$ bits per boundary pixel to encode a nominally scaled m-region map at a resolution of $2^n \times 2^n$. We use the term boundary pixel to denote a pixel that is intersected by a colour boundary and thus forms part of the chain code. Note that the reconstruction of an image from its chain code is a non-trivial problem[16].

Representing maps as images composed of pixels at a fixed resolution is becoming increasingly important for instance in geo-data processing. This is due both to the technological imperatives of data manipulation and output and the use of remote sensing (satellites) for data acquisition[9]. After a lengthy processing cycle, remotely sensed data is typically interpreted as a nominally coded map in the above sense. The number of code classes is typically rather low (e.g. 8 - 64) and often the homogeneous areas become large (hundreds or thousands of pixels). For good quality cartographic work about 100 lines per millimeter of output image are needed. Satellite image frames contain up to 6000 X 6000 pixels and many of these frames are needed to cover a country such as Finland.

The above should justify the relevance of studying image encoding in the case that resolution is high with respect to the amount of detail on a map. Specifically, in this paper we present some new variants of schemes for encoding pixel trees and report on their asymptotic behaviour as resolution is increased. We present empirical statistics concerning both two- and three-dimensional images showing the scope of relevance of the asymptotical analysis and justifying the attention given to binary pixel trees. We also show that the method of encoding bit planes separately is not efficient for maps. Finally we point to an extension: paged pixel trees, offering an attractive compromise between efficient storage and access.

PIXEL TREES

Consider an image represented by a $2^n \times 2^n$ array of pixels - i.e., a geometric structure at a fixed spatial resolution (denoted hereafter by n). Each pixel may be related to a code ("colour") describing it. For instance, when representing a polygon network by an image, the code would be the label associated with the underlying polygon.

There are various more compact representations of images than the above pixel array. We discuss mainly what we have called pixel trees. They seem to present a good foundation for managing pixel based data.

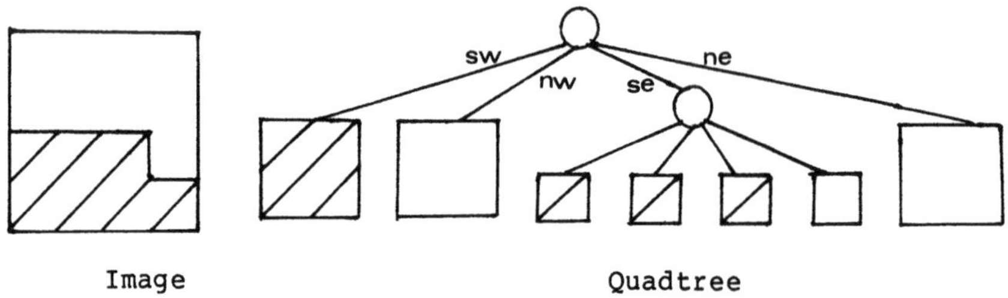

Figure 1. An image and the corresponding quadtree (n = 2).

Pixel trees have been much studied in the literature[3,5,7,10,18] under the name of quadtrees (figure 1). We use the more general term because division into two parts is at least as natural and simple as division into four parts when defining a tree (figure 2)[11].

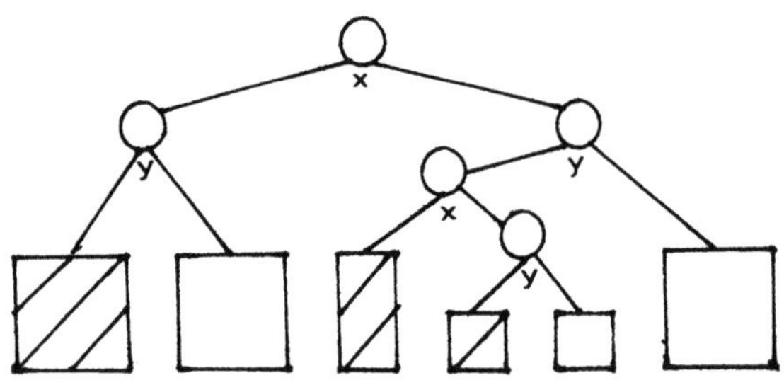

Figure 2. Binary pixel tree of the image in figure 1.

Figure 3 describes a similar binary tree corresponding to the octree[15] representation of a three-dimensional image. In the rest of this section we shall consider only two-dimensional images with the understanding that all the encodings presented generalize in a straight forward way to three dimensions.

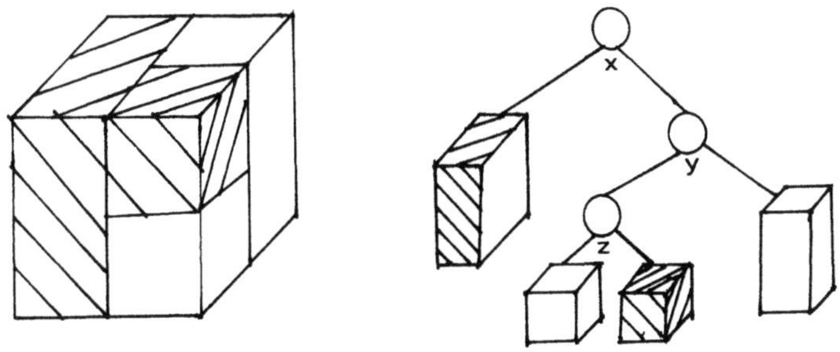

Solid Binary tree

Figure 3. A solid and its binary tree representation.

The conventional representation of a quadtree is a tree structure with each node containing at least four pointers, one to each son-quadrant (NW,NE,SW,SE), and a colour code. An extra colour code, 'gray', means that the corresponding node is not uniform and has been subdivided.

There are a number of ways of representing a quadtree more efficiently from a space standpoint than described above[5,10]. A very compact linear representation is obtained by transforming the tree into a bit string according to definition 1[10]:

Definition 1. The bit string encoding of a pixel tree is obtained as follows:

- the nodes are processed in preorder, i.e. first the root and then recursively its left son followed by its right son
- an interior node (i.e. having descendants) receives the code '1'
- a leaf receives the code '0' to which is appended the colour of the leaf, described by, say, 8 bits
- a leaf at the pixel level (i.e., at the bottom of the tree) does not need to be encoded by 0 because by virtue of the fixed resolution the branch is known to end.

The code for the quadtree in figure 1 would become ('B' = 'black' and 'W' = 'white')

10B0W1BBBW0W,

and for the binary tree of figure 2

110B0W110B1BW0W.

Various techniques may be used to further compress the code produced according to definition 1. For instance, in the case of a binary tree it is useful to maintain the guarantee that no leaf has the same colour as its brother. In the black-and-white case this lets us encode with a common bit both brother leaves at the lowest level because there are only two combinations ('black','white') and ('white','black'). In the following, we use the codes '1' and '0' respectively for these colour pairs. This device does not apply as well to quadtrees because there are more combinations.

The following discussion should intuitively justify the claim that asymptotically still better compression is possible as resolution is increased. Figure 4 is a typical B/W subimage corresponding to a subtree of a binary pixel tree at high resolution: As resolution is increased with respect to image detail a typical subtree of a fixed size will contain only one of the two colour pair codes.

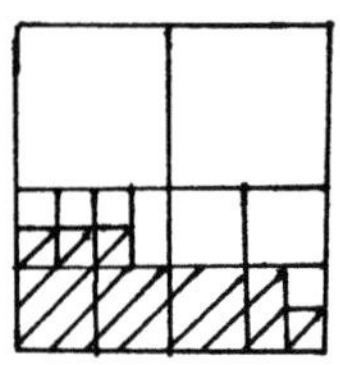

Figure 4. A typical image corresponding to a subtree of a binary pixel tree.

The code corresponding to figure 4 is

11110B11BW1BW10B11BW0W0W1110B0W110B1BW0W0W.

Here 'BW' and 'WB' denote for clarity the two colour pair codes '1' and '0'. In order to encode this string further we shall extract from it the three structural components defined below.

Definition 2. The three components of the linear code of a pixel tree are: A) the structure of the tree, B) the codes of the lowest level leaves and C) the colour codes of the higher level leaves.

For figure 4 the components of definition 2 become:

A) 1111011110110011100110100; the structure of the tree

B) 1111; the colour pair codes of leaves at the lowest level

C) 110010100; the colour codes of the higher level leaves.

Each of the above components has different properties that can be used to enhance the coding efficiency. Based on the discussion on figure 4 above, we may say that the code series B is spatially coherent. This means that asymptotically, as resolution is increased with respect to image detail, it will contain long runs of the codes '0' and '1'. We may say that the local entropy of code component B is asymptotically zero. This can be utilized in the following "change code".

Definition 3. The change code of a B/W binary pixel tree is formed as follows:

- separate the three code components A,B and C of definition 2
- retain component A without modification
- code the first colour pair code of series B ordinarily; thereafter code: '0' = 'same as previous code' and '1' = 'change in code'
- code the first colour code of component C ordinarily; thereafter code changes as above
- apply a code compression technique to components B and C.

Based on the informal discussion above, without going into the details of code compression, we assert the following "theorem". A formal proof of this kind of a statement would only be possible if also the image generation mechanism were formally defined.

"Theorem" 1. Asymptotically, as resolution is increased with respect to image complexity, the average number of bits per colour pair needed by the use of the change code of definition 3 for code component B approaches zero.

ANALYSIS USING GEOMETRIC PROBABILITY

In practical experiments (reported in more detail later) with high resolution B/W images definition 1 has resulted in an average of 1.2 bits per quadtree node. The best binary tree representation (definition 3) has utilized an average of 0.9 bits per node and required slightly less space than the quadtree encoding. In the following we shall use a simplified stochastic model of a B/W image to explain these characteristics "asymptotically". Our model is based on geometric probability[14,20]. It embodies more formally and in a very simplified way the discussion related to figure 4 in the previous section.

The basic concept of geometric probability is a random (straight) line. We shall study images generated by one random line: the area on one side of the line is defined to be white and on the other one black. At any fixed resolution the more precise definition to be given below corresponds to a colouring of all pixels of the image and we may consider the asymptotic behaviour as resolution is increased.

We shall not go into definitions and results of geometric probability but consider the concept of a random line as a primitive. See[14,19] for more theory and discussion. All we need is the following basic result given here without proof.

Theorem 2. Let K and its subset K1 be bounded convex sets. The probability that a random line intersects K1 if it is known to intersect K is L1/L, L and L1 being the perimeters of K and K1. The perimeter of a straight line segment is defined as twice its length.

Theorem 2 suffices as a basis for all the derivations reported here. The following is a more formal definition of a random image providing a "worst case" colouring of the pixels intersected by the line.

Definition 4. The asymptotic stochastic model of a B/W image is formed as follows. Let U denote the unit square $[0,1] \times [0,1]$. At resolution n the image under consideration is represented by a partitioning of U into a grid of $2^n \times 2^n$ square cells, pixels. The brother of a pixel is defined as the brother of the corresponding leaf in a complete binary pixel tree. Let G be a random line intersecting U. The random image corresponding to G is formed to satisfy the following rules:

- each pixel completely on the same side of G as the point (0,0) is coloured black and each pixel completely on the other side white
- each pixel intersected by line G is made to receive the opposite colour as compared to its brother.

Definition 4 leads to a random pixel tree, in which all pixels intersected by G are leaves at the lowest level and it is not possible to combine brother leaves. This assumption is conservative in making the number of leaves in a random pixel tree greater than what it would be using any other method of classifying the intersected pixels. The definition makes possible a theoretical analysis without much affecting its results. Based on it and theorem 2 we can deduce expected characteristics of random images. In the present paper we only refer to the results, though formulated as theorems. The proofs are presented elsewhere[22].

Definition 4 corresponds closely to that used by Hunter and Steiglitz[6] in their analysis of the worst case size of a quadtree corresponding to a polygon. They show that at resolution n the quadtree of a polygon with perimeter p (measured in resolution units) contains at most 16p + 16n - 11 nodes. Our goal is to derive a better bound for the expected size of random pixel trees assuming the chosen data generation model.

Next we define more precisely some image statistics and in theorem 3 give their expected values in our random image generation model.

Definition 5. The scan line j0 of an image is the set of pixels with coordinates of the form (i,j0). The number of colour changes (ncc) in a random image is the number of scan lines intersected by the random line G. The chain code of a random image is the set of boundary pixels, i.e. pixels intersected by G. Its cardinality is denoted by nbp.

Theorem 3. The expected number of colour changes in a random image is approximately 2^{n-1} and the expected number of boundary pixels is approximately 2^{n}.

The number of colour changes is approximately equal to the number of code words in a run length code. Thus the result of theorem 3 is identical to the observation of Pavlidis[17] that a chain code often contains twice the amount of code words compared to a run length code. A chain code can be represented by 2-3 bits per boundary pixel[4,16].

To describe the performance of pixel trees we need the following notation:

nn: total number of nodes

nl0: number of leaves at the lowest level

nl1: number of leaves at higher levels

r: nl1/nl0

nb: number of bits required by an encoding.

The number of leaves and the total number of nodes determine each other uniquely. Therefore, because the number of bits required per leaf is different at the lowest level and other levels, the ratio r is important in estimating space requirements. The following lemma describes its behaviour.

<u>Lemma 4</u>. In a random binary pixel tree, r approaches 2/3 from below asymptotically as $n \to \infty$. In a quadtree it approaches similarly 1/2.

The following lemma combines the results of theorem 3 and lemma 4.

<u>Lemma 5</u>. In a random binary pixel tree the expected number of leaves at the lowest level is related to the number of boundary pixels by:

$$nl0 = (3/2)nbp$$

and in a quadtree by:

$$nl0 = 2nbp.$$

Because the number of boundary pixels is fixed, lemmas 4 and 5 tell us that a quadtree has 4/3 times the number of lowest level leaves and 6/5 times the total number of leaves of a binary pixel tree.

Now we can formulate the main theorems on the expected size of random pixel trees.

<u>Theorem 6</u>. The expected size of an encoding of a random quadtree formed according to definition 1 satisfies:

$$nb = 5nbp = (5/4)nn.$$

<u>Theorem 7</u>. The expected size of an encoding of a random binary pixel tree formed according to definition 3 satisfies asymptotically:

$$nb_3 = (9/10)nn = (9/2)nbp.$$

The corresponding size according to definition 1 becomes:

$$nb_1 = (21/20)nn = (21/4)nbp.$$

From theorems 6 and 7 we see that the best encoding scheme that we have been able to devise for binary pixel trees (definition 3) is asymptotically better than our best scheme for quadtrees (definition 1). Statistical methods of compressing the three code series of definition 3 might make improvements of the above results possible and even reverse this conclusion. However, it is improbable that we could quite reach the efficiency of a chain code. Considering theorem 3 it is also improbable that we could reach the efficiency of the best two-dimensional state change codes[8] for B/W images.

EFFICIENT ENCODING OF MULTICOLOUR PIXEL TREES

After treating in some depth the asymptotical B/W case we shall only informally show that similar results should apply to multicolour images. We have to change definition 3 somewhat to obtain an asymptotically efficient code for them.

Definition 6. The change code of a multicolour binary pixel tree is formed as follows:

- separate the three code components A,B and C of definition 2
- retain component A without modification
- code the first colour pair code of series B ordinarily; thereafter code: '0' = 'same as previous code' and '1' = 'change in code'; append new colour pair code to '1'
- for component C maintain a two colour buffer of least recently used colour codes and divide C into two bit streams, C1 and C2; if the colour of a leaf is in the buffer, insert code '0' into C1 and a one-bit code designating the buffer slot into C2; otherwise insert '1' into C1 and the new colour code into C2.
- apply a code compression technique to components B and C1.

Figure 5 presents an asymptotically typical subtree of a multicolour pixel tree.

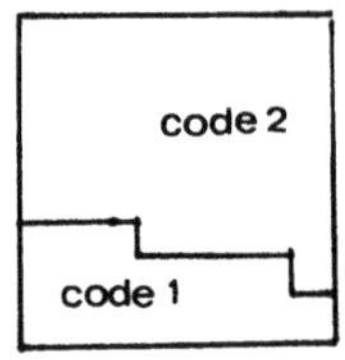

Figure 5. A typical subtree of a binary multicolour pixel tree.

We see that, again, asymptotically for a binary pixel tree the codes for series B and C1 are locally constant and that the series C2 can locally be represented by 1 bit per leaf. Thus, without more formalism we can state our main result. For concreteness we have formulated it assuming colour boundaries to locally resemble segments of random lines. However, the result is qualitatively valid also without this assumption.

Theorem 8. Assume that boundaries of colour areas locally behave as random lines as resolution is asymptotically increased with respect to image detail. In this case a multicolour binary pixel tree can asymptotically be represented by an average of 9/2 bits per boundary pixel. Similarly, a multicolour quadtree can asymptotically be represented by an average of 5 bits per boundary pixel.

When resolution is high the result of theorem 9 is better than the best run length encodings described by Pavlidis[17]. However, complicated chain encodings, that encode each colour boundary segment only once, remain more compact than the new code. For many purposes the code of definition 8 is easier to process than these code types.

In practical applications the size of the colour buffer is a design parameter. The size of two is only asymptotically efficient. A very simple code is obtained if we use a three colour buffer and let '11' designate 'new colour' and the other three codes the three current colours.

EXPERIMENTAL RESULTS

As in[21] we have utilized the random Dirichlet tessellation as a data generation tool to model polygon networks (figure 6). Ahuja and Schachter[1] call it a random mosaic image model.

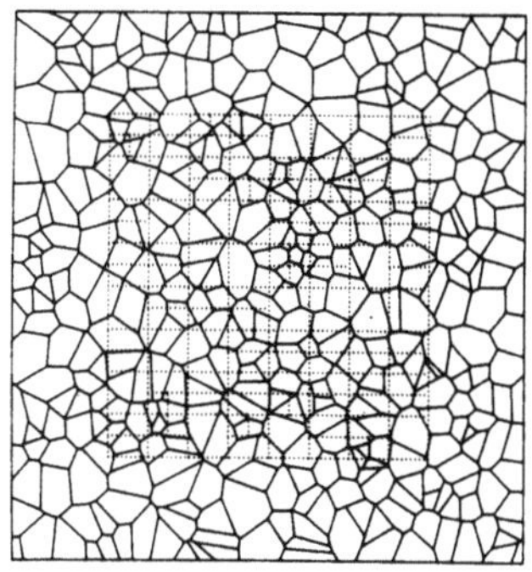

Figure 6. A random Dirichlet tessellation of 400 polygons, each the locus of points closest to one of the 400 random centers. The dashed grid corresponds to an EXCELL[20,21] data structure.

To study the performance of encoding schemes for pixel trees we have transformed the tessellation into an image with the number of each polygon attached to each pixel classified as belonging to it. In order to avoid complicated classifications of boundary pixels we have utilized the restriction of definition 4 when forming the image. Actually, we have formed the image only implicitly while building the pixel tree. Using a similar procedure we have also constructed pixel trees corresponding to a black disk embedded in a square background.

From a multiarea Dirichlet tessellation we have formed a B/W image by randomly allocating the two colours, each to one half of the areas.

None of the above image generation models corresponds directly to the random line model. However, the following tables (for instance row 'r' in table 1 and row 'rl' in table 2) show that the assumptions of that model seem valid, even for moderate resolutions.

resolution	10		11		12	
type	bin.	quad	bin.	quad.	bin.	quad
nl0	6016	8016	12040	16048	24088	32112
nl1	3968	3952	7976	7956	16000	15976
r	0.660	0.493	0.662	0.496	0.664	0.498

Table 1. Statistics describing the binary pixel tree and quadtree of a black disk.

	B/W						256 colours					
resol.	7		9		11		7		9		11	
type	bin.	quad	bin.	quad	bin.	quad	bin.	quad	bin.	quad	bin.	quad
nl0	56	76	220	295	783	1021	66	84	283	373	915	1243
nl1	23	16	137	131	518	521	20	14	150	137	589	574
r	0.40	0.21	0.62	0.44	0.66	0.51	0.31	0.17	0.53	0.36	0.64	0.46
rl	0.17	0.19	0.17	0.26	0.18	0.26	0.14	0.15	0.16	0.23	0.18	0.25

Table 2. Statistics describing B/W and colour coded pixel trees corresponding to random 256 area Dirichlet tessellations. Row rl is the ratio of the number of leaves at the next to lowest level to that on the lowest level. According to the random line model the expected values for rl are 1/6 for a binary pixel tree and 1/4 for a quadtree.

Table 3 describes the size (in bits) of the encodings of binary and quadtrees formed at various levels of resolution to correspond to 256 center Dirichlet tessellations. Table 3 corresponds to the encoding formed according to definition 1, i.e., without code compression.

	Size of tree encoding			
	B/W		8 bit code	
n	bin.	quad	bin.	quad
6	4069	3988	28194	28556
7	12447	11939	76784	81294
8	29424	28820	177566	192475
9	63109	62460	390773	429553
10	121644	120864	793676	872332
11	233856	232208	1440128	1623872

Table 3. Size in bits of binary and quadtree encodings formed according to definition 1. The largest images (n = 11) correspond to $4X10^6$ pixels. In this case the binary tree (8 bits) contains approximately 160000 leaves and the same amount of interior nodes while the quadtree contains 190000 leaves and 64000 interior nodes. The uncompressed pixel array would require $32X10^6$ bits.

From table 3 we see that, even without code compression, the size of the 256 colour tree (8 bit code) is less than 8 times the size of the B/W (one bit) tree. We have not programmed a complete code compression procedure corresponding to the method of colour buffers. However, simple experiments with a three colour buffer have shown that the results of table 3 (8 bit code) can be easily further compressed by at least a factor of three or four.

From the simulations we have arrived at the following conclusions:

1. The results derived from geometric probability seem to remain valid for more complex models of image generation.

2. For B/W images the quadtree encoding of definition 1 is more efficient than the binary one.

3. For 256 colour images the binary encoding of definition 1 is more efficient than the quadtree one. This is explained by the lesser number of leaves in a binary tree. Much further compression is possible with the colour buffer scheme.

4. The asymptotic compression ratios predicted by theorems 7-9 seem approachable at moderate values of resolution.

5. The technique of separately encoding each bit plane of a map is not efficient when compared to encoding the complete area partition, even by the method of definition 1.

For the B/W images described above, at a resolution of 10, the basic encoding scheme that we have used is about four times as efficient as that proposed by Gargantini[5].

Many of the above results go over - in a qualitative sense - also to the three-dimensional case. As a confirmation we performed experiments on a unit sphere at resolution $2^7 \times 2^7 \times 2^7$. In this case the binary tree has 136344 leaves and its encoding according to definition 1 requires 203495 bits while the octree has 148024 leaves and requires 209249 bits.

EXTENSIONS

Compared to other efficient image coding techniques pixel trees facilitate operations on and access to the images. However, the linear encoding discussed above is not suitable for efficient access to parts of a tree. A compromise between efficient compaction and access may be obtained by applying the extendible cell method[20,21] to form a paged pixel tree. It consists of pages corresponding to subtrees and a directory facilitating efficient access by location to these pages. Both parts of the structure can be modified dynamically if the image is updated. Also, many operations could be performed in parallel.

Figure 7 describes the basic idea of a paged pixel tree. We have shown[21] that it requires about twice as much space as the non-paged variant but still remains very compact compared to other representations offering similar efficiency of access. We recommend such a structure for the processing of maps at a very high resolution.

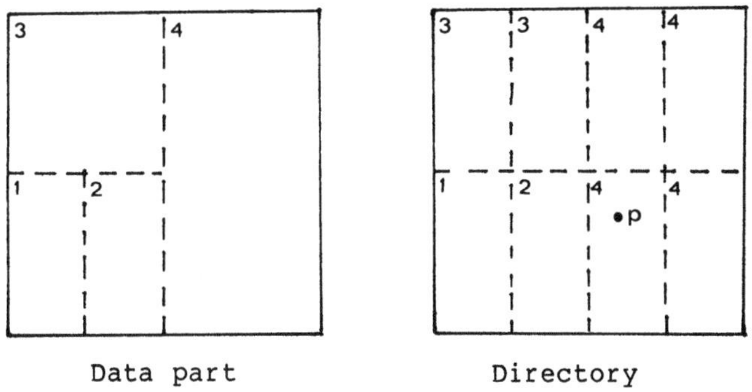

Figure 7. Example of basic concepts of a paged pixel tree. The image is divided into four data cells (rectangles), the subimage in each of which can be encoded in less than pagesize (say 4096) bits. The directory is an array of elements each corresponding to a rectangle of minimal size and indicating the data cell containing it. The cell corresponding to some pixel p is retrieved by first calculating the corresponding directory array index.

CONCLUSIONS

We have shown that pixel trees form an efficient basis for encoding both B/W and multicolour images, especially at high resolution. For nominally coded multicolour images (maps) we have demonstrated a new kind of encoding based on the use of a colour buffer. All the encoding schemes apply directly to images of any number of dimensions.

Based on our results binary pixel trees should be given increasing consideration as data structures and image encoding schemes.

We have demonstrated that geometric probability provides a very simple model to help understand the general behaviour of image data structures. Maybe surprisingly, on the basis of simulations the results derived from this simple model seem to hold for a large class of maps. More empirical work is needed to determine the practical validity of this finding.

ACKNOWLEDGEMENTS

The Finnish Academy funded this work. I thank Hanan Samet for his careful reading of the manuscript and Martti Mantyla and Heikki Saikkonen for comments on an earlier version.

REFERENCES

1. N. Ahuja and B. Schachter, Image models. Comp. Surv. 13(1981)4.
2. A. Blaser (ed.), Data base techniques for pictorial applications, Springer Verlag, Lecture Notes in Computer Science, 1980
3. C.C. Dyer, The space efficiency of quadtrees, Computer Graphics and Image Processing, 19(1982), 335-348
4. H. Freeman, Computer processing of line drawing images, Comp. Surv., 6(1974)1, 57-97
5. I. Gargantini, An effective way to represent quadtrees. Comm. ACM 25(1982)12, 905-910
6. R. Hunter and A.H. Robinson, International digital faximile coding standards, in 8
7. G.M. Hunter and G. Steiglitz, operations on images using quadtrees, IEEE PAMI-1, 1979
8. Special issue on digital encoding of graphics, Proc. IEEE 68(1980) 755-929
9. J. Jimenez and J.L. Navalon, Some experiments in image vectorization, IBM J. Res. and Dev. 26(1982)6, 724-734
10. E. Kawaguchi and T. Endo, On a method of binary-picture representation and its application to data compression. IEEE, PAMI-2(1980)1
11. K. Knowlton, Progressive transmission of grey scale and B/W images by simple, efficient and lossless encoding schemes. IEEE Proceedings 68 (1980), 885-896
12. M. Kunt and O. Johnsen, Block coding of graphics: a tutorial review, in 8, 770-786
13. B. Mandelbrot, Fractals:,Form, Chance and Dimension, W.H. Freeman and Co, San Francisco, 1977
14. R.E. Miles A survey of geometrical probability in the plane, Computer Graphics and Image Processing, 12, 1980
15. D. Meagher, Geometric modeling using octree encoding, Computer Graphics and Image Processing, 19(1982), 129-147
16. T.H. Morrin, II, Chain-link compression of arbitrary black-white images, Computer Graphics and Image Processing 5(1976), 172-189
17. T. Pavlidis, Techniques for optimal compaction of pictures and maps, Computer Graphics and Image Processing 3(1974), 215-224
18. H. Samet, Region representation: quadtrees from boundary codes, CACM 23(1980)3, 163-170
19. L.A. Santalo, Integral Geometry and Geometric Probability, Addison-Wesley, 1976
20. M. Tamminen, Performance analysis of cell based file structures, to appear in Computer Graphics and Image Processing
21. M. Tamminen, Efficient geometric access to a multirepresentation geo-database, submitted for publication. (Also Report-HTKK-TKO-B52, Helsinki University of Technology, Espoo, 1983.)
22. M. Tamminen, Encoding pixel trees, submitted for publication. (Also Report-HTKK-TKO-B51, Helsinki University of Technology, Espoo, 1983.)

IMAGE PROCESSING WITH HIERARCHICAL CELLULAR LOGIC

S. L. Tanimoto
Department of Computer Science, FR-35
University of Washington
Seattle, Washington 98195
U.S.A.

Introduction

The use of pyramids, cones, and quadtrees to represent and process images is a way to incorporate aspects of <u>hierarchy</u> into low-level image processing. Hierarchy is important in providing multiple levels of image representation, in terms of resolution or of abstraction. Hierarchy was present in the early perceptron models [Rosenblatt 62], was incorporated in computer graphics [Warnock 67], into data structures [Klinger 71], and into machine vision models [Uhr 71], [Hanson and Riseman 74], [Hanson and Riseman 80]. Hierarchy in machine vision is also suggested by the structure of biological vision systems [Uhr 80].

An important capability in image analysis is to be able to compute not only local features and global features, but also intermediate features and features that span the scale of local to global. A number of studies have been done to assess the possibilities of local/global processing using hierarchical computation structures [Tanimoto & Klinger 80], [Dyer and Rosenfeld 77], [Rosenfeld 79], [Granlund 81]. When one considers such computations in a parallel-processing framework, it is desirable to have a good model for the kinds of data processing one wants to do. This paper summarizes a model called <u>hierarchical cellular logic</u> and the applications for it in image processing. The details of this logic are described in [Tanimoto 83c, 83d, 83e]. For a discussion of the architecture aspects, see [Tanimoto 83b], [Dyer 81]. The reason for utilizing cellular logic as a paradigm for image analysis is that it is possible to build parallel hardware for cellular logic operations in a straightforward way [Preston et al 79], [Duff 76].

NATO ASI Series, Vol. F18
Computer Architectures for Spatially Distributed Data
Edited by H. Freeman and G. G. Pieroni

Hierarchical Cellular Logic

Hierarchical Domains. The system we shall present consists of a class of data objects and operations that work on those objects. Thus we begin with the general structure of the data objects. We call such objects "pyramids", and they have a structure referred to by the term "hierarchical domain", which designates, in turn, a set of cells.

We define a *cell* to be a 3-tuple, whose integer components may be considered to be the coordinates of the cell. In general, the form of a cell is: (k,i,j). We say that it occurs in "level" k, "row" i, and "column" j. We define a *hierarchical domain* with L+1 levels to be the set of cells:

$$\{(k,i,j) \text{ such that } -1 < k < L+1, \text{ and } -1 < i < 2^{**}k, \text{ and } -1 < j < 2^{**}k\} .$$

For a given integer k, the kth *level* consists of the cells of a hierarchical domain whose first coordinate is k. The largest is level L, and it is also called the *base* level. The smallest is level 0, consisting of the single cell (0,0,0) and we call it the *root* of the hierarchical domain.

By a *pyramid* we mean a function which maps each cell of a hierarchical domain to a value (in some given range). If the range of values is {0, 1} then the function is called a binary pyramid or *bit pyramid*. Some other types of pyramids include integer pyramids, byte pyramids, real pyramids and complex pyramids. This definition is related to some others that have appeared in the literature [Tanimoto and Pavlidis 75], [Tanimoto 77], [Schneier 81].

We define the *neighborhood* of a cell to be a set of fourteen cells that are either spatially adjacent or adjacent in an embedded quadtree. Cells that are in the base, at the sides or at the root have incomplete neighborhoods. For simplicity in the discussion, we shall assume that "dummy cells" exist around the border of the hierarchical domain thereby completing the neighborhoods of border cells. The standard neighbors are listed below, here given numbers N1 to N14, names (e.g. "father") and their coordinates in terms of the home cell (k,i,j).

N1	"father"	(k-1, i div 2, j div 2)
N2	"northwest"	(k, i-1, j-1)
N3	"north"	(k, i-1, j)
N4	"northeast"	(k, i-1, j+1)
N5	"west"	(k, i, j-1)
N6	"home"	(k, i, j)
N7	"east"	(k, i, j+1)
N8	"southwest"	(k, i+1, j-1)
N9	"south"	(k, i+1, j)
N10	"southeast"	(k, i+1, j+1)
N11	"northwest son"	(k+1, 2i, 2j)
N12	"northeast son"	(k+1, 2i, 2j+1)
N13	"southwest son"	(k+1, 2i+1, 2j)
N14	"southeast son"	(k+1, 2i+1, 2j+1)

Here "div" indicates truncated integer division as in Pascal. The nine neighbors in level k (the level that contains the home cell) make up the *lateral neighborhood*. The remaining five cells together with the home cell (again) comprise the *quadtree neighborhood*. The pyramidal neighborhood is diagrammed in figure 1.

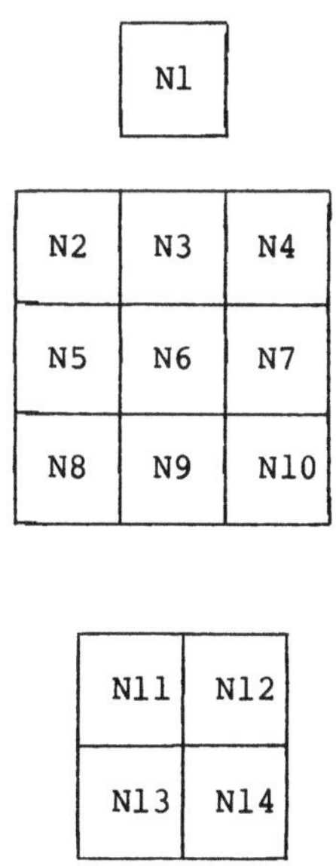

Figure 1. The neighborhood of a cell.

Constant Bit Pyramids. There are several particular bit pyramids which are useful in describing algoritms. We use 0 and 1 to denote bit pyramids that are everywhere 0 and everywhere 1, respectively. By Qk, where k is an integer, we indicate a bit pyramid containing 0 at all cells except those in level k, where all cells have value 1. Each cell can be classified into one of four primitive son types: Northwest, Northeast, Southwest or Southeast. There are also four composite son types: North, South, East and West. A bit pyramid in which precisely all the Northwest sons have value 1 is designated QNW. Other bit pyramids have similar definitions: i.e. we have QNE, QSW, QSE, QN, QS, QW, QE. Note that (for example)

$$\mathrm{QNE} = \mathrm{QN} * \mathrm{QE}$$
$$\mathrm{QN} = \mathrm{QNW} + \mathrm{QNE}.$$

Cellular Logic Operations. There are two kinds of cellular logic operations in the hierarchical cellular logic. They both operate on bit pyramids. The first kind is boolean. If X and Y are bit pyramids then X <op> Y is defined to be the bit pyramid whose cell (k, i, j) has the value X [(k, i, j)] <op> Y [(k, i, j)], where <op> is one of +,*, -, or (+).

The second kind of operation is matching. We define a pattern to be a vector of fourteen elements, each of which is either 0, 1, or D. A pattern is a specification for a neighborhood condition. The occurrence of a D signifies a "don't care" entry. An example pattern is the following:

VertEdge1 = [D 1 D 0 1 D 0 1 D 0 D D D D].

This can be graphically illustrated as follows:

```
   D

 1 D 0
 1 D 0
 1 D 0

  D D
  D D
```

A pattern such as this can be matched to each neighborhood of a binary image in either a strict of a liberal fashion. We define AND_Match [Pattern] (X) to be a function (which depends upon Pattern) that maps the bit pyramid X to a new bit pyramid. At each cell, the new value is defined as follows:

$$Y\,[(k,\ i,\ j)] = \underset{n=1}{\overset{14}{\mathrm{AND}}}\ (\mathrm{Pattern}[n] \overset{A}{=} X\,[C[N](k,\ i,\ j)]\ )$$

where the binary operation $\overset{A}{=}$ is defined in the following table:

$\overset{A}{=}$	0	1
0	1	0
1	0	1
D	1	1

The other matching operations OR_Match[Pattern] (X) is defined analogously.

$$Y\,[(k,\ i,\ j)] = \underset{n=1}{\overset{14}{\mathrm{OR}}}\ (\mathrm{Pattern}[n] \overset{V}{=} X\,[C[n](k,\ i,\ j)]\ )$$

where the operation $\overset{V}{=}$ is defined as follows:

$\overset{V}{=}$	0	1
0	1	0
1	0	1
D	0	0

<u>Restricted</u> <u>Function</u> <u>Application</u>. One concept useful in describing cellular logic operations is that of restricting the application of an operation to the cells at which a given bit pyramid (other than the argument of the operation) has value equal to 1. Such restrictions are defined as follows where F is a unary operation and <op> is a binary operation.

$$[F|Z](X) = (F(X) * Z) * Z) + (X * -Z)$$

$$X\ [\langle op\rangle|Z]\ Y = ((X \langle op\rangle Y) * Z) + (X * -Z).$$

If the bit pyramid Z contained is in the interior of an object and zeros elsewhere, a restriction of F to Z applied to X would limit the effects of F on X to those cells within the object as defined by Z.

Iteration. In order to express the repeated application of a function, we use "exponential" notation:

$$F^n(X) = \begin{cases} X & \text{if } n = 0 \\ F(F^{n-1}(X) & \text{otherwise} \end{cases}$$

Often there arise situations where it is convenient to specify indefinite repetition. In other words, it may be known that repeatedly applying some function F to a bit pyramid eventually provides a stable result. We use an asterisk as an exponent to indicate such a "repeat until no change" control designation. When the result never becomes stable, the expression involving the construct has an undefined value.

$$F^*(X) = \begin{cases} F^m(X) & \text{if there exists m s.t. } F^m(X)=F^{m+1}(X) \\ \text{undefined otherwise} & \end{cases}$$

Bit Pyramids for Binary Images

Let us suppose that B is a bit pyramid which represents some binary image. That is, it is everywhere 0 except in its base level, where it contains a binary image of 1s and 0s. We define several kinds of bit pyramids that are constructed from a bit pyramid such as B.

The OR pyramid. Assuming Psons represents the pattern which contains 1s at the positions corresponding to the four sons of the extended neighborhood, and which contains "don't care" entries everywhere else, we then define

$$ORPYR(X) = [OR\_Match(Psons)|(1-QL)]^L(X)$$

Here each cell (except those in the base) receives the logical OR of the values of its four sons, and this is repeated until the data has moved all the way up to the root. An important property of an OR pyramid is that there exists a path of 1s from the root to any 1 in the base.

The AND pyramid. A similarly constructed pyramid is the following:

$$\mathrm{ANDPYR}(X) = \lfloor \mathrm{AND\_Match}(\mathrm{Psons}) \mid (1\text{-}QL) \rfloor^{*} (X)$$

An important property of AND pyramids is that each level above the base tends to filter out more and more of the objects that are not "dense" and "compact". Note the use of indefinite repetition here; one often gets by with fewer than L iterations when building an AND pyramid.

The COUNT-OF-TWO Pyramid. Whereas the OR and AND pyramids are extremely liberal and conservative, respectively, in the reduced representations they give at higher pyramid levels, to the original binary image, there are two more-compromising kinds of pyramids. The first of these is the COUNT-OF-TWO pyramid. In this case, each cell receives value 1 if two or more of its sons have value 1.

Let Ppair1, Ppair2, ..., Ppair6 be the six patterns which contain 1s at exactly two son positions, with Ds everywhere else. Then

$$\mathrm{CNT2}(X) = \mathop{\mathrm{OR}}_{n=1}^{6} \mathrm{OR\_Match}(\mathrm{Ppair}\lfloor n \rfloor)\ (X)$$

$$\text{COUNT-OF-TWO-PYR}(X) = \lfloor \mathrm{CNT2} \mid (1\text{-}QL) \rfloor^{*} (X).$$

The COUNT-OF-THREE Pyramid. Having a similar definition is COUNT-OF-THREE-PYR(X) in which a cell gets value 1 if it has at least three sons with value 1.

Applications

Typical Applications in Image Processing. In order to illustrate how hierarchical cellular logic can be used, we describe generally how some well-known problems in image processing can be solved.

Key Point Selection. The selection of seed points for region growing is one recurring problem. Bright spots are good candidates for objects in many industrial and medical images. With binary images, points interior to large objects are desired as seed points for object extraction algorithms. With hierarchical cellular logic we can easily find key points in an image by building a pyramid structure for the image, and doing a top-down search in it.

In binary images one can define several types of key points: the leftmost uppermost point containing 1; the center of mass of the objects; the center of the smallest rectangle that encloses the objects and has sides parallel to the image borders; etc. Using hierarchical cellular logic, one class of key points is easily defined.

We assume that it is desired to obtain, quickly, a bit pyramid X containing a single 1 which must lie in the base level and in the interior of one of the connected regions of another given bit pyramid Y. That is, X must satisfy X = X * Y, and X must only have one cell with value 1.

A solution using hierarchical cellular logic is to construct ORPYR(Y) and then steer a 1 down the hierarchical domain from the root, so that at each step it is within the set of cells containing 1 in ORPYR(Y), and therefore finishes up in a 1's region in Y. Such a procedure is efficient, since it uses a number of steps proportional to L. At each step, care must be taken to ensure that no more than one son of the currently selected cell becomes selected.

The basic step of this procedure is applied once at each level (except L) starting with k=0. It places a 1 in level k+1 at one of the four sons of the cell marked 1 in level k. It begins by marking any northwest son in level k+1 whose father is marked 1, provided the cell itself has value 1 in ORPYR(Y). Then it marks northeast sons that satisfy that condition plus the condition that their west neighbor is not already marked (this resolves ties). The other two types of sons are similarly handled. Logical expressions describing this top-down marking are:

$$X_0 = Q0$$

$$X_{k+1,NW} = \mathrm{ORPYR}(Y) * QNW * \mathrm{Project}(X_k)$$

$$X_{k+1,NE} = (\mathrm{ORPYR}(Y) * QNE * \mathrm{Project}(X_k)) * -\mathrm{ShiftEast}(X_{k+1,NW})$$

$$X_{k+1,SW} = (ORPYR(Y) * QSW * Project(X_k)) * -ShiftSouth(X_{k+1,NW}) * -ShiftSouthWest(X_{k+1,NE})$$

$$X_{k+1,SE} = (ORPYR(Y) * QSE * Project(X_k)) * -ShiftSouthEast(X_{k+1,NW}) * -ShiftSouth(X_{k+1,NE}) * -ShiftEast(X_{k+1,SW})$$

$$X_{k+1} = X_{k+1,NW} + X_{k+1,NE} + X_{k+1,SW} + X_{k+1,SE}$$

Here, Project(X) is defined as OR_Match(Pfather, X), where Pfather is a pattern with value 1 in the father position and Ds everywhere else. ShiftEast(X) is OR_Match(Pwest, X), where Pwest is a pattern with value in the west neighbor position and Ds elsewhere; it has the effect of translating a bit pyramid one cell toward the east. ShiftWest, ShiftSouthWest, and ShiftSouthEast are similarly defined.

Since each basic step requires no more than a fixed number of operations of hierarchical cellular logic, and there are L levels at which the basic step must be applied, the time needed to select the key point from the constructed pyramid is on the order of L. This is far less than the time that would generally be necessary using conventional, non-hierarchical cellular logic operations to shrink objects down to points.

The point found by the above procedure is a function of the structure of the OR pyramid in which the search is performed. With an OR pyramid, the leftmost uppermost (i.e. westernmost northernmost) point containing a 1 is found. If several objects are present in the image, the keypoint found is not necessarily in the largest one or even a relatively large one.

If one changes the pyramid used, the selection method may be encouraged to find keypoints that lie in significantly large objects. One can build a binary pyramid from an image B by starting with the two or three bottom levels of a COUNT-OF-TWO, COUNT-OF-THREE, or AND pyramid, and then using the OR_Math(Psons) function to construct the remaining levels up to the root. This causes fewer paths from root to base to exist and these paths tend to lead to the larger objects. It is also possible that no paths exist in the new pyramid, although paths existed in the OR pyramid. Through a more adaptive procedure, pyramids can be constructed for any nonzero binary image, that are guaranteed to have at least one path from the root to the base. Such a procedure is sketched below.

In order to ensure at least one path, we can begin with the binary image B in the base. At each step, we construct one more level of the pyramid above the last one constructed. We successively try ANDing, the CNT2 transform, the CNT3 transform, and ORing the sons of each node at the level to be computed. The first of these transforms that produces something other than a level full of zeros is used for that level. During the Lth step, the root is assigned the value 1.

Fast Fill. A number of commercially available graphics systems provide an operation called "polygon fill", "paint", or "region fill", which causes a connected set of pixels of a two-dimensional digital image to be labelled with a given value. This operation is often the bottleneck in interactive graphics programs that present pictures made up of colored-in regions.

The region-filling problem may be stated as follows: One is given two binary images, A and B, such that A has a 1 at only a single cell (the "seed" pixel), and such that B consists of one or more connected components (of 1's), one of which includes the seed cell. From these, it is desired to produce a third binary image C which has 1's precisely at those cells which comprise the connected component in B which includes the seed pixel in A. This problem may be stated in other ways in which one may allow non-binary values at cells or have a region of 0's to be filled in rather than a region described by 1's bounded by 0's, etc. Such problems are minor variations on the one treated here.

A straightforward solution in HCL to the region-filling problem is:

$$C = \mathrm{FlatFill}(X,Y) = [\mathrm{OR\_Match}(\mathrm{Plateral})|Y]^{*}(X)$$

where Plateral = D11111111DDDD. In each iteration of the OR_Match function application, the labelling moves one cell further out from the seed cell. However, this propagation is restricted to take place only at cells where Y is a 1. Thus the number of iterations required is equal to the length of the longest path in Y between the seed cell and another cell belonging to the same connected component in Y. The diameter of a region is the longest such distance possible in the region, for any placement of the seed cell within the region. Note that the distance in this case is the minimum number of "chess king move" steps required to get from one cell to another. The FlatFill function requires a number of steps on the order of the diameter of the region to be filled.

An alternative HCL solution allows (in the general case) the propagation to use higher levels of the hierarchical domain, and it achieves much faster filling when the region is large and relatively compact.

$$\text{PyramidFill}(X,Y) = [\text{OR\_Match}(\text{Pall}) | \text{ANDPYR}(Y)]^*(X)$$

where Pall = 1111111111111. PyramidFill requires a preliminary step, the construction of ANDPYR(Y), which itself may require up to L iterations of an AND_Match operation. However, this operation may be performed just one time and many regions in Y may be labelled by PyramidFill. For a large, compact, region (one relatively free of holes, cracks and isthmuses), the labelling propagates out from the seed cell not only laterally but up into higher levels of the hierarchical domain. Successive iterations have the effect of spreading the label across the region very rapidly because the diameter of the region is much reduced at such levels. The labelling then propagates back down filling in large areas of the region in level L at once.

The results of computing FlatFill and PyramidFill are similar. The results in level L are identical. As explained, PyramidFill labels some cells in upper levels and these are also part of its result. They can be eliminated by ANDing with QL. For regions of the appropriate type, PyramidFill requires a number of steps proportional to the logarithm of the diameter. Not counting the construction of ANDPYR(Y), in the worst case, PyramidFill uses the same number of steps as FlatFill.

Binary Edge Detection. Two edge detection procedures for handling noisy binary images have recently been described [Gangoli and Tanimoto 83]. They may both be described effectively with HCL expressions. For brevity, only the first is described here. Let B be the bit pyramid containing the input binary image in level L. Then the following definitions compute the clean edge image in E.

E0(X) = [AND_Match(Psons) | (1-QL)](X)

E1(X) = E0(X) * OR_Match(Pedge, E0(X))

E2(X) = OR_Match(Plateral, E1(X))

E3(X) = Project(E2(X))

EdgeHull(X) = AND_Match(Plateral, E3(X))

EdgeHull2(X) = EdgeHull(-X)

E4(X) = OR_Match(Plateral, EdgeHull2(X))

CleanEdges1(X) = EdgeHull(X) * E4(X)

E = CleanEdges(B)

Here E0(X) generates level L-1 only of ANDPYR(X). E1(X) generates a rough edge representation. EdgeHull(X) represents the edge image with exterior noise removed. EdgeHull2(X) represents edges with interior noise (only) removed. The final clean edge image is obtained by growing the internally cleaned edges enough to obtain overlap with the externally cleaned ones, and then taking the intersection of these two bit pyramids.

Progressive Refinement of Images. It is interesting to note that in interactive graphics applications in which there is a bottleneck in transmission bandwidth between an image source and the user's CRT, a hierarchical technique for transmission may sometimes be appropriate. The potential advantage of the scheme to be described is that rough versions of the entire image arrive on the display early, so that the user may obtain an overall impression of the image long before all its details arrive [Sloan and Tanimoto 79]. The transmitting agent first creates a bit pyramid Trans(X) from the original binary image stored in level L of X.

$$\text{Trans(X)} = \lfloor \text{AND\_Match(PNWson)} \,|\, (1\text{-QL}) \rfloor^{*} \text{(X)}$$

Where PNWson = DDDDDDDDDD1DDD. Then the transmitter sends selected data from this pyramid in a particular order: Beginning with the root, and ending with level L, the levels are scanned in a raster-scan order, and the bits visited are transmitted in a stream, but the cells which are northwest sons are skipped over, and their values not sent. The root is considered in this special case not to be a northwest son, so that its value is sent.

The receiver, in synchrony with the transmitter, fills a hierarchical domain with the received values, again passing over northwest sons. However, the receiver interleaves two other acitivities with the filling process. One of these activities is the projection of values downward in the hierarchical domain, and the other is the reading of values out of level L to refresh a display. The projection downward serves two purposes. One of these is to get data to level L where it can be displayed. The other is to replace northwest son data that was extracted from each sibling group before transmission. Assuming that Y is the pyramid resulting just after cell (k, i, j) has been filled, and that Y' is the pyramid just after the projection has been done (and before the next cell is filled), we have:

$$Y' = \mathrm{RProject}_k^{1-k}(Y)$$

where

$$\mathrm{RProject}_m(X) = \left[\mathrm{AND\_Match(Pfather)}\,\middle|\,(1\text{-}Qm)\right](X).$$

This new projection function differs from Project in not allowing level m to change. That is RProject copies data down from level m without destroying the contents of level m itself. After each projection, the image to be displayed is in level L. If the original image shows large, compact solid-colored objects, these objects will be visible in the display long before all the data has arrived. It is easy to see, also, that the data bits transmitted are exactly those of the original image, but that the ordering is a different one from the usual raster-scan order.

Other Applications. Although the operations and applications mentioned above involve only bit pyramids rather than integer pyramids, one can define integer pyramids in terms of bit pyramids. It is then a straightforward matter to perform hierarchical bit counting [Rosenfeld 79], [Tanimoto 83e] and apply that to local property counting [Dubitsky et al 81], [Tanimoto 83e]. One can also then construct efficient sorting algorithms and perform median filtering of images [Tanimoto 83a].

Conclusions

In order to have image analysis algorithms which take into consideration both the local and global characteristics, it behooves one to use a hierarchical computational approach. Cellular logic operations are well matched to parallel computing hardware because they consist of highly-regular local transformations of cellular configurations. Traditional two-dimensional cellular spaces can be augmented to form hierarchical domains, adding global power to operations. Bit pyramids can be manipulated like binary images by operations of a hierarchical cellular logic.

Applications of hierarchical cellular logic to problems of local feature counting, determining key points of regions, and labelling compact regions result in efficient algorithms that require on the order of log N time to compute. The approach can also be employed in computer graphics for such tasks as filling polygons and transmitting pictures in a progressive manner.

References

Dubitsky, T., Wu, A.Y., and Rosenfeld, A. (1981) Parallel region property computation by active quadtree networks. IEEE Trans. on Pattern Recog. and Machine Intelligence, Vol. PAMI-3, No. 6, pp626-633.

Duff, M.J.B. (1976) CLIP4: A large scale integrated circuit parallel image processor. Proceedings of the Third Int. Joint Conf. on Pattern Recognition, Coronado, Calif. pp728-733.

Dyer, C.R. (1981) VLSI pyramid machines for image processing. Proceedings of PRIP '81: The IEEE Conf. on Pattern Recognition and Image Processing, Dallas, TX, August.

Dyer, C.R. and Rosenfeld, A. (1977) Cellular pyramids for image analysis. Tech. Report No. 544, Computer Science Center, Univ. of Maryland, College Park MD.

Gangolli, A.R. and Tanimoto, S.L. (1983) Two pyramid machine algorithms for edge detection in noisy binary images. Info. Proc. Letters (to appear).

Granlund, G.H. (1981) The GOP parallel image processor. In Digital Image Processing Systems, Bolc, L. and Kulpa, Z., eds. McMillan, London.

Hanson, A.R. and Riseman, E.M. (1974) Design of a semantically-directed vision processor. Technical Report. Dept. of Computer and Information Sciences, Univ. of Massachusetts, Jan.

Hanson, A.R. and Riseman, E.M. (1980) Processing cones: a computational structure for image analysis. In [Tanimoto and Klinger 80], pp101-131.

Preston, K., Duff, M.J.B., Levialdi, S., Norgren, P.E., and Toriwaki, J.-I. (1979) Basics of cellular logic with some applications in medical image processing. Proc. of the IEEE, Vol. 67, No. 5, pp826-855.

Rosenblatt, F. (1962) Principles of Neurodynamics: Perceptrons and the theory of brain mechanisms. Washington D.C.: Spartan Books.

Rosenfeld, A. (1979) Picture Languages. NY: Academic Press.

Schneier, M. (1981) Two hierarchical linear feature representations: edge pyramids and edge quadtrees. Computer Graphics and Image Processing, Vol. 17, No. 3, Nov. pp211-224.

Sloan, K.R., Jr., and Tanimoto, S.L. (1979) Progressive refinement of raster images. IEEE Trans. on Computers, Vol. C-28, No. 11, Nov. pp871-874.

Tanimoto, S.L. (1977) A pyramid model for binary picture complexity. Proc. IEEE Conf. on Pattern Recognition and Image Processing, Troy, NY, June, pp25-28.

Tanimoto, S.L. (1983a) Algorithms for median filtering of images on a pyramid machine. Technical Report No. 83-01-04, Dept. of Computer Science, FR-35, Univ. of Washington, Seattle WA 98195. Also to appear in Computing Structures for Image Processing, M.J.B. Duff, (ed.), London: Academic Press, 1983.

Tanimoto, S.L. (1983b) A pyramidal approach to parallel processing. Proc. 10th Int. Symposium on Computer Architecture, Stockholm, Sweden, June.

Tanimoto, S.L. (1983c) Cellular logic in a hierarchical framework. Proc. Third Scandinavian Conf. on Image Analysis, Copenhagen, Denmark, July, pp237-243.

Tanimoto, S.L. (1983d) Cellular logic operations with hierarchical extensions. Proc. Soc. Photo. Inst. Eng. Vol. 435, Conf. on Architecture and Algorithms for Digital Image Processing, San Diego, August.

Tanimoto, S.L. (1983e) A hierarchical cellular logic. (submitted for publication).

Tanimoto, S.L. and Klinger, A. (eds., 1980). Structured Computer Vision: Machine Perception Through Hierarchical Computation Structures. NY: Academic Press.

Tanimoto, S.L. and Pavlidis, T. (1975) A hierarchical data structure for picture processing. Computer Graphics and Image Processing, Vol. 4, pp104-119.

Uhr, L. (1972) Layered "recognition cone" networks that preprocess, classify and describe. IEEE Transaction on Computers, Vol. 21, pp758-768.

Uhr, L. (1980) Psychological motivation and underlying concepts. In [Tanimoto and Klinger 80], pp1-30.

Warnock, J.E. (1969) A hidden-surface algorithm for computer-generated half-tone pictures. Technical Report No. 4-15, Dept. of Computer Science, Univ. of Utah, Salt Lake City, UT.

CONSIDERATIONS ON PYRAMIDAL PIPELINES FOR SPATIAL ANALYSIS OF GEOSCIENCE MAP DATA

T. Kasvand and A. G. Fabbri (*)
National Research Council Canada, Ottawa, Canada, K1A 0R8
(*) Geological Survey of Canada, Ottawa, Canada, K1A 0E8

ABSTRACT

In the geosciences the visual aspect derived from data bases and the quantitative results are fundamental. Digital image processing has been demonstrated to represent a useful tool in geology. Two examples of geological applications are described in this contribution to show which computational aspects would benefit by special architectures.

The theory of mathematical morphology provides a statistical background that supports processing images by particular local operators termed "structuring elements". Some forms of pipeline architectures are envisaged which, if available at moderate cost, could greatly facilitate the spatial analysis of geoscience data.

INTRODUCTION

In geology, and in most fields of the geosciences, the quantitative and visual aspects of results derived from data bases are fundamental. Commonly, hand-drawn maps and computer-generated contour maps are used to synthesize the knowledge acquired by surveys over a given topographic area in which one or more particular characteristics are considered; e.g., bedrock geology, soil classification, land use, geophysical and geochemical anomalies, or mineral resources. Particularly, the generation of thematic maps requires that several types of data covering the same area be combined to define areas in which terrains assume desired attributes corresponding to expert-knowledge models.

NATO ASI Series, Vol. F18
Computer Architectures for Spatially Distributed Data
Edited by H. Freeman and G. G. Pieroni

Such terrain classification must be expressed in a quantitative manner to lead to statistical estimation and spatial data analysis. Examples of data integration and subsequent statistical analysis have been described by Kasvand et al. (1981) and Agterberg et al. (1981). Furthermore, flexibility and automation in visual representations are needed to accommodate modifications of the geological models required for most realistic classifications. Image processing is a tool suitable for such purposes.

Besides this macroscopic aspect of terrain classification, much work has been done in quantitative characterization of microscopic images of crystalline materials by stereologists, geologists, metallographers, ceramists, etc. Such images can be considered as micromaps in which the silhuettes (profiles) of mineral grains or other objects are separately identified and analyzed.

In particular, the theory of mathematical morphology (Matheron, 1967,1975, Serra, 1982) can be used in the analysis of textures; i.e., local neighborhood (structuring element) transformations are computed which lead to exact morphological characterizations (Fabbri and Masounave, 1981). The definition of textural properties in crystalline materials is important to explain the physical behaviour of the material and also the genetic aspects implied by geological models not necessarily in image form (Fabbri et al., 1983).

As demonstrated by Kasvand (1983), image processing in geoscience represents a tool particularly well suited for spatial data analysis so that we can consider some form of computerized vision to assist the geologist. A system of computer programs for metallurgy was demonstrated by Moore (1968) and the development of specialized image processing devices (image or texture analyzers) started at about this time (Fisher 1967). An image processing system based on general-purpose computers for analyzing geological images was proposed by Fabbri (1980). A more extensive approach to image processing of geological data is considered by Fabbri (1983). This contribution analyzes two classes of geological image processing to identify the computational aspects which could greatly benefit from specialized architectures.

COMPUTER PROCESSING

The computational aspects of processing geoscience data can be subdivided into the following three classes,

(I) primarily interactive,

(S) sequential, and

(P) "pipelineable".

Table I shows a sequence of steps for the digitization of line drawings of maps, or microscopic images of grains, and for preprocessing binary boundary images to compute labeled images from which to extract binary images of silhouettes or profiles. The computational aspects I, S, and P are identified in the table. Figure 1 shows some computational aspects in terms of types of processing required and the form of the input and output data. For preprocessing and processing of binary and labeled images, the P identifies the pipelineable aspects.

In general, many individual image processing operations may be viewed as transformations (T) of an input image (I) into an output image (O), i.e., O=T(I). The transformation T may involve the entire input image I for the computation of one output pixel in O, such as the Fourier transform, or only a certain local neighbourhood N is involved, for example as in thinning or edge detection. If the processing is, or can be reduced to, a local neighbourhood operation, it is potentially "pipelineable". The word "pipeline", however, only refers to a particular hardware realization of the process, while the concept itself is much more general.

The cluster of pixels in N may be viewed as a generalized sensor (S), where each of the pixels in N is an elementary sensor, say a photodiode. The cluster of sensors S over N computes a specific function of the inputs. The generalized sensors S may be replicated, as seems to be the case in biological vision, to produce a parallel processing machine. Since replication of the hardware is, or at least has been, expensive, the generalized processors are kept fundamentally very simple, while relying on the interaction between them.

To trade hardware costs and complexity for time, one generalized processor may be used (per operation) to scan the image. Such a scanner would directly produce the desired output image, or whatever other data are to be extracted from the image. However, when considering the necessary sequences of image processing operations, as outlined here for a particular application, it is desirable to store the input images as well as many processed versions of these images. To avoid the addressing of individual pixels, the contents of the image are made to flow or are "streamed" past the processor, which at each "clock cycle" has new inputs in N, to generate one or more output pixels. Hence the name "pipeline" processing. In order for this realization to be economical, the neighbourhood N should be small.

In brief, the basic concepts to consider are the following.

(i) In an image-processing system a balance is needed between (a) speed of operation, (b) expense of hardware, and (c) ease of programming.

(ii) Among the many image-processing operations, a frequently occurring one is the so-termed "local operator" or neighbourhood transformation (Levialdi, 1983). Examples of local operations which are directly pipelineable are; (a) filtering, (b) eroding or shrinking, (c) dilatating or expanding, (d) thinning and skeletonizing, (e) transformations by structuring elements (mask matching, template matching, correlation), (f) relaxation, and (f) Boolean operations. Some versions already exist in hardware form (Sternberg, 1979, 1980, Preston et al., 1979, Gillies, 1978). By modifying the algorithms for traditionally "random access" type operations, (such as area and pixel sequence labeling, slope calculations, and even contour following and chain coding), these may also be computed iteratively by mostly using pipeline achitectures.

(iii) A basic constraint on local operators to be pipelineable is the neighbourhood size N (otherwise a parallel processing machine results). The spatial extent of the input is limited to a neighborhood N of m x n pixels, which is much smaller than the size of the entire image.

(iv) Simplifying constraints for hardware design are; (a) the output of the m x n neighborhood is a single pixel, and (b) the same algorithm is used for the entire image.

(v) In most cases the output is another image.

(vi) The operations may be both iterative and hierarchical.

PROCESSING	output data
(I) ONLINE DIGITIZATION BY GRAPHIC TABLET	tables of vectors
(S) VECTORS->RASTER CONVERSION	binary image of contours or boundaries for submap
(S) PATCHING OF BINARY IMAGES OF SUBMAPS	binary image of mosaic for submaps
(I) ONLINE EDITING OF BINARY IMAGES	edited binary image of mosaic
(P) LINE THINNING OF BINARY IMAGES OF LINES	binary image of thin lines
(S) LABELING OF CLOSED AREAS (COMPONENTS)	component-labeled image
(I) ONLINE LABELING OF MAP UNITS (PHASES)	table of phase labels and of corresponding components
(S) EXTRACTION OF PHASE-LABELED IMAGE or EXTRACTION OF ONE BINARY IMAGE FOR EACH PHASE	phase-labeled image or binary image for each phase
SUBSEQUENT PROCESSING	?

TABLE I; digitization, preprocessing, and input/output data sequence for geological applications. I, S, and P indicate interactive, sequential, and pipelineable processes, respectively.

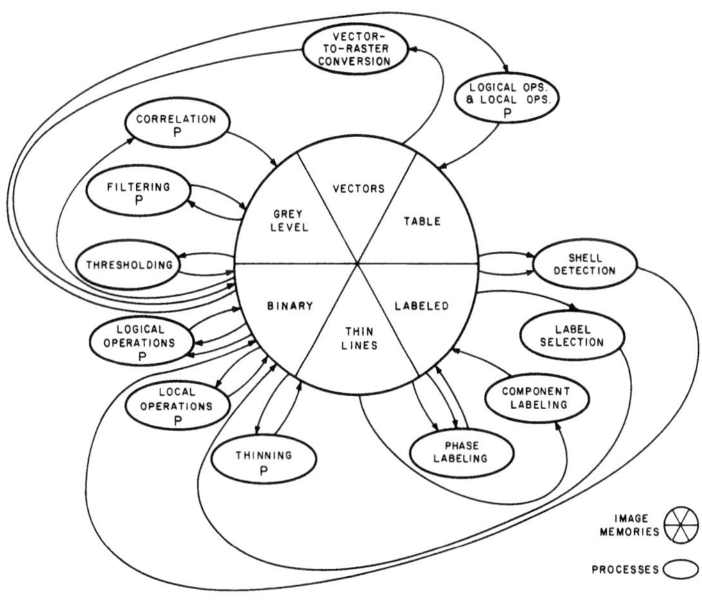

Figure 1. Computational aspects of processing binary and labeled images for geological applications. P indicates pipelineable processes.

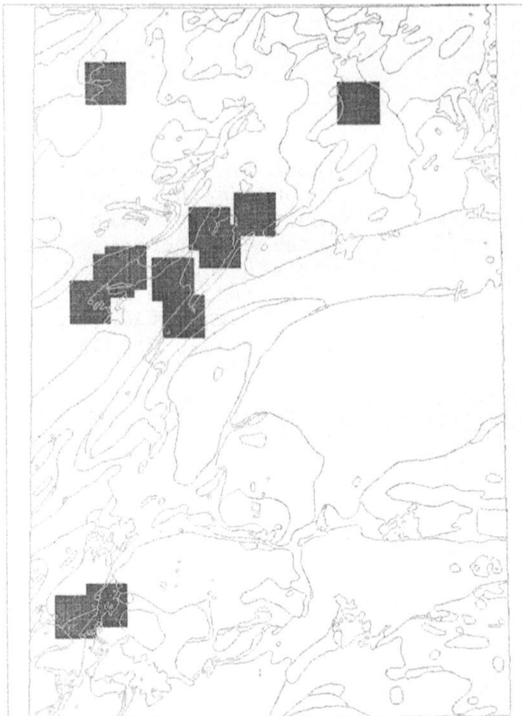

Figure 2. A geological boundary binary image of dimension 760 x 1004 pixels in Northwestern Manitoba, Canada. One pixel corresponds to a square on the ground of 167 m side. The 12 partly overlapping squares represent 10 km cells centered around 12 uranium occurrences known in the study area.

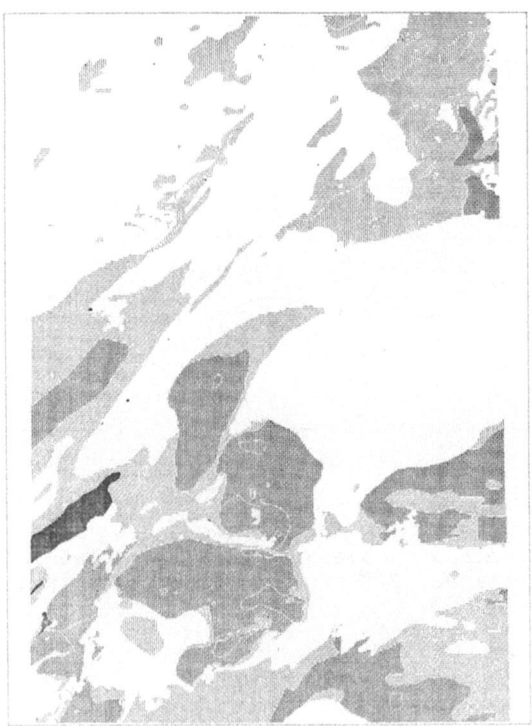

Figure 3. Four groups of map units extracted from the boundary image in Figure 2; horizontal lines represent aphebian pelitic metasediments, black represents aphebian calc-silicate rocks, vertical lines represent the hudsonian white and pink granite pegmatites, and cross-hatching represents arckean igneous and metamorphic rocks. The four groups are identified as image sets G1 to G4 in the text and in Figure 7.

Figure 4. Coincidence (black areas) between EU/ETH highs (>0.20, horizontal lines) and aeromagnetic anomaly lows (<2100 gammas, vertical lines). The two geophysical-anomaly image-sets are identified as A1 and A2 in the text and in Figure 7. EU/ETH is the ratio of equivalent uranium to equivalent thorium concentrations detected by low flying aircraft.

Figure 5. Dilatations and erosions (local neighborhood operations) of the binary image of aphebian pelitic metasediments; the black lines represent the edge pixels of the black areas after three and five successive dilatations. The white lines represent the edge pixels after three and five successive erosions. This pattern illustrates how distance relationships can be obtained by computing simple transforms.

Figure 6. Example of a thematic map in which the four geological map units in Figure 3 have been subdivided into the following two themes. (A) are terrains of the four units corresponding to the coincidence between the two anomalies in Figure 4 (EU/ETH highs and aeromagnetic lows), and (B) are archean rock terrains corresponding to the coincidence between the two anomalies (not shown) of aeromagnetic highs >2500 gammas and gravity highs >-65 milligals. The themes represent the conditions in the vicinity of the uranium occurrences shown in Figure 2. The black indicates terrains within 1 km from aphebian calc-silicate rocks (image set G2 in the text and in Fig, 7).

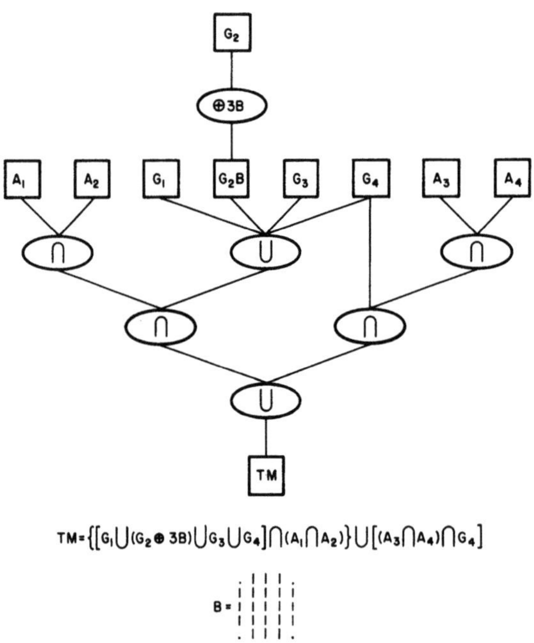

Figure 7. Processing structure for thematic mapping corresponding to the pattern shown in Figure 6. The concept of logical operation between image sets and of transformations by local neighborhood operators is symbolized by the expression for TM.

TWO GEOLOGICAL EXAMPLES

Let us have, in digitized and registered form, the following binary images obtained by labeling several boundary binary images (as shown in Fig. 2); sets G1 to G4, four different groups of geological map units (see Fig. 3), sets A1 to A4, four different geophysical anomaly intervals (two of these are shown in Fig. 4), and set B, a pseudooctagonal structuring element of 5 pixels x 5 pixels shown in Figure 7. The black pixels in B are indicated by 1's, and the "don't care" pixels by dots. Also, in Figure 7, the symbol (+) indicates a dilatation of an image set by the set B.

Examples of a logical operation between A1 and A2, intersection, and of transformations of G1, erosions and dilatations, are shown in Figures 4 and 5, respectively.

An example in thematic mapping can be represented as an "agglomerative" processing structure, shown in Figure 7, which corresponds to the image set shown in Figure 6. Map unit set G2 is dilatated three times (three successive 25 neighbors expansions) to represent all the pixels either coinciding with the unit itself or within 1 km from its boundary (in the present case each pixel corresponds to a square area of side 167 m).

An experiment for extracting the theme: "all areas similar to areas mineralized in uranium" (uranium mineralization 10 km square neighborhoods are shown in Fig. 2) has produced the thematic map set TM, shown in Figure 6, which can be identified by the expression in Figure 7. The latter consists of several logical operations and local neighborhood transformations.

The number (proportion) of black pixels in set TM can be considered as the probability that a random pixel, translated at random throughout the entire image space (also dilatated by 3B) coincide with pixels belonging to set TM. A convenient number of such themes can be extracted for a given area to identify all modes of occurrences of uranium and other types of mineralizations (see Fabbri, 1983).

Opening and closing functions are used in mathematical morphology to characterize granulometry (grain-size distribution) and interparticle distances, respectively. While granulometry is of interest, for example, for classifying porous sandstones which are potential oil reservoirs (granulometry of the pores and of the grains), a distribution of interparticle distances can be of importance for improving the extraction of minerals. For this we have to identify an optimum grind to separate most of the mineral particles, i.e., reducing the ore to a convenient minimum grain size.

An example of the processing structure to compute a "closing function" is shown in Figure 9. The corresponding transforms are the binary image sets shown in Figure 8. The closing function is generated by a process in which, from an image set A, a family of images is produced in a "divisive" processing structure. In Figure 9, B is the structuring element used for erosions (symbol (-)) and dilatations (symbol (+)) to produce the closing transforms. B1 and B2 are used for computing erosions leading to "object counting", i.e., connectivity number (= number of object - number of holes) for the square raster images shown in Figure 8. The numbers of 4-connected objects in Figure 8 are 139, 62, 48, 43, 34, and 22, respectively, for 0 to 5 closing iterations. For iterations 6 to 8 (not shown here) the numbers are 18, 11, and 5.

The connectivity number for each iteration can be used to histogram the frequency of particles at successive unit distances in the two directions of the raster. This represents a characterization "in number", i.e., weighted in number of particles (or better, connectivity numbers). Alternatively, the counting of the black pixels before and after each closing iteration can be used to compute a characterization "in measure", i.e., weighted according to areas (number of pixels in closing residues, or of pixels which changed value in the transformation). These numbers appear on top of the illustrations in Fig. 8.

For the five iterations shown in Figure 8, 32 transforms by local operators (or structuring elements) are needed, as shown in Figure 9. The number of transforms required increases very quickly with the number of iterations, especially if separate closing functions are required (as is generally the case) for the different directions of the raster. Linear directed structuring elements are used for this purpose and many more transformations have to be computed.

Clearly, this type of computations can be too slow on a sequential machine and should be conveniently obtained on a pipeline processor.

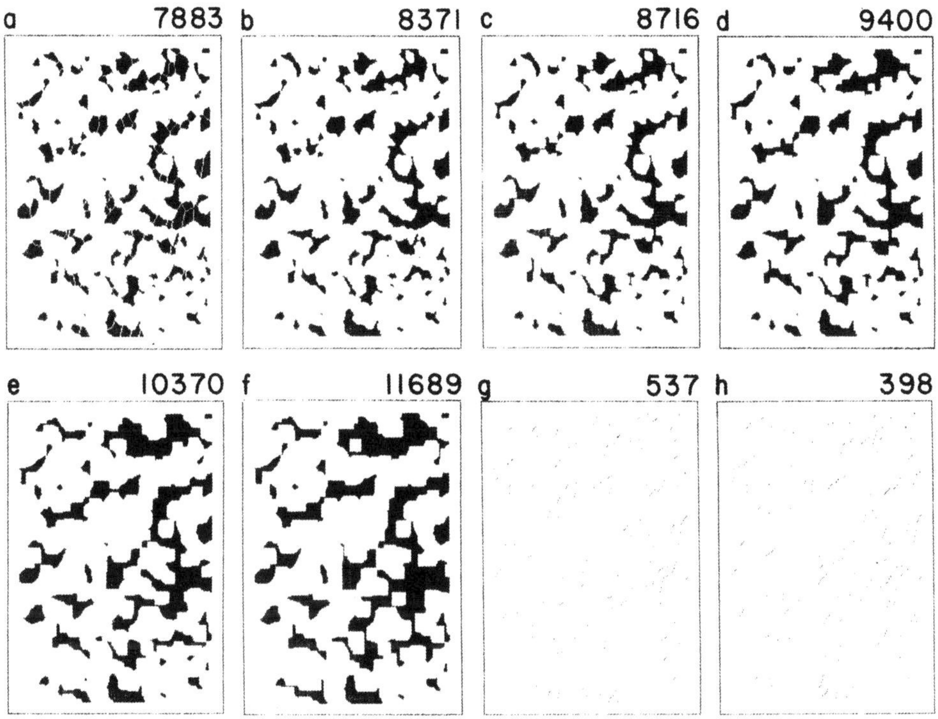

Figure 8. Characterization of interparticle distances for a binary image of plagioclase profiles from a granulitic rock by successive closing transformations. Closings are obtained by a 3 x 3 black pixel structuring element. The number of black pixels is printed above each image or transform.
(a) The original image of dimension 180 x 252 pixels mapped into a larger image space of 200 x 272 pixels; there are 139 profiles (objects) in this image. (b) to (h), results of one to five closing transformations leaving 62, 48, 43, 34, and 22 "4-connected objects", respectively. (g) and (h) are the images of the black pixels which turned to white during the erosions of the image in (a) by the structuring elements B1 and B2, respectively, illustrated in Figure 9. B1 and B2 are used to compute the "connectivity number". The difference between the two counts of 537 and 398 is 139. Five successive black pixel counts for 6 to 10 closings are 13614, 16213, 18112, 21477, and 24567.

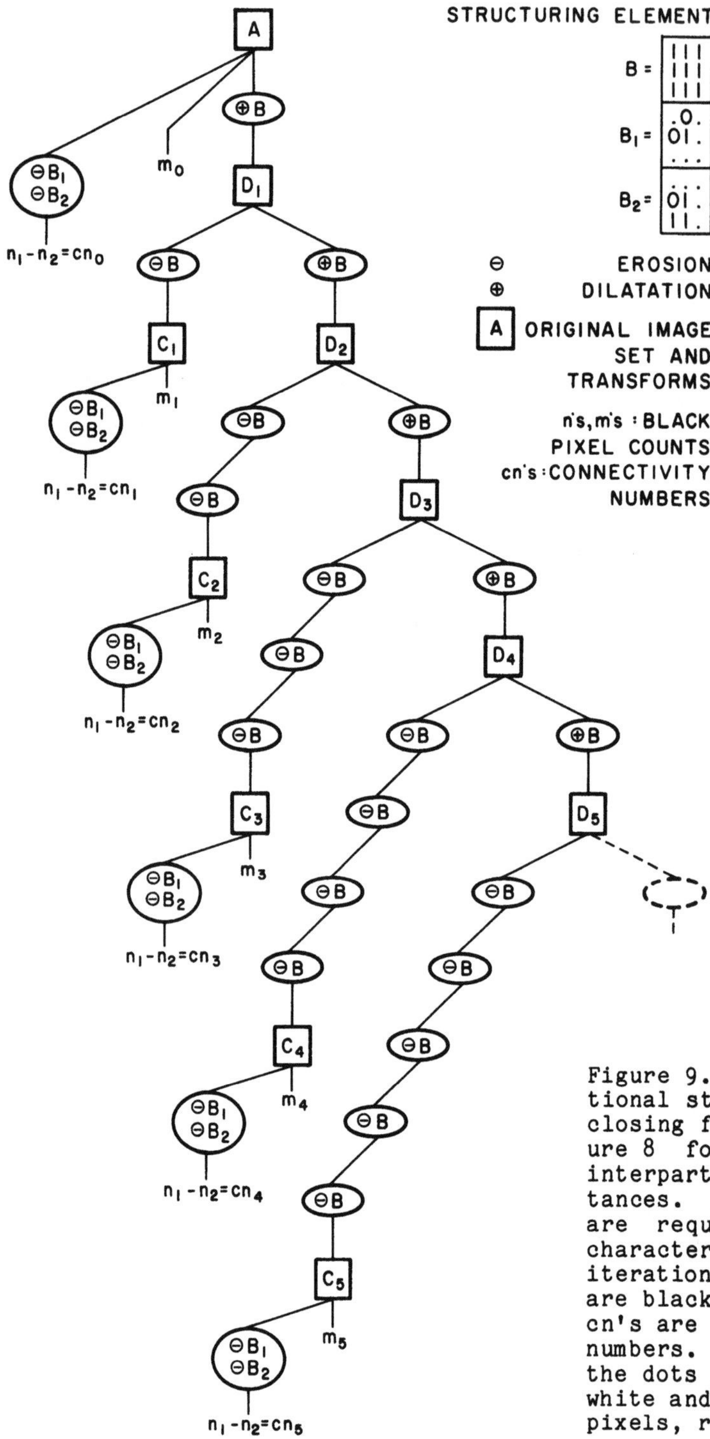

Figure 9. The computational structure for the closing function of Figure 8 for histogramming interparticle distances. 32 transforms are required for characterizing 5 closing iterations. n's and m's are black pixel counts; cn's are connectivity numbers. 1's, 0's and the dots identify black, white and "don't care" pixels, respectively.

CONSIDERATIONS ON DESIRABLE ARCHITECTURES

From the experience gained in geological applications (Fabbri, 1983) a basic pipeline processor can be envisaged so that image pixels are loaded in a shift register and then shifted past program set logic in the pipeline processor. The results can either be loaded into another image memory or back into the same image memory after a suitable delay (see Fig. 10).

A simplified sketch of a pipeline processor is shown in Figure 11. Processing is done row-by-row, and input and output are separate. Edge conditions above, below, and on both sides of the image have to be considered for proper mapping of the local neighborhood.

Figure 12 shows an example of hierarchical processing using only one wraparound memory (self-destructive processing). In Figure 13 a more elaborate multi-memory and multi-pipeline system is exemplified.

A "pyramidal pipeline" in which each processor has its own "circulating" shift-register memory is sketched in Figure 14. In this instance, after initialization we need only to read one new row of pixels into each pipeline processor, i.e., one row delay per layer of processors. This configuration makes a pipeline operation as close as possible to a parallel one.

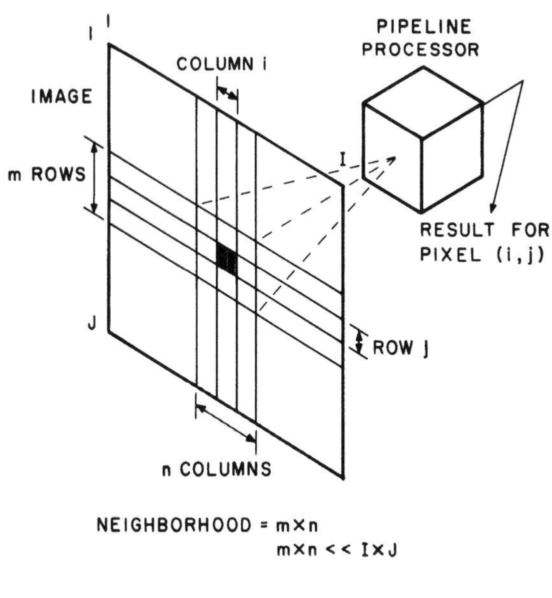

Figure 10. Skematic diagram of the basic pipeline processor. The local operator neighbourhood is m x n, the image size is I x J, m x n << I x J. This sketch illustrates the use of the pipeline processor also as a scanner, if the image is the scene and proper light deflection is provided.

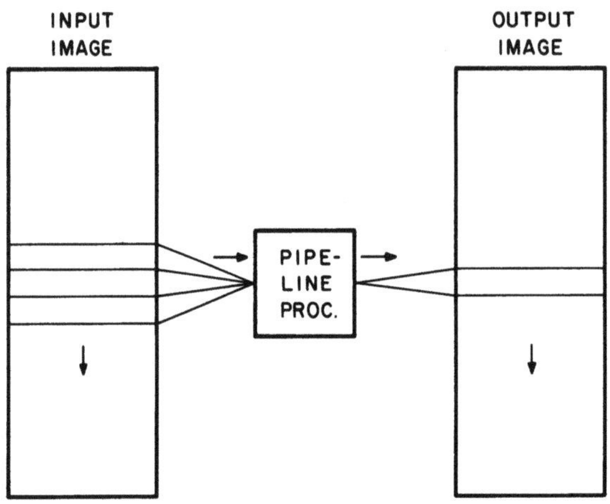

Figure 11. A pipeline example with separate input and output image memories.

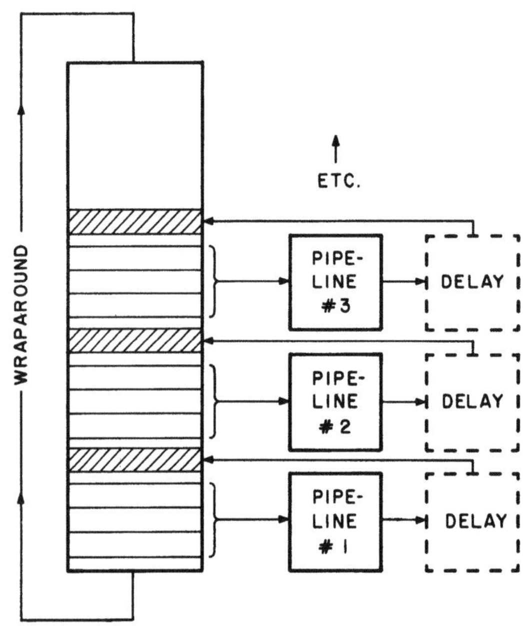

Figure 12. Example of hierarchical processing using only one wrap around memory. The results from each pipeline are suitably delayed, in order not to produce interference between the inputs and outputs (unless some form of implicit or recursive operation is actually intended). Pipeline 2 can go into action as soon as there are enough results from pipeline 1, etc. One processing cycle needs about two passes around the memory. Obviously, the input image is destroyed, and some stopping conditions have to be provided.

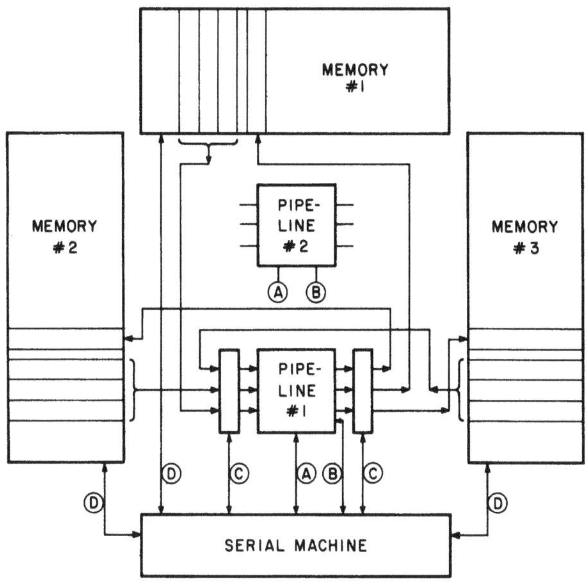

Figure 13. Example of a multi-memory and multi-pipeline system. The basic structure shown in Fig. 12 has been elaborated by including multiple memories, switches, and connections to a serial machine, where A indicates connections for controlling the pipeline processors, loading the programs and structuring elements, etc., B represents global outputs such as counts, for example, C shows switching of the inputs and outputs, controlled by the serial machine, D represents connections between the image memories and the serial machine.

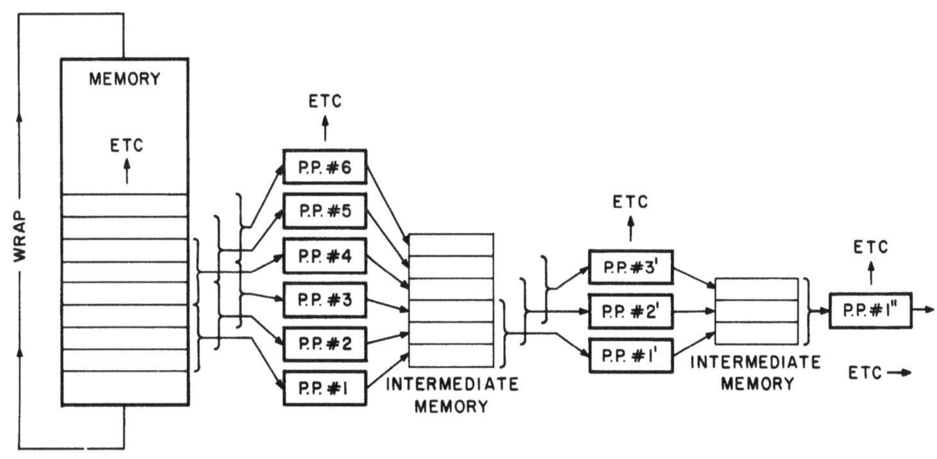

Figure 14. Example of pyramidal pipeline. The first "layer" of pipeline processors is represented by 1, 2, 3, ..., the second layer by 1',2', 3', ..., etc. Between each layer of processors there is intermediate memory to provide inputs to the next layer. If properly designed, the structure in Fig. 13 could be used to simulate the pyramidal machine. It is a very interesting question to what level of complexity such designs should be carried, since there does not appear to be any "upper limit" to the possibilities.

CONCLUDING REMARKS

The pipeline architectures described in this contribution are of necessity very skematic, nevertheless they are a direct response to a large number of problems in the geosciences in which image processing for spatial data analysis is applicable and desirable. Possibly, computer processing will be performed in future by machines that, while working in a real time (or seemingly so), will be affordable to a very large community by no means restricted to geologists.

It is a major contribution of the theory of mathematical morphology that the statistical significance of local operators and set theory approach to image processing can be used extensively in texture analysis and is becoming familiar to an increasing number of applied scientists.

ACKNOWLEDGEMENTS

The authors are grateful for the collaboration and assistance provided by the Electrical Engineering Division of the National Research Council of Canada. The Geological Survey of Canada has supported this research.

REFERENCES

Agterberg, F. P., Chung, C. F., Divi, S. R., Eade, K. E., and Fabbri, A. G., 1981, Preliminary Geomathematical Analysis of Geological, Mineral Occurrence and Geophysical Data, Southern District of Keewatin, Northwest Territories; Geol. Surv. Can., Open File 718, 31 p.

Fabbri, A. G., 1980, GIAPP: Geological Image Analysis Program Package for Estimating Geometrical Probabilities; Computers and Geosciences, v. 6, p. 153-161.

Fabbri, A. G., 1983, Image Processing of Geological Data; Stroudsburg, Pennsylvania, Hutchinson Ross Publ. Co., book in press.

Fabbri, A. G. and Masounave, J., 1981, Experiments on the Characterization of Metamorphic Textures from a Micrograph of an Amphibolite; Jour. of Microscopy, v. 121, p. 111-117.

Fabbri, A. G., Kasvand, T., and Masounave, J., 1983; Adjacency Relationships in Aggregates of Crystal Profiles: Proc. NATO Adv. Study Inst. on "Pictorial Data Analysis", Bonas, France, Aug. 1-12, 1982, R. Haralick and S. Levialdi, eds., New York, Springer-Verlag, in press.

Fisher, C., 1967, An Image Analysing Computer; Bio-Medical Engineering Journal, v. 2, p. 351-357.

Gillies, A. W., 1978, An Image Processing Computer which Learns by Example; in Nevatia, R., ed., Image understanding systems and industrial applications; Proc. of the Soc. of Photo-Optical Instrumentation Engineers, SPIE, Aug. 30-31, 1978, SanDiego, California, v. 155, p. 120-126.

Kasvand, T., 1983, Computerized Vision for the Geologist; Math. Geol., v. 15, p. 3-23.

Kasvand, T., Fabbri, A. G., and Nel, L. D., 1981; Digitization and Processing of Large Regional Geological Maps; Nat. Res. Council. Canada, Elect. Eng. Divn., report ERB-938, 91 p.

Levialdi, S., 1983, Neighborhood Operators; An Outlook; in, Haralick, R. M., and Levialdi, S., Eds., Pictorial Data Analysis; Proc. of 1982 NATO Adv. Study Inst., Bonas, France, Aug. 1-12, 1982, New York, Springer-Verlag (in press).

Matheron, G., 1967, Elements pour une Theorie des Milieux Poreux, Paris, Masson et Cie, Eds., 166 p.

Matheron, G., 1975, Random Sets and Integral Geometry, John Wiley and Sons, New York, 261 p.

Moore, A. G., 1968, Automatic Scanning and Computer Processes for the Quantitative Analysis of Micrographs and Equivalent Subjects; in Cheng, G. C., Ledley, R. S., Pollock, D. K., and Rosenfeld, A., Eds.; Pictorial Pattern Recognition; Washington D. C., Thompson Book Co., p. 275-326.

Preston, K. Jr., Duff, M.J.B., Levialdi, S., Norgren, P.E., and Toriwaki, J-i., 1979, Basics of Cellular Logic with some Applications in Medical Image Processing, Proc. IEEE, v. 67, p. 826-858.

Serra, J., 1982, Image Analysis and Mathematical Morphology; New York, Academic Press, 610 p.

Sternberg, S.R., 1979, Parallel Archtecture for Image Processing. Proc. of third Internat. IEEE Compsoc., Chicago.

Sternberg, S.R., 1980, Cellular Computer and Biomedical Image Processing. To be published in, Lecture Notes in Bio-Mathematics, Springer-Verlag.

AN INTERPOLATION METHOD ON TRIANGULAR NETWORKS FOR SURFACE MODEL ARCHITECTURES

Walter Kropatsch

Institute for Image Processing and Computer Graphics
Technical University and Research Center
Graz, Austria

1. Introduction

In many application fields, such as geodesy, cartography, and surveying large surfaces are represented by triangular networks (3, 11, 12, 17). These networks must be manipulated and modified frequently as they are generated. Afterwards, the graphical presentation of these surfaces should be pleasing to the eye of a critical observer.

Another aspect is the accuracy of the surface interpolation. Most often, the input data are not precise. For the final result, however, high quality is required. It is therefore necessary to have an appropriate means to perform this task. Interpolation methods are needed that allow interactive and fast data manipulation while maintaining a high quality output. Based on our previous experience with raster models (9), we have developed a method that has given satisfactory results.

The interpolation principle of our procedure is based on the Bezier method, named after P. E. Bezier of Renault (1) who developed a broad concept of interpolation by blending in his UNISURF method. It has properties of polynomials, splines, and parametric techniques, plus advantages for interactive modelling. The Bezier technique has found a wide field of application in computer graphics, where most of the relevant literature deals with Bezier curves (7, 13, 14). Bezier surfaces, which are constructed over a quadrangular grid in the original UNISURF proposal, are not, however, as often used. Other structures, such as triangular networks, also may be useful. A comparison between the various types of networks and the advantages in using triangular structures under certain circumstances are presented in the following sections. It is shown that such networks have a special property in the graph theoretic sense. We expanded, therefore, the Bezier technique to triangular networks.

We analysed some of the properties of this surface representation that are of special interest for interactive modelling. Most of them derive directly from the Bezier method, with some showing interesting new features with respect to triangles.

NATO ASI Series, Vol. F18
Computer Architectures for Spatially Distributed Data
Edited by H. Freeman and G. G. Pieroni

From a practical point of view, the applicability of the method to irregular structures must be considered. We found that there are ways of transforming irregular networks to regular ones. Hence the interpolation method can also be applied to irregular structures if these are preprocessed before interpolation.

The Bezier technique can also be used like a spline. It is possible to build frameworks of curves and surfaces with a given degree of continuity at the joints. This also applies to the triangular method with some additional nice side effects. For example, the tangential plane at the corners can be derived directly from the control points in the neighborhood of this corner.

Modelling was the primary reason for developing the triangular method. Basic modelling steps have been designed so that the operator has neither to deal with derivatives nor with curvature parameters. The input is restricted to just data points. They are guides or controls to the shape of the surface. The manipulation process can be easily learned, as it is reduced mainly to such operations as picking up a control point and moving it around, whilst simultaneously visualizing the corresponding surface modifications.

Since the Bezier technique develops a single equation for each variable, computer storage, input and output transactions, and computation are decreased. This is in contrast to the frequently used spline method (15), which requires a separate equation for each configuration of points. The new technology of parallel machines permits standard, "good old" algorithms to be examined for their degree of parallelism. In the case of Bezier algorithms, and especially the triangular method, most of the processing can be done in parallel. Some of these ideas are treated in the last section by means of remarks on architectures for the display of such surfaces.

2. Why Triangular Networks?

The task of representing and manipulating a non-analytical surface needs basic elements that are the means to modify a given surface. In many applications these basic elements are points that are measured in a vector space. There exist methods that approximate a surface defined by a pile of points without any additional specifications. Such methods often fall under the category of statistics, where a general model, such as least squares (10,16) or stochastic functions (4), is assumed.Other methods prescribe the use of additional location dependent information (2). Such information can be given by neighborhood relations among the points.

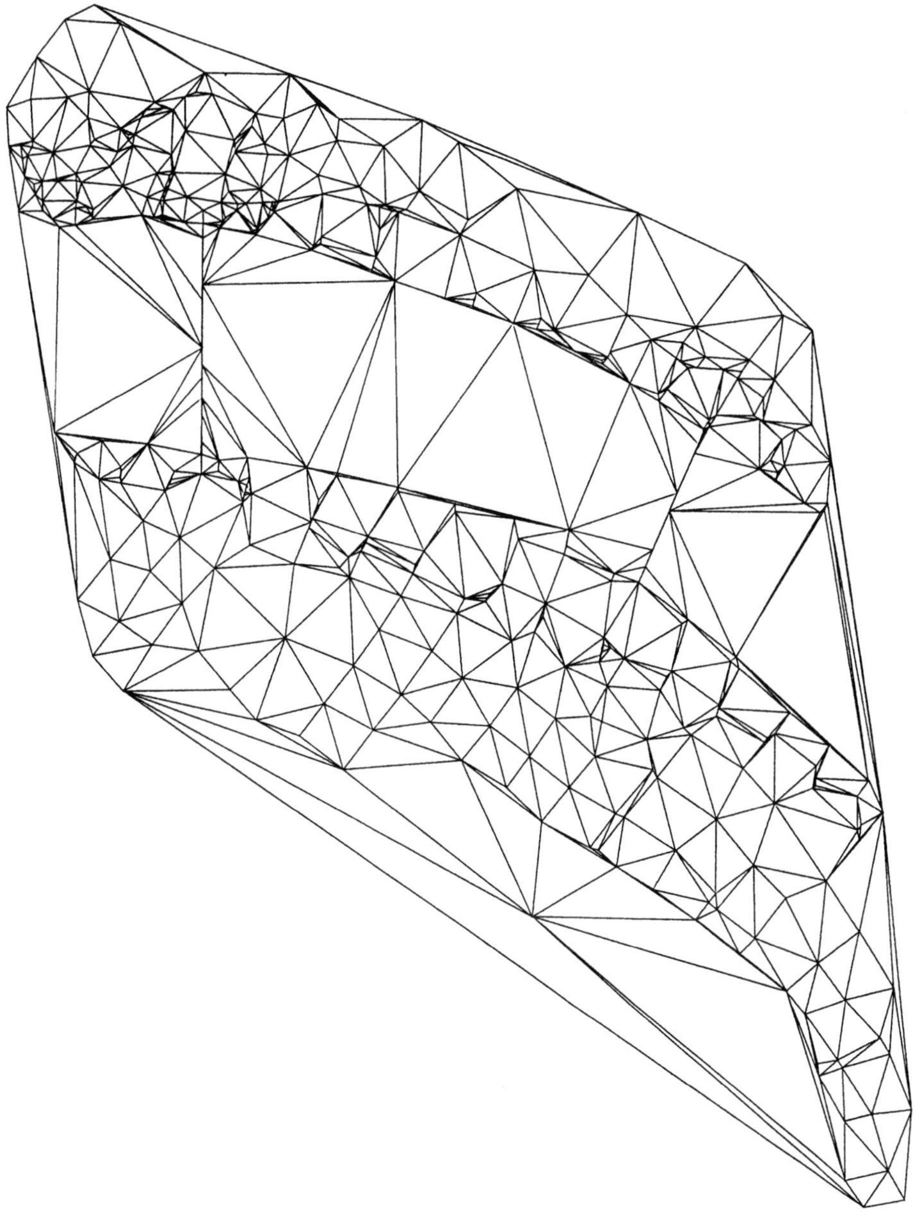

Figure 1: Triangular network

The combination of points P and neighborhood relationships E form a graph G=(P,E). In graph theory, the relationships are called edges (E). Since the graph G is supposed to represent relations on a surface, it must be planar. If the number of edges is not sufficient to interpolate a surface, it is expanded automatically or interactively by adding new edges.

An expansion of the planar graph can lead to a quadrangular grid. Most interpolation methods are based on such grids (8): Coons surfaces (5), Ferguson surfaces (6), Bezier-UNISURF surfaces (1), and so on. Quadrangular grids have several advantages. They often come from curve interpolation methods that are expanded to surfaces by simply taking the cross product of the two curves. Another advantage of quadrangular grids is the fact that they can be stored as matrices within the computer. This facilitates enormously the task of accessing single elements of the grid at random. Sometimes the x-y coordinates of the points are chosen on a rectangular grid and encoded implicitly in the indices of the matrix. This reduces storage space, but introduces an inflexibility to respond to varying point densities.

If the set of edges is expanded to its maximum size, the resultant graph is a triangular network. The set of edges of a triangular network is a maximum in that any further addition of an edge joining two points of the existing net will hurt the planarity of the graph. The rationale for using triangular networks is confirmed by the fact that in geodesy and surveying such networks are frequently used to represent the earth's surface. A typical example is shown in figure 1. In these applications, the surface within the triangles is approximated by the plane through the three corners of the triangle. The approximation model is, therefore, the polyhedron with only triangular faces. Our method maintains the concept of the triangular network, as well as allowing higher order surfaces to be defined over the net.

3. The Interpolation Principle

We developed a formula for representing and interpolating surfaces. That is strongly related to the UNISURF method of Bezier. A review of the concept of Bezier curves is given below, in order to apply their generation principle to the primitive element of our surfaces, the triangle.

The simplest case of a curve is a straight line between two points, say P0 and P1. Any point P on this line segment may be represented in the parametric form of a line: $P(t)=(1-t)*P0+t*P1$. The parameter t varies from 0 to 1 when the line is followed from P0 to P1. Let us call this line segment C(1,Pi,t). The first parameter (1) stands for the degree of the curve, which is linear in this case, the second denotes formally the sequence of the points P0 and P1 for i=0,1.

To proceed to higher order curves we designate the above defined straight line segment C(1,Pi,t) as a primitive element. Substituting the notion "point" in the previous paragraph by "straight line segment" we define a curve between two line segments:

$$C(2,Pi,t)=(1-t)*C(1,Pi,t)+t*C(1,P(i+1),t) .$$

The degree of the resulting curve is now quadratic. The two line segments (P0,P1) and (P1,P2) must meet each other at a common point (P1). The combined curve C(2,Pi,t) is then defined by the sequence of the three points P0 P1 P2. The recursion step can be applied to higher order curve segments in the same way. To combine two curves of the order n, it is necessary that the last n-1 points of the first curve appear in the first n-1 locations of the second curve. The overlap region is, therefore, n-1 points long, with only one point being added at each end of the curve. The explicit formula of a Bezier curve is then:

$$C(m,Pi,t) = \sum_{i=0}^{m} \binom{m}{i} * t^{i} * (1-t)^{m-i} * Pi$$

The simplest non-trivial case of a surface is the plane. Every three linear independent points in a vector space span a plane. We take the triangle spanned by the three points P(1,0,0), P(0,1,0), P(0,0,1) as our primitive element. Any point X within the triangle may be represented by the following 3-parametric form of a plane:

$$\begin{aligned} X(a,b,c) &= a*P(1,0,0) + b*P(0,1,0) + c*P(0,0,1) \\ \text{with } 1 &= a + b + c \quad . \end{aligned}$$

The parameters a, b and c vary from 0 to 1. Let us denote the primitive triangle with respect to the straight line segment S(1, P(i,j,k), a, b, c). Again, the first parameter signifies linearity. The second parameter defines formally the three corner points, where the integer indices are all non - negative and sum up to 1. They specify the configuration of the points (figure 2a). The third, fourth, and fifth parameters define the actual location of the point X within the triangle.

As in the case of the Bezier curve we proceed to higher order surfaces by combining low order primitives. Replacing the points P(1,0,0), P(0,1,0) and P(0,0,1) of the previous paragraph by the appropriate triangles, we define a surface of degree 2:

$$\begin{aligned} S(2,P(i,j,k),a,b,c) = {} & a*S(1,P(i-1,j,k),a,b,c)+b*S(1,P(i,j-1,k),a,b,c) \\ & +c*S(1,P(i,j,k-1),a,b,c) \end{aligned}$$

where a+b+c=1 and i+j+k=2 .

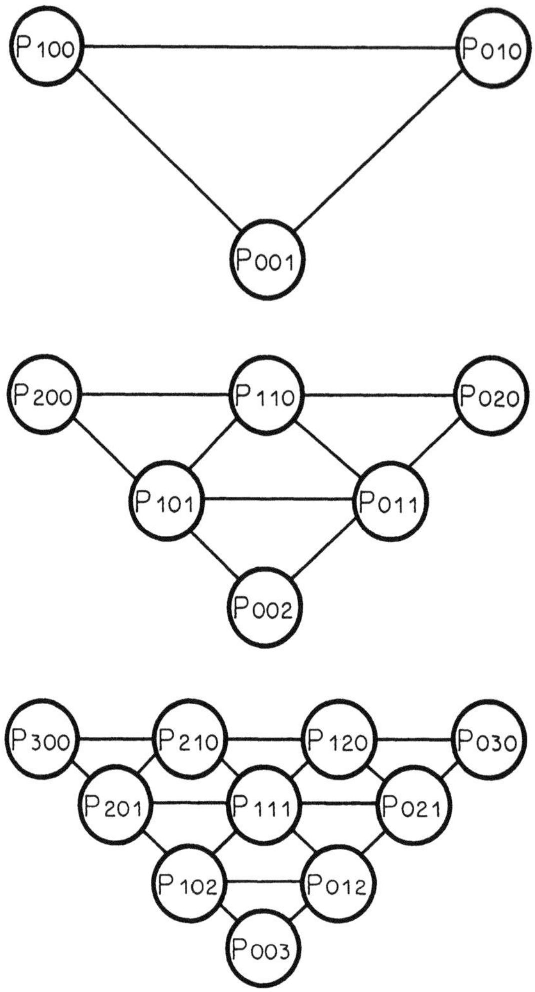

Figure 2: Point configurations for orders 1 (a), 2 (b) and 3 (c)

The configuration of the 6 points is shown in figure 2b. The meeting condition for the three triangles to be integrated is a little more complicated than in the case of curves. It says that P(1,1,0) is a corner point of the two upper triangles, that P(1,0,1) is a corner point of the two left - hand triangles, and that P(0,1,1) is a corner point of the two right - hand triangles.

A recursive application of an analogue of the step just described leads to high order surfaces. An example of the point configuration of a third order surface is shown in figure 2c. The necessary meeting condition for high order combinations can be formulated in the following way: Three triangular surfaces of the order n may be combined to form a surface of the order n+1, if any two of them overlap each other along one side except for the two corner points. For the rest, only the two borders opposite to each other shouldn't overlap. In the example of figure 2c, triangles T1= (P300, P210, P120, P201, P111, P102), T2= (P210, P120, P030, P111, P021, P012), and T3= (P201, P111, P021, P102, P012, P003) are combined to the configuration of figure 2c. The overlap for triangles T1 and T2 consists of the three points P210, P120, P111.

The explicit formula for a triangular surface takes the following form:

$$S(m,P(i,j,k),a,b,c) = \sum_{\substack{i+j+k=m \\ i,j,k\geq 0}} \frac{m!}{i!j!k!} * a^{i} * b^{j} * c^{k} * P(i,j,k)$$

4. Properties

The here presented surface formula is defined by a set of control points in a regular order. For each control point, there is associated a weight. They form a set of special blending functions (13, 14). The control points are organized in a triangular network, which we call a "characteristic network" in analogy to the notion "characteristic polygon" used by Bezier (1) for his curves.We distinguish two types of control points: knots and guiding points. There are three knots in the characteristic network. They build the corners of the net and lie on the surface. The guiding points form the nodes of the network and lie off the surface, but, nevertheless, provide control over the shape of the surface.

Our surface function is a vector-valued function, where a point on the surface is defined by three parameters, a, b, and c, which are positive and sum up to one. It has, therefore, all the properties that parametric functions have. One of the most important of them is that the computation of the vector components is independent of each other. Hence, it can be done in parallel by special computer hardware. Another advantage is its non-dependence on a particular coordinate system. Any coordinate transformation can be applied without any effect to the surface.

Each component of a point on the surface is the scalar product of the data points with the corresponding values of the blending function.These weights characterize the location of the point within the network,regardless of the actual surface. This allows precomputation of the weights, if the same parameter values are used during modification and display.

Another useful property concerns the surface border. The surface border between two knots is a Bèzier curve of the same degree as the surface. It is generated by the border polygon connecting the two knots. This shows again the strong relationship between the Bezier curves and our surfaces. Another property of Bezier curves that holds true for triangular surfaces is that they lie always within the convex hull of all control points.

The partial derivatives of the surface play an important role in the construction of tangential planes, and for continuity considerations at the joint between two surface patches. A usefull property of the triangular surface is the following:

$$\frac{dS(m,P(i,j,k),a,b,1-a-b)}{da} = S(m-1,m*(P(i+1,j,k)-P(i,j,k+1)),a,b,1-a-b)$$

This means that the partial derivative of a surface of degree m is again a surface, but of degree m-1, with control points that are forward differences of the original control points enlarged by a factor of m. A consequence of this formula is the fact that the tangential planes at the corners are built by the three control points of the corner triangles.

As in the case of Bezier curves, interpolation points on the surface can be constructed using primitive geometric operations. Intermediate points derived in the construction process can be used as control points for a new subsurface, which will be part of the original surface and of the same degree. More generally, it can be stated that each surface segment can be generated by the same formula (and degree) using appropriate control points. These can be calculated, as in the case above, from the original control points. The formula can be computed by substituting the three parameters a, b, c by expressions of new parameters a', b', c'. Rearranging the terms of the sums makes the appearences of a', b', c' explicit, and the new control points will appear as functions of the original ones.

A further advantage of our triangular surface is the speed of calculation. Many of the common techniques for evaluating polynomials, such as Horner's rule or incremental methods, can be used efficiently. Hierarchical subdivisions work especially fast, because they can be designed to need only additions, subtractions and divisions by two, which are implemented as shift operations.

The linear dependence of the surface from the data favors linear combinations of surfaces that are completely performed on the control points. Adding surfaces to each other and building the difference between two surfaces are simple operations.

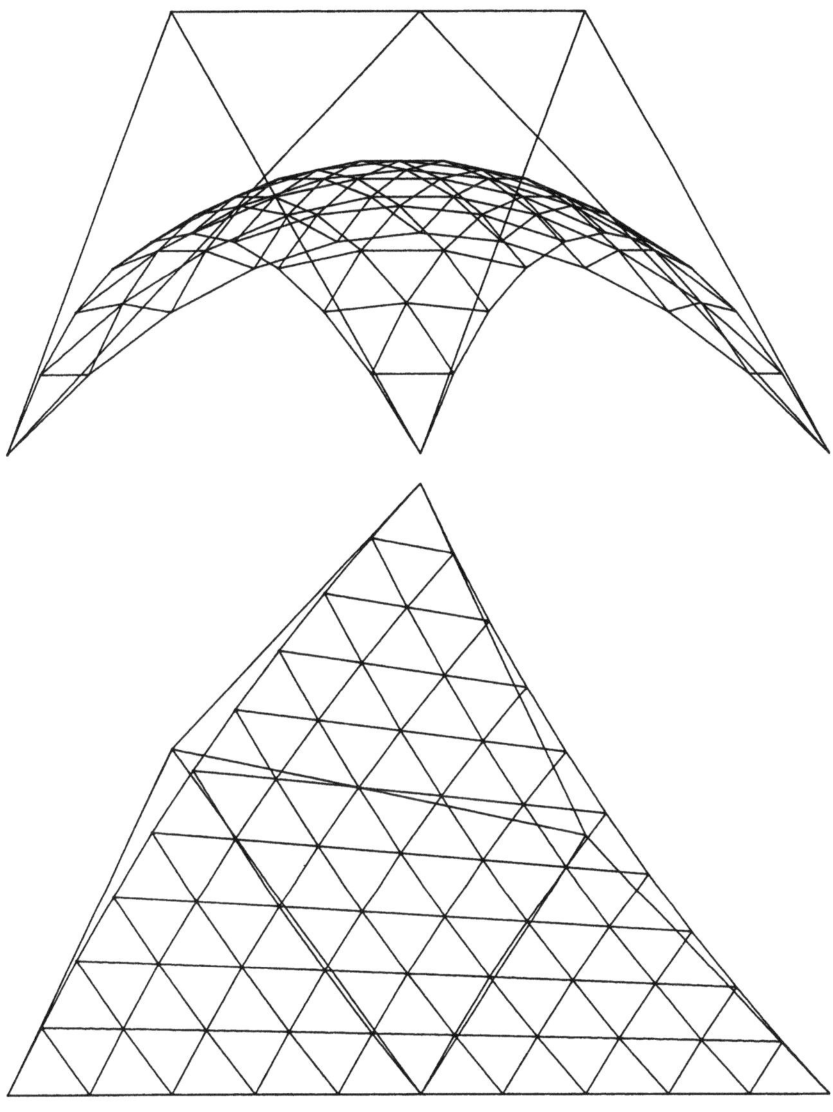

Figure 3: Interpolated surface and control points

Finally, we consider the data compaction capacity of the triangular surface compared with an approximation by polyhedrons. This is evident in the following example (figure 3). The characteristic network needs only six control points while an approximation by plane triangles giving acceptable smoothness requires 66 points!

5. Irregular Networks

In practice, when data are measured in the field, they won't fit exactly with our interpolation model.Arbitrarily located points in three-dimensional space can be linked together to form, in general, an irregular network. The notion "irregular" in this context refers to topology, but not to geometry.

The conceptual difference between geometrical and topological regularity can be seen in the two examples of figure 4. Both represent triangular networks. Obviously, the left - hand example is geometrically irregular, while the other contains only congruent triangles. More difficult to see is the property that a network is topologically regular. This is the property we need for our interpolation method.

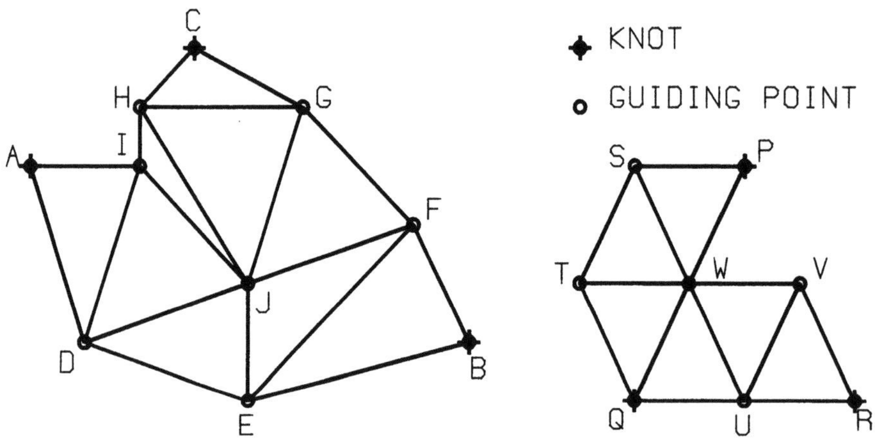

Figure 4: Topological and geometrical regularity of triangular networks

In previous sections, control points of the characteristic net have been classified into knots and guiding points. For the present purpose, the latter can be subdivided into border points and inner points of the net. In our examples, A,B,C and P,Q,R are knots, D,E,F,G,H,I and S,T,U, V,W are border points, and J is an inner point. The right - hand example has no inner point.

With this distinction, we define the topological regularity of a triangular network. The number of edges adjacent to a control point in the net is called "the degree" of this point. Using this notion, together with our point distinction, we require for a regular net that

a) the degree of a knot is 2,
b) the degree of a border point is 4, and
c) the degree of a inner point is 6.

We furthermore know that the total number of control points used for interpolating a surface of degree n is (n+1)*(n+2)/2. This imposes another constraint on the regularity of the net, and it allows the calculation of the interpolation degree n from the number of control points. A detailed counting of the distinct types of points adds three new conditions:

d) the number of knots must be 3,
e) the number of border points must be 3*(n-1), and
f) the number of inner points must be (n-1)*(n-2)/2 .

Conditions a) through f) permit an unambiguous definition of a topologically regular triangular network: all points of the net must be classified according to their degree by conditions a), b) and c), and their number of occurrences must satisfy conditions d), e) or f).

In the examples shown in figure 4, it can now be verified that the left - hand example is topologically regular, while the other is not.

In order to be able to interpolate the surface from an irregular net, we need a method that transforms such a net into a regular one. Let us first study the reverse case: how can we modify a regular net to receive a given irregular net? Consider figure 4: If we merge points A and D geometrically, then the edge AD will disappear and edges AI and AD will coincide. Merging G with J takes away edge GJ and merges the incident edges HG with HJ and FG with FJ. The resulting structure is topologically equivalent to the right - hand example, if the following point identification is done:

C - P, (AD) - Q, B - R, H - S, I - T, E - U, F - V, (GJ) - W.

We see that merging adjacent points geometrically modifies the topology of the net significantly and produces a smaller net that is, in general, topologically not regular. To perform the reverse operation, namely to create a topological regularity on a given irregular net, we invert the applied basic step. In the merging process, two distinct points of the net became geometrically identical. The inversion of this process duplicates a point of the irregular structure. This point splits into two topologically distinct points. However, these are located at the same place in geometric space.

In our example, we can interpolate the topologically irregular right-hand net by applying the method to the left - hand structure with following geometrical settings:

A:=Q, B:=R, C:=P, D:=Q, E:=U, F:=V, G:=W, H:=S, I:=T, J:=W.

The above decribed method permits the triangular interpolation to be applied to irregular networks. However, there are still some problems that have to be solved in the future.

6. Piecewise Concatenation

A complex shape usually cannot be modelled by a single surface, but requires several surfaces pieced together end-to-end. Such joints are used to introduce sharp edges within the surface "network". In other cases, a joint is introduced to increase versatility. A shape that cannot be described by a single surface can often be described by several surface patches joined together. An important consideration when creating joints is to control the order of continuity at the joint.

Zero-order continuity means that the two surfaces meet along a curve, which, in our case, is a Bezier curve. First-order continuity requires that the tangential planes along the joint curve be identical.

The border curve of a surface is defined by the control points at the corresponding border of the characteristic net. Two Bezier curves are identical if their characteristic polygons are the same. This means for our zero-order joint of two surfaces that the control points along the joint must be geometrically identical in both surfaces. Sharp edges are typical examples for zero-order joints.

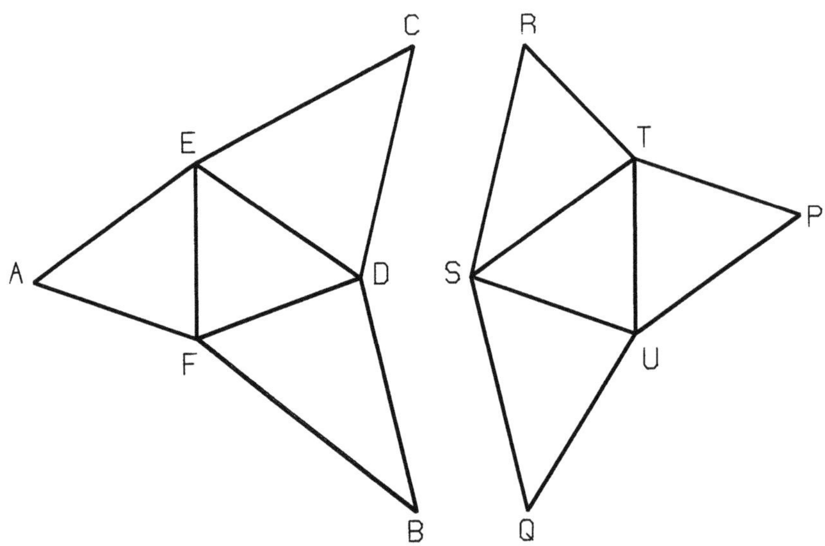

Figure 5: Piecing together two surfaces of order 2

Figure 5 shows an example of two surfaces of order 2 in which the knots are named A,B,C for surface I, and P,Q,R for surface II. The guiding points of surface I are D,E,F and S,T,U for surface II. The joint should be between B,C and Q,R. Zero-order continuity in this example requires that B=Q, C=R and D=S. All other control points can be chosen arbitrarily.

First-order continuity requires zero-order continuity at the joint. Furthermore, corresponding border triangles must lie within the same plane on both sides of the joint. In the example of figure 5, the points D,F,B,U and C,D,E,T must both lie within a plane. This condition is necessary, but is still not sufficient. A sufficient condition in this example can be derived from the differentiation property of the surface (see section 4):

$$U = D + p*(F - D) + q*(B - D)$$
$$T = C + p*(E - C) + q*(D - C)$$

with 2 free parameters p and q.

If we define a topological distance on the characteristic net, then a continuity constraint for the order n includes all control points of the characteristic net that have a topological distance less than or equal to n from the joint polygon. The topological distance between two points A and B of the net is defined to be the minimum number of edges in the net that must be traversed when travelling along the edges of the net from A to B. It turns out that a continuity of the order n along a joint curve involves a "local" neighborhood of this joint that is of the same order n.

7. Modelling

By modelling a surface we mean the generation and interactive modification of the shape of a surface by manipulating simple primitives. The aim of modelling is to build a model in the computer that corresponds to its realistic counterpart, and which can be used for simulation purposes. In order to be an efficient instrument, the basic operations must be easy to handle and should work by means of primitive elements that are familiar to the human operator.

Essential primitives of our surface model are points, edges, and the degree of the interpolation polynomial. Manipulating such primitives is easy and comfortable, and is a common tool in CAD (Computer Aided Design) applications. In our case, however, they are used to model smooth surfaces in three dimensions.

Basic modelling steps in the triangular surface model are:

a) changing the shape of the surface by moving a specified point,
b) modifying a specific component of a characteristic point (e.g. the height),
c) merging adjacent points geometrically to achieve predefined topological configurations, and
d) incrementing the degree of the interpolating polynomial without changing the geometrical appearence of the surface, with the mind of increasing the amount of detail later on.

Steps a), b), and c) require the identification of a point. There are standard graphic commands and procedures performing this task in two dimensions. For step a), however, 3-dimensional identification is needed. The convential way of doing this is to use a 2-dimensional projection of the characteristic net that is unambiguous in the neighborhood of the point of interest. Once the point is identified, it can be modified by manipulation with a joystick or a trackball. To achieve the necessary user feedback, the corresponding surface changes must be shown on the display screen simultaneously.

Steps a) and b) modify the geometry of the surface, but leave the topology of the underlying characteristic net unchanged. In contrast to this, step d) augments the number of nodes in the net without any change to the geometry of the surface. The (m+1)*(m+2)/2 characteristic points P(i,j,k) of the net of degree m are replaced by (m+2)*(m+3)/2 points Q(i,j,k) using the formula:

$$Q(i,j,k) = (i*P(i-1,j,k) + j*P(i,j-1,k) + k*P(i,j,k-1))/(m + 1).$$

The surface spanned by P(i,j,k) is identical with the surface spanned by Q(i,j,k):

$$S(m, P(i,j,k), a, b, c) = S(m+1, Q(i,j,k), a, b, c)$$

This can be verified easily by multiplying S(m, P(i,j,k), a, b, c) by (a + b + c), which sums up to 1 by definition. After rearranging the sums and the new indexing of P, the result can be resumed to S(m+1, Q(i,j,k), a, b, c) with Q(i,j,k) as defined above.

8. Model Architectures

The presented model for representing surfaces allows the complete separation of the manipulation processes from the interpolation processes. The processing of the surface can be performed on the control points only. However, before displaying a picture of a surface, it must be interpolated.

Since actual display processors have high processing capacities, the task of interpolation can be dedicated to the display processor (17), or to a special purpose processor that is interconnected with the display control in parallel. It then delivers the interpolated data to the display processor or an intermediate refresh memory. This special purpose processor can be built from components available on the open market, as the interpolation consists of the calculation of the weights and a scalar product for every interpolated point.

The advantages of such a structure are evident: complex data manipulations are performed only on a highly reduced data set, namely the control points. High quality can be achieved by the interpolation model, which is flexible and easy to manipulate. The data transmission from the processing unit to the display is restricted to the control points only, if the interpolation is done there. The integration of an interpolation module in the display device would enlarge the basic graphic entities of that device.

9. Concluding Remarks

An interpolation model was presented that works on triangular networks. The interpolation principle is strongly related to the Bezier technique. The interpolation formula is linear with respect to the control points, and of degree n with respect to the blending functions. The control points are organized in a topologically regular network of triangles. Some of the important properties of the model were reviewed. A method was presented for applying the interpolation model to irregular networks. Piecing together several surface patches brings into question the continuity at joints, which can be easily handled by the described interpolation model. Finally, some basic steps for interactive modelling gave an idea of what can be done when editing such surfaces. Some remarks on hardware architectures showed the effectiveness of the model for such implementations.

10. References

1. P. Bezier (1972): Numerical Control. Mathematics and Applications, John Wiley & Sons, London 1972.

2. W. Boehm (1975): "Zur Approximation von raeumlichen Flaechen mittels geeigneter Netze". Angewandte Informatik, 3/75 , pp. 99-103.

3. K. Brassel (1975): "Neighborhood Computations for large Sets of Data Points", in AUTO - CARTO II, proc. intl. symp. on computer - assisted cartography. September 21-25, 1975.

4. E. Clerici, K. Kubik (1973): "The Theoretical Accuracy of Point Interpolation on Topographic Surfaces". Dienst Informatieverwerking, Dec. 1973.

5. St. A. Coons (1976):"Surfaces for Computer-Aided Design of Space Forms". Technical report MAC-TR-41,M.I.T.,Cambridge,Mass., June 1976.

6. J. Ferguson (1964): "Multivariable Curve Interpolation". JACM, April 1964.

7. W. K. Giloi (1978): Interactive Computer Graphics. Prentice-Hall, pp. 134-140.

8. S. Glaenzer (1977): Ein Beitrag zur Darstellung glatter Flaechen. Dissertation, TU-Graz, Nov. 1977.

9. "The Graz-Terrain-Model",User Guide (1983). Programmdokumentation am Institut für digitale Bildverarbeitung und Grafik.

10. K. Kraus (1972): "Interpolation nach kleinsten Quadraten in der Photogrammetrie". Bildmessung und Luftbildwesen, 1/1972, pp. 7-11.

11. G. L. Lawson (1972): "Generation of a Triangular Grid with Application to Contour Plotting". Sect. 914, Techn. Mem. No. 299, Febr. 1972, JPL.

12. A. Mirante, N. Weingarten (1982): "The Radical Sweep Algorithm for Constructing Triangulated Irregular Networks". IEEE, Tr. on Computer Graphics and Appl., May 1982, pp. 11-21.

13. W. F. Newman, R. F. Sproull (1979): Principles of Interactive Computer Graphics. New York: McGrawHill; pp.315-320.

14. T. Pavlidis (1982): Graphics and Image Processing. Springer Verlag Berlin-Heidelberg-New York.

15. H. Spaeth (1973): Spline-Algorithmen zur Konstruktion glatter Kurven und Flaechen. R. Oldenburg Verlag, Muenchen 1973.

16. E. Stark, E. Mikhail (1973): "Least Squares and Non-Linear Functions". Photogrammetric Engeneering, 1973.

17. G. Zumofen, M. Leoni (1977): Neue Programmsysteme zur Berechnung und Darstellung von Isolinien mit Hilfe von Kleincomputern. Zeitschrift Vermessung,Photogrammetrie, Kulturtechnik 6-77.

INTRODUCTION TO A SIMPLE BUT UNCONVENTIONAL MULTIPROCESSOR SYSTEM AND OUTLINE OF AN APPLICATION

R. Lindner
Computer Science Department
Technical University of Darmstadt
D-6100 Darmstadt, Germany

1. Introduction to a Homogeneous Multiprocessor Kernel (HoMuK)

1. 1. The philosophy of the system

The smaller and the cheaper microprocessors become the more tempting is it to step back from high-speed and high-power single processors and make use of multi(micro)processor systems instead.

Prerequisite for this major change seems by now that efficient solutions are found for software (system and application software) adaptation to the new hardware structures. This is a very lengthy process and will require some more years of experience - longer in any case as users are willing to wait.

Therefore, a solution for the nearest future is very desirable. The The philosophy of such a system must be assembling as much as possible standard hardware in such a way that as much as possible standard software may be used and doing this in a way that the advantages of multiprocessor systems are maintained. These advantages may be high computational power for one task (e.g. under real time conditions), high availability for many users (or communication links) or high adaptability to many different applications. Additionally, the system shall be extendable to very large numbers of modules in order to achieve advantages (especially speed up) to a very high degree.

NATO ASI Series, Vol. F18
Computer Architectures for Spatially Distributed Data
Edited by H. Freeman and G. G. Pieroni

In order to meet all these requirements, cellular automata as a solution were removed because they have too large impacts on the software. Systems coupled by common memory were put aside because of the problems with memory access conflict which occur as soon as many modules are active. Pipeline structures as a basic concept were excluded because of too high sensitivity to applications. At least the very simple common bus structure was chosen and stress was laid to overcome the system bus bottleneck.

This paper will therefore from the hardware point of view focus on the problems of internal system communication. Concerning programming, HoMuK systems allow to go around many of the software problems as the system modules are able to operate standalone and are only losely coupled to other system modules. System interconnection may be done on process level. In cases, however, where a tight coupling of modules is required, a very effective special bus technique (multiple-write) may be used and will help to compensate the disadvantages of losely coupled systems.

System intercommunication is a hardware/software matter. While the basic hardware is fix for HoMuKs, the system software is partly subject of application dependent decisions. In order to provide extensive flexibility, the fix system software is reduced to an absolute minimum and may be enriched by users of the system to a very high degree.

There are further means to adapt HoMuK systems to special applications. Most simple is to install special processors in the modules of a HoMuK. More complicated (from the software point of view) is providing for private communication links between modules of a HoMuK or even to assemble several HoMuK systems and create a new hardware structure.

1. 2. Multiple-Write - the special feature of the system bus

If many processors are expected to exchange information on one common bus, there is no way aside simultaneous writing to the bus by several or even all processors. This has been prohibited in the past for reasons which will be seen from the following example.

The result of the wired-AND combination of four data words is shown in figure 1 and appears to be without remarkable information. The only information on the bus is that no processor accesses the bus with a lower value data word. One has to reduce the data word to the trivial length of one bit to get valuable information: in this case single bit wired-AND result on the bus is identical with the lowest bit placed on this bus line by the accessing processors (this technique is frequently used in multiprocessor systems for bus control lines such as ready or acknowledge). If this type of comparison could be realized for a whole word of n bit length, this would be an important advance.

	Original Processor Data	Negating Driver Gates	Low Active Processor Data
Processor P(1) Data	0 1 0 0 0 0	----->	1 0 1 1 1 1
Processor P(2) Data	1 0 0 1 0 0	----->	0 1 1 0 1 1
Processor P(3) Data	1 0 1 0 0 1	----->	0 1 0 1 1 0
Processor P(4) Data	1 0 1 0 1 0	----->	0 1 0 1 0 1
		Wired-AND Bus Data:	0 0 0 0 0 0

Figure 1: Simultaneous open-collector bus access by 4 processors

This advance can be obtained! It is, of course, not available for free. It costs extra hardware and extra time on the bus. This is the disadvantage of the new bus access technique. The additional hardware costs are reasonably low, however, and - which is much more important- the additional bus time required is not dependent on the number of processors involved but only on the length of the data word. There is a linear relationship between the amount of additionally required bus time and the number of bits in the data word. Figure 2 shows the network which is necessary for the new bus access technique.

The bus itself (if not to be extended) does not differ from a convenbus and has a most significant bit line db(n-1), a medium significant one db(i) and a last significant one db(0). The processor P(j) acces-

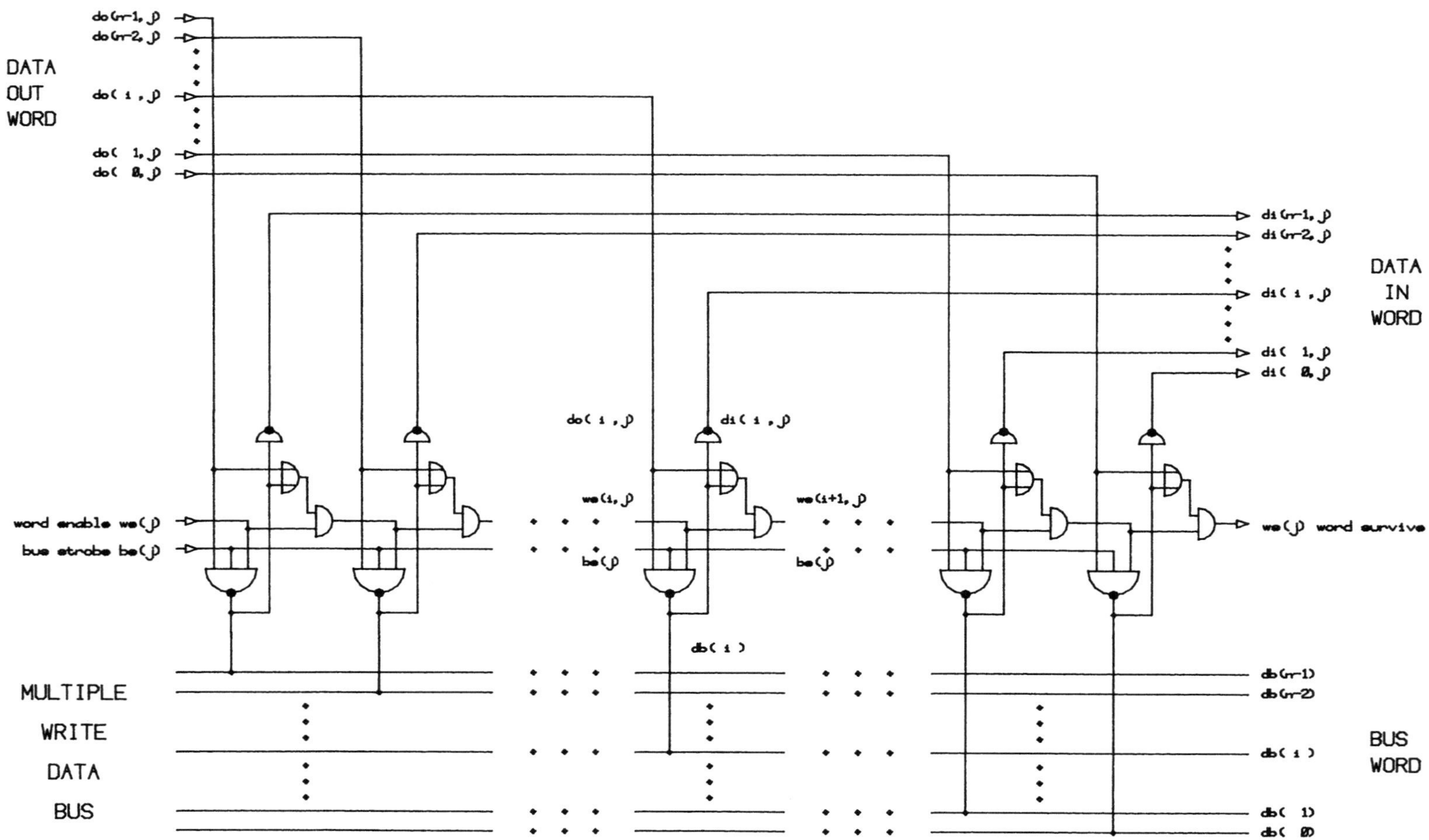

Figure 2: Multiple-write bus driver circuitry for processor P(j)

sing the bus has an output data word DO(j) and an input data word DI(j). It generates a bus strobe signal bs(j) as conventionally usual and uses it to connect or to isolate its output data to or from the bus. Bus access is realized by inverting open-collector NAND bus drivers. Negative logic is used on the bus, therefore the bus receivers for the input word are inverting as well.

Up to these details everything is done as usual in conventional systems. The additional hardware for the new access technique is a third input for the NAND bus driver and 2 additional gates for each bit stage. Also new are an additional control signal 'word enable' we(j) and a resulting signal 'word survive' ws(j).

The function of the access network is as follows. The additional 2-input-OR gates perform the comparator function of the special bus access: they generate a '0' signal 'lose' in the case where the examined processor P(j) has a data bit do(i,j)='0' and the appropriate bus line db(i) holds a '0' value, too, meaning that there is at least one processor P(k) accessing this bus line with do(i,k)='1' (negated) and therefore 'wins' against processor P(j) in this stage.

The result is a '0' signal at the output of the 2-input-OR gate in stage i of processor P(j) which induces a '0' signal at the output of the following 2-input-AND gate. This 'lose'-signal ripples through all following (less significant) stages of processor P(j). The effect of this mechanism is, that any processor 'losing' in any stage i replaces all its less significant output data bits from the bus. After a certain settling time (sum of the delay times for the three gates in the single stage and the loading time for the bus capacitance) the next less significant stage is ready for the same competition between all processors which did not lose in an earlier bit stage. Supposing n bit data word length, after n delay times only the processor (or the processors if there are several containing the same largest data word) with the largest data word generates a 'word survive' signal '1', all others lose and generate a '0'. At least, the bus contains the 'winning' largest word in negative logic.

From figure 3 can be seen how the largest data word DO(4) 'wins'. Processor P(1) loses in stage 5, processor P(2) in stage 3 and processor P(3) in stage 1. Processor P(4) is the only one 'surviving'. The bus contains the 'winning' data word DO(4) in negative logic. All processors may read it back negating it as data input DI. From this example can be seen how pairs of data bits are responsible for comparison delays under worst case conditions.

```
                               Original        Negating   Low Active
                               Processor       Driver     Processor
                               Data            Gates      Data
                                                          (small characters
                                                          represent disabled
                                                          noneffective bits)

Processor P(1) Data   Ø 1 Ø Ø Ø Ø   ----->     1 • 1 1 1 1
Processor P(2) Data   1 Ø Ø 1 Ø Ø   ----->     Ø 1 1 • 1 1
Processor P(3) Data   1 Ø 1 Ø Ø 1   ----->     Ø 1 Ø 1 1 •
Processor P(4) Data   1 Ø 1 Ø 1 Ø   ----->     Ø 1 Ø 1 Ø 1
                                               -----------
                                    Multiple-
                                    Write
                                    Bus Data:  Ø 1 Ø 1 Ø 1
```

Figure 3: Simultaneous multiple-write bus access by 4 processors

The whole system is a distributed asynchronous bitsequential comparison network. Everyone, familiar with elementary logic, will see this easily. Like any asynchronous network the system needs some time for signal settling. Each stage has 3 levels of logic (bus access, OR gate and AND gate) and one bus line which needs some time to become stable. Assuming the use of standard SSI logic and a medium sized bus system (e.g. one large rack with 16 to 32 processors) the worst case delay for each pair of stages may be 100 nanoseconds. This means 800 ns settling time for a 16 bit word. In normal microprocessor systems this will still be less than the microprocessors require for preparing the readback of the result.

1. 3. The criterium for Multiple-Write applicability

The simultaneous multiple-write access of n processors to the common system bus reduces n data words to a single one. The information resulting from this process is the winning (the largest) data word which is automatically distributed in the system and the information for each processor, whether its own data 'won' or not. In negative logic also the smallest data word may be determined and, more general, by computing the distance to a reference data word and comparing these distances, the 'best fit' may be determined for many processors in a single multiple-write data cycle.

To make more clear, what the multiple-write technique can do, two applications are outlined which cannot profit from this technique:

- Unrestricted simultaneous multiple data exchange.

  Though this restriction is trivial, again and again people who get to know the multiple-write technique start arguing against this nonavailable (and by now impossible) feature. It would be a revolution to have it - this technique doesn't.

- Search for a known value.

  If the data which is searched for is already known, it may be broadcasted and every processor may check it against its own data. Though broadcasting is a standard feature of a multiple-write bus, the multiple-write feature itself is not used in this case.

Frequently the misunderstanding occurs that the multiple-write technique is a special technique and cannot be used for standard applications. Correctly one should say that this technique is the most general data transport mechanism and includes all other mechanisms from its nature. This will become evident from the following examples:

- A single processor writes to and a single processor reads from the bus.

  This is the standard data transfer in conventional systems. In multiple-write technique, the reading processor may disable its data output (word enable we(j)) and therefore is not effective on the bus. The ripple mechanism of the multiple-write drivers is not effective because the only written word 'wins' trivially.

- A single processor writes to and several processors read from the bus.

  This means broadcasting. The write access to the bus does not differ from the one used for the simple transfer described above. Therefore there is no different behavior for multiple-write and conventional bus technique. In any case broadcasting requires additional means for group addressing and extended handshake. Multiple-write bus installations will include these as any broadcasting buses else.

- Several processors write to and several processors read from the bus.

  This is the new field of multiple-write. The ripple-chains in the bus drivers are effective now and the bus protocoll has to wait for data signals settling. On the other hand the competition results from multiple-write are obtained. Bus extension is no longer trivial as the direction of data flow is no longer definit. Outputs to and inputs from the bus must be separated which doubles the number of bus lines und leads to a hierarchical structure of the overall system.

From the above examples can be seen, that the multiple-write bus technique adapts to the conventional transfer techniques automatically just depending on the number of writers to and readers from the bus. It will be useful, though, to install an additional transfer protocol on the bus which is designed with respect to high speed block transfer. Then the multiple-write technique may be used for general purpose simple transfer, broadcasting of single data and ,of course, for competition while large data blocks may be transferred using the simple high speed protocol taking some initial control overhead in account.

After the above general remarks and examples where the multiple-write technique gives no profit, two typical applications for this technique will be outlined: one very low level system function and one basic and frequent user application.

- Bus arbitration supported by multiple-write technique.

  Conventionally, special bus arbiters with privat lines to all processors in a multiprocessor system or daisy chains connecting all processors in a fixed hardware manner are used for this purpose. One multiple-write cycle, however, may have the same effect. Watching one interrupt line, the actual system master (which may be any one of the processors in the system and which may change from time to time) has the information whether there is a service request in the system by one or by several processors.

  By broadcasting a response command to all processors, the system master may induce all processors with pending service request to participate in a multiple-write cycle, sending their priority with their (fix) individual address in the lower part of the word. The system master reads the 'winning' word and with it gets the address of the requester with the highest priority (or the highest unique individual address if there is a priority conflict). All requesters have simultaneously the information whether their request was accepted or not.

- Fast sorting by using the multiple-write technique.

  The multiple-write technique is ideally suited to merge operations. So sorting may be distributed by distributing the set of keys well balanced to the processors of the multiprocessor system, sorting the partial sets locally and merging the resulting sorted lists by multiple-write cycles. Every multiple-write cycle gives the next element for the final sorted list. If conflicts between equal keys may occur and multiple keys must not be reduced, individual address concatenation must be used as described in the example above. Long keys may be handled in a sequence of multiple-write cycles.

  Having the support of linear n-way merge, sorting can be performed about linearly at all. With p processors in the multiprocessor system the local sorting time goes down in the order of p*log(p) and becomes easily neclectable in comparison with the constant time required for previous data distribution and final result merging. It is easy to obtain a good efficiency in systems of moderate size. With 16 processors and 1000 keys to be sorted, a speed up factor of 9.6 can be obtained which means an efficiency factor of 60%. The larger the sets of keys to be sorted are, the larger may be the number of processors in a multiprocessor system working efficiently and the larger are the speed up factors.

1. 4. System control mechanisms

The homogeneous multiprocessor kernel HoMuK is built from modules which are connected to each other by a common system bus with the multiple-write feature installed.

The modules themselves contain at least three components: the CPU, private ROM/RAM and the interface to the system bus (the bus coupler). These components are interconnected by the resident bus of each module. At least one module contains random access mass storage like a disk and I/O peripherals.

The first implementation of HoMuK will make use of the MC68000 CPU in all modules, will contain 16k byte PROM and 256k byte RAM in each module and a VME resident bus. One module will be connected to a 20 Mbyte winchester disk and a VT100 display terminal. The operating system of this module will be FLEXOS which is not widely spread used - its advantages are that it is almost completely written in FORTRAN and the implementers team knows it in details. Other operating systems might serve as well under comparable conditions.

Figure 4 shows the system functions of HoMuK. The two transfer protocols are known already from the description above like the service request interrupt function. The appearance of a reset and restart function is trivial. So the following discussion will focus on the control cycle which is the means for system control.

In figure 4 the terms 'master', 'slave' and 'outsider' are used. These are the different roles any module may play. In the work state of the system there is always exactly one actual system bus master. This module is the only one being allowed to initiate bus cycles (control, transfer or multiple-write). Addressing of partners for the master is performed by a control cycle. Modules being adressed by such an action remain in this adressed state until other modules are adressed by another control cycle. Addressed modules are in the slave role. All modules being neither master nor slave are outsiders.

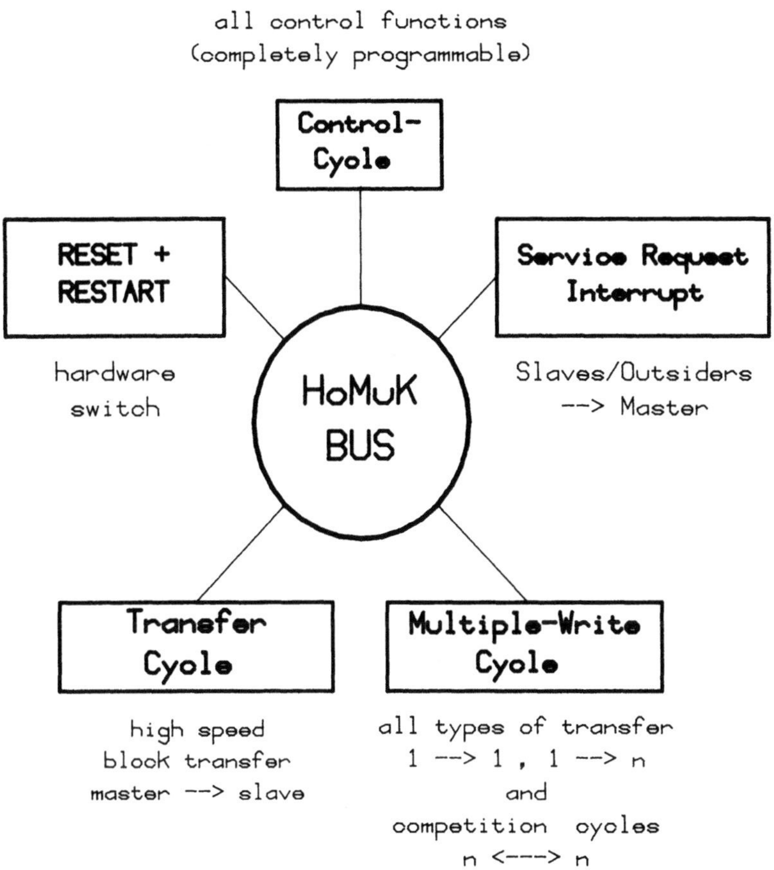

Figure 4: Overview over all HoMuK bus functions

Any module may play any one of the three roles. It is possible to change the master role over from one module to another. As during such an action the system runs through a critical phase where it may have two masters or none at a time, the system has a special interlocked state, the control state. The normal state of the system is the work state. Any control cycle sets the system to the control state which will be maintained until all addressed modules and the master have released the control interlock separately. During the control state of the system, no system bus cycle can be initiated and service request interrupts are disabled.

The control cycle itself is a two-phase operation. The first phase is addressing, the second phase is command. In the first phase the modules which shall be controlled are addressed. Two types of address may be used: individual address or group address. The address types are specified by two bits of the address word.

The individual address of a module is a fix address. It is coded in a switch register on the bus coupler board and has to be unique in the system. The group address is programmable and can be set by the module processor (only if the module is in control state). It is stored in a register on the bus coupler, also. By giving the same group address to several modules, system structures may be founded and changed at runtime. The two address specification bits allow another two address modes. One of them is very useful and means 'all'. It may be used for system bootstrap and service request inquiry.

The data phase of any control cycle is the transfer of a single command word. This is evaluated in all addressed modules and starts an appropriate response. The software module doing this is the communication handler which is programmable itself.

From figure 5 can be seen how this control mechanism works. Any control cycle activates (by interrupt) that section of the communication handler which is located in the ROM area of the local memory. Here is checked whether the control word is the command for receiving binary code. If this is true, the program continues with this function, receives some parameters for the transfer and receives and stores the code. If the command was any one else, the program branches to the continuation of the communication handler starting at a reserved location in the RAM area of the local memory. This memory contents must have been loaded earlier (during system bootstrap) using the first mentioned function.

The mechanism outlined above appears to be a very flexible one and avoids any restrictions concerning the implementation of the total system and the later use. Very low level programming remaines possible even for the system user who may define his one application specific commands.

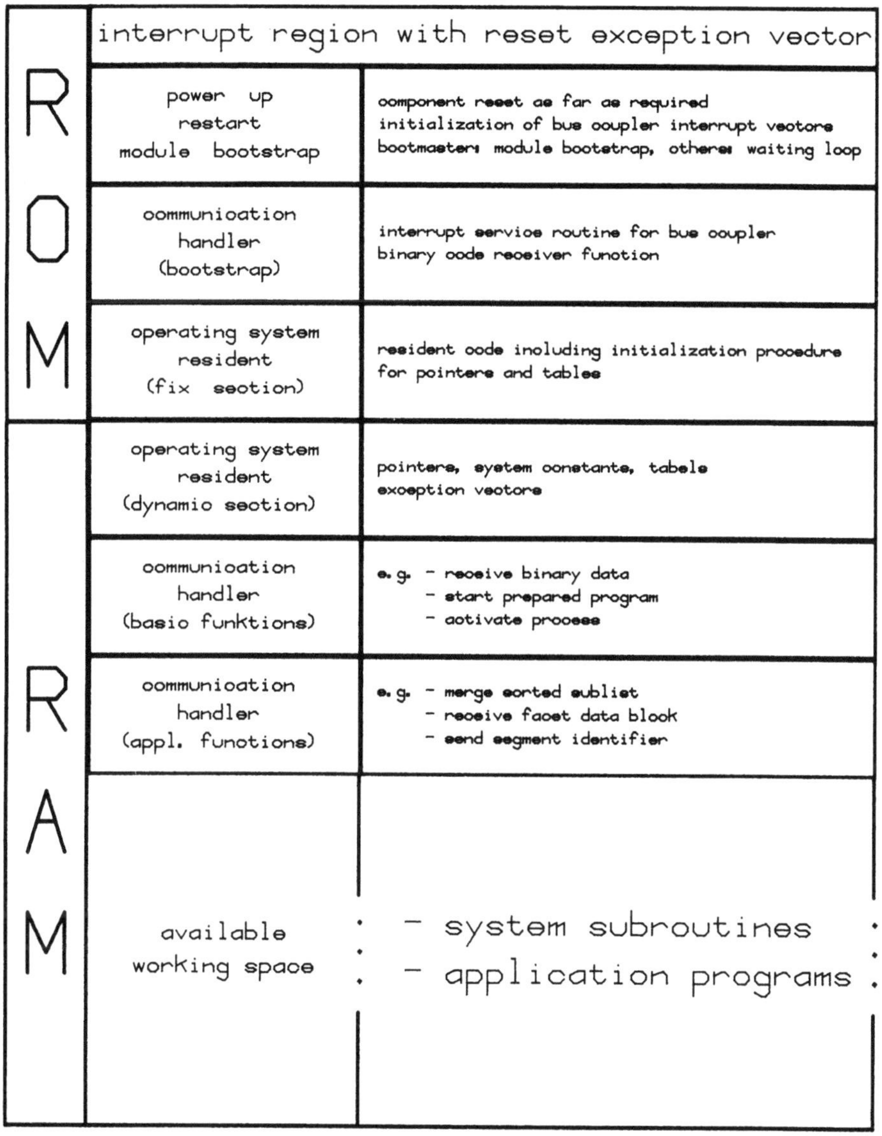

Figure 5: Structure of memory contents for a HoMuK module

It is planned to implement a basic set of functions for the communication handler, allowing a system control on the process level (load, start, terminate process, inquire status etc.). This task is still in the design phase and will be ready at the completion of the system hardware in fall 1983.

2. Distributed Scan Conversion - a HoMuK Application

2. 1. Architectural concepts for distributed raster scan conversion

It can be shown that there is no way to refresh complex pictures fast enough using a single processor. To obtain sufficient computational power, multiprocessors are required. This statement is valid for real time scan conversion of scenes with medium or larger complexity and for high-quality raster output (including transparancy, refraction and reflection) as well. Subsequently we shall focus on real time scan conversion.

The required parallelism may be applied in order to approach either of the two basic concepts: 'one processor for each pixel' or 'one processor for each picture primitive' (e.g. plane triangular facets). Having complex pictures in mind, for either one of the two concepts the required number of processors is quite high. The concept 'one processor for each picture primitive' will require some hundreds up to some thousands of medium complex processors, the concept 'one processor for each pixel' will require a quarter up to one million very simple processors. Comparing both approaches, the concept 'one processor for each pixel' seems to induce more technical problems than the other one because any processor must know about the complete scene. Otherwise the data distribution comes out to be scan conversion itself and must be performed again and again after any transformation. Subsequently we will focus on the approach 'one processor for each picture primitive', which seems to be the more practicable one.

Merging of the individual results of the large number of processors turns out to be the main problem of the approach 'one processor for each picture primitive'. As long as only 2-dimensional pictures are involved there seem to be no problems of this kind because only one processor at a time (for a distinct pixel location) is expected to produce video information. All processors may access the video bus using three-state or open-collector techniques. Bus load problems can be solved by installing a hierarchical multi-level-bus system where the levels are pipelined to be fast enough. Actually, however, even in pure 2-dimensional systems conflicts between processors on the same pixel location occur. These conflicts are induced by rounding inaccuracies in the raster scan arithmetic. These inaccuracies cannot be avoided completely and induce conflicts as soon as facets neighbour each other. If three-state technique is used for video-bus access, the bus drivers of the processors may be damaged as a result of such conflicts. In the case of open-collector access some unexpected video data may be produced on the video-bus which may be tolerated.

In the case of 3-dimensional picture data, conflicts of processors on the same pixel location must be solved. As a consequence of the large number of processors the well known priority control using 'daisy-chain' techniques is not at all fast enough to meet the strict timing requirements of real time raster output. The solution desired is one which leads to displaying only those pixels which are nearest to the viewing point. This means a demand for solving the hidden surface problem on pixel level. As in a real time system with hundreds of processors there is no time left for any central control, the community of processors has to decide autonomously who shall place its video information on the video-bus.

There are two approaches to realize this demand. One is pipelining the processors and in this way get as many separate bus time slices as there are processors. Every processor has its individual local time, receives the results from the chain of preceeding processors, combines it with its own data and sends it to the succeeding chain of processors. In this way there are no bus access conflicts. The main problem, however, is the length of the pipeline which causes long time delays and makes it difficult to realize any information feed back in the system. Information feedback may serve functions like identification of primitives (pick) or looping on pixels in order to obtain high-quality pictures.

The second approach uses a common bus, and all processors which are involved in the appearance of the actual pixel access this bus simultaneously using the multiple-write technique. This approach shall be outlined here.

Figure 6 shows the structure of a prototype system which is build now build now at the Technical University Darmstadt. Two common busses connect the modules of the multiprocessor system. The whole system is an extended HoMuK system. The kernel appears in the upper left part of figure 6 while the extensions are module extensions and the raster system. The whole system is a pilot and experimental one. For really

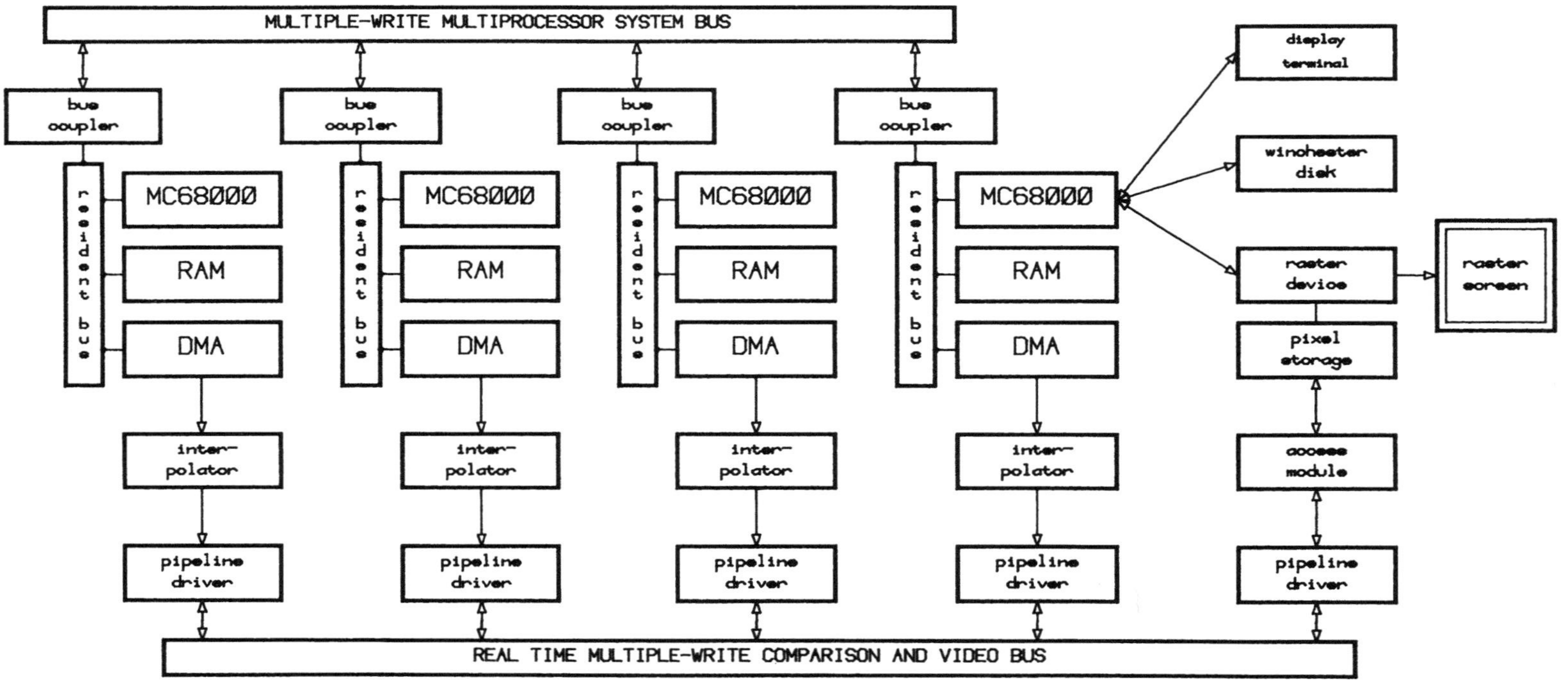

Figure 6: Structure of a HoMuK rasterscan extension

powerful and as well economical machines much more modules are required and the modules must be much more simple. VLSI is the key for this solution. Most technical and software problems, however, can be found and solved using a small machine.

2. 2. Frame preprocessing with HoMuK

The double bus multiprocessor will use the system bus for frame preprocessing. One group of the HoMuK (the system master and a slave group) will perform this task which includes transformations and clipping. Also the task of splitting up patches or other primitives into simple, plane areas (e.g. facets) shall be performed here. These operations are ideal for distribution because they are restricted to the data of single primitives.

Another very important process of frame preprocessing in this multiprocessor system is the preparation of data distribution. The facets must be distributed to the scan modules in such a way that no module gets two or more facets which are intersected by the same scan line. Distribution preparation includes sorting and cannot be performed without taking into account the complete set of facets. Operations of this kind can substantially be supported by the multiple-write feature of the system bus.

2. 3. Pixel calculation and merging of parallel results

The pixel calculation is performed in several levels of computation. The basic function is simple interpolation and results in the values for location and appearance of each pixel. As a pixel output rate of 10 millions per second is the required minimum, standard microprocessors are much too slow for this task. The solution of this problem in the described machine is discrete interpolation hardware. In figure 6 the blocks named 'interpolator' are responsible.

The interpolators get their data from the module processors and are controlled by the displays clock and sync-signal generator. This generator (which is part of the raster device) also controls the module processors which are involved in scan conversion. This is done by interrupts.

The module processors compute the key data for the interpolators and are supported by DMA to transfer these data blocks. Key data are facet frame constants (interpolation increments and entry position) and facet line constants (start values, entry position and segment length). The line constants must be transferred for every scan line (every 64 microseconds). The module processor will be rather busy to compute all these values. It should be seen, that a processor like the MC68000 is not the appropriate tool for this job. In commercial raster machines a very simple special processor would do the job even better (and much more economically).

The interpolation includes the three color channels and the z coordinate which is required for the pixel distance competition. This pixelwise hidden surface elimination is performed on the second bus of the system.

As the pixel data rate is too high for a standard multiple-write protocol, a pipeline technique is used to obtain the required speed. The pixel stream is a one-directional one. Z values which lost may be dropped. Therefore a readback of the competition result to the processors is not necessary for control purposes.

Figure 7 shows the structure and the circuitry of the pipeline version of the multiple-write bus driver. The result of the competition is to be seen in the upper right corner of the figure. This word survive signal ws(j) concerns a word which has been input to the driver 7 clock periods before. The result ws(j) is used to control the video output of the processor to the video bus. The video signal (result of the color interpolation) is delayed to meet with the appropriate control signal.

Z-coordinate input is from the left. The competition is bitwise performed instead of wordwise and this results in the higher cycle frequency. At any clock period 6 bits of 6 different sequential words are in competition. The competition for one word requires 6 clock periods. At any clock period one word result is obtained. So the whole mecha-

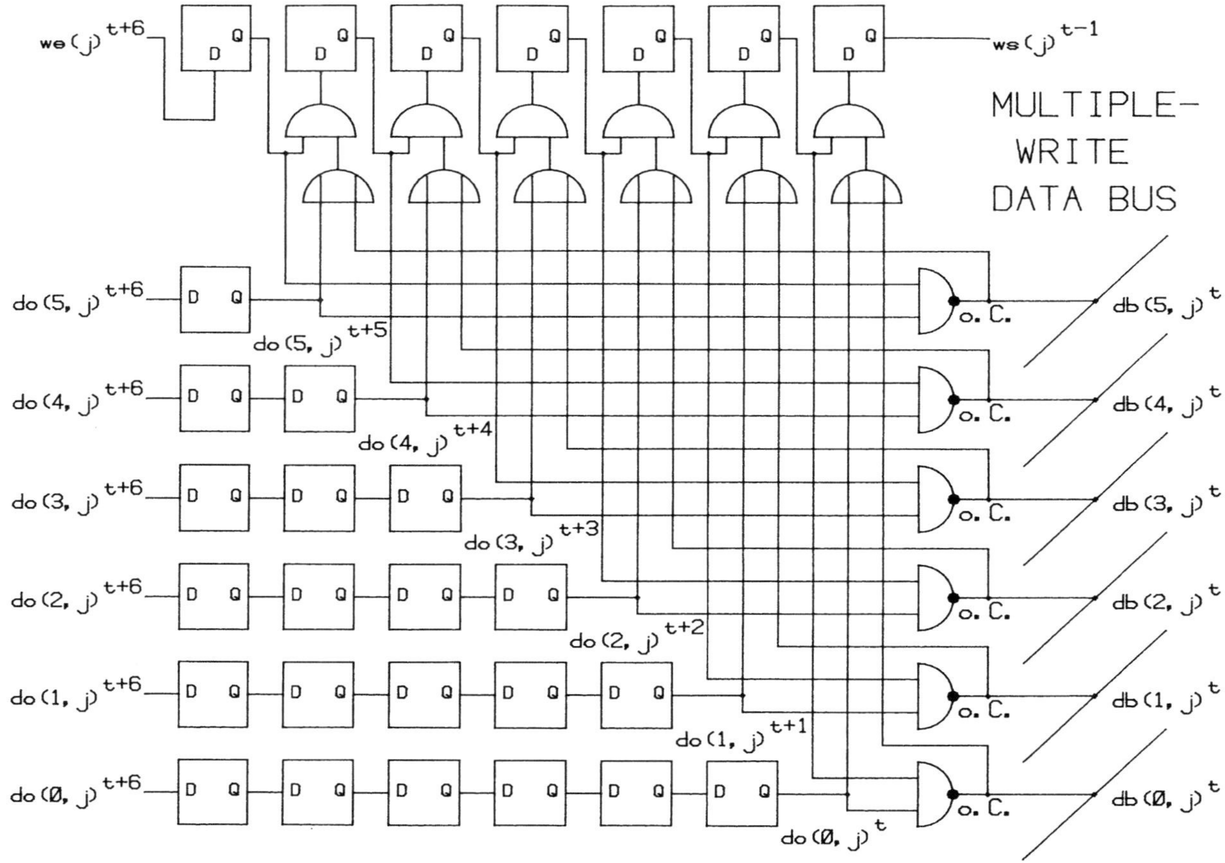

Figure 7: Pipeline multiple-write bus driver circuitry

nism leads to a higher output rate and costs a small delay which is not important on this oneway dataflow.

From this description the efficiency of the double bus concept and the flexibility of the group and master/slave-outsider design will become evident. Processors in the outsider role are able to do extensive processing as long as they do not need external data.

2. 4. Real Time Hidden Surface Merge

The machine outlined here with its only 4 processors cannot do very much effect without an additional special feature not yet mentioned. In any case it is planned to enlarge the system to 16 modules and make it much more powerful.

The special feature is the integration of the raster device into the realtime hidden surface elimination. For this purpose, the pixel memory of the raster device contains for every pixel the presentation (color information) and additionally the z value in 12 bits accuracy. This makes it possible, to mix real time scan information from the multiprocessor with static pixel storage information and move objects through a static 3D scene with hidden surface elimination in real time. Also, the real time system can be used as a very fast loader for the pixel storage. It can be expected, that the machine - as soon as the hardware is complete - will be a powerful raster output device for highly interactive applications.

REFERENCES

(1) Lindner, R.: Rasterdisplay-Prozessoren - Ihre Bedeutung, Konzepte und Verfahren, D17 Darmstädter Dissertation, Fachbereich 20, Technische Hochschule Darmstadt, November 1979 (in German)

(2) Gemballa, R., Lindner, R.: The Multiple-Write Bus Technique, Computer Graphics and Applications, Volume 2, Number 7, September 1982

(3) Bittner, H. et. al.: HoMuK - Ein Homogener Multiprozessor-Kern, Forschungsbericht GRIS 83-5 des FG GRIS, Fachbereich 20, Technische Hochschule Darmstadt, März 1983 (in German)

PARALLEL PROCESSING

S. Castan
Laboratoire CERFIA
I.U.T. INFORMATIQUE
50A, chemin des Maraîchers, Toulouse, FRANCE

INTRODUCTION

Image processing is certainly an area where conventional serial Von Neuman Computers are not well suited, and people try to develop various parallel computer architectures adapted for spatially distributed data. These parallel computers, allow to develop high-performance systems by replication of computers, or computer sub-systems. This replication of hardware may allow similar processing of different data to occur simultaneously, or allow different hardwares to handle distinctly different parts of the problem.

These machines are termed parallel, and both parallelism and pipelining have the same origin and are hard to separate in practice.

Both techniques attempt to increase the performance of some function by increasing the number of simultaneous operating hardware units. For a conventionally designed module to do some generic function, either technique can be used to derive a new design running up to N times faster.

In the pipeline design the basic module is split into N pieces. In the pure parallel design the basic module may be replicated N times with all replications running simultaneously on different data.

In the first part of this paper we examine some aspects of the pipeline processing, and in the second part we describe a multi-level architecture for image processing built in our laboratory.

NATO ASI Series, Vol. F18
Computer Architectures for Spatially Distributed Data
Edited by H. Freeman and G. G. Pieroni

PART I

PIPELINE PROCESSING

1. INTRODUCTION

Pipelining and overlapping are general multiprocessing techniques using precedence requirement, these techniques are consistently applied to a high-performance general-purpose machine design, which incidentally shows the power of distributed control in a tagged architecture.

Overlapping and pipelining are essentially job-partition and management techniques that encompass possible precedence constraints.

So a total job is partitioned into individual subjobs to be parcelled out to different working units. This way the handling of each subjob may not itself be done faster, but the entire job is completed much sooner.

But arbitrary partition is often impractical some jobs cannot be partitioned, the subjobs may not be identical in nature. Effective partition also depends on the capabilities of the working units and control mechanism available. All these problems are generaly interwoven. Sometimes a job may be divisible in several mutually exclusive ways, and the fact that it could be done one way does not imply that it must be so partitioned.

If a job is symmetrically partitioned into identical tasks, the working units can be identical in make up, and the processing can be synchronised in time, simplifying the control. The broader term "synchro parallelism" to depict this phenomenon of identical units working in unison is generaly used.

Some subjobs often show interdependencies, restricting their concurrent execution. One of the most common among these is the precedence constraint, which demands that the subjobs must be processed in a certain prescribed order. Precedence constraints may seem to preclude multiprocessing, as the total time cannot be shortened if the subjobs have to follow one another. But when the number of task to do, is big enough, concurrent handling is possible.

2. PIPELINE ARCHITECTURE

So the pipeline approach is to split the function to be performed into smaller pieces and allocating separate hardware to each piece, termed a stage. Instructions or data, flow the stages of a digital computer pipeline at a rate that is independent of the length of the pipeline (number of stages) and dependent only on the rate at which new entries may be fed to the input of the pipeline.

This rate inturn depends on the time for one piece of data to traverse a simple stage, a computer pipeline may do more than simply move its contents unchanged from one location to the next as does a physical pipeline.

As a particular item flows though either pipeline, it occupies only one stage at a time. Simultaneously, an item that enters the pipeline before this item occupies a stage farther down the pipeline, and an item that enters after the referenced item occupies a previous stage. As time goes on, the stage vacated by one item is occupied by the one immediatly following it.

This concurrent use of many stages by different terms is called "overlap", and the maximum rate at which new items may enter the pipeline depends strictly on the longest time required to traverse any single stage and not on the number of stages.

3. OVERLAP DESIGNS OR DYNAMIC PIPELINE

In a computer system, there can be overlap at different level :

-between the processor and the I/O units.

- between instruction preparation and execution ; overlapping at a finer level is also possible.

In the case of overlapping between processor and I/O units, there is no precedence issue. All I/O is handled one processor, and all computation by another, and most communication is through a common memory module. A typical task in this system would alternate between the computational and I/O processors while the execution of some other task is overlapped by using the other processor. The partitioning of the basic function is dynamically changing and even the time per subjob is not predictable in advance.

- an example of precedence constraints is the concurrent handling of instruction preparation (I) and execution (E), with I setting up the stage for E in every instruction as shown in figure 2.

The programmer's view is that, at any time, at most one instruction is being processed, and that within the instruction there is a precise processing order. For the jth instruction let Ij the instruction preparation and Ej the subsequent execution, T(Ij) and T(Ej) the corresponding handling times as shown in figure 2(a).
We have there precedences Rules : R1 : Ij precedes Ej, R2 : Ij precedes IJ+1, Ej precedes Ej+1, R3 : Ej precedes Ij+1. The overall processing time for n instructions for this conventional processor is :

$$T = \sum_{1}^{n} [T(Ij) + T(Ej)]$$

With an overlapped processor as shown in figure 2(b).

If we permit Ej to be concurrent with Ij+1 most of the time, using

R4 : Ej precedes Ij+2

The overall processing time is

$$T = \sum_{0}^{n} \text{Max } [T(Ej), T(Ij+1)] \text{ with } T(E_1) = 0 \; ; \; T(I_n) = 0$$

4. PIPELINE DESIGN

A simple pipeline is a time synchronised assembly line with neither side branches nor feedback.
Consider a collection of M processing units (S1, S2,...,SM) : the jth member can accept an input aj do a local work wj within the time interval tj and produce an output bj at the end of the interval (figure 3) and is ready to accept new inputs.
One can string there M units together, one after the other, for the purpose of doing work Σ Wj. (as shown in figure 4).

The data matching condition is $bj = aj+1 \; \forall \; j$
and the time matching condition is $tj = \tau = ct \forall j$
There are three states
1. Starting this pipeline at time t1 and supplying a1 at every cycle
2. Steady state reached at time $t = (s+M)\tau$

Where $s\tau$ is a fixed start up time that is required to set up the pipeline for the vector.
bM emerges at every cycle (with overlapping), the pipeline is filled, every stage is busy, the jth stage doing work Wj, the steady-state work rate is there Σ Wj per cycle. At the steady-state finishes one task cycle, insensitive to the size of the task, and independant of the number of stages required.
3. Draining state
The time to perform the operation on a vector of length n is therefore

$$t_{pipe} : [s + M + (n-1)]\ \tau \qquad (1)$$

the maximum rate of producing result is :

$$r_{\infty}\ pipe = \tau^{-1}$$

Figure 5 illustrates the different ways of performing an arithmetic operation on pipelined architecture. As an example, we take the problem of adding two floating point vectors xi an yi (i = 1,2,.. ..n), to obtain the sum vector zi = xi + yi (i = 1,2,..n).
The operation of adding any pair of the above element ($x = e.2^p$, $y = f.2^q$) may be divided into four sub-operations which, we will assume take the same time to complete.
There are : 1. Compare exposent : from (p-q) ;

2. Shift x with respect to y,(p-q) places in order to line up the binary points ;

3. Add the mantissa of x to the mantissa of y ;

4. Normalise by shifting the result Z to the left until the leading non zero digit is next to the binary point.

5. PERFORMANCE ON VECTORS

The caracterisation of performance of the computer during a single arithmetic operation on a vector of length n by the following generic formula :

$$t = r_{\infty}^{-1}\ (n + n1/2) \qquad (2)$$

has been recommended by Calahan and Ames (1979).

The two parameters r_∞ and nl/2 introduced by Hockney (1977), completely describe the hardware performance of the idealised generic computer and give first-order description of any read computer. These characteristic parameters are called :

1. r_∞ : the maximum or asymptotic performance.

The maximum rate of computation in units of equivalent scalar operation performed per second. For the generic computer this occurs asymptotically for vector of infinite length (hence the subscript). The common unit for floating-point execution is Millions of floating-point operations per second (megaflop/s or M flop/s).

2. nl/2 : the half performance length nl/n2 :

the vector length required to achieve half the maximum performance.

If we consider a vector arithmetic operations take a time :

$$T = b + cn \qquad (3)$$

then

$$t = \frac{T}{a} = \frac{c}{a}(n + b/c) \qquad (4)$$

by comparison with (2)

r_∞ = a/c and nl/2 = b/c.

If we speed up all the circuits of a computer by the same factor K (by dividing b and c by K).

(decreasing the clock period) increase the asymptotic performance by this factor, but does not alter nl/2.

So r_∞ is characteristic of the computer technology used and plays no role in the choice of the best algorithm.

nl/2 on the other hand, is a measure of the amount of parallelism in the computer architecture. It varies from nl/2 = 0 for serial computer to nl/2 = ∞ for an infinite array of processors, and it provides a quantitative one-parameter measure of the amount of parallelisms in a computer architecture.

So the relative performance of different algorithms is determined by the value of nl/2 because this parameter does not appears as a factor in equation (3).

The vector length n measures the parallelism in the problem, and ν = nl/2/n measures how parallel a computer appears to a particular problem.

If $\nu = 0$ or small, an algorithm designed for a sequential environment will be the best, if ν is large an algorithm designed for a highly parallel environment will be the best.

6. MEASUREMENT OF $n1/2$ AND r_∞

In a M stages pipeline computer the time to compute a vector length n is :

$$t = [s + M + (n-1)]\,\tau \qquad (1)$$

Whence, by comparison with (2) one obtains the pipeline computer

$$n1/2 = s + M - 1 \qquad (5)$$

and

$$r_\infty = \tau^{-1} \qquad (6)$$

Figure (6) give the time t plotted against the vector length, the graph obtained is a straight-line :

$$t = r_\infty^{-1}\, n + n1/2 * r_\infty^{-1}$$

the negative of the intercept of the line with the n axis gives the value of $n1/2$, and the slope is r_∞^{-1}.

7. PROGRAM PERFORMANCE

The generic formula (2) can be used to define some other numbers that characterise performance of a computer on actual program with finite vector length. These are :

7.1. The average performance

$$r = n/t = r_\infty (1 + x^{-1}) \qquad (7)$$

with $x = n/n1/2 = \nu^{-1}$

7.2. The vector efficiency

$$\eta = r/r_\infty = (1 + x^{-1})^{-1} \qquad (8)$$

Figure (7) shows the relation between vector efficiency and vector length, we note from the definition that :

- $\eta = 0{,}5$ when $n = n1/2$
- the efficiency asymptotically approachs unity as the vector length increase to infinity.

We can examine the performance of a computer on vectors that are both long and short compared with its half-performance length.
For long vectors : $n >> n1/2$, and $x \rightarrow \infty$ we have from equation (7)

$$t = \frac{n}{r_\infty} \text{ and } r = r_\infty$$

Thus the processing time is proportional to the vector length and the performance is constant
For short vectors $n << n1/2$, $x \rightarrow 0$

$$t = n1/2/r_\infty = \Pi_\infty^{-1}$$

and $r = n\,\Pi_\infty$
Thus the processing time is constant, and the performance is proportional to vector length.

8 - TIMING AND CONTROL

Efficient use of a pipeline demands that there be a timely source of inputs to drive it.
Whithout such a stream, successive stages in the pipeline become idle. An other problem is in scheduling when each input starts through the pipeline to guarantee both high performance and avoidance of internal conflicts. If the pipeline is purely linear (ie) each stage connecting to only a single succeeding stage, the scheduling would be trivial : imputs would be given to the pipeline as they arrive at a rate of one per clock pulse. But real pipeline are much more complex, some stages may require different time periods, there may be feed back from a stage to a previous one, or multiple paths out of a stage to later stages, more than one stage may be used by an input at one time. There may be dependencies between inputs that force certain ordering to the computations involving these inputs, and sometimes for multifunction dynamically configured pipelines, the path to be taken through the pipeline may vary at each input. All these factors place constraints on new starts and make the performance of a pipeline very sensitive the procedure used for scheduling and control its activities.
The development of procedures for scheduling pipelines has been studied by several groups. Ramanoorthy and Li (1975) have shown that this problem is a member of the "NP" complete problem.

Despite the intrinsic difficulty of the general case, there exist subclasses of pipelines for which optimal good scheduling algorithms exists. The restrictions are :

- the execution time for all stages is a multiple basic clock ;
- one a computation starts through a pipeline, its time-pattern of stage usage is fixed.

This model is good for a lot of real pipelines, in vector processors for instance.

The scheduling procedures assume that the exact pattern of stage usage is known for each input before it is started through the pipeline. These pattern may be described in a two dimensional tabular description named : reservation table. Such reservation table represents exactly one pattern taken be one data input.

An initiation of a reservation table occurs when a computation is started, and corresponds to the start of a single function evaluation. Then the pipeline's controller must reserve for that initiation at the appropriate time the stages called out by the reservation table. If there are two or more initiations to use the same stage at the same time is a collision and must be avoided by both the scheduling algorithm and the controller executing it.

Figure (8) illustrates a reservation table for a pipeline having three stages. Table A has a compute time of 7 time units. (each evaluation table represents exactly one evaluation of a given function).

A reservation table corresponds to one or more pipeline having the same data flow. Figure 9 diagrams a pipeline that would support the above reservation table A. Each stage takes exactly one cycle for its operation.

A very important parameter in determining the performance of a pipeline is the latency, or number of time units, separating two initiations of the same or different reservation tables. A latency may have any positive integer including 0. Figure 10 illustrates the effects of different latency values between various combinations of the reservation table of figure 7.

We can notice that not all latencies are permitted. For a static pipeline a latency of 0 is impossible because both evaluations would attempt to use the same hardware stages at exactly the same moments, in figure 7 a latency of 2 for reservation table A causes dual use of stage 2 during time 3 and 5 and this is never allowed. In general a latency value that results in a conflict is said to cause a collision.

9. PARALLEL ALGORITHMS

In order to obtain the optimum performance from any computer it is necessary to tailor the computer program to suit the architecture of the computer.

We make no attempt to survey parallel algorithm in all major area of numerical analysis, we shall examine the matrix multiplication problem that demonstrate a variety of approaches.

We will define the performance of a computer program to be inversely proportional to the CPU time consumed during the execution of the program. This is not the only definition of performance that could have been given. We might have asked for minimum cost on a particular computer installation or for the least use for memory.

The performance of a computer program depends both on the suitability of the numerical procedure : the algorithm that is used to solve the problem, and on the skill with which the algorithm is implemented on the computer by the programmer or the compiler. If the parallelism in the algorithm matches the parallelism of the computer we have a chance that a high performance code can be written by an experimented programmer.

At any stage within an algorithm, the parallelism of the algorithm is defined as the number of arithmetic operation that are independent and can be performed in parallel. On a pipelined computer the data for the operations would be defined as vectors and the operations would by performed as one vector instruction, the parallelism is then the same as the vector length. On the pipelined computer without vectors registers, such as CYBER 205, the average performance (equation 7) increases monotonically as the vector length increases, and one can only say that the natural hardware parallelism is as long as possible. On pipelined computer with vector registers such as CRAY I, the performance is best for vector length that are multiples of the number of elements held in a vector register.

So the objective of a good programmer is to find a solution that makes the last match between the parallelism of the algorithm and the natural parallelism of the computer.

9.1. Matrix multiplication

Matrix multiplication is a very simple example of matrix manipulation and illustrates the different ways in which a simple algorithm should be restructured to suit the architecture of the computer on which it is to be executed. Let the elements Cij of the product matrix are related to the elements Aij and Bij of the matrices being multiplied by the equation.

$$Cij = \sum_{k=1}^{n} Aik * Bkj \qquad 1 \leq i,j \leq n$$

9.1.1. Inner product method

On serial computer matrices are computed using a nest of three loops, using FORTRAN code :

```
    DO 1  I = 1,N
    DO 1  J = 1,N
    DO 1  K = 1,N
1 C(I,J) = C(I,J) + A(I,K) * A(K,J)                    (9)
```

Where we assume that all elements C(I,J) of the matrix are set to zero before entering the code.

The assignment (9) forms the inner product of the ith row of A and the ith column of B.

9.1.2. Middle product method

The middle product method is obtained by interchanging the order of the DO LOOP in the code (9)

```
    DO 1 J = 1,N
    DO 1 K = 1,N
    DO 1 I = 1,N
1 C(I,J) = C(I,J) + A(I,K) * B(K,J)                    (10)
```

Every term in the loop over I can be evaluated in parallel. The addition +, is a parallel addition of n elements, and the multiplication *, is the multiplication of the scalar B(K,J) by the vector A(I,K). The parallelism of the middle product is n compared with 1 for the original inner-product algorithm.

9.1.3. Outer-product method

The outer-product method is obtained by moving the loop over K in the code (9) to the outside, as follow :

```
    DO 1 K = 1,N
    DO 1 I = 1,N
    DO 1 J = 1,N
1 C(I,J) = C(I,J) + A(I,K) * B(K,J)                          (11)
```

One term of the inner product may be evaluated in parallel for all n^2 element of C. The multiplication operation is an element by element multiplication of an n*n matrix made by duplicating the Kth column of A and an n*n matrix made by duplication of the Kth row of B. The addition operation is an element - by element addition of n*n elements.
So the parallelism has been increased from n to n^2, compared with the middle product method. The outer product algorithm is suitable for an array processor that has the same dimension as the matrix, but it is suitable for a pipelined computer with a large value of $n1/2$.
The ratio of the performance of the outer-product method P_O, to the performance of the middle-product method P_m, is in the ratio of the time to perform n vector operations of length n, to time to perform one vector operation of length n^2.

$$\frac{P_O}{P_m} = \frac{n(n+n1/2)}{n^2+n1/2} = \frac{1 + n1/2/n}{1+n1/2/n^2} \begin{array}{l} \sim 2 \text{ for } n1/2 = n > 1 \\ \sim n1/2 \text{ for } n^2>n1/2>n \end{array}$$

There are advantages to the outer-product algorithm in pipelined computer when $n^2 > n1/2 > n$.

10. CONCLUSION

Overlapping and pipelining are important multiprocessing tools for improving system performance, when the task subdivisions show distinct precedence linkages. The duration of a task no longer presents an obstacle for performance if there are enough task to exploit the decentralized computing power.
In overlap processing the machine exercise internal processing freedom to gain performance, as long as it produces the correct out come of computation at all user interfaces.

Pipelining unifies the protocols by time pulses, thus it belong to the category of tightly-coupled multiprocessing like synchro-parallelism.

Both are in turn with the requirement of modern VLSI micro electronics. Synchro-parallelism provides circuits systematicity, and pipelining reduces interconnections via orderliness in the time domain.

As VLSI technology advances, associative control will become inexpensive and self-optimization should add flexibility to high coupling ; systematic structures akin to cellular logic and data flow machines may also become economical enough to merit serious study.

BIBLIOGRAPHY

S.C. Flynn et al. : Introduction to Computer Architecture (Second edition S.R.A. Inc. 1980)

M.J.B. Duff, S. Levialdi : Languages and Architectures for Image Processing.(Academic Press. 1981).

K.S. Fu (ed.) T. Ichikawa (ed) : Special Computer Architectures for Pattern Processing. (CRC Press Inc. Boca Raton Florida 1982).

R.W. Hockney, C.R. Jesshope : Parallel Computers (Adam. Hilger Ltd. Bristol 1981.).

P.M. Kodge : The Architecture of Pipelined Computers. (Mc Graw Hill book Company 1981).

R.H. Kuhm, H.D. Padua : "Tutorial Parallel Processing." 10th Int. Conf. on Parallel Processing. Bellaire Michigan U.S.A. 1981.

K. Preston Jr, L. Uhr : Multicomputers and Image. Processing. Algorithms and Programs. (Academic Press 1982.).

L.S. Haynes et al. : A Survey of highly parallel Computer. Computer Sciences Press Jan. 1982.

L. Sydney : Introduction to the Configurable highly parallel Computer. Computer Sciences Press Jan 1982.

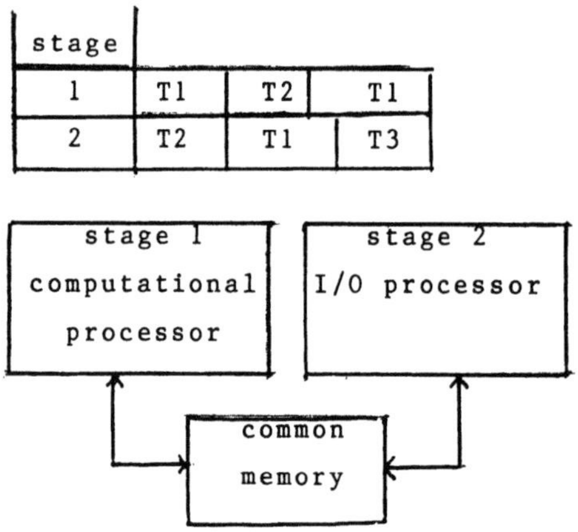

Figure 1

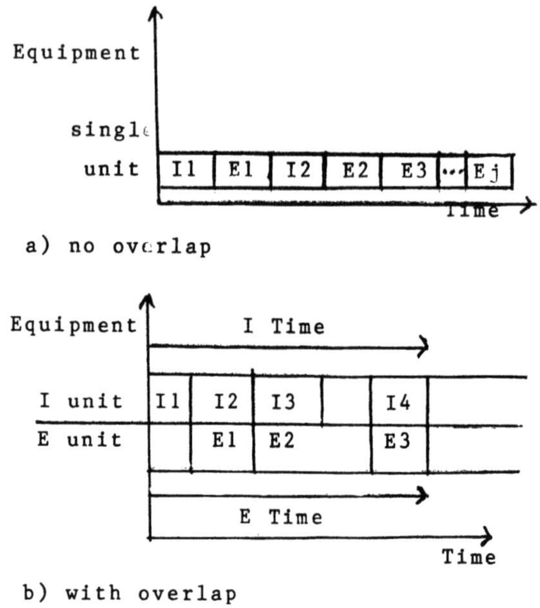

Figure 2

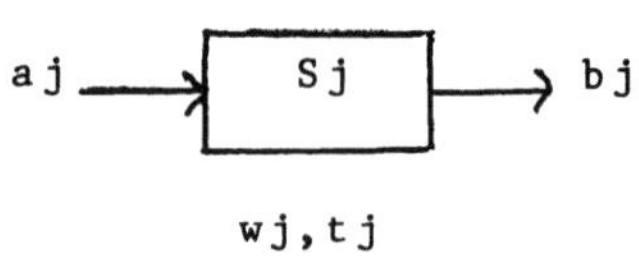

Figure 3

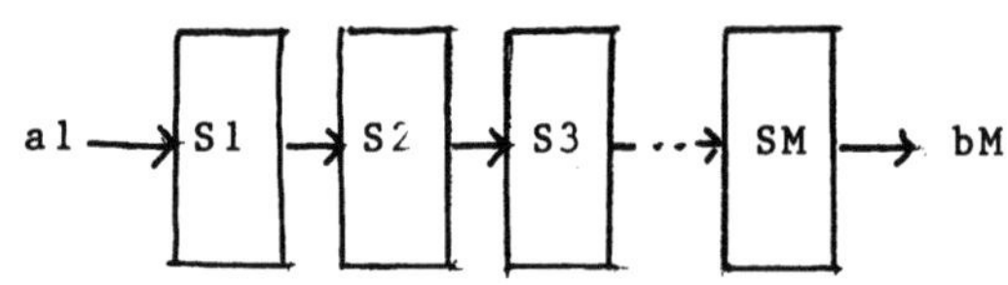

Figure 4

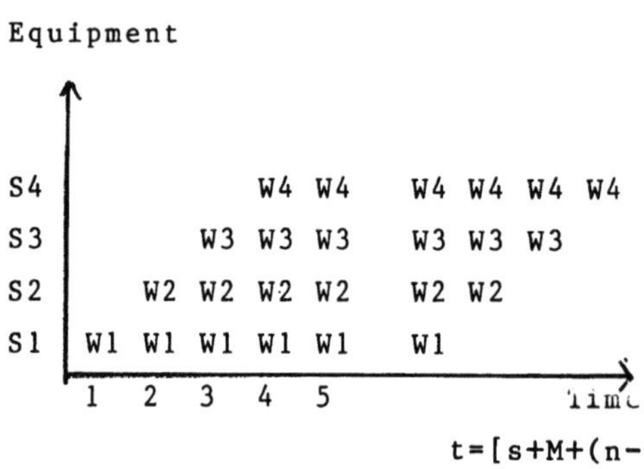

Figure 5

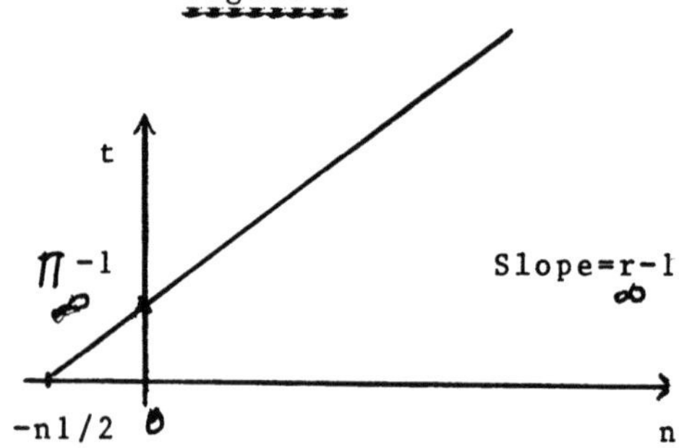

Figure 6

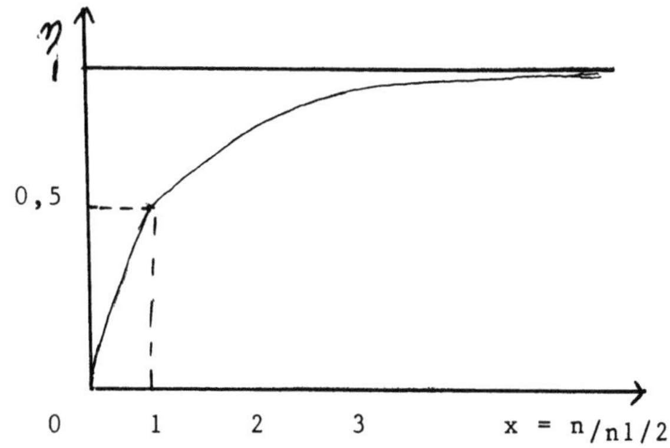

Figure 7

Stage \ Time	0	1	2	3	4	5	6
1					A		
2		A		A		A	
3	A		A		A		A

A Latency = 0

Figure 8

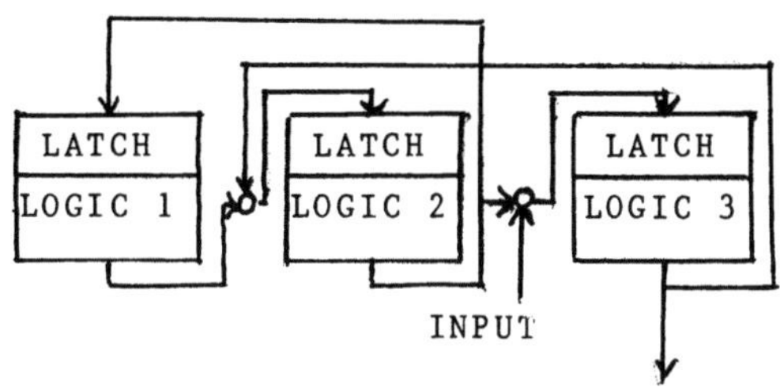

Figure 9

Stage \ Time	0	1	2	3	4	5	6	7
1			A1	A2	A1	A2		
2		A1	A2	A1	A2	A1	A2	
3	A1	A2	A1	A2			A1	A2

A,A Latency = 1

Stage \ Time	0	1	2	3	4	5	6	7	8
1			A1		(A1A2)		A2		
2		A1		(A1A2)		(A1A2)		A2	
3	A1		(A1A2)		A2		A1		A2

A,A Latency = 2 collision (circled)

Figure 10

PART II

A MULTI-LEVEL ARCHITECTURE FOR IMAGE PROCESSING AND PARALLEL IMAGE PROCESSING ALGORITHMS

1. INTRODUCTION

Image processing is certainly an area where conventional serial computers are not well suited, and people try to develop various parallel computer architectures adapted for spatially distributed data. In image processing we can define two main levels of activity : the pixel level processing, generally working on a given neighborhood, to compute any local transform ; and the region level processing, working on different subimages, to compute more global transform

To solve any specific problems, there are hardwired systems providing the best result when used in the particular problem for which they were designed. But very often it is necessary to design a general purpose image processing machine, and these machines must have identical performances when they work at pixel or at region levels.

In order to achieve that goal there are two solutions, the first one being a reconfigurable machine and the second one involving a multi-level architecture.

With this motivation, we have designed a three levels parallel machine. The first level is of a multiple Single Instruction stream Multiple Data stream type. Which it makes possible to perform plain treatment directly at memory level ; the second level is a Multiple Instruction stream, Multiple Data stream type, and the third level is the byte level.

2. GENERAL ARCHITECTURE

The system SY.MP.A.T.I. is a double data bus oriented structure :

a - A fast bus used to exchange data at T.V. rate ; on this bus are connected one or more image-processors in which pictures are stored and may be processed in a S.I.M.D. mode.

Specialized hardwired modules may also be connected to this bus in order to solve specific real time problems.

b - An inter-processor bus connecting standard processors, making it possible to perform parallel algorithms in a M.I.N.D. mode.

This bus permits the following possibilities :

-Sending the operating code of a procedure to a free processor before running it ;

- Exchanging information blocks between two processors, for example the result of one procedure called by another ;

- Exchanging information between a processor and an image memory.

Such exchanges are made transparent for the processors concerned because they are stopped by the bus manager in order to get the maximum input/output rate.

These two buses are connected to each other through a transfer module, and the whole system is managed by resource allocator as shown in figure 1.

2.1.The S.I.M.D. Memory structure

2.1.1. The column structure : The memory is structured in a S.I.M.D. way, each S.I.M.D. module may contain 512 x 512 eight-bit pixels. The data are column strutured, so the neighbors of the same column are in the same block, and the close-line neighbors are in the neighboring blocks.

Each column of the image is contained in a memory block, and to each block is attached a processing unit. All the processing units communicate with each other through a shifting loop (figure 3).

It seems it would be satisfactory to have one column per memory block, in order to have a row processor with 512 processing units since we are working on 512 x 512 pixel images. For economical reasons we use only 16 blocks (figure 2). It is the minimum number in order to be compatible with TV rate, considering the dynamic RAM we use to build the memory (1 μs cycle).

2.1.2. The shifting loop : Modulo 16 opérations are made possible with the shifting loop as shown in figure 3 the extremity of which is composed as shown in figure 4 :

- two registers to store the left or the right pixel of the 16 point-segments being considered.
- one register to initialize some or all of the 16 registers of the shifting loop.
- a set of gates which make it possible to establish communication with the fast bus, to shift left or right, and to perform I/O and circularly shifting.

2.1.3. The processing-units structure : each processing unit consists of the following components as shown in figure 6. :

- an arithmetical and logical unit in order to process some plain local expressions,
- an eight registers to function as a scratch pad for storing some intermediate results, or to avoid memory accesses,
- an indicator set where the ALU indicators may be stored ; this is necessary to process conditional computation as the 16 ALUs work in an associative way. That structure shows that memory access and ALU processing cannot be run simultaneously, but memory access and shifting loop, or ALU processing and shifting loop, may be run simultaneously.

2.1.4. The command unit : This unit manages the 16 blocks (memory and processing units). Procedures are running in microprogrammed mode, with two level micro-instructions :

- "short" micro-instructions that give the sequence of the micro-program,
- "long" micro-instructions that command the different parts of the image-memory.

2.2. Specialized modules : On the fast bus, specialized modules are connected for processing specific problems. For example, there are three modules for image input-output :

- An image digitizer at TV rate
- An image synthesizer to visualize image content on a TV monitor
- An input-output module to manage the connection with another computer
- Many other modules may be added in order to process classical algorithms such as histograms, etc.

2.3. The standard processors

Each standard processor has its own memory large enough to store the image region which is to be processed. The size of each region and the number of regions depends on the algorithm being performed and on the image being analyzed.
The parallelism to be performed has to be explicitly indicated by the programmer ; different resource allocation strategies may be used in the operating system. We adapted a strategy based on a dynamic tree of resource requests.

3. S.I.M.D. ALGORITHMS

In the S.I.M.D. structure of the memory, it is possible to compute algorithms at pixel level, proceeding row by row.
In the following algorithm we suppose that we have a row processor adapted in size to the image and we are going to examine some classical local transforms generally used in image processing. On the SY.MP.A.T.I. S.I.M.D. processors, any neighborhood may be used since the inter-block communication is done by the fast shifting loop ; but eight neighbors 8(N) or four neighbors 4(N) are faster than larger neighborhood because block j has a direct connection with blocks j±1.
We shall see some algorithms running in parallel row be row working on two memories. Generally some algorithms are available for array processors, while others run sequentially, row by row, working on the same memory (each row working in parallel).

3.1. Grey weighted images

Let A be an (n * n) grey weighted image, and a_{ij} one pixel. We consider that when we process row i, all the column j are processed at the same time.
Let a'_{ij} be an another point of the memory located in an extra memory of the same size and in the same block.
Let the neighbors of the element a_{ij} be denoted by

		column j-1	j	j+1
	i-1	a_3	a_2	a_1
row	i	a_4	a_{ij}	a_0
	i+1	a_5	a_6	a_7

3.1.1. Averaging over a neighborhood

$$a'_{ij} \leftarrow (a_0 + a_1 + a_2 + a_3 + a_4 + a_5 + a_6 + a_7) / 8$$

3.1.2. Medial filter

$$a'_{ij} \leftarrow \text{the median of } (a_0, \ldots, a_7)$$

3.1.3. Sobel

For all a_{ij} we compute :
$X = (a_1 + 2a_0 + a_7) - (a_3 + 2a_4 + a_5)$ and
$Y = (a_3 + 2a_2 + a_1) - (a_5 + 2a_6 + a_7)$ in two scans.

3.2. Binary images

Let 1 be the pattern F and 0 be $\overline{F}$ (complement of F).
Dilation and shrinking are very useful algorithms in image e restoration.

3.2.1. Dilation

$a'_{ij} \leftarrow a_0 \cup a_1 \cup a_2 \cup a_3 \cup a_4 \cup a_5 \cup a_6 \cup a_7$

3.2.2. Shrinking

$a'_{ij} \leftarrow a_0 \cap a_1 \cap a_2 \cap a_3 \cap a_4 \cap a_5 \cap a_6 \cap a_7$

3.2.3. Transform distance

We will use the following definition of 8 neighbors for the components of F and 4 neighbors for the components of $\overline{F}$. The distance function used is for the component of F :
$d\ [(i,j),(k,l)] = \max\ \{(i,j),(j-l)\}$
Let the neighborhood be $N(P) = \{a \in (a_{i,j})\ /\ d(P,a) \leq n-1\ \ , \forall\ i = 1,2,...$
The neighborhood is a square (2n-1) on each side
We will say P is of order n iff we have.
$N_n(P) \in F$ and $N_{n+1}(P) \cap \overline{F} = \phi$.
The following algorithm computes the order of each pixel belonging to F.

3.2.3.1. Parallel Transform distance

For all $a_{ij} > 0$ do $a'_{ij} \leftarrow \min\ (a_0, a_1,...,a_7) + 1$.
The number of iterations is equal to the number of the largest order N_{max} minus one, (and is a function of the thickness of the pattern).

3.2.3.2. Parallel generation

The dual problem is that from the transform distance results we want to generate the corresponding binary image.

For all a_{ij} do : a'_{ij} Max $(a_0, a_1, \dots, a_7) - 1$. We stop when we have a binary image. The number of iterations if : $N_{max} - 1$.

These two algorithms have a processing time dependent on the size of the pattern, and it is sometimes useful to know to processing time for any pattern. The following algorithm is sequential. It runs in two scans on the same memory, the first one is top-down the second is bottom-up, running row by row in parallel.

3.2.3.3. Sequential Transform distance : For all $a_{ij} > 0$

1°) Top-down :

$a_{ij,j} \leftarrow \min (a_{ij}, a_{i,j+1}, a_{i,j-1})+1;$

IF $a_{i+1,j-1} = 0$ THEN $a_{i+1,j} \leftarrow 1$ endif.

IF $a_{i+1,j+1} = 0$ THEN $a_{i+1,j} \leftarrow 1$ endif.

2°) Bottom-up :

$a_{ij} \leftarrow \min (a_{ij} - 1, a_{i+1,j}, a_{i+1,j-1}, a_{i+1,j+1}) + 1.$

3.2.3.4. Sequantial generation : For all a_{ij}

1°) Top-down :

$a_{i+1,j} \leftarrow \max(a_{i+1,j} + 1, a_{i,j}, a_{i,j+1}, a_{i,j-1}) - 1$

2°) Bottom-up :

$a_{i,j} \leftarrow \max(a_{i,j+1}, a_{i+1,j}, a_{i+1,j+1}, a_{i+1,j-1}, a_{i,j+1}, a_{i,j-1})-1$

3.2.3.5. Applications

3.2.3.5.1. Dilation

We compute a transform distance of an image, increase each point by a given value, and generate the corresponding new image.

3.2.3.5.2. Shrinking

We compute a transform distance of an image, decrease each point by a given value, and generate the corresponding new image.

3.2.3.5.3. Contour detection

We compute a transform distance of an image, and the resulting set of points N_1 give the contour of the image.

3.2.3.5.4. Skeleton

We compute a transform distance. An element is then in the skeleton if none of its four neighbors has a value larger than its own.

3.2.3.5.5. Correction of branches and isolated points

$\forall P \in F$ so that $N_n(P) \subset F$

We make $p \leftarrow 0$ iff the set $[V_{n+1}(P) - V_n(P)] \cap \overline{F}$ is

a) - closed loop (isolated point), or

- open on one side only (branch).

This algorithm keeps the closed loop in F and has been used very successfully to extract patterns obscured by a very large random noise, and,

b) if we add in condition "a" the case of a non connected set, then the algorithm erases a closed loop of a given size.

3.2.3.5.6. Correction of holes and cuts

$\forall P \in F$ so that $N_n(P) \subset \overline{F}$

We make $P \leftarrow 1$ iff the set $[V_{n+1}(P) - V_n(P)] \cap F$ is :

a) non-connected (break)

b) connected : closed loop (hole)

c) open on one side only (local irregularities). This algorithm makes a spatial smoothing.

CONCLUSION

This double structure machine shows the ability to perform local algorithms at the S.I.M.D. memory level ; the flexibility of the system allows working on different sizes of neighborhoods. This multiple level structure shows the ability to perform algorithm at the region level processing, working on different subimages, or to compute global transform in the M.I.M.D. mode, and to perform local algorithms at the S.I.M.D. memory level. We give some classical algorithms adapted to run in S.I.M.D. mode in parallel or sequential way. Among these algorithms some gives very good result in feature extraction such as contour or skeleton, and in image restoration such as dilation, shrinking, and to filter pattern obscured by a very large random noise.

BIBLIOGRAPHY

G.H. Barnes et al : The ILLIAC IV Computer. Trans. IEEE on Comp. C-17, 746, 1968.

A. Rosenfled : Picture Processing by Computer (Academic Press 1969).

C. Timsit, R. Boudarel : "PROPAL II : Une Nouvelle Architecture de Calculateur Adapté au Traitement du Signal". GRETSI, Nice, France, 1977.

M.J.B. Duff, D.M. Watson, E.S. Deutsh : "A Parallel Computer for Array Processing" Proc. I.F.I.P. Congress, Stockholm, Sweden 1974, pp 94-97.

W.K. Pratt : Digital Image Processing (John Wiley and Sons 1978).

J.L. Basille, S. Castan, J.Y. Latil :" Structure Logique et Physique de l'Information dans un Multiprocesseur Adapté au Traitement d'Images". GRETSI, Nice, France 1979.

J.L. Basille, S. Castan, J.Y. Latil : "A Two-Level Parallel Structure. SY.MP.A.T.I. Application to Chromosome Analysis", IVth European Chromosome Analysis Workshop, Edimbourg, Scotland 1981.

J.L. Basille, S. Castan, J.Y. Latil :" Système Multiprocesseur Adapté au Traitement d'Images, in Languages and Architectures, ed. by M.J.B. Duff and S. Levialdi (Academic Press 1981) pp 205-215.

J.L. Basille, S. Castan, J.Y. Latil :" A Typical Propagation Algorithm on the line Processor SY.MP.A.T.I. The Region Labelling" in Multi-Computer and Image Processing Algorithms and Programs, ed. by K. Preston Jr., L. Uhr (Academic Press 1982) pp 99-111.

J.L. Basille S. Castan, M. Al Rozz : "Parallel Architectures Adapted to Image Processing and their Limits." in Computing structures for image Processing, ed. by M.J.B. Duff (Academic Press 1983).

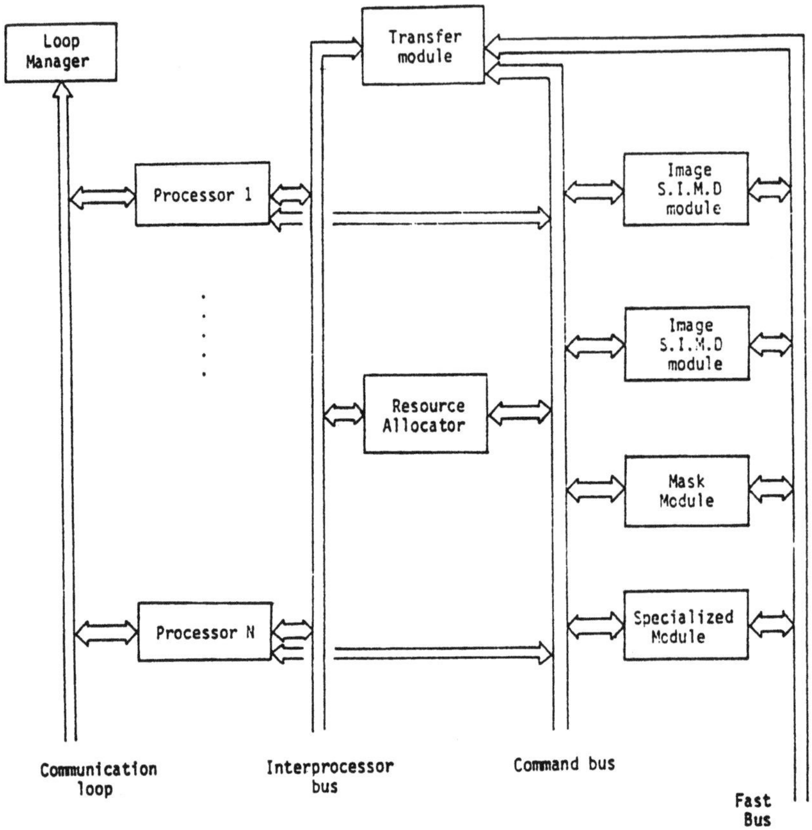

Figure 1 - The general SY.MP.A.T.I. structure

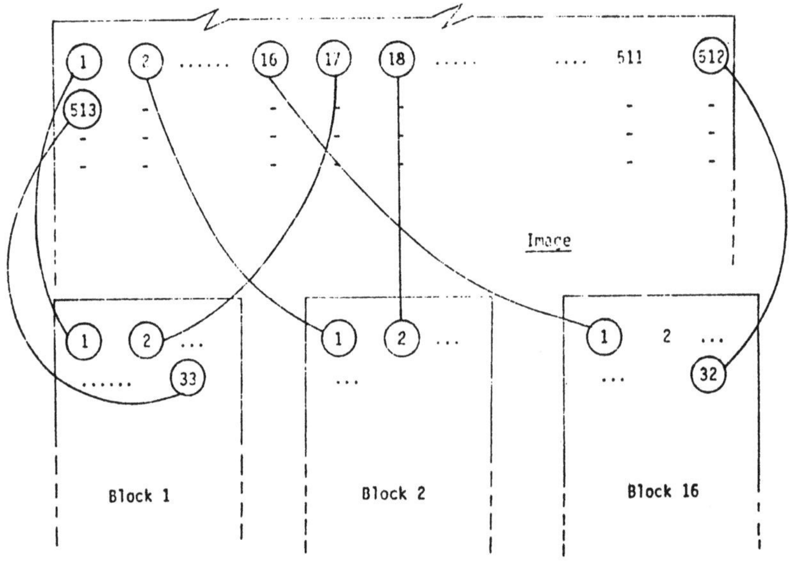

Figure 2 - Image location / Memory address correspondance

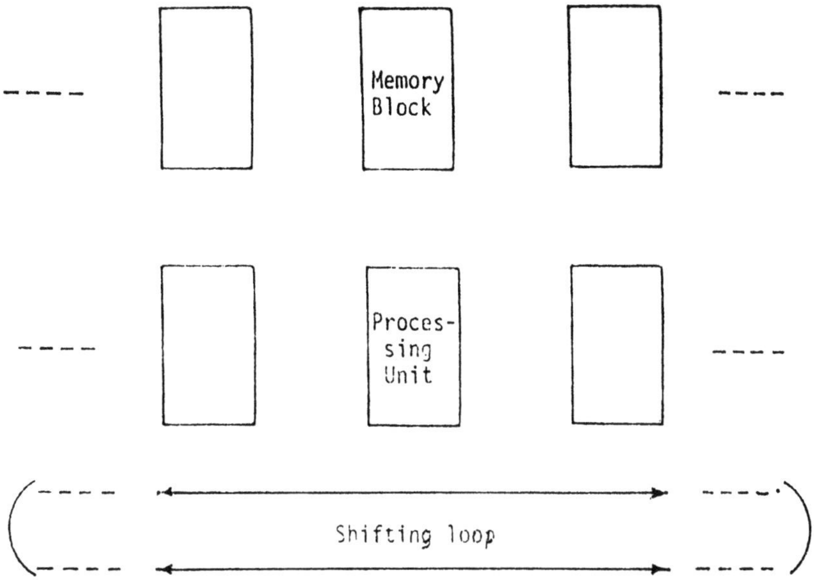

Figure 3 - The column structure
of one S.I.M.D. image
memory of SY.MP.A.T.I.

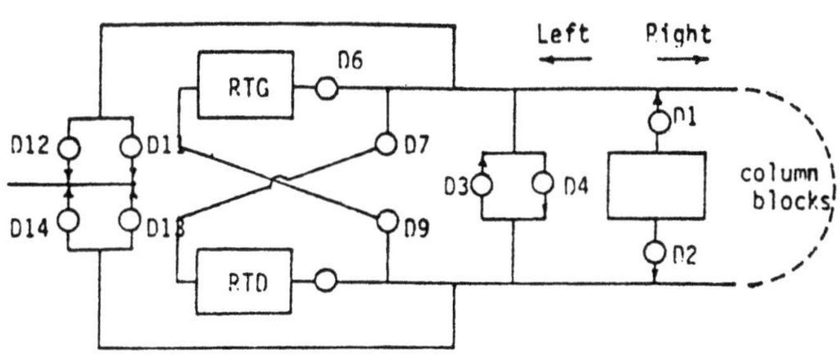

Figure 4 - The extremity of the
shifting loop

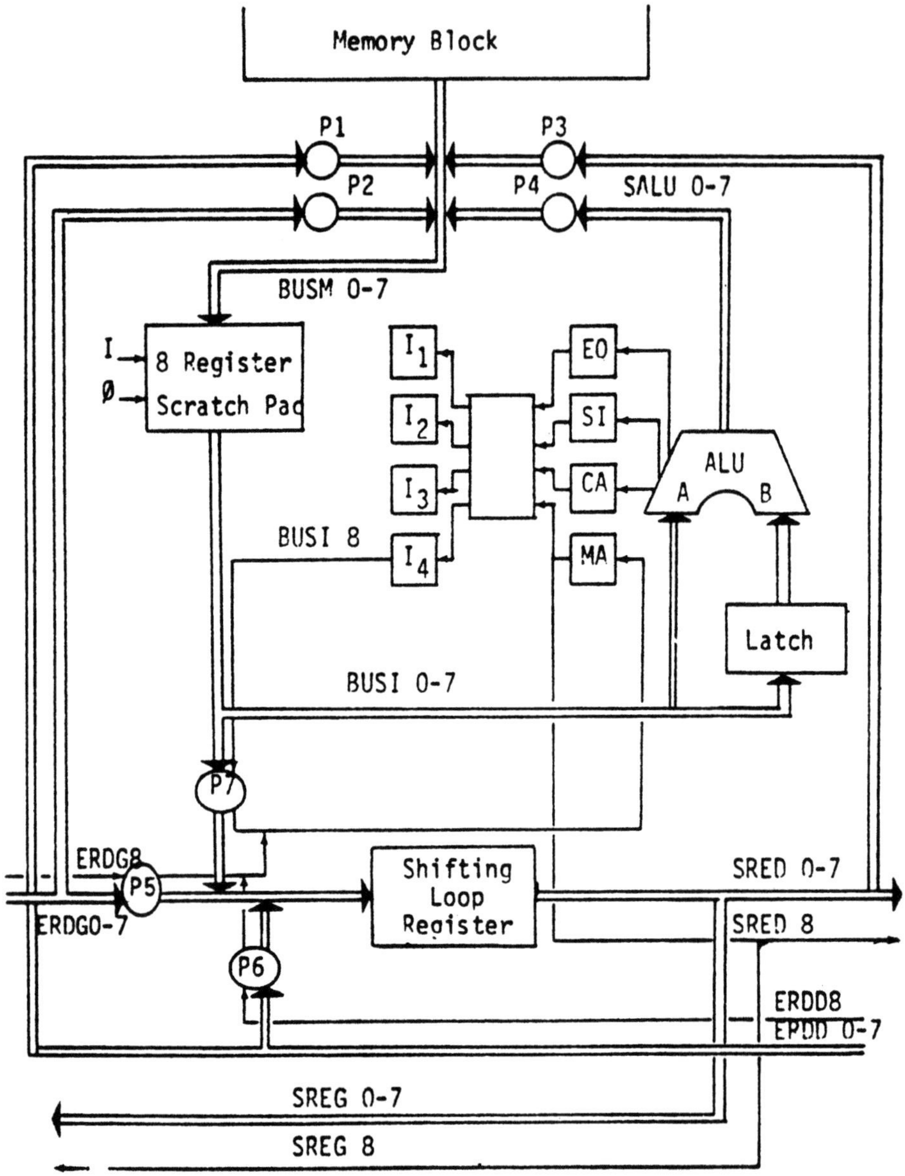

Figure 5 - The Processing unit

PARALLEL ALGORITHMS FOR HYPOTHESES GENERATION IN CONTINUOUS SPEECH

Renato DE MORI
Department of Computer Science
Concordia University
1455 de Maisonneuve Blvd.
Montreal, Quebec, H3G 1M8, Canada

Abstract

The paper describes the conception of the auditory, syllabic and lexical components of a Speech Understanding System (SUS) as a Society of Experts.

Experts cooperate in extracting and describing acoustic cues, generating and verifying phonetic hypotheses and accessing a large lexicon.

The knowledge of each Expert is described by a frame language which allows integration between structural and procedural knowledge. Structural knowledge deals with relations between facts like acoustic cue descriptions and phonetic feature hypotheses. Procedural knowledge deals with rules for the use of relations, the generation of contextual constraints for relation application and for the extraction of new cues in specified contexts.

The main purpose of the research proposed here is that of providing at the same time a model for Computer Perception and algorithms useful for designing complex systems operating in real-time.

Introduction

The conception of Speech Understanding Systems (SUS) as perceptual models is useful for designing machines capable of performing more ambitious tasks than the ones actually achieved by commercial machines and laboratory prototypes, offering the challenge of experimenting new parallel algorithms and non-conventional system architectures.

Central to the organization of an SUS is the representation of knowledge structured on several levels of abstraction and the control strategy that has to use the knowledge efficiently (see, for example, Reddy [1]).

This paper describes a new knowledge-based system for interpreting speech patterns in a task-independent multi-speaker environment.

Central to the conception of this system is the idea that the interpretation of speech patterns is controlled by rules applicable to segments of the speech signal having approximately the duration of a syllable. This is consistent with the conclusions drawn from experiments on the storage time of a pre-perceptual auditory memory (Massaro [2]).

In contrast with other approaches which use syllables as units for speech

NATO ASI Series, Vol. F18
Computer Architectures for Spatially Distributed Data
Edited by H. Freeman and G. G. Pieroni

recognition or for lexical access (Mermelstein [3], Smith and Erman [4], Kohda and Nakatsu [5]), here the generation of syllabic hypotheses is not based on matching spectral segments of speech with prototypes. Rather, it is controlled by rules that take into account context-constraints, bottom-up information and top-down predictions imposed by lexical hypotheses. Rules also control the extraction of acoustic cues which may depend on the hypotheses to be generated or verified. The use of lexical-dependent constraints in syllable hypothesization is consistent with perception models (Massaro [2], Massaro and Oden [6], Marslen-Wilson [7]).

Syllable hypothesization is based on the hierarchical application of relations involving acoustic cues extracted from the signal or spectral transformations of it and phonetic features. The selection of relations to be applied is controlled by a planning system described by a frame language. This language is introduced for representing knowledge about how to interpret the speech signal and its transformations. It describes the available knowledge and how it can be used and updated.

Knowledge is shared, in the model proposed in this paper, among Experts. They cooperate in extracting acoustic cues from the signal and its numerical transformations, in generating hypotheses about bounds of syllabic segments and about phonetic feature hypotheses inside the segments.

A high degree of parallelism can be achieved with such a model allowing to design real-time systems with complex tasks.

The knowledge of each expert can be updated, particularly for what concerns the specification and the use of contextual constraints whose importance has been stressed in previous works [8,9].

The attempt to conceive an SUS as a knowledge-based system is also on the line of recent researches in Computer Vision [10,11] in the hope of finding good models for Computer Perception.

Most of the SUSs described in the literature (Bahl et al. [12], Smith and Erman [4], Woods et al. [13], Vintsjuk [14]), perform lexical access using phone hypotheses or syllabic hypotheses obtained by a translation process from phone hypotheses. The knowledge used for generating these hypotheses is speaker-dependent and gives little importance to contextual effects.

Klatt [15] has proposed a pattern matching technique for lexical access in which different coarticulation instances are represented by different sequences of template spectra. Template spectra are speaker-dependent and it is hard to define a comparison metric that gives importance to the relevant cues of the spectra.

A recent work by Knipper [16], on the line of the approach proposed here, introduces "speaker-independent fields of existence" for spectral cues useful for characterizing the place of articulation of sonorant consonants in a prevocalic context. These fields specify shapes and domains in a frequency-time-energy space for transitions of energy concentrations corresponding to coarticulation instances.

All the above mentioned works have introduced valuable contributions to the conception of SUSs. Nevertheless, they have left many problems open, particularly those related to speaker-independence and the acquisition of new knowledge.

The system proposed here is based on rules which capture many speaker-independent relations between phonetic features and acoustic cues. These rules are a kernel that can be enriched when new knowledge is acquired regarding new pronunciations and new languages.

Particular attention has been devoted so far to improving the knowledge used for segmenting continuous speech into Pseudo-Syllabic Segments (PSS) and to find reliable features for constraining the access to a large lexicon.

Interaction Between Auditory, Syllabic and Lexical Knowledge

Based on models for speech perception [2,7] and on past experience on speech pattern interpretation [8] three main levels of computational activities are proposed for generating lexical hypotheses from the speech signal. The interaction of these activities is sketched in Fig. 1. Following this scheme, the speech signal is processed by "auditory activities" which extract acoustic cues and provide a description of them. Some acoustic cues, like peaks and valleys of time evolutions of energies in fixed bands of the signal, are analyzed first because they do not require any contextual constraint to be applied for their extraction and interpretation. These acoustic cues are related to phonetic features, like 'vocalic' with rules that are context-independent because their application does not depend on any contextual constraints. These acoustic cues will be called primary acoustic cues and the related phonetic features will be called primary phonetic features.

A description of primary acoustic cues and of some prosodic cues mainly related to duration and loudness of possible vocalic segments are sent as a message, indicated as DES1 in Fig. 1, to the lexical level.

Based on DES1 and higher level constraints, depending on syntax and semantic predictions, a set of initial word hypotheses is selected by the lexical activities. Primary phonetic features are obtained from DES1 and used for lexical access. The reason for using such an approach is that primary phonetic features are less affected than other detailed features, like place of articulation, by system imprecision, mispronunciation and dialectal variations. Any difference between the phonetic features of an utterance and the phonetic features of the basic form of the word they correspond to can be taken into account using concepts of error-correcting parsing. Allowed errors of primary phonetic features can depend on the position.

Lexical expectations (LE) in terms of Pseudo-Syllabic Segments (PSS) and descriptions of acoustic cues more detailed than the primary ones are sent to a syllabic level at which syllabic hypotheses are generated. Syllabic hypotheses are indicated as SYLL in Fig. 1.

Generation of hypotheses inside a PSS may require the extraction of further acoustic cues which won't be in competition with the ones already available but will be just added to them. Requests from the syllabic level are indicated as REQ1 in Fig. 1 and the corresponding answers from the auditory level are indicated as DES2.

Generation of lexical hypotheses may start at different time instants. For example, if a set of lexical hypotheses L11 is started at time T1, another set of lexical hypotheses can start at time T2. The interval I12 = T2 - T1 can just correspond to the duration of a PSS. The proliferation of lexical hypothesis generation can be suspended by a 'Focus-by-Inhibition' mechanism that inhibits the generation of new sets of hypotheses or the growing of already existing ones when another set of hypotheses started at a given time instant has reached an evidence such that the probability that the set contains the right candidate is very high.

Inhibition may be stopped at the end of the generation of hypotheses which caused it. After this end point, generation of new hypotheses can restart.

The sub-lexical activities require short-term-memories capable of storing hypotheses and descriptions for a time interval having approximately the duration of a syllable. Short-term-memories of such dimensions have been postulated to be used in human perception.

Generation of hypotheses with the scheme of Fig. 1 is a problem solving activity having a "parsimonious control strategy" because there is only one flow of top-down and bottom-up information.

Outline of an Expert System for Interpreting Speech Patterns

The achievement of complex tasks such as speech understanding and speech recognition can be conceived in the framework of distributed problem solving.

One motivation for taking such an approach is that a model with parallel execution of tasks can be used for designing a modular, unconventional architecture based on distributed processing and capable of achieving real-time performances far beyond the capabilities of classical sequential computers.

Another important motivation is that if knowledge for problem solving is distributed, it is often possible to update separately each piece of knowledge when new scientific results or new experience pertinent to that knowledge becomes available.

A third motivation for this approach is that it allows implementation of a control strategy capable of scheduling sensory procedures which extract new cues from the data when this is necessary for growing an interpretation hypothesis.

In many cases, cues cannot be extracted if the context in which they have to be extracted is not specified. For example (see Demichelis et al. [19] for details), formant loci are important cues for the recognition of plosive consonants but their extraction can be performed only after having hypothesized the existence of a plosive sound before or after a vowel and having detected the voice onset interval.

With this view, a system has been designed for which the extraction of acoustic cues and generation of syllabic hypotheses is the result of a pluralism of cooperating activities performed by many processes. This cooperation of computational activities has been conceived using the paradigm of an Expert System Society [20]. The Society executes parallel algorithms derived from a task-decomposition of the complex hypothesis generation mechanism. Each Expert is associated with a Long Term Memory (LTM) containing the specific Expert's knowledge and a Short Term Memory (STM) where data interpretations are written.

For example, the computational activities for extracting acoustic cues are performed by a group of Experts referred to as the Auditory Expert Society (AES). Analogously, the generation of syllabic hypotheses is performed by a Syllabic Expert.

Experts are computing agents which execute reasoning programs using structural and procedural knowledge in an integrated form. For example, they must be able to perform the extraction of cues when the evidences of already existing hypotheses call for the application of rules that involve cues that have not been extracted yet.

Conflict resolution can often be achieved after the execution of disambiguation procedures involving the extraction of 'ad hoc' cues from the data in a well-specified context.

The main characteristics of the Expert System proposed in this paper are the following.

First, the structures of the Experts define task decomposition. Task decomposition has been based on previous experience with SUS and separates the execution of sets of algorithms that can be performed in parallel and/or require disjoint pieces of knowledge. Communication between cooperating tasks is performed by message passing.

Second, the procedural knowledge is integrated as much as possible with the structural one using semantic attachments. This represents an effort for explicitly representing procedures in the attempt of formalizing a simulation structure for speech perception.

Third, part of the knowledge of some Experts can be related to a planning scheme similar to Sacerdoti's NOAH [21].

A short outline of the structure of the Experts will be presented now before introducing more details on knowledge representation. Data structures generated by Expert instantiations as well as data descriptions and hypotheses are allocated into the Expert STM. An instantiation may communicate with other instantiations of the Expert that created it or with other Experts or their instantiations. For this purpose, each instantiation of Expert EXP_j is associated with a message queue MQ_j.

This computation model differs remarkably from the blackboard model [22] for speech understanding. In fact, in the blackboard model, computational activities are triggered asynchronously by the appearance of an event in a common blackboard. In the model proposed here, Experts do not communicate through a common data-base and are provided with an elaborate control strategy. This strategy is made of planning algorithms controlling the selection of pieces of knowledge applicable to the data in the Experts STMs. These algorithms are described by a frame language.

Another peculiar aspect of this system is that it contains various types of knowledge-driven cue extraction algorithms. These algorithms are applied when the control strategy needs to execute sensory procedures for producing new facts useful for continuing the interpretation process.

An introductory description of the Experts of the Auditory Society is given in the following.

Fig. 2 shows the Experts EXP_j ($1 \le j \le 5$) of the Auditory Society their LTM and STM and their communication links.

Each circle in Fig. 2 represents an Expert that can generate many instantiations of it.

The speech signal is sampled, quantized, stored into a "SIGNAL-STM" and transformed by a Data Acquisition Expert (DAE). DAE looks for the starting point of a sentence by using a set of rules for this purpose. When this point has been detected, AEPDST starts transmitting messages to another Expert called Waveform Cue Descriptor (WCD).

WCD extracts cues from the speech waveform and describes them. These descriptions are based on peaks and valleys of the signal loudness and peaks of zero-crossing densities of the signal derivative. It is planned to make this expert capable of describing other waveform features using syntactic pattern recognition techniques [4].

The LTM of WCD, denoted LTM/2/, contains an attributed grammar that controls the coding of waveform features. Waveform Feature Descriptions are sent to a Primary Phonetic Feature Descriptor (PPFD) that uses them for requesting the execution of sensory procedures.

For this purpose, PPFD sends messages to a SIGNAL-PROCESSING-EXPERT (SPE) that performs various signal transformations depending on the requests it receives. SPE can perform, for example, an analysis based on Linear Prediction Coefficients (LPC) or a Fast Fourier Transformation (FFT). The time resolution of these analyses may depend on the type of request that has been received.

The information produced by SPE can be stored into the "Acoustic Data" STM or into a Gross Spectral Feature (GSF) STM.

Syllabic hypothesization is performed by a SYLLABIC EXPERT (SE). The SYLLABIC EXPERT receives lexical expectations and an unambiguous description of acoustic cues, generates and sends syllabic hypotheses to the lexical level. These hypotheses are affected by degrees of plausibility.

The PPFD Expert generates hypotheses about phonetic features that are related to acoustic cues with Context-Independent Rules (CIR). This set of phonetic features, called Primary Phonetic Features (PFF), is defined in Table 1.

TABLE I

Primary Phonetic Features

Symbol	Primary Phonetic Feature
VF	Front vowel
VC	Central vowel
VB	Back vowel
VFC	Front or central vowel
VCB	Central or back vowel
VW	Uncertain vowel
NI	Nonsonorant interrupted consonant
NA	Nonsonorant affricate consonant
NC	Nonsonorant continuant consonant
SON	Sonorant consonant
NIV	The /v/ or a NI consonant
SONV	A sonorant or the /v/ consonant

For this purpose, SCE sends messages to a SIGNAL-PROCESSING-EXPERT (SPE) that performs various signal transformations depending on the requests it receives. SPE can perform, for example, an analysis based on Linear Prediction Coefficients (LPC) for vocalic hypotheses or a Fast Fourier Transformation (FFT) for hypotheses of nonsonorant-continuant sounds.

The information produced by SPE is stored into the "Acoustic Data" STM. The knowledge of SPE is stored into LTM_5. SPE can also carry a dialogue with GSF-DESCRIPTOR.

Syllabic hypothesization is performed by a SYLLABIC EXPERT (SE). The SYLLABIC EXPERT receives lexical expectations and an unambiguous description of acoustic cues, generates and sends syllabic hypotheses to the lexical level. These hypotheses are affected by degrees of plausibility.

The organization of knowledge stored into the Long-Term Memories of the GSF DESCRIPTOR, the SYLLABIC CUE EXTRACTOR and the SYLLABIC EXPERT are described by means of a frame language that will be introduced in the next Section.

A Frame Language for Describing Expert's Knowledge

Generalities

Experts like the SYLLABIC one, the GSF-DESCRIPTOR and the SYLLABIC-CUE-EXTRACTOR have a complex LTM knowledge.

The knowledge of these Experts contains context-sensitive rules, controls the extraction of spectral cues from the speech data, produces a description of the extracted cues, and generate phonetic hypotheses.

The algorithms for producing descriptions of acoustic data and for generating hypotheses from descriptions are expressed in a frame language. This language is suitable for integrating structural and procedural knowledge, for handling context-sensitive relations, for propagating constraints, for performing inferences, for making default assumptions when the cues extracted from the data cannot be interpreted by the system's knowledge, for specifying the use of sensory procedures capable of extracting cues and features from the data when this is required for growing hypotheses or for generating new ones.

A <u>frame</u> is an information structure made of a frame-name and number of slots. A <u>slot</u> is the holder of information concerning a particular item called <u>slot filler</u> (Minsky [20]). Slot-fillers may include descriptions of events, relations, results of procedures, invocation of other frames.

Slots can be filled by the results of sensory procedures invoked for extracting cues from the data. In such a case, a slot is considered filled only if the required information has been found in the data.

TABLE 1

<u>Rewriting rules of the frame-structure grammar</u>

```
<FRAME>                    := (<NAME> <SLOT-LIST>)
                                                          k>0
<SLOT-LIST>                := (<NAME> [(<DESCRIPTION>)])

<DESCRIPTION>              := (described-as <CHDES>)
                                                            k>1
                           := (<CONNECTIVE> <DESCRIPTION>       )
                           := (not <DESCRIPTION>)
                           := (filled-by <FRAME>)
                           := <CONDITIONAL>
                           := (result-of <PROC >)

<CONDITIONAL >             := (when <PREDICATE EXPRESSION >
                                   <DESCRIPTION >
                              [(else <DESCRIPTION>)])
                           := (unless <DESCRIPTION ><DESCRIPTION>)
                           := (case <NAME> of
                                                                   k>1
                              (<DESCRIPTION> filled-by <FRAME>)       )

<CONNECTIVE>               := or
                           := and
                           := xor
                           := sequence

<PREDICATE EXPRESSION>     := <PREDICATE >
                           := (not <PREDICATE>)
                                                           k>1
                           := (<CONNECTIVE> (<PREDICATE>          ))

<PROC>                     := F-<function>
                           := P-<procedure >

< NAME >                   := any string of characters

< CHDES >                  := any cue or hypothesis description
```

Very often, the content of already filled slots acts as contextual constraint specifying the signal interval in which the sensory procedure has to be executed.

Filling a slot may be conditioned by the verification of a relation involving predicates; evaluation of predicates may require the calculation of functions defined by semantic attachments. A slot can also be filled by a disjunction or a conjunction of frame instantiations. All the possible slot filling structures are defined by a context-free grammar whose rewriting rules are shown in Table I.

The terminal symbols of this grammar are written in lower case letters. The non-terminal ones are in upper-case. The starting symbol is <FRAME>. Cues and hypotheses descriptions are usually "well-formed formulae" of the predicate calculus or temporal sequences of them. Brackets contain optional items. An exponent k applied to a base means that the content of the base is repeated k times in a sequence.

The LTM of an Expert contains a collection of algorithms, each one having a frame structure.

When the execution of an algorithm is invoked, for example by a received message, an <u>instantiation</u> of the first frame of the corresponding structure is created into the Expert's STM. The Expert executes the algorithm by attempting to fill the slots of the invoked frame.

The attempt to fill a slot may instantiate another frame and this operation can be done recursively.

Filling a slot by a <u>described-as</u> <CHDES> slot description corresponds to the generation of descriptions of acoustic cues or interpretation hypotheses.

When all the slots of a frame instantiation are filled, the frame instantiation is complete.

The execution of a procedure can be invoked by the attempt of filling a frame slot in a frame instantiation. A procedure in a given instantiation has access to the content of those slots that have been already filled in that instantiation.

Many procedural rules used here are derived from knowledge related to speech perception (Massaro [2]), spectrogram reading, speech production (Fant [23]) and the experience gained in designing rule-based speech recognition systems.

Filling a slot by a <u>filled-by</u> <CHDES> slot description corresponds to the instantiation of a frame represented by its NAME.

Filling a slot with a connective of descriptions may cause the invocation of other frames whose instantiation may require the execution of procedures for extracting new cues or evaluating evidences of hypotheses. Parameters to be used by these procedures are specified by names of already filled slots.

The connective <u>sequence</u> specifies that a slot has to be filled with frames describing a temporal sequence of events such that the (i+1)-th event has to begin near the end of the i-th one. This implies the evaluation of a time consistency predicate whenever data are analyzed or descriptions are generated by frames in the sequence.

The need for these different types of connectives depends on the nature of the speech interpretation task in which some events are temporal sequences of facts for which the order is essential as for strings of symbol in a language. Some other events, instead, are conjunctions or disjunctions of facts appearing in the same time interval. These facts can be handled as elements of a set in any order.

Executing a connective statement invoking many frame instantiations corresponds to the creation of concurrent processes, one for each invoked frame. These processes may cooperate by setting up constraints and contexts or by generating hypotheses and descriptions. For example, the invocation of a frame for a vowel that follows a consonant may generate a context constraint to be used by the frame invocation that creates descriptions and hypotheses about the consonant.

Depth-first or breadth-first strategies can be used for controlling the growth of frame instantiations. Heuristic knowledge is used for setting constraints and placing conditional statements in order to keep small the average number of frames for which instantiation cannot reach completion.

Conditionals may involve preconditions that have to be checked before proceeding in slot filling. They are often used to avoid creating a network of instantiations if some necessary conditions for the success of such an operation are not met.

Eventually, default conditions may also appear in the descriptions of frame slots.

Synchronization, constraint creation and propagation are performed by procedures executed for slot filling. A discussion of these issues will be presented in a future work.

Writing an algorithm in the frame language allows one to express complex inference and cue-extraction rules, to prepare constraints and contexts and to verify preconditions before applying knowledge for generating descriptions about cues and hypotheses after the corresponding signal segment has been analyzed.

Frame instantiations that remain incomplete do not contribute to the generation of descriptions because this is usually the last step of a frame instantiation. Each Expert supervises its frame instantiations and decides when to remove an instantiation from its STM.

The introduction of the frame language should be completed with a formal presentation of its semantic. This presentation is omitted in this paper for the sake of brevity. Rather, when pieces of knowledge will be described in the following using the frame language, some explanations will be given in order to allow one to understand how knowledge is represented and used.

It is important to point out that the deductive part of the speech understanding components described here is not as crucial as the specification of when and how sensory procedures have to be used for finding cues in the data. Patterns of cues, once detected, become facts that may drive the system inference toward the generation of interpretation hypotheses.

The frame language is also suitable for describing meta-rules of control knowledge as well as structural rules.

The control knowledge selects relevant modules of structural knowledge with a planning activity in analogy with the NOAH planning system proposed by Sacerdoti[21]. This analogy is justified by the following considerations.

1. Frame invocation corresponds to the expansion of a plan into more detailed sub-plans, each sub-plan being related to the attempt of filling a slot of the frame.
2. Filling a sequence of slots in a frame is the execution of a sequence of sub-plans.
3. A slot that can be filled by a conjunction or a disjunction of frame invocations, represents the splitting of a plan into a conjunction or a disjunction of more detailed sub-plans in a non-linear way.
4. Conditional statements verify whether it is worthwhile expanding a plan into a more detailed network of sub-plans.

A Network for Lexical Access

A new solution for accessing a large lexicon in continuous speech is proposed. The words of a lexicon and their relations with syllables, acoustic and prosodic cues are represented by a network similar to semantic networks used in Artificial Intelligence for knowledge representation. The network for lexical representation is generated by a graph grammar in which rules are applied either when suitable acoustic cues are detected in the signal or when model driven predictions are made. The piece of network generated by the application of a set of rules contains nodes and links. Nodes are processes capable of executing algorithms. Links are channels through which messages between processes can be exchanged. The type of a link specifies the type of message that can be exchanged. The model exhibits a high degree of parallelism and allows to efficiently perform intersections of large sets of descriptions. Some nodes correspond to word classes which are hypothesized when some sets of sufficient conditions are detected in the data.

Lexical access is an operation that humans, unlike the classical computers, do very quickly and apparently easily. As this operation seems to be primarily an intersection of large sets involving word representations, discourse predictions and descriptions of physical events detected in the speech signal, concepts from Fahlman's semantic networks [25] are worth to be considered for this purpose.

A graph grammar that generates networks for word hypothesization in continuous speech will be introduced. These networks are similar to semantic networks whose nodes are processes capable of executing algorithms and of communicating among them through links. The type of the links specify the type of messages the links can convey. Some of the link types introduced here are derived from Fahlman NETL [25].

Organization of the Lexical Knowledge

Human performances in lexical access can be achieved only with system structures having high parallel processing capabilities in contrast with conventional computer architectures.

A model of lexical organization and access will be introduced in the following. Let us call this model Lexical Network. The main components of the Lexical Network are nodes and links. Each node is associated with a name, a knowledge and a set of procedures it can perform in order to attempt to match its knowledge with interpretations of the input data. Procedures execute algorithms written in the frame language introduced in [8]. Their main purpose is that of setting top-down constraints for the application of relations between a phonetic feature and acoustic cues. Details of these relations that may require the execution of sensory procedures for extracting new cues from the data are given in [8] and [26].

Links establish relations between nodes and have associated descriptions of relations. These relations may specify types of messages or signals that can be exchanged between nodes. The whole lexical network is controlled by a supervisor that monitors the lexicon behaviour. The Lexical Network will be described by a graph grammar in which nonterminal symbols are represented by strings of lower case letters and terminal symbols are represented by strings of capital letters with indices in lower case letters. The start symbol is 'lexicon'. These rules generate pieces of network used for word hypothesization. Some of these rules are given in the following.

Rule <u>RL1</u>

lexicon := wcs(1) |wcs(2) |.... |wcs(c) |.... |wcs(g)

The symbol | represents a disjunction of items which can be generated by the nonterminal symbol on the left-hand side of the rule.
Rule RL1 states that the Lexical Network is a collection of structures corresponding to word classes. Each word W(i) may belong to one or more word classes WC(c) depending on the variety of its pronunciations. WC(c) is the label of a node in the graph generated by rewriting the nonterminal symbol wcs(c).

A word class WC(c) is characterized by a stress pattern sp(c) and a sequence of syllable types. A <u>virtual copy</u> link connects the node WC(c) with the words of the class. This connection is shown in the graph produced by Rule RL2. A virtual copy link is represented by a thick arrow and corresponds to the fact that when a word class is activated because some sufficient conditions are met in the data, this property is inherited by all the word nodes which are virtual copies of the class. The nonterminal symbol words(c) is used in Rule RL2 for generating virtual copies of WC(c).

Rule <u>RL2</u>

wcs(c) := WC(c)

stress sp(c)

syllabic

syltypes(c)

words(c)

The nonterminal symbol syltypes(c) appearing in RL2 is used for generating the phonetic feature structure of the syllables of WC(c) (see [3] for details). This is shown by the following rule RL3.

Rule RL3

syltypes(c):= SYLT(c,1) precedes SYLT(c,2)

sufficient condition syltype(j) sufficient condition

syltype(k)

suffsylt(k,m) suffsylt(j,n)

Rule RL3 establishes that the syltypes of class WC(c) are represented by two nodes SYLT(c,1) and SYLT(c,2). The double thick arrow connecting SYLT(c,1) with 'syltype(k)' means that the first syllable type of WC(c) is equivalent to the structure that will be generated by 'syltype(k)'. The same is for SYLT(c,2).

SYLT(c,1) precedes SYLT(c,2) in time. Each node is also linked with a set of sufficient conditions. When these sufficient conditions are met, because they contain features that have been detected in the data by sensory procedures, the node pointed by the arrow becomes active.

When all the sufficient conditions of a word class are detected and the relations between them are verified, the node syltypes(c) becomes active and this activity is inherited by WC(c). If data provide enough evidence for matching one of the stress patterns in sp(c), WC(c) becomes active and enables a network expansion by the application of the following rule RL4.

Rule RL4

words(c):= W(c,1)|W(c,2)|....|W(c,i)|...W(c,I(c))

I(c) is the number of items on the right-hand side of the rule.

Each word W(c,i) of the class WC(c) inherits the properties of the class and is characterized by a node labelled by its orthographic representation W(i). Furthermore, a word W(i) has a set of syntactic and semantic scopes represented by links between the node W(i) and the semantic and syntactic components of the Speech Understanding System.

Links are also established between the node W(i) and nodes representing the fixed part of W(i) and its termination. The fixed part of W(i) is represented by sequences of syllabic segments. Further parts of the Lexical Network are generated by the following rules.

Rule RL5

w(c,i):= W(i) synt(i)
synt-scope
sem-scope sem(i)
fixed-part termination
ctx
fp(i) D(i) d(x)
precedes

Rule RL6

D(x):= DSINGULAR(x) | DPLURAL(x)

In many languages, the common names have different terminations for singular and plural mostly affecting the last syllable. For this reason it is necessary to spearate the fixed part and the termination in the subnetwork of a word. This is realized by the two links reaching the node W(i); the first one is connected to the node fp(i) representing the fixed part; the second one is connected to the node D(i) representing the termination. D(i) is equivalent to a prototype for terminations denoted as d(x) which, in turn, belongs to a set of terminations.

D(x) is connected, for example, to two possible typical terminations, linked with the syntactic categories 'singular' and 'plural'. Many languages like French, Italian and Spanish may have very complex termination sets for verbs. The dashed line between nodes D(i) and fp(i) is labelled 'ctx' and represents the fact that phonemes in D(i) may act as context constraints in the rules relating phonetic features of fp(i) with acoustic cues.

The nonterminal symbol fp(i) generates the fragment of network defined by the following rules.

Rule RL7

fp(i):= syll(i,1,1) syll(i,1,j) syll(i,1,J(ij))
precedes precedes
:= syll(i,2,1) syll(i,2,j) syll(i,2,J(i2))
precedes precedes
.
.

Rule RL7 establishes that fp(i) is a disjunction of references of syllables syll(i,l,j),

1 = l = L(i), 1 = j = J(il). The last syllable of each reference is usually incomplete and has to be completed by the termination or some part of it.

A-priori probabilities can be associated to each reference. The structure of each syllabic node is defined by the following rule.

Rule RL8

syll(i,l,j):= S(i,l,j) ..to S(i,l,j+l)

DGR

acceptable
degradations

sl(k)

DGR ADGR(i,l,j)

from S(i,l,j-l) DGR

Each syllable S(i,l,j) is an instantiation equivalent to a syllable represented by the node sl(k). For example the /mo/ of Montreal is an instantiation of the syllable /mo/.

The node S(i,l,j) is activated if a set of acceptable degradation of sl(k) has been hypothesized starting from the data. The set of acceptable degradation is contained in the node ADGR(i,l,j).

References

[1] - D.R. Reddy (1976)
Speech Recognition by Machine: A Review.
Proceedings IEEE, vol. 64, pp. 501-531.

[2] - D.W. Massaro (1980)
Letter and Word Perception.
Elsevier North-Holland,New York

[3] - P. Mermelstein (1975)
Automatic Segmentation of Speech into Syllabic Units.
J.A.S.A., vol. 58, pp. 880-888.

[4] - A.R. Smith and L.D. Erman (1981)
NOAH - A Bottom-Up Word Hypothesizer for Large Vocabulary Speech Understanding Systems.
IEEE Trans. On Pattern Analysis and Machine Intelligence.
vol. PAMI-3, pp. 41-51.

[5] - M. Kahda and R. Nakatsu (1978)
An Acoustic Processor in a Conversational Speech System.
Review of the Electrical Communication Laboratories (NTT),
Japan, vol. 26, pp. 1436-1504.

[6] - D.W. Massaro and G.C. Oden (1978)
Integration of Featural Information in Speech Perception.
Psychological Review, vol. 85, pp. 172-191.

[7] - W.D. Marslen-Wilson (1980)
Speech Understanding as a Psychological Process
In Spoken Language Generation and Understanding.
Ed. By J.C. Simon, Reidel Publ. Co.
Dordrecht, The Netherlands, pp. 39-68.

[8] - R. De Mori (1983)
Computer Model of Speech Using Fuzzy Algorithms
Plenum Press, New York

[9] - R. De Mori and P. Laface (1980)
Use of Fuzzy Algorithms for Phonetic and Phonemic Labelling of Continuous Speech.
IEEE Trans. On Pattern Analysis and Machine Intelligence, vol. PAMI-2, pp. 136-148.

[10] - D. Marr
Vision
Freeman, San Francisco, 1982.

[11] - J.K. Tsotsos (1980)
A Framework for Visual Motion Understanding.
Ph.D. Thesis, Dept. of Computer Science, University of Toronto

[12] - L.R. Bahl, J.K. Baker, P.S. Cohen, F. Jelinek, B.L. Lewis and R.L. Mercer (1978)
Recognition of a Continuously Read Natural Corpus.
Proc. IEEE-ICASSP (Tulsa, OK), pp. 422-425.

[13] - W.A. Woods, M. Bates, G. Brown, B. Bruce, C. Cook, J. Klovstad, J. Makhoul, B. Nash-Webber, P. Schwartz, J. Wolf and V. Zue (1976)
Speech Understanding Systems.
Final Technical Progress Report. Volumes I-V.
Report N. 3438, Bolt Beranek and Newman, Cambridge, MA.

[14] - T.K. Vintsjuk (1976)
Generative Grammars and Dynamic Programming in Speech Recognition with Learning.
Proc. IEEE-ICASSP (Philadelphia, PA), pp. 446-449.

[15] - D.H. Klatt (1979)
Speech Perception: A Model of Acoustic Phonetic Analysis and Lexical Access.
J. Phonetics, vol. 7, pp. 279-312.

[16] - A.V. Knipper (1981)
Acoustic Events in CV Syllables with Liquid and Nasal Sounds.
Signal Processing, vol. 3, no. 4, pp. 389-396.

[17] - R. De Mori, A. Giordana, P. Laface (1982)
Speech Segmentation by Semantic Syntax-Directed Translation.
Pattern Recognition Letters, vol. 1, no. 2, pp. 121-124.

[18] - D.W. Shipman and V.W. Zue (1982)
Properties of Large Lexicons: Implication for Advanced Isolated-Word Recognition Systems.
Proc. IEEE-ICASSP-82, Paris, pp. 546-549

[19] - P. Demichelis, R. De Mori, P. Laface and M. O'Kane
Computer Recognition of Plosive Sounds Using Contextual Information.
IEEE Trans. on Acoustic Speech and Signal Processing (to appear).

[20] - M. Minsky (1975)
A Framework for Representing Knowledge.
In the Psychology of Computer Vision, Ed. by P. Winston, McGraw-Hill.

[21] - E.D. Sacerdoti (1977)
A Structure for Plans and Behaviour.
Elsevier North-Holland, New York.

[22] - L.D. Erman, F. Hayes-Roth, V.R. Lesser and D.R. Reddy (1980)
The HEARSAY-II Speech Understanding System. Integrating Knowledge to Resolve Uncertainty. Computing Surveys, vol. 12, pp. 213-258.

[23] - G. Fant (1960)
Acoustic Theory of Speech Production.
Mouton Co., The Hague.

[24] - R. De Mori, R. Gubrynowicz and P. Laface (1979)
Inference of a Knowledge Source for the Recognition of Nasals in Continuous Speech.
IEEE Transactions ASSP vol. 27, no. 5.

[25] - S.E. Fahlman (1979)
NETL: A System for Representing and Using Real-World Knowledge.
MIT Press.

[26] - R. De Mori, A. Giordana, P. Laface and L. Saitta (1982)
An Expert System for Speech Decoding.
Proc. AAAI Conference, Pittsburgh, PA, pp. 107-110.

NATO ASI Series F

Vol. 1: Issues in Acoustic Signal – Image Processing and Recognition. Edited by C. H. Chen. VIII, 333 pages. 1983.

Vol. 2: Image Sequence Processing and Dynamic Scene Analysis. Edited by T. S. Huang. IX, 749 pages. 1983.

Vol. 3: Electronic Systems Effectiveness and Life Cycle Costing. Edited by J. K. Skwirzynski. XVII, 732 pages. 1983.

Vol. 4: Pictorial Data Analysis. Edited by R. M. Haralick. VIII, 468 pages. 1983.

Vol. 5: International Calibration Study of Traffic Conflict Techniques. Edited by E. Asmussen VII, 229 pages. 1984.

Vol. 6: Information Technology and the Computer Network. Edited by K. G. Beauchamp. VIII, 271 pages. 1984.

Vol. 7: High-Speed Computation. Edited by J. S. Kowalik. IX, 441 pages. 1984.

Vol. 8: Program Transformation and Programming Environments. Report on an Workshop directed by F. L. Bauer and H. Remus. Edited by P. Pepper. XIV, 378 pages. 1984.

Vol. 9: Computer Aided Analysis and Optimization of Mechanical System Dynamics. Edited by E. J. Haug. XXII, 700 pages. 1984.

Vol. 10: Simulation and Model-Based Methodologies: An Integrative View. Edited by T. I. Ören, B. P. Zeigler, M. S. Elzas. XIII, 651 pages. 1984.

Vol. 11: Robotics and Artificial Intelligence. Edited by M. Brady, L. A. Gerhardt, H. F. Davidson. XVII, 693 pages. 1984.

Vol. 12: Combinatorial Algorithms on Words. Edited by A. Apostolico, Z. Galil. VIII, 361 pages. 1985.

Vol. 13: Logics and Models of Concurrent Systems. Edited by K. R. Apt. VIII, 498 pages. 1985.

Vol. 14: Control Flow and Data Flow: Concepts of Distributed Programming. Edited by M. Broy. VIII, 525 pages. 1985.

Vol. 15: Computational Mathematical Programming. Edited by K. Schittkowski. VIII, 451 pages. 1985.

Vol. 16: New Systems and Architectures for Automatic Speech Recognition and Synthesis. Edited by R. De Mori, C.Y. Suen. XIII, 630 pages. 1985.

Vol. 17: Fundamental Algorithms for Computer Graphics. Edited by R.A. Earnshaw. XVI, 1042 pages. 1985.

Vol. 18: Computer Architectures for Spatially Distributed Data. Edited by H. Freeman and G.G. Pieroni. VIII, 391 pages. 1985.

MIX
Papier aus verantwortungsvollen Quellen
Paper from responsible sources
FSC® C105338

If you have any concerns about our products,
you can contact us on
ProductSafety@springernature.com

In case Publisher is established outside the EU,
the EU authorized representative is:
Springer Nature Customer Service Center GmbH
Europaplatz 3, 69115 Heidelberg, Germany

Printed by Libri Plureos GmbH
in Hamburg, Germany